THE

VIDEO GAME

GUIDE

VOLUME 2

1990-1999

First Edition

Peter Cruickshank

First published in the UK in 2023 by Peter Cruickshank

ISBN 978-1-7392384-0-7

British Library Cataloguing in Publication Data.

A catalogue record for this book is available from the British Library.

Publisher's Note

Although the information in this book is believed to be accurate and true at the time of going to press, neither the author nor publisher can accept any legal responsibility or liability for any errors or omissions that may have been made.

Facebook.com/thevideogameguide

A glossary of terms can be found at the back of this book.

DEDICATION

To everyone who has ever found thrills, suspense, glory, wonder, escapism, love, loss and life in a video game.

Contents

Contents ... *v*

INTRODUCTION ... *3*

1990 ... *5*

1991 ... *31*

1992 ... *61*

1993 ... *84*

1994 ... *117*

1995 ... *145*

1996 ... *167*

1997 ... *197*

1998 ... *227*

1999 ... *261*

NOTES ... *289*

Glossary ... *313*

Sources Used ... *325*

Index ... *329*

ACKNOWLEDGMENTS

First, I would like to thank Iain Stirling who unwittingly helped sow the seeds for this series of books with our passionate talks about computer games of the 1980s and 90s during a holiday to Disney World with our families in 2019. Steff El Madawi for giving initial editing pointers and advice. My chief editors Steph Dagg and her son Benji Dagg for all their hard work. Paul Johnson, Ed Pulis and Alice Tennant for proofreading the original book. Krzysztof for his beautiful icons on the front cover, check out his work at http://dycha.net/ To everyone who has advised and listened to me hark on about what would, one day, become the Video Game Guide. Finally for the support of my loving wife, Catherine who has let me indulge in my passion.

INTRODUCTION

My first experiences with video games go back to the late 1970s, playing arcades such as Space Invaders (1978), Asteroids (1979) and Galaxian (1979). My family's very first video game console here in the United Kingdom was a Binatone TV Master System (1976). Although this book is encyclopedic in nature, I would like to state that video games are as much about the passion and the emotions they evoke within us as anything else. For it is our personal experiences that make them important to us and have a lasting effect on us for many years to come.

All these experiences are as real as anything that happens in our everyday lives. For every game mentioned in this book, there is someone out there on whom it has had a significant impact. From the most primitive, purely text-based adventure and roguelike games, where the player's imagination did the grunt work, to the vast immersive open-world games of today. All of these experiences should be cherished.

When we consider how far video games have come over the last seventy years we can only imagine where the future will take us and how they will evolve. We can predict that video games will look even more real and become even more immersive and that all of this is only the beginning.

I wanted to write a book about video games that focuses as much on their origins as it does on their more contemporary embodiments (covered in later volumes); that acknowledges games not only from Japan and the USA but from other parts of the world too. I wanted to give the reader exposure to not only triple-AAA titled blockbuster games but also to indie and casual games. This book also covers many of the hardware innovations over the years and I hope this will give the reader an idea of the 'complete' history of video games while also acting as reference material and guide.

Peter Cruickshank

Note: A Glossary of terms can be found at the back of this book.

Video Game

Noun

A game played by electronically manipulating images produced by a computer program on a monitor or other display.

(Oxford Dictionary)

1990

1990s Introduction

Although 3D graphics had been around for over a decade in video games, it wasn't until the 1990s that players would see a real evolution from 2D sprite-based games to 3D becoming the dominant way in which graphics would be presented to us. 3D graphics seemed to be the future direction of gaming, yet such was the eagerness that some titles struggled to make the transition from 2D to 3D, proving that just because you could do a thing it does not necessarily mean you should do that thing. The breakthrough into 3D would forever change the way people played games on the PC. In the previous decade, a game made for the Atari 800 or the Commodore 64 would 'always' run on that computer. Now players found the necessity for what was known as a '3D hardware accelerator', what would later become known as graphics cards, to run ever-more demanding games. This was the beginning of the concept of the modern 'modular PC' where each major component of the PC can easily be removed and replaced, thus eliminating the need to replace the entire unit. With enough money PCs would always spearhead graphic fidelity. Typical consoles of the time could attain resolutions of 320 x 240 or 640 x 480. A PC with a high-quality graphics card could facilitate a resolution of 800 x 600 including impressive lighting effects and higher frame rates. The PC platform not the Arcade would represent the shape of things to come.

Yet it was not only in the realms of graphics where video games would see a revolution. Perhaps just as significant was the evolution of gameplay and game mechanics. Games such as stealth action-adventure Metal Gear Solid (1998), action-adventure RPG The Legend of Zelda: Ocarina of Time (1998) and first-person shooter Half-Life (1998) would all bring vast depths of narrative, character and other innovations to their respective genres, the likes of which had not been experienced ten years before. Whilst many genres have their roots in the previous decades, it was in the 1990s that some of them would firmly establish themselves. For example, the grandfather of the first-person shooter, Wolfenstein 3D (1992), and its father, Doom (1993), both spearheaded by id Software, arrived on the home computer. Meanwhile, the survival horror genre would fully awaken from its slumber in 1996 with Capcom's Resident Evil for the PlayStation.

With titles like Mortal Kombat (1992), Doom (1993) and Postal (1997), the nineties appeared to be a time of ultra-violent games. The 1993 US Senate inquiries attempted to stamp down on these games, which were believed to be affecting America's youth, leading to the establishment of the Entertainment Software Rating Board (ESRB). The rest of the world soon followed suit with their own standard of ratings. However, rather than stifling mature content, this allowed the proliferation of such themes since developers were free to make any kind of game they wished and were happy to receive an 'M' for Mature or 'AO' Adults Only rating.

A couple of other notable advances in technology came with how games were distributed and displayed. For the most part, games moved from floppy disks and cartridges to the CD-ROM, which held hundreds of times more data than a floppy and almost ten times that of a typical games cartridge. The first commercial example of HD Graphics was playable to the public in the form of Hi-Ten Bomberman, deriving its name from a higher resolution, ten-player version of the popular Bomberman game. It was showcased at the 'Super Caravan' gaming event in 1993, hosted by Hudson Soft and shown at forty-four venues across Japan. However, it wouldn't be until the early 2000s that video games would achieve high-definition resolution in the mainstream commercial sector.

Yet there was an even more significant, emerging technology that would define the future of gaming: the internet. It is true that network gaming began in the 1970s, however, it was in the 1990s that Internet gaming really took off, and games such as Neverwinter Nights (1991), The Shadow of Yserbius (1991-1996), SimCity 2000 (1993) and Doom II: Hell on Earth (1994) were just the beginning of this exciting new facet of video games.

Throughout the end of the 1980s and the beginning of the 1990s, there had been a brutal console war between Nintendo, with its Super Nintendo Entertainment System (SNES), and Sega, with its Sega Genesis/Mega Drive. With rumours of the next generation of consoles on the horizon, it seemed that the next console war would be between these two titans. The Nintendo market had been aimed chiefly at young children, while the Sega Genesis's sweet spot was centered around teenagers. However, there was a new contender with the Sony PlayStation, focusing on young people with enough disposable income to pay for their own games rather than relying on their parents' income. The PlayStation far outsold both the new Nintendo 64 and the Sega Dreamcast and shook the gaming world.

Since the late eighties, arcade manufacturers had been constantly seeking new innovations in creating an experience that players could not get in the home. By the end of the nineties the gap between the arcade and home experience, which at one point had been huge, had become so narrow as to become non-existent. Personal computers and consoles offered far more immersive and in-depth experiences than arcades could, despite every gimmick and conceivable idea developers could come up with. By the end of the millennium, arcade cabinets which at one point in the eighties could be found in almost every conceivable catering and entertainment outlet in the West had almost disappeared. Only in Japan did arcades still enjoy a degree of popularity. Many games in the 1970s and 1980s would begin in the arcades and then see ports to the current home computers and consoles. With the slow decline of arcade games in the West, this trend would change. By the end of the 1990s, hardly any games on a home or handheld platform found their origins in the flagging arcades. Perhaps this is why this was not only a decade of technological evolution but also a true revolution in so many aspects of game design. No longer was the industry partially reliant on arcade ports (which were based on a business strategy of short gameplay to make as much money as possible) and their respective clones, but on some genuinely new and innovative gameplay.

Microsoft Entertainment Pack 1

Date of release: 1990

Region: USA

Developer: Microsoft

Publisher: Microsoft

Platform: Windows

The Microsoft Entertainment Pack (MEP) was made up of seven games and a screensaver. These included Minesweeper, Pegged (peg solitaire), Taipei (Mahjong), Tetris, TicTactics (Tic-Tac-Toe/Noughts & Crosses), and two card games (Cruel and Golf). Three more packs followed including classic games like FreeCell, Pipe Dream, Rodent's Revenge and Chess.

The MEPs were intended for casual gaming and are significant for three reasons. Firstly, for the enormous amount of time accumulated by people in offices and at home who played these games for many years all over the world. Secondly, for the millions who still thought video games were for children yet suddenly found themselves playing such games. Finally, they were a precursor of what was to come almost a decade later with the advent of casual gaming on mobile devices.

Klax

Date of release: February 1990

Region: USA

Developer: Atari Games

Publisher: Atari Games

Platform: Arcade

Designed by Dave Akers and Mark Stephen Pierce, Klax is a single or multiplayer 3D Puzzle game. The aim of Klax is to get three blocks of the same colour in a row and achieve the highest score possible, vertically earning 50 points, horizontally 1000 points, and diagonally 5000 points. Each row is called a Klax. When a Klax is achieved, the blocks disappear. Each level requires the player to achieve a specific number of Klax to proceed to the next level. The 3D blocks roll towards you down one of five columns, where you can collect them and quickly drop them into the well in an attempt to make a Klax before collecting the next block. If you do not collect the block then it simply drops down, possibly thwarting the player's attempt to create a Klax. A flashing block can be used as any colour. The well is only five blocks deep. If the well fills without achieving the current goal then the game is over. There are 100 levels in Klax.

The game was one of the most successful and addictive Tetris-inspired games and was soon ported to many 8- and 16-bit home computers and consoles. Klax was the last 'official' game (homebrew games are still made) to be released for the now ancient Atari 2600 (1977).

Game Genie

The Game Genie, also known as the Power Pack, was released in 1990 by Camerica and Galoob for the Nintendo Entertainment System. Developed by Codemasters, the Game Genie is a cheat device, although it was marketed as a 'game enhancer.' Using the Game Genie, a player could 'start on any level, access more power, more speed, more weapons, infinite lives, jump higher and punch harder.' To use the Game Genie, players simply slotted their game into the device and then put the Game Genie into the console. Using codes from a book included with all Game Genies, the player could access many helpful features.

Although not the first such device to be produced, the Game Genie for the NES was the first to be commercially successful, selling over five million units. Nintendo attempted to sue Galoob before they could release their product. However, they were unsuccessful. Other similar 'game enhancers' were developed for the Game Boy, Sega Genesis/Mega Drive, Game Gear, and Super Nintendo Entertainment System.

Railroad Tycoon

Date of release: 1990

Region: Worldwide

Developer: MPS Labs

Publisher: MicroProse

Platform: Multiple 16-bit home computers

Designed by Sid Meier (of Sid Meier's Pirates! (1987) and F-19 Stealth Fighter (1988)) and Bruce Shelly of MPS Labs, Railroad Tycoon is a single-player simulation game. The aim of the game is to build up and manage a railway company, choosing between the roles of Investor, Financier, Mogul or Tycoon. The player can pick between working in Eastern USA, Western USA, England or Europe. Railroad Tycoon features the building of different tracks and stations, an engine shop for manufacturing trains, a stock market system, and the management of the supply and demand of goods.

Railroad Tycoon was highly praised at the time of its release for its attention to detail and clever game mechanics, selling over 400,000 units. Railroad Tycoon has spawned several very successful sequels with Railroad Tycoon II (1998), Railroad Tycoon 3 (2003) and Sid Meier's Railroads! (2006).

Railroad Tycoon won best PC game at the 1990/1991 Golden Joystick Awards

Nintendo World Championship

The Nintendo World Championship was a tournament held in twenty-nine cities in the USA in March 1990. There were three age groups: 11 and under, 12-17, and 18 and above. The original championship ran for three days, with three winners, one for each category. The three winners of each city then went on to the World Final in Los Angeles, California, in December. The finalists played a special Nintendo World Championship cartridge, on which were three customised variations of Rad Racer (1987), Super Mario Bros (1985) and Tetris (NES 1989).

The three winners of the NWC were Erin Schroeder (11 and under), Thor Aackerlund (12-17), and Robert Whitemanin (18 and above). Each winner was awarded $10,000, a 1990 Geo Metro Convertible, 40-inch television, and a gold-painted Mario trophy.

The NWC NES game cartridge is one of the most valuable video games in existence. There are thought to have been only 90 copies of the grey version and 26 gold cartridges. These cartridges do not crop up for sale very often. However, when they do, they have been known to sell for around $20,000. Two other NWCs have taken place since 1990: one in June 2015 and the other in October 2017.

Neo Geo

Neo Geo refers to the release of two products in Japan in April 1990 by SNK Corporation: the Neo Geo Multi Video System Arcade Cabinet, and the Neo Geo Advanced Entertainment System home console. The Neo Geo MVS was an arcade cabinet, of which there were four versions: 1 slot, 2 slot, 4 slot and 6 slot. This referred to the number of game cartridges that could be slotted into the arcade cabinet's motherboard. The cartridges themselves were huge, being almost the same size as a contemporary video game console. Cartridges could be exchanged by owners to maintain the appeal of the machine. The possibility of keeping popular games while exchanging other games for new ones made for an innovative approach and a tidy profit.

SNK also produced a more portable, console version of the cabinet in the form of the Neo Geo Advanced Entertainment System for use in Japanese video game stores and other commercial venues such as bars and hotels. However, due to high demand, this console eventually became available as a luxury home console arcade cabinet in 1991, costing $649.99. This was a very high price when considering that the Super Nintendo Entertainment System, also released in 1991, would cost $199. However, the Neo Geo home console was head and shoulders above its rival consoles and computers, being able to display a possible 4,096 colours from a palette of 65,536, perfectly reproducing the arcade experience which in 1990 was still unmatched when it came to graphics and sound.

The Neo Geo products would go on to sell around one million units in total. Some of the most notable games for the Neo Geo are Samurai Showdown II (1994), Metal Slug (1996), The Last Blade (1997), Blazing Star (1998), King of Fighters 98: The Slugfest (1998), Shock Troopers: 2nd Squad (1998) and Garou: Mark of the Wolves (1999).

Games were produced for the Neo Geo up until 2004, making it one of the longest-supported arcade system in video game history.

Fire Emblem: Ankoku Ryu to Hikari no Tsurugi/Fire Emblem: Shadow Dragon and the Blade of Light

Date of release: April 1990

Region: Japan

Developer: Intelligent Systems

Publisher: Nintendo

Platform: Famicom

Designed by Shouzou Kaga, Keisuke Terasaki, Gunpei Yokoi and with music by Yuka Tsujiyoko, Fire Emblem: Ankoku Ryu to Hikari no Tsurugi (known as Fire Emblem: Shadow Dragon and the Blade of Light in the West) is a single-player, turn-based, tactical role-playing game. You play as Prince Marth, who was driven from his kingdom by the evil sorcerer Gharnef and the Shadow Dragon, Medeus. The aim of the game is to rally your army and reclaim the throne. The narrative of the game is played out as a series of battles on a 2D grid-based map. The player must defeat the enemy army's commander to progress to the next part of the game. There are 21 different classes in the game, all with different abilities and attributes such as health points, movement, strength, physical and magical defence, skill, and evasion. These classes comprise Knights, Paladins, Axemen, Archers, Magicians, Priests, Commandos, Shooters and Hunters, as well as character units, which level up after gaining experience on the battlefield. Classes are strong against certain other classes while being weak against others. Terrain also must be taken into account as it affects player movement and evasion stats.

Fire Emblem would help bring about an emerging trend in tactical/strategy games similar to Desert Commander (1988). Despite being a critical disaster due to its bad graphics and being seen as too complex for many players, Fire Emblem: Ankoku Ryu to Hikari no Tsurugi spawned many sequels in the now highly-successful and popular Fire Emblem series.

Some of the most notable games in the Fire Emblem series are Fire Emblem (2003), Fire Emblem: The Sacred Stones (2004), Fire Emblem: Path of Radiance (2005), Fire Emblem: Radiant Dawn (2007), Fire Emblem: Awakening (2012), Fire Emblem: Shadows of Valentia (2017), and Fire Emblem: Three Houses (2019).

1989/1990s Golden Joystick Awards

The 1989/1990s Golden Joystick Awards was hosted in London on 11th April.

Populous (1989) wins Most Original Game of the Year.

Myth (1989) wins Best Graphics of the Year.

Chase HQ (1987) wins Best Soundtrack of the Year.

The Untouchables (1989) wins Game of the Year.

Smash TV

Date of release: April 1990

Region: USA

Developer: Williams

Publisher: Williams

Platform: Arcade

Designed by Eugene Jarvis (Defender (1981), Robotron: 2084 (1982)), Smash TV is a single-player or two-player co-op multidirectional shooter. To quote the game material: 'The Year is 1999. Television has adapted to the more violent nature of man. The most popular form of television remains the game show. One show, in particular, has dominated the ratings. That show is Smash TV.' The player character is one of the lucky contestants and must battle their way through waves of various enemies in a series of arenas on live TV. The player or players must deal with masses of lethal enemies which pour out of the four doors leading into an arena. These include thugs with baseball bats, floating droids, electric-pulse-generating orbs, mutant lizard men, walking time bombs and end-of-level bosses. As if this was not enough, the player must also deal with, mines, wall-mounted turrets and tanks. Power-ups, such as speed-up, spinning shurikens, triple shot, rocket launcher and smart bombs, can be collected to help deal with your opponents. Players can collect cash and prizes that litter the arena for extra points. The game's final boss is the game show host, who has been transformed into a nightmarish giant half-man, half-tank, killing machine.

Smash TV was essentially a more advanced version of Eugene Jarvis' earlier game Robotron: 2084 (1982). The core gameplay is the same, however, it introduced an undercurrent of social commentary and was influenced by similar concepts in the movie The Running Man (1987). Smash TV drew in players with its over-the-top violence and ridiculous amounts of enemies.

Smash TV was ported to various 8-bit and 16-bit home computers and consoles.

Raiden

Date of release: April 1990

Region: Worldwide

Developer: Seibu Kaihatsu

Publisher: Tecmo

Platform: Arcade

Raiden is a single-player or co-op vertical-scrolling shoot 'em up. In the year 2090, Earth has been invaded by aliens known as the Crystals. As a Vanquish Defence Pilot, you control a Fighting Thunder aircraft. The player's goal is simple: defeat the aliens. Raiden features many of the usual game mechanics of this genre, such as different power-ups, throughout its eight stages. However, Raiden did have a couple of unique features. Players could shoot at one another's craft to generate a special destructive projectile. Whenever a player's craft was destroyed, the shrapnel caused by the explosion would damage enemy ships.

Raiden was another in a long line of vertical-scrolling shoot 'em ups, yet it was precisely what many players of the time still enjoyed. After a slow start, Raiden sold well with around 17,000 units shipped and was ported to some of the consoles.

It was successful enough to spawn several sequels with Raiden II (1993), Raiden DX (1994), Raiden III (2005), Raiden IV (2007) and Raiden V (2016).

Alpha Waves/Continuum

Date of release: August 1990

Region: France

Developer: Infogrames

Publisher: Infogrames

Platform: Atari ST

Designed by Christophe de Dinechin, Alpha Waves (known as Continuum in North America) is a single-player, third-person, 3D platform game. Alpha Waves can be played in two modes: 'Action Mode,' where the player must explore as many rooms as possible before the timer runs out, and 'Emotion Mode,' where the player is free to explore with no time limit. The player controls a simple geometric shape which bounces on a 'foot' of sorts from one platform to another. Each successive bounce on the same platform gains the player more height, akin to a trampoline. The shadow cast by your shape gives you a good idea of your position in the 3D world and allows you to successfully use the platforms to reach the level's exit and enter the next room.

The game was praised for its originality, offering a unique audio-visual experience. Despite its graphics and quaint gameplay, however, others found it a boring game with little replay value.

Alpha Waves was also ported to the Amiga and MS-DOS. It is regarded by some as a milestone in 3D gaming.

Corporation/Cyber-Cop

Date of release: 1990

Region: France

Developer: Synthetic Dimensions

Publisher: Virgin Games

Platform: Amiga

Designed by Kevin Bulmer and Bill Allen of Synthetic Dimensions, Corporation (known as Cyber-Cop in North America), is a single-player, first-person shooter and role-playing game. The aim of Corporation is to infiltrate and expose the illegal activity of the Universal Cybernetics Corporation (or U.C.C.). The player begins the game by choosing a character, each with different skills, two of which are androids. They are given a certain amount of money to spend on equipment. From there, the player must move through each level of the building, dispatching enemies such as robots and genetically modified monsters. The game features a paper doll interface, hacking, key cards to access new areas, and body modifications and enhancements.

At the time, the game was renowned for its 3D graphics. 3D games had been around for some time now yet were becoming even more common on home computers and consoles. Most 3D first-person games were from the point of view of a vehicle. Corporation was a taste of what was to come – the advent of the popular character-driven, first-person shooter such as Wolfenstein 3D (1992), Doom (1993) and System Shock (1994).

Corporation was ported to the Atari ST, MS-DOS, and the Sega Genesis/Mega Drive.

Pit Fighter

Date of release: August 1990

Region: USA

Developer: Atari Games

Publisher: Atari Games

Platform: Arcade

Designed by Gary Stark, Mark Pierce, Paul Kwinn and Rob Rowe, Pit Fighter is a single-player or multiplayer (3-player maximum) fighting game. The aim of Pit Fighter is to progress through as many rounds as possible and to make the most money. The player or players begin by choosing one of three characters: Buzz, the ex-professional wrestler, Ty, kickboxing champion, and Kato, third-degree black belt. They must punch, kick and use their unique special move to defeat their opponents. The stages feature interactive objects on hand, such as bar stools, crates, knives and even motorcycles, to help dispose of challengers. Once all the opponents have been defeated, the surviving players receive money dependent on health remaining.

The characters in the game were digitised from videos of real performers. Even though this was not the first example of this technique in a video game, it would inspire other developers. Pit Fighter was certainly a precursor to the immensely popular Mortal Kombat (1992) series.

Despite being vastly inferior compared to games such as Mortal Kombat, Pit Fighter was well-received at the time. Pit Fighter was ported to various 8-bit and 16-bit home computers and consoles, with varying degrees of success.

Out Zone

Date of release: August 1990

Region: worldwide

Developer: Toaplan

Publisher: Tecmo

Platform: Arcade

Designed by Naoki Ogiwara, Out Zone is a single-player or multiplayer co-op vertical scrolling run and gun game. In the year 2097, aliens menace the human race. You play as one of two cyborg mercenaries and must stop the aliens.

Out Zone features standard power-ups and energy boosts sometimes found in this genre throughout the seven levels of the game, each of which has a boss at the end.

The game was praised for its colourful graphics and smooth, fast-paced gameplay. It was well received in the arcades but tragically was never ported to any computer or console.

Wing Commander

Date of release: September 1990

Region: USA

Developer: Origin Systems

Publisher: Origin Systems

Platform: MS-DOS

Designed by Chris Roberts (who would years later spearhead the crowdfunded game Star Citizen), Wing Commander is a single-player, first-person, space flight simulation game. Wing Commander is set in the year 2654 aboard the Tiger's Claw, a Bengal-class Strike Carrier. The aim of the game is to play your part as a fighter pilot, typically destroying enemy ships with the ultimate aim of leading a successful strike on the Kilrathi High Command Starbase. The gameplay is similar to other space flight simulation games with an emphasis on dogfighting. The game heavily features cutscenes and in-game music, giving the game a real 'Star Wars' or 'Battlestar Galactica' feel.

Wing Commander was a milestone in space flight simulation, which began with games like Spasim (1974), Star Raiders (1979) and Elite (1984). It would inspire LucasArts to develop their own games within this genre, beginning with Star Wars: X-Wing (1993).

Wing Commander was a huge hit on the numerous home computers and consoles it was ported to. It went on to spawn numerous sequels, expansions and remakes, including Wing Commander II: Vengeance of the Kilrathi (1991), Wing Commander III: Heart of the Tiger (1994), Wing Commander IV: The Price of Freedom (1996) and Wing Commander:

Prophecy (1997).

Captive

Date of release: 1990

Region: USA

Developer: Mindscape

Publisher: Mindscape

Platform: Amiga, Atari ST, and MS-DOS

Designed by Anthony Crowther and with music by Chris Crowther, Captive is a single-player, first-person, pseudo-3D role-playing game. You play as Trill, who was cryogenically frozen for 250 years for a crime he did not commit in 2127 AD. Trill awakes two years early in a cell with a briefcase next to him. The briefcase gives him (and therefore, the player) access to four droids and a ship. The aim of the game is to explore several underground facilities located on different planets and destroy the generators which power the force field which prevents him from leaving the space station.

The gameplay is basically the same as Dungeon Master (1987), where the player controls a party exploring the game world and defeating numerous enemies, only with a science fiction theme. Captive features real-time combat and the same effective paper doll interface as Dungeon Master, where players can swap out different droid body parts, essentially upgrading them. These can be found in the 'dungeons' or bought and sold in shops. The game was applauded for its plot and challenging puzzles.

Warlords

Date of release: October 1990

Region: Australia

Developer: Strategic Studies Group

Publisher: Strategic Studies Group

Platform: Amiga and DOS

Warlords was released in Australia in 1990 by Strategic Studies Group for Amiga, MS-DOS and Mac. Developed by Steve Fawkner, Roger Keating, Stephen Hart and Greame Whittle, Warlords is a single-player or multiplayer turn-based fantasy strategy game. The players fight for dominion of the Kingdom of Illuria. The game can be played by between one to eight people, each taking turns, with the computer running any of the remaining factions not player-controlled. The factions in Warlords are The Sirians, The Storm Giants, The Grey Dwarves, The Orcs of Kor, The Elaville (Elves), The Selentines, The Horse Lords, and Lord Bane. The main interface is split vertically into two halves with the right depicting the entire kingdom of Illuria, while the left shows the player's immediate surroundings as seen from above. The player uses their varied unit types to attempt to control the most cities on the map, thus winning the game. Warlords also features heroes, each with unique abilities to empower friendly units, along with ruins, libraries, and temples where hidden relics and allies can be found.

Warlords spawned several sequels with Warlords II (1993), Warlords III (1997) and Warlords IV (2003) each adding new mechanics and improved graphics to the series. The game also inspired a trilogy of spinoff games in the form of the Warlords Battlecry series (2000-2004).

Rampart

Date of release: October 1990

Region: USA

Developer: Atari Games

Publisher: Atari Games

Platform: Arcade

Designed by John Salwitz (720° (1986)), Rampart is a single-player or multiplayer (maximum of 3 players) shooter strategy and puzzle game. The aim of Rampart is to destroy the attacking enemy ships while defending your territory when playing in single-player mode, or to destroy your opponents' castles if playing in multiplayer mode. In both modes, the player must rebuild their castles and capture more land. Rampart is a rather unique game. The first part of the gameplay has the players shooting cannonballs at the enemy or each other. The players must then rebuild parts of their fortifications using different shapes in a puzzle/strategy section of the game under the constraints of a time limit before the next attack commences. The game also features the placement of additional cannons and essentially what amounts to cannon upgrades. It is these game mechanics in Rampart which make it a precursor to the tower defence subgenre.

Rampart was ported to most of the popular platforms of the time.

Powermonger

Date of release: October 1990

Region: UK

Developer: Bullfrog Productions

Publisher: Electronic Arts

Platform: Amiga and Atari ST

Powermonger is a single-player or two-player (using a modem link), fantasy/medieval, real-time strategy game, and is the follow-up to the very popular god game Populous (1989). The aim of Powermonger is to control the map by overcoming the enemy and killing the captains of their armies. The game world is made up of a series of 195 islands. The player starts on small islands and works their way up to progressively larger ones, which are more difficult to conquer. The majority of the screen is taken up by a map and the surrounding control interface. The map is a 3D-textured polygonal landscape that shows only a tiny fraction of the map and scrolls in much the same way as Populous. The player can orbit and zoom in or out of the map for easy orientation. The game begins with the player conquering small villages and drafting any survivors into their army. The dead fly away as angels. Farms, the slaughtering of sheep or pillaging of an enemy's food supply will keep your army's bellies full. Weather conditions, such as rain and snow, can affect gameplay. The player can 'invent' such things as pikes, crossbows and catapults to use against the enemy. Boats need to be constructed to reach the other islands. Enemies are colour-coded to easily identify who is who.

With its 195 islands, Powermonger was rather a large game for the time. A match between two players using two computers hooked together would have been a truly epic spectacle in 1990.

The game was fairly well-received, with its AI and game mechanics highly praised. Powermonger was ported to a handful of 16-bit home computers and consoles. A World War I expansion set was released for Powermonger in 1991.

The Secret of Monkey Island

Date of release: October 1990

Region: USA

Developer: Lucasfilm Games

Publisher: Lucasfilm Games

Platform: 16-bit home computers

Designed by Ron Gilbert, Greg Hammond, Dave Grossman and Tim Shafer, The Secret of Monkey Island is a single-player point-and-click, pirate adventure set in the Caribbean. You play as Guybrush Threepwood, whose aim is to be a pirate. Noted for its colourful humour, the narrative has the player attempt to complete three trials set by the pirate leaders on Mêlée Island. However, when Guybrush meets the beautiful governor Elaine Marley, everything changes. Elaine is abducted by the infamous ghost pirate LeChuck and his undead crew. The remaining part of the game involves the player putting together a crew and sailing off to Monkey Island in an effort to save Elaine and somehow stop LeChuck.

The developers of The Secret of Monkey Island originally drew inspiration from the Pirates of the Caribbean ride at Disneyland. The game was the fifth to use Lucasfilm Games' propriety SCUMM (Script Creation Utility for Maniac Mansion) game engine, somewhat evolved since its initial creation in 1987.

The Secret of Monkey Island was highly praised, yet only sold around 100,000 units when it was released: a good but not great outcome. However, with the subsequent sequels, the series gained traction and the original game received the respect and retrospective accolade it deserved. Often cited as one of the most significant games in video game history, The Secret of Monkey Island is admired for its puzzles, narrative, memorable music and, most notably, humour. The trading insults game mechanic, used as a way to win swordfights, is just one of many examples of this humour. The Secret of Monkey Island is perhaps one of the wittiest video games ever released.

The Secret of Monkey Island spawned four sequels with Monkey Island 2: LeChuck's Revenge (1991). The Curse of Monkey Island (1997), Escape from Monkey Island (2000) and Tales of Monkey Island (2009).

Game Gear

The Game Gear was released in Japan in October 1990 by Sega. The Game Gear is an 8-bit, fourth-generation, cartridge-based handheld game console, with a resolution of 160 x 144 pixels. It could display 32 colours from a palette of 4096, boasting 8KB of RAM and 16KB of video RAM and sold for $149.99 in America, where it was eventually released in 1991. The Sega Game Gear featured a standard D-Pad, two controller buttons and a start button. Like the Atari Lynx, and unlike the Nintendo Game Boy, the Game Gear's display had a backlight.

The Game Gear was Sega's attempt to enter the handheld market, meant to compete with the aforementioned Game Boy, Lynx and the NEC's Turbo Express due to be released at the end of 1990. As well as its own games, the Game Gear was able to play Sega Master System games by using an adapter that slotted into the cartridge port. A TV tuner accessory was also available, which plugged into the console, in the same way, allowing the buyer to watch television.

Even though it could not achieve the same incredible success as the Game Boy, the Game Gear easily outsold both the Lynx and the Turbo Express with over 10 million units, in some ways marking it as a success. However, it was often criticized for its power consumption (with its batteries lasting 3-5hrs) and its game library. Sega never followed it up with another handheld game console.

Some of the most notable games for the Game Gear are Prince of Persia (1992), Shinobi II: The Silent Fury (1992), Sonic the Hedgehog 2 (1992), Land of Illusion starring Micky Mouse (1993), Streets of Rage 2 (1993), Shining Force II: The Swords of Hajya (1994) and Gunstar Heroes (1995).

Super Famicom/Super Nintendo Entertainment System

The Super Famicom (what would be known as the Super Nintendo System or SNES, released a year, later in America) was released in Japan in November 1990 by Nintendo. Designed by Masayuki Uemura, the Super Famicom is a fourth-generation, 16-bit, cartridge-based home video game console. Even though the now-ageing original Famicom/NES was still holding its own against technically more powerful machines such as the PC Engine/TurboGrafx-16 (1987) and the Sega Genesis (1988), Nintendo knew that if they wanted to compete, they would have to develop a 16-bit console of their own. When the original Super Famicom first launched, its initial shipment of 300,000 units sold out within the first few hours. The Super Famicom shipped with 128KB of RAM and could output at a resolution of 512 x 448 pixels, with a possible 256 different colours on screen from a palette of 32,768.

The Super Famicom and SNES would become the best-selling fourth-generation home console selling 49 million units in total.

Some of the most notable games for the Super Famicom/SNES are Super Mario World

(1990), Super Castlevania IV (1991), The Legend of Zelda: A Link to the Past (1991), Super Mario Kart (1992), Star Fox (1993), Street Fighter II Turbo: Hyper Fighting (1993), Chrono Trigger (1995), Donkey Kong Country (1994), Final Fantasy III (AKA Final Fantasy VI) (1994), Super Metroid (1994), Earthbound (1995) and Super Mario RPG: Legend of the Seven Stars (1996).

Castle of Illusion Starring Mickey Mouse

Date of release: November 1990

Region: Worldwide

Developer: Sega

Publisher: Sega

Platform: Sega Master System, Game Gear & Genesis/Mega Drive

Designed by Emiko Yamamoto, Yoshio Yoshida and Stephen L. Butler, Castle of Illusion Starring Mickey Mouse is a single-player, side-scrolling platform game. The aim of the game is to rescue Minnie Mouse from the evil witch Mizrabel. To defeat Mizrabel, Mickey must find seven gems, each one gained by defeating a Master of Illusion boss located at the end of each one of the six levels within the Castle. The six levels are the Enchanted Forest, Toyland, the Storm, Dessert Factory, the Library, and the Castle. At the end of the game, Mickey must defeat Mizrabel to be reunited with Minnie. Mickey's main aim of defeating a multitude of enemies is by jumping on their heads, which gives him additional height to reach higher levels and items like apples. By throwing them, these can also be used to defeat enemies.

Castle of Illusion Starring Mickey Mouse was renowned for the quality of its graphics, animation, smooth and responsive gameplay, sound, and music. In 1998, it was ported to the Sega Saturn. A remake with improved graphics and sound was developed and released in 2013.

Castle of Illusion had three major sequels: Land of Illusion Starring Mickey Mouse (1992), World of Illusion Starring Mickey Mouse and Donald Duck (1992) and Legend of Illusion Starring Mickey Mouse (1995).

King's Quest V: Absence Makes the Heart Go Yonder!

Date of release: November 1990

Region: USA

Developer: Sierra On-Line

Publisher: Sierra On-Line

Platform: various home computers and the NES

King's Quest V is a single-player, point-and-click adventure game. The game begins with the evil wizard Mordack using magic to make Castle Daventry vanish. As King Graham, the player must rescue the rest of the royal family, defeat the wizard, and return the castle to its proper place.

King's Quest V featured Improved VGA (Video Graphics Array) graphics and was the first King's Quest game to replace text-based input with a point-and-click interface. It was also the first King's Quest game to make the transition to voice acting, the quality of which became a matter of contention. King's Quest V became another firm favourite with fans, selling over 500,000 units.

Super Mario World/Super Mario World: Super Mario Bros. 4

Date of release: November 1990

Region: Japan

Developer: Nintendo EAD

Publisher: Nintendo

Platform: Super Famicom

Designed by Takashi Tezuka and Shigeru Miyamoto with music by Koji Kondo, Super Mario World (known as Super Mario World: Super Mario Bros. 4 in Japan) is a single-player or multiplayer, side-scrolling platform game. The aim of Super Mario World is to save Princess Toadstool and Dinosaur Land from Bowser. As with previous Mario games, the player controls either Mario or his brother Luigi and must defeat numerous enemies, including bosses, collecting coins and power-ups to achieve their goal. Some familiar power-ups make an appearance in Super Mario World such as the Super Mushroom (increasing Mario in size), the Fire Flower (allowing Mario to throw fireballs), and the Starman (Invincibility). New power-ups in Super Mario World include the feather (turning Mario into Cape Mario giving him the ability to spin attack enemies and fly) and, most significantly, the introduction of Yoshi, a power-up dinosaur companion, whom Mario rides. Yoshi can eat and spit out enemies. When Yoshi eats a Yellow Koopa, he gains the ability to ground pound, damaging nearby enemies. Blue Koopas allow him to fly, and Red Koopas give him the ability to spit a spread-shot volley of fireballs. Mario himself has the new ability of the Spin Jump, an extra powerful jump, to defeat enemies and destroy blocks.

The development team for Super Mario World added as many new features as possible to set it apart from the previous Mario games and establish it as a fresh new game for the Super Famicom/SNES 16-bit platform with its ability to display 256 colours on the screen. To this end, Super Mario World featured: large enemies, Mode 7 scaling and rotation, mosaic pixelation transitions, multiple scrolling backgrounds, and up to 128 simultaneous moving sprites. Twenty-four of the ninety-six levels have hidden levels or second exits. The developers threw everything they had at the game, along with the kitchen sink.

Super Mario World was one of the original Super Famicom/SNES launch titles. With the huge success of the original Famicom/NES and the integration of Mario into Japanese and American culture, Super Mario World was a phenomenal success. Super Mario World revolutionised platform gaming and video games as a whole, selling over twenty million units. This made it the most successful game released in 1990 and the best-selling game for the Super Famicom/SNES. It is often cited as one of the greatest video games of all time.

F-Zero

Date of release: November 1990

Region: Japan

Developer: Nintendo EAD

Publisher: Nintendo

Platform: Super Famicom

F-Zero is a single-player, third-person, futuristic racing game. The game is set in the year 2560, where the player chooses one of four high-speed hovercars in the F-Zero tournament. The aim of the game is to win the race while avoiding hazards, such as high-powered magnets and slip zones.

F-Zero used a technique called Mode 7 Scrolling which enabled it to appear as if the hover cars were travelling at speeds in excess of 400 km/ph. Players were stunned by the incredibly smooth gameplay only previously seen in arcade versions of games like Hang On (1985) and Out Run (1986), and as such the game was highly praised by critics and consumers alike. Its only downside was its lack of a multiplayer feature.

F-Zero inspired a 51-episode anime series called F-Zero: GP Legend and spawned a series of sequels, most notably F-Zero X (1998).

G-Loc: Air Battle

Date of release: November 1990

Region: Worldwide

Developer: Sega AM2

Publisher: Sega

Platform: Arcade

Developed by Yu Suzuki, G-Loc: Air Battle is a first-person and third-person, single-player, air combat simulation game. The aim of the game is simple: complete the current mission within the allotted time to continue. Missions often require the player to shoot down several enemy planes.

G-Loc: Air Battle was the culmination of Yu Suzuki's experiments with arcade cabinets in the shape of a bike, starting with Hang-On (1985), which the player straddled and pushed side to side to take the corners on the screen. Space Harrier (1985) and Out Run (1986) moved with the action with both featuring movements across three axes. After Burner (1987) moved even further, tipping players almost onto their front and back. G-Loc: Air Battle could spin the player 360 degrees in any direction. Arcade games were still holding their own against home video games with these unmatched innovations.

The game was ported to some of the most popular home computers and consoles of the time. However, these ports were pretty lacklustre as they lacked the 360-degree freedom of movement found only on the arcade versions.

Turbo Express/PC Engine GT

The Turbo Express, known as the PC Engine GT, was released in Japan and North

America (though never in Europe) in December 1990 by NEC Home Electronics. It is a fourth-generation, cartridge-based, 16-bit, handheld console that had a backlit LCD. Its display was the same size as Nintendo's Game Boy and had a resolution of 400 x 270 pixels with 481 colours drawn from a 512-colour palette. The TurboExpress sold for $249.99. A link cable was available to facilitate player versus player or cooperative play with two TurboExpress handhelds. A TV tuner was also available. Its biggest draw was the fact that it could play original PC Engine/TurboGrafx games. To play Japanese PC Engine games on the TurboExpress handheld, however, you needed a convertor.

To be able to play near-arcade-quality versions of games like Street Fighter II on a handheld device in 1990 was mind-blowing. However, on the negative side, its batteries did not last long and the price was fairly high when compared to the Game Boy, the market leader at the time.

Some of the most notable games for the TurboExpress/PC Engine GT are: Military Madness (1988), Blazing Lazers (1989), Bonk's Revenge (1989), Neutopia II (1991), Splatterhouse (1990), Bomberman '93 (1992) and Street Fighter II: Championship Edition (1999)

StarTropics

Date of release: December 1990

Region: USA

Developer: Nintendo R&D3

Publisher: Nintendo

Platform: NES

StarTropics is a single-player action-adventure game. You play as Mike, a fifteen-year-old boy, who goes to visit his uncle, Dr Jones, on C-Island, Coralcola. The aim of StarTropics is to rescue your uncle who has been abducted. You are given a yoyo to use as a weapon (later Mike can use more powerful weapons such as a baseball and a shooting star) to deal with various enemies you may encounter on the island. The majority of the game is seen from a 2D top-down perspective.

StarTropics plays very much like the Legend of Zelda games, where the player deals with enemies and must make their way through a series of different 'dungeons'. While StarTropics also features puzzles and bosses, it is its narrative that makes it a compelling and quirky game. A great deal of emphasis is placed on interacting with the many interesting characters scattered throughout the game who help progress the plot. For example, Mike finds a submarine and, with the help of a droid, encounters a talking dolphin who asks Mike to help find her missing son. He eventually finds a message in a bottle from his uncle, informing him he's been captured by aliens! Once Mike has found his uncle, he must find three 'magic cubes' on the alien spaceship and defeat the 'Prime Invader, Zoda.'

StarTropics is often compared to The Legend of Zelda. Even though it is indeed true that there are similarities, StarTropics is a great game in its own right. The gameplay and mechanics are solid, and the narrative is involving and endearing.

StarTropics spawned one sequel with Zoda's Revenge: StarTropics II (1994).

Commander Keen in Invasion of the Vorticons trilogy

Date of release: December 1990

Region: USA

Developer: id Software

Publisher: Apogee Software

Platform: MS-DOS

'Marooned on Mars,' was the first in the 'Commander Keen in Invasion of the Vorticons' trilogy of games and was released as a shareware game, meaning that it was free to play, albeit limited in available content. The other two episodes were released in the traditional method. Designed by Tom Hall, John Carmack, John Romero and Adrian Carmack, and with music by Robert Prince, Commander Keen is a single-player, side-scrolling platform game. You play as eight-year-old boy genius Billy Blaze, who also goes under the pseudonym 'Commander Keen.' While exploring Mars, your spaceship (made from household items) is dismantled and stolen by the Vorticons. The aim of the game is to find the stolen parts in the Vorticon fortresses. The gameplay consists of platform jumping, shooting enemies, and collecting items. Key cards grant access to other fortresses. The game is non-linear, meaning the player can leave a fortress at any time and access any other fortress on the Martian surface, providing they have the corresponding key card.

In the second game of the trilogy, 'The Earth Explodes,' Commander Keen must disable the Vorticon cannons aimed at famous landmarks on Earth. In the final game, 'Keen Must Die!,' Commander Keen must defeat the 'Grand Intellect,' with the result being that the Vorticons (whom you've been killing all this time) now hail you as a hero.

Commander Keen was significant to PC gaming as it was the first PC platform game that had been expertly programmed by John Carmack using a new technique called Adaptive Tile Refresh to allow for smooth scrolling. The game was very well-received and became something of a cult classic. This first trilogy of games spawned an entire series, with games such as Commander Keen in Keen Dreams (1991), Commander Keen in Goodbye, Galaxy (1991), Commander Keen in Aliens Ate My Babysitter (1991) and Commander Keen (2001).

Speedball 2: Brutal Deluxe

Date of release: December 1990

Region: UK

Developer: The Bitmap Brothers

Publisher: Image Works

Platform: Various 8-bit and 16-bit home computers

Speedball 2: Brutal Deluxe is a single-player and multiplayer futuristic sports game, and the sequel to Speedball (1988). The aim of Speedball 2 is to score more points than the opposing team in each game with the ultimate goal of winning the league. The players score points by throwing the ball through their opponent's goal by any means necessary. However, there are other ways to score points. Violence in the game is encouraged to make it as entertaining as possible for the masses.

The pitch is over three times larger than in the original Speedball and there are nine players per team (with another three as subs), instead of the previous five. Gameplay consists of two 90-second halves, making Speedball 2 a fast-paced game. As well as scoring goals to earn points, players can also increase their score by severely injuring an opposing player, throwing the ball against bounce domes on the pitch, and throwing the ball against the stars on the wall. If the player can throw the ball up the multiplier ramp, then all points scored while the multiplier is activated will be doubled. There are warp gates down the sides of the pitch to allow players to easily get the ball from one side of the pitch to the other. Coins can be picked up for use between games. Other power-ups appear and when picked up affect the entire team for a short time, usually around six seconds. These include tokens which freeze opponents, reverse their directional input, reduce the opposing players' attributes to the minimum, gives you possession of the ball, prevents the ball from entering your goal and makes your team immune to tackles.

The game also features team positioning, the buying and selling of players, improving different player attributes at the gym, and increasing attributes by purchasing additional armour.

Speedball 2: Brutal Deluxe was praised for its intense and fun gameplay, fantastic graphics, and great music and sound (notably the sardonic cry of "Ice-cream Ice-cream" should an own goal be scored). Several remakes have been released over the years, yet none have had the impact of the original. Speedball 2: Brutal Deluxe won Best Soundtrack at the 1990/1991 Golden Joystick Awards. It is often cited as one of the greatest video games of all time.

1990 Notable Omissions

Act Raiser. Alex Kidd in Shinobi World. Aliens. Alien Storm. B.A.T. Blood Bros. Bomberman (PC Engine). Cisco Heat. Crystalis. Columns. Conflict: Middle East Political Simulator. Devil's Crush. Double Dragon III: The Rosetta Stone. Dr. Mario. Eidos Interactive is founded. Final Lap 2. Galaxian 3: Project Dragoon. Ghostbusters. G-Loc: Air Battle. It Came From the Desert Remake. James Pond: Underwater Agent. Journey to Silius. Kwik Snax. Liquid Kids. Lotus Esprit Turbo Challenge. Mado Monogatari. Mega Man 3. Metal Gear 2: Solid Snake. Michael Jackson's Moonwalker. NAM-1975. Nintendo sues Color Dreams. Out Zone. Parodiusda! From Myth to Laughter. PGA Tour Golf. Pilotwings. Pistol Daimyo no Boken. Rabbit Jack's Casino. Red Baron. Revolution Software Limited is founded. Rick Dangerous 2. Rise of the Dragon. Rodland. Robocop 2. Rolling Thunder 2. Sega Master System II. Snake Rattle 'n' Roll. Snake's Revenge. Snow Bros. Space Gun. Steel Gunner. Star Control. Super Cars. Super Glove Ball. Supremacy: Your Will Be Done. Team 17 is founded. The Killing Game Show. Trog. Turrican. Ultima VI: The False Prophet. Wings. World Stadium '90. X-Out.

1991

Lemmings

Date of release: February 1991

Region: UK

Developer: DMA Design

Publisher: Psygnosis

Platform: Amiga

Designed by David Jones, Russel Kay and Mike Daily of DMA Design, Lemmings is a single-player or two-player puzzle game. The aim of Lemmings is to safely guide as many Lemmings to the designated level exit. The game begins with a short and quaint cutscene featuring the cutesy, green-haired lemmings. At the beginning of each unique level, the lemmings drop through a trap door and proceed to walk quite often towards their doom, varying from a fatal drop or blundering into a lava pit. The player must use the tools at the bottom of the screen to assign the lemmings to perform specific roles. These include: climber – climbs vertical surfaces, floater – an umbrella opens up to ensure safe descent, blocker – blocks lemmings and turns them in the other direction, bomb – explodes a lemming, bridge builder – self-explanatory, basher – digs horizontally, and miner – digs diagonally down. The player could also click the 'Nuke' button, which would explode all remaining lemmings should the level be turning into a lost cause and, if nothing else, is very entertaining to watch. There is a time limit to get all your lemmings to the exit. When the timer reaches zero, the remaining lemmings begin to explode. This means that even if the player has failed the game, it offers something unique and entertaining. In two-player mode, the screen is split vertically, and each player competes to save the most lemmings.

Lemmings was highly praised by critics and loved by consumers. At the time it was one of the few completely original ideas for a videogame. It was amusing and delightful in its presentation. The mechanics and puzzle elements mixed with the clever level design were nothing short of genius. It went on to be one of the most widely ported games in history and spawned several remakes and sequels including Oh No! More Lemmings (1991), Lemmings 2: The Tribes (1993), All New World of Lemmings (1994), 3D Lemmings (1995) and Lemmings Revolution (2000).

Lemmings was the most successful computer game of 1991 and has sold more than twenty million units across various platforms since its initial release.

id Software is founded

id Software is founded in the USA in February 1991 by John Carmack, Adrian Carmack, Tom Hall, and John Romero. id Software's initial release was the first Commander Keen game (1990) before going on to work on a series of first-person shooter games with Hovertank 3D (1991), Catacomb 3-D (1991), culminating in the release of Wolfenstein 3D (1992). However, even this paled compared to the release of the phenomenal Doom (1993) and Quake (1996). id Software is known for turning these games into very popular franchises such as Wolfenstein (1992-2008), Doom (1996-current date) and Quake (1996-current date).

Blizzard Entertainment is founded

Blizzard Entertainment was founded originally under the name Silicon Synapse, Inc., in California USA in February 1991 by Michael Morhaime, Frank Pearce and Allen Adham. The company initially worked on ports of other games until developing their own titles from 1993 onwards. Blizzard are best known for their Warcraft series (1994-current date), Diablo series (1997-current date), StarCraft series (1998-2015), Hearthstone (2014-current date) and Overwatch (2016-current date).

The Simpsons

Date of release: March 1991

Region: USA

Developer: Konami

Publisher: Konami

Platform: Arcade

The Simpsons is a single-player or multiplayer, side-scrolling beat 'em up, based on the popular US animated sitcom of the same name. The aim of The Simpsons is to rescue the kidnapped Maggie Simpson. Up to four players can play cooperatively, choosing to be either Homer, Marge, Bart or Lisa Simpson, each with their own signature attack. The Simpsons must fight through waves of various enemies to defeat Mister Burns and save Maggie. The game features many of the characters and references to specific, well-known gags from the show.

Konami had a huge amount of success in America with a similar four-player game, Teenage Mutant Ninja Turtles (1989), and was keen to capitalise on another well-known franchise. The Simpsons was perfect. It followed very similar gameplay and mechanics to Teenage Mutant Ninja Turtles, such as boss fights and cutscenes.

The Simpsons was also another arcade game that could make a lot of money. Players would not want to let their teammates down and would readily pump more coins into the cabinet with a little peer pressure. The game was a firm favourite in the arcades and was exported to the Commodore 64 and MS-DOS. The arcade incarnation would be the second Simpsons video game. The first was Bart vs. the Space Mutants (1991), released only a month earlier on the NES. Other notable Simpsons games are The Simpsons: Road Rage (2001), The Simpsons Hit & Run (2003), The Simpsons Game (2007) and The Simpsons: Tapped Out (2012).

Street Fighter II: The World Warrior

Date of release: March 1991

Region: Worldwide

Developer: Capcom

Publisher: Capcom

Platform: Arcade

Designed by Yoshiki Okamoto, Noritaka Funamizu, Akira Nishitani and Akira Yasuda, and featuring music by Yoko Shimomura, Street Fighter II: The World Warrior (typically referred to simply as Street Fighter II) is a single-player or two-player fighting game, and the sequel to Street Fighter (1987). The aim of the game is to defeat your opponent by reducing their health bar to zero and thus deliver a knockout (KO) in a best-two-out-of-three match. In the original Street Fighter, there were only two playable characters, whereas in Street Fighter II there are up to eight: Ryu, E. Honda, Blanka, Guile, Dhalsim, Zangief, Chun Li, and Ken. They hail from various parts of the world. This roster of playable fighters has given us some of the most well-known characters in video game culture. The player controls their character using an eight-directional joystick and six buttons for light, medium, and heavy punch, and light, medium, and heavy kick. What really elevated Street Fighter II was its special combination attacks, also known as special moves or combos. Each character had a handful of combos that a skilful player could master and chain together at the opportune moment, to give them an advantage in combat.

It cannot be understated the impact Street Fighter II had in video game history. It is arguably the most significant game ever in the fighting genre, making most of its predecessors feel clunky in their gameplay by comparison. Whereas the previous decades of fighting games had been dominated by martial arts games like Karate Champ Player vs Player (1984) and International Karate+/Chop N' Drop (1987), Street Fighter II would set the trend for more fantastical characters with their supernatural special moves, inspiring almost every fighting game that would come after it, such as the Mortal Kombat series (1992-current date), Fighters History (1993) and Killer Instinct (1994).

In April 1992, Street Fighter II: Championship Edition was released. This was the same game, yet featuring four additional characters and mirror matching, meaning different players could choose the same character if they so wished. The game was a phenomenal success throughout the world and received a multitude of awards, as well as being cited by some as the best video game of all time.

Street Fighter II was ported to most of the popular gaming platforms of the time and inevitably went on to spawn a multitude of sequels and variations, some of the most notable of these being Street Fighter II Turbo: Hyper Fighting (1992), Super Street Fighter II Turbo (1994), Street Fighter Alpha 2 (1996), Street Fighter Alpha 3 (1998), Street Fighter III: 3rd Strike (1999), Ultra Street Fighter IV (2014) and Street Fighter V: Arcade Edition (2018). Street Fighter II would go on to be the third best-selling arcade game of all time. In fact, at the time supply could not keep up with demand and queues would build up around machines. Some venues simply couldn't get their hands on enough machines, so popular was the game. Street Fighter II sold around 200,000 cabinets, bringing in an estimated $2.3 billion by 1995!

Shining and the Darkness/Shining in the Darkness

Date of release: March 1991

Region: Japan

Developer: Climax Entertainment

Publisher: Sega

Platform: Sega Genesis/Mega Drive

Shining and the Darkness, known as Shining in the Darkness in the West, is a single-player, first-person, turn-based, tactical dungeon crawler RPG, and the first game in the Shining series. The aim of the game is to travel through the labyrinth, rescue Princess Jessa and your father, and defeat the evil sorcerer Dark Sol. The player picks up members of their party who accompany them and help defeat the various enemies found in the labyrinth. Combat is turn-based, with each player possessing different abilities, earning experience points and levelling up. The game features similar elements found in most JRPGs, ranging from the Shrine, which allows the players to save, cure ailments, revive party members and remove curses, to the Tavern which allows the player to talk to NPCs (non-player characters) and sleep, restoring all hit points (HP) and magic points (MP). There are also three different shops where the player can sell and buy equipment, namely the Weapons Dealer, the Armorer, and the Alchemist.

The game used a scaling sprite technique to give the impression of moving through a labyrinth from a first-person perspective.

First-person, turn-based dungeon crawlers had been around for years on home computers. However, they were a little rarer on consoles, and while many players in Japan and America were familiar with Dragon Quest, Final Fantasy, and Phantasy Star, Shining in the Darkness was for some European gamers their first experience of a JRPG.

Shining in the Darkness was highly praised for its graphics, sound, script and its combat mechanics: using an icon-based menu system was considered especially innovative. The game spawned several sequels, including Shining Force (1992), Shining Force II (1993), Shining Force CD (1994), Shining Force III (1997) and Shining Force: Resurrection of the Dark Dragon (2004).

1990/1991s Golden Joystick Awards

1990/1991 Golden Joystick Awards is hosted in London on 4th April.

Midnight Resistance wins Best Graphics of the Year.

Robocop 2 wins Best Soundtrack of the Year.

Railroad Tycoon wins PC Game of the Year.

Rick Dangerous 2 wins Game of the Year.

Eye of the Beholder

Date of release: 1991

Region: USA

Developer: Westwood Associates

Publisher: Strategic Simulations Inc

Platform: MS-DOS

Eye of the Beholder is a single-player, first-person, 3D, party-based RPG. It is the first in the Eye of the Beholder trilogy and the sixth Advanced Dungeons & Dragons video game to be released. The aim of Eye of the Beholder is to investigate and deal with the evil spreading from beneath the city of Waterdeep. You control a party of four adventurers, which can be expanded to six (two of which are NPCs) later in the game. The player can choose between male or female human, elf, half-elf, dwarf, gnome, and halfling. With its tabletop counterpart, the player can choose from six classes (Warrior, Thief, Mage, Cleric, Paladin and Ranger) and allocate the adventurer's stat attributes and alignment. Eye of the Beholder plays similarly to other games in the then-burgeoning genre. It features real-time combat with monsters, puzzles and traps to contend with, over forty different magic spells, and the paper doll interface for equipping armour, weapons, and managing a character's inventory. There are twelve levels. At the end of the game, the player must defeat Xanathar, the titular Beholder, a floating mass of flesh and tentacles, with one huge cyclopean eye, gaping maw and ten surrounding eyestalks. The Beholder is one of Dungeons and Dragons' most iconic monsters, appearing in every edition of the traditional tabletop RPG game since its first publication in 1974.

Eye of the Beholder was highly praised when released and was seen as a progressive next step from Dungeon Master (1987). It sold over 150,000 units and was soon ported to the Amiga, Sega CD, SNES and PC-98. It soon spawned two sequels in what would become the trilogy. Players could import their characters from the original game to Eye of the Beholder II: The Legend of Darkmoon (1991) and from the second game to the third, Eye of the Beholder III: Assault on Myth Drannor (1993).

Hovertank 3D

Date of release: April 1991

Region: USA

Developer: id Software

Publisher: Softdisk

Platform: MS-DOS

Designed by Tom Hall, John Carmack, John Romero and Adrian Carmack of id Software, Hovertank 3D is a single-player, first-person, vehicular combat game. The aim of Hovertank 3D is to rescue all the people in each city before a nuclear strike destroys everything. Various mutated enemies and enemy tanks seek to prevent you from accomplishing your mission and must be dealt with accordingly. A radar displays enemies and the people who need rescuing, and a timer informs the player how much time is left until the nuclear strike.

Despite looking rather primitive by today's standards, Hovertank 3D is extremely significant. The game engine John Carmack wrote for it was used (with further refinement) for Catacomb 3D (1991) and subsequently Wolfenstein 3D (1992). This then would lead to one of the biggest landmark games in the first-person shooter genre: Doom (1993). Even though there had been similar 3D FPS games such as Maze War (1973), Hovertank 3D would pave the way for the birth of the modern-day FPS.

Micro Machines

Date of release: 1991

Region: Worldwide

Developer: Codemasters

Publisher: Camerica

Platform: NES

Micro Machines is a single-player or multiplayer racing game, based on Galoob's popular Micro Machines toy line. The aim is to finish in first or second place to qualify and progress to the next race. The premise is that the player will be taking control of their very own Micro Machines toy vehicle and race around the real-world environments, seemingly giant from the game's perspective. There are four participants in each race, one or two of which can be controlled by the players, while the other vehicles are controlled by the game. The player can choose between eleven different vehicles, each with different abilities. The game is played from a 2D top-down perspective with the camera following the lead vehicle. Vehicles include sports cars racing around a school desk, tanks on the garage floor, helicopters in the garden, Formula One cars on the pool table, buggies racing in the sandpit, powerboats in the bathtub, and 4x4s on the kitchen table. Each track has obstacles and hazards which slow your vehicle down, such as running through spilt glue or syrup.

Micro Machines was highly acclaimed by critics and very popular with gamers. It was praised for its immensely fun gameplay (racing these miniature vehicles around such novelty tracks turned out to be tremendously enjoyable), and for its highly competitive and unique gaming experience.

The game was soon ported to the popular consoles and the Amiga. It also spawned a series of sequels with Micro Machines 2: Turbo Tournament (1994), Micro Machines Military (1996), Micro Machines V3 (1997), Micro Machines (2000), Micro Machines V4 (2006) and Micro Machines World Series (2017).

Bungie is founded

Bungie was founded in Washington USA in May 1991 by Alex Seropian. Bungie is best known for the Marathon series (1994-96), Myth series (1997-98), Halo series (2001-2010) (after this time the Halo series has been developed by 343 industries) and Destiny series (2014-current date).

Time Traveller

Date of release: 1991

Region: USA

Developer: Virtual Image Productions

Publisher: Sega

Platform: Arcade

Designed by Rick Dyer, Time Traveller is a single-player, LaserDisc holographic interactive movie game. The player controls cowboy Marshal Gram who must rescue Princess Kyi-La and save the universe from the evil time lord Vulcor. The player used a joystick to move Gram in one of four directions and a button for Gram to fire his pistol. As this was a LaserDisc game, the player did not move the character in real-time. Instead, on-screen prompts told the player in which direction to move the joystick and which way to shoot. This would then result in either a successful animation being played where Gram would dispatch the threat or a failure animation showing a brief death scene. The player only had a very short amount of time to initiate the correct input meaning that they had to focus and hold their nerve lest they make a mistake.

What set Time Traveller apart from other LaserDisc games or games that used real-life actors was that it was the world's first holographic video game. The holographic effect was achieved by reflecting the television screen on a curved mirror, making it seem like these figures were standing on a miniature stage. Sega intended to develop this new technology and expand it to multiplayer games hoping that, like traditional video games, it would evolve into something very lucrative. However, despite its brief success with the game making $1 million a week, it was not to be. The novelty of the game soon wore off and visitors to the arcades turned their attention back to games like Street Fighter II (1991) and Mortal Kombat (1992). Return on the game plummeted and Time Traveller seemed to be a flash in the pan.

Sonic the Hedgehog

Date of release: June/July 1991

Region: USA/ Japan

Developer: Sega Team

Publisher: Sega

Platform: Sega Mega Drive/Genesis

Designed by Yuji Naka, Shinobu Toyoda and Hirokazu Yasuhara of the newly-formed Sonic Team, Sonic the Hedgehog is a single-player, side-scrolling, platform game. The player must stop the game's antagonist Dr Eggman (Dr Robotnik in the West) by collecting the six Chaos Emeralds before Eggman/Robotnik can and free your captured animal friends. You play as Sonic, a blue hedgehog, who runs at supersonic speed through each level, collecting gold rings. The player can run, jump and perform a spin attack, gain a boost in speed if Sonic is already going fast enough to pass through tunnels, do loop-the-loops, go over bridges and bounce off springboards unhindered by hazards such as spikes or a variety of enemies. Sonic begins the game with three lives. A life is lost if he collides with any hazards or enemies while not in possession of any rings, which act as a layer of protection. A life is immediately lost, however, should he, fall down a bottomless pit, drown, or fail to finish the level within the allotted time. Sonic's score is based on how many rings are collected and how much time has elapsed upon completing the level. An extra life is awarded if Sonic manages to collect 100 rings. There are six unique environments, known as zones. These are Green Hill Zone, Marble Zone, Spring Yard Zone, Labyrinth Zone, Star Light Zone, Scrap Brain Zone and then the Final Zone in Sonic the Hedgehog, each with three levels, or acts. At the end of each zone, there is a boss battle against Eggman/Robotnik, with a final decisive fight at the end of the game

Sega needed a mascot to compete with Nintendo's Mario, to better launch a brand they could build on and sell their console and more games. Sonic was inspired by Felix the Cat and Mickey Mouse and was originally going to be named 'Mr Needlemouse.' Players loved the character of Sonic the Hedgehog and the exciting breakneck speed of the game, only possible via an algorithm developed by Yuji Naka. Nothing like this had ever been seen in the platform genre. Some Western critics praised the game while others said it was too fast and difficult. However, the consensus among players was that this was not the case, which could easily be seen by its successful sales and the plethora of its ports and many sequels. Some of the most notable of these are Sonic the Hedgehog 2 (1992), Sonic CD (1993), Sonic the Hedgehog 3 (1994), Sonic & Knuckles (1994), Sonic Adventure 2 (2001), Sonic Colours (2010), Sonic Generations (2011) and Sonic Mania (2017).

Sonic the Hedgehog was also the title of a live-action feature film in 2020 (spawning its own sequel Sonic the Hedgehog 2 (2022)) which set the record for the most successful opening weekend for a video game-based film.

Sonic the Hedgehog was the most successful video game of 1991 and has sold in excess of 23 million units across various platforms since its initial release.

Battletoads

Date of release: June 1991

Region: USA

Developer: Rare

Publisher: Tradewest

Platform: NES

Designed by Tim Stamper and Chris Stamper, Gregg Mayles and Kev Bayliss, with music by David Wise, Battletoads is a single-player or two-player, cooperative, side-scrolling platform beat 'em up. The aim of Battletoads is to rescue Pimple, a fellow Battletoad, and Princess Angelica from the Dark Queen. The players control Battletoads Rash and Zitz. Gameplay involves the players dealing with a variety of enemies, ranging from giant rats with sunglasses to killer snowmen, by punching, kicking (both included a huge fist or punch animation to emphasize humour and perspective), head-butting and using objects to hit or throw at these enemies. Battletoads features a variety of gameplay elements, with players able to ride on the back of flying animals or vehicles. The game also features the player battling a boss as seen from the boss's perspective (which was rather unique), and a section featuring vertical abseiling down a shaft while fending off enemies. In fact, the game contains many vertical-scrolling sections and typically features the Battletoads riding on the back of a giant snake to proceed to the next level.

It is easy to see how the enormous success of Teenage Mutant Ninja Turtles (1989/90) had a huge influence on Battletoads. The game is often noted for its graphics, gameplay, humour and high level of difficulty. It was ported to the Sega, Game Gear and Amiga platforms over the next couple of years. It also spawned several sequels. Some of the most notable are: Battletoads in Battlemaniac (1993), Battletoads & Double Dragon (1993) and Battletoads Arcade (1994). It was not often that a console game was ported to the Arcade. This was just another example of how the dynamics between home and Arcade gaming was changing.

4D Sports Boxing

Date of release: June 1991

Region: Canada

Developer: Distinctive Software

Publisher: Mindscape

Platform: Various 16-bit home computers

4D Sports Boxing is a single-player, 3D, sports fighting game. As in real boxing, the aim of the game is to win the fight either by knockout or by a points score attributed by the game. In the gym, the player can choose their speed, power and stamina, as well as more aesthetic attributes including a custom name. The game is very unusual in the way it switches from a third-person to a first-person perspective while you attempt to pummel your opponent.

4D Sports Boxing was another early attempt to introduce 3D polygon graphics into a specific genre. It was well-received, perhaps encouraging other game publishing companies to dip their toe in and develop 3D games themselves.

Neverwinter Nights

Date of release: June 1991

Region: Canada

Developer: Bioware

Publisher: Infogrames

Platform: Windows

Neverwinter Nights is a Massive Multiplayer Online Role-Playing Game or MMORPG. It is the eleventh Advanced Dungeons & Dragons video game and the first MMORPG to display graphics. Running from 1991 to 1997 on the America Online Internet Service Provider, Neverwinter Nights was the eighth D&D game to use the Gold Box engine. As with other D&D games, the player begins by choosing their character's race, sex, class, allegiance and name, generating randomised character stats. The game window is split into three sections: a first-person perspective or map view of your surroundings, your current character status, and a dialogue box. The information displayed changes depending on whether the player is browsing wares in a shop or is in combat. Combat is turn-based, with the screen splitting in two, displaying an isometric view of the players, their enemies and the environment. The other side of the screen displays the combatant's current actions.

As the game was online, players could help one another or even fight against each other. Hundreds of players could participate in a game at any one time. Neverwinter Nights was the first video game to feature Clans and PvP combat in a MMORPG. It also featured different ranked PvP ladders for players to progress.

The game was highly praised for its well-balanced and diverse combat and the ability to play with so many players online when such a concept was relatively new to most gamers. Neverwinter Nights began with a humble player base of 50 people in 1991, reaching 500 by 1995, and making it to 115,000 players in 1997. It peaked at an average of around 2,000 active players online.

Neverwinter Nights would pave the wave for more MMORPGs, such as The Shadow of Yserbius (1991-96), Ultima Online (1997-current date), EverQuest (1999-current date), RuneScape (2001-current date) and World of Warcraft (2004-current date). Though not direct sequels, there have been other AD&D video games using the Neverwinter title, such as Neverwinter Nights (2002) and Neverwinter Nights 2 (2006), both including several expansion packs.

Seiken Densetsu: Final Fantasy Gaiden/Final Fantasy Adventure/Mystic Quest

Date of release: June 1991

Region: Japan

Developer: Square

Publisher: Square

Platform: Game Boy

Designed by Koichi Ishii, Seiken Densetsu: Final Fantasy Gaiden (known as Final Fantasy Adventure in America and Mystic Quest in Europe, and often referred to simply as Seiken in Japan) is a single-player, action JRPG. The aim of the game is to stop the dark lord Glaive and the evil sorcerer Julius from taking the power of the Tree of Mana. The gameplay is similar to The Legend of Zelda (1986), although Seiken has more emphasis on RPG elements, such as stats and levelling-up.

Seiken was highly praised and is considered to be one of the best action RPGs for the Game Boy. Seiken is the first Final Fantasy spin-off game and the first game in the popular Mana series. The others are Seiken Densetsu 2/Secret of Mana (1993), Seiken Densetsu 3/Trials of Mana (1995) and Seiken Densetsu 4/Dawn of Mana (2006). The Mana series also spawned several spin-off games of its own.

Final Fantasy IV/Final Fantasy II

Date of release: July 1991

Region: Japan

Developer: Square

Publisher: Square

Platform: Super Famicom

Designed by Hironobu Sakaguchi and Takashi Tokita, Final Fantasy IV (known as Final Fantasy II in the West) is a single-player JRPG. The aim is to stop the sorcerer Golbez from getting four elemental crystals and destroying the world. The player controls Cecil, a Dark Knight at the story's outset, as well as other party members, each with their own abilities. While it has many familiar elements from the previous games, Final Fantasy IV saw radical improvements in the series, and not just because it was the first Final Fantasy game on a next-generation platform with improved 16-bit graphics and sound. Final Fantasy IV had a much stronger and more sophisticated narrative than its relatively generic predecessors. It also introduced the 'active time battle' system as opposed to the more turn-based system of the previous games. This system gave the gameplay more urgency and was popular enough to become a part of future Final Fantasy games.

Final Fantasy IV was highly acclaimed upon release and is often cited as one of the best of the many Final Fantasy games. The game has been released on multiple platforms over the decades and is thought to have sold around four million units in total.

Final Fantasy IV was released in the West with a reduction in difficulty: enemies were made significantly weaker and attack options for player characters were taken out to simplify the game. Final Fantasy II and III had never been released in the West and so Final Fantasy IV was released there as Final Fantasy II. This would cause a lot of confusion in the future when Final Fantasy VII was released in 1997, leaving many players wondering just what had happened to the other games. For clarification, below is a chronological breakdown of the first seven Final Fantasy games:

Final Fantasy was released in Japan and the West in 1987.

Final Fantasy II was released in Japan in 1988 but was never initially released in the West.

Final Fantasy III was released in Japan in 1990 but was never initially released in the West.

Final Fantasy IV was released in Japan in 1991 and released in the West as Final Fantasy II, also in 1991. For the most part, Western players were unaware that they were playing the fourth game in the series and not the second.

Final Fantasy V was released in Japan in 1992 but was never initially released in the West.

Final Fantasy VI was released in Japan in 1994 and released in the West as Final Fantasy III, also in 1994. For the most part, Western players were unaware that they were playing the sixth game in the series and not the third. Since then, players in the West have had the opportunity to play these missing Final Fantasy games.

Final Fantasy VII was released in Japan and the West in 1997. From this point on the Final Fantasy games were released under the same name.

Duke Nukem

Date of release: July 1991

Region: USA

Developer: Apogee Software

Publisher: Apogee Software

Platform: MS-DOS

Duke Nukem is a single-player, multi-scrolling platform game. The aim is to defeat Dr Proton, who wants to rule the world. You play as Duke Nukem and must shoot the numerous robot enemies and find the exit to the next level. Health, gun power-ups and items such as keys allow the player to progress through the game, which starts with the player in the enemy's underground base, then in Dr Proton's lunar space station, and finally in Earth's nuclear-devastated future.

The game was moderately successful, selling around 70,000 units. Duke Nukem has spawned numerous sequels and even though the first two games, Duke Nukem (1991) and Duke Nukem II (1993), were multi-scrolling 2D platform games, it would be the first-person 3D release, Duke Nukem 3D (1996) by developer 3D Realms, which would become a phenomenal success and leave a lasting legacy in video game history.

Streets of Rage/Bare Knuckle: Furious Iron Fist

Date of release: August 1991

Region: Japan (released in the West in the following months)

Developer: Sega

Publisher: Sega

Platform: Sega Genesis

Designed by Noriyoshi Ohba, Hiroaki Chino and Hiroshi Momota, and with music by Yuzo Koshiro, Streets of Rage, known as Bare Knuckle: Furious Iron Fist in Japan, is a single-player or multiplayer, side-scrolling beat 'em up. The aim of Streets of Rage is to put an end to the crime syndicate which has taken over control of the city. You play as one of three ex-police officers, Adam, Axel or Blaze, who quit because of the corruption within the police force. The players must fight their way through a multitude of enemies using hand-to-hand combat or a variety of weapons, such as knives, batons, glass bottles, metal pipes and even a pepper pot (which momentarily stuns enemies), allowing them the opportunity to deliver some much-needed justice. Special moves involve your buddies turning up in a car and napalming your enemies. Only one of these special moves can be performed per life. At the end of each stage, the players must defeat a boss, with a confrontation with the final boss at the end. The game gives the player a choice as to whether to join the crime syndicate or not, allowing for multiple endings.

Sega wanted to develop a game similar to Double Dragon (1987) or Final Fight (1989) for the Genesis. Streets of Rage was very well received and is often referred to as one of the best games for the Sega Genesis/Mega Drive. It spawned several sequels with Streets of Rage 2 (1992), Streets of Rage 3 (1994) and Streets of Rage 4 (2020).

Hunter

Date of release: August 1991

Region: USA

Developer: Activision

Publisher: Activision

Platform: Amiga and Amiga ST

Designed by Paul Holmes, Hunter is a single-player, third-person, 3D action-adventure game. The aim is dependent on the game mode, ranging from a specific mission-based game, such as assassinating a target, to action mode, where the player has a list of objectives to carry out but may do them in any order. The player controls a soldier who can walk, swim and use a variety of weapons, such as guns, bombs and a missile launcher, to name but a few. The game also features a multitude of vehicles, including boats, cars, tanks and helicopters. One of Hunter's most intriguing features is its real-time 24-hour clock system. If the player plays during the day, then it is daytime in the game, and should they play at night then it is correspondingly night in the game. Hunter also features 3D polygonal graphics.

Although the graphics may seem primitive by modern standards, they were somewhat impressive in 1991. Hunter, although not well-known, is a significant milestone in video game history for several reasons. Even though commonplace today, third-person 3D action-adventure games featuring a character who was free to roam in the game world was very rare. The player was usually limited in movement in games, such as in Space Harrier (1986) and Xybots (1988). In Hunter, the player's character was free to roam the game world and free to complete missions in any way they saw fit. This was five years before such mechanics would be established with Super Mario 64 in 1996 and ten years before the acclaimed sandbox open-world approach found in Grand Theft Auto III (2001).

Super Mario World released in America

Super Mario World was released in America in August 1991, almost a year after its release in its native country of Japan. American gamers had fallen in love with the first three Mario games on the NES, and the excitement of a new Mario game reached a fever pitch through Nintendo's marketing and teasers. Super Mario World was an unprecedented success on the SNES and would become the best-selling game on the system, with over 20 million units.

Starblade

Date of release: September 1991

Region: Japan

Developer: Namco

Publisher: Namco

Platform: Arcade

Designed by Hajime Nakatani, Starblade is a single-player, first-person, 3D, space rail shooter. The aim is to defeat the Unknown Intelligent Mechanized Species threatening the mother planet by first destroying the Red Eye superweapon and then the mechanical fortress, Iceberg. Starblade comprises ten missions. Gameplay involves shooting enemy fighters as well as larger ships' gun turrets and weak spots. Your ship's movement is controlled by the game, so there is a large emphasis on making gameplay as exciting a cinematic experience as possible by having your ship flying close to huge capital ships, inside immense enemy structures, and warping through hyperspace. Along with the incredible stereo sound allowing the developers to control the games pace and narrative, Starblade gave players something they'd never experienced before: the sit-down arcade cabinet featured a concave mirror to emphasise a sense of depth and featured vibration in the seat and yoke to make the game even more immersive.

Starblade was influenced by many science-fiction films, especially the originally Star Wars trilogy (1977-83) and The Last Starfighter (1984). Starblade is, in fact, an evolved version of the Star Wars (1983) Arcade. However, whereas Star Wars featured wireframe 3D graphics, technology had evolved so that Starblade used 3D flat-shaded polygons. The game would inspire other 3D video games such as Star Fox (1993) and Panzer Dragoon (1995).

While the game was ported to a few CD-ROM game consoles, the incredible arcade experience could not be replicated in the home and much of its appeal was lost.

Steel Talons

Date of release: 1991

Region: USA

Developer: Atari games

Publisher: Atari games

Platform: Arcade

Steel Talons is a single-player, first-person or third-person, 3D, combat flight simulator. The aim is to complete the nineteen missions by destroying a variety of enemies. The player controls an AT1196 Steel Talons combat helicopter and can choose to start the game with a training mission against the computer, or in the two-player cabinet version to battle head-to-head. The helicopter is armed with a machine gun, rockets and air-to-surface guided missiles. It is controlled with a joystick for direction and a lever for altitude. Radar and a virtual camera help the player select and lock onto targets.

Steel Talons was another example of a game that used 3D flat-shaded polygons to great effect. The game was a fun experience, especially when playing head-to-head against a friend. However, the lines between what was possible graphically in the arcades and what was possible on the 16-bit home platforms were beginning to blur. Games liked Steel Talons, and certainly the aforementioned Starblade (1991), still had the edge, but for how much longer? The trend seemed to predict that home computers and consoles would one day be as good as their arcade counterparts.

Steel Talons was ported to a handful of 16-bit consoles and the Atari ST.

Road Rash

Date of release: September 1991

Region: USA

Developer: Electronic Arts

Publisher: Electronic Arts

Platform: Sega Genesis

Designed by Carl Mey and Randy Breen of Electronic Arts, Road Rash is a single-player or multiplayer, third-person, vehicular combat and racing game. The aim is to finish in the first three places of the race by any means necessary. Competitors race on motorbikes and can either punch, kick or use melee weapons (taken from other riders) to knock other racers off the track. There are five tracks to race on. If the player wins the race, money is awarded and is used to purchase new and improved bikes at the bike shop.

Up to twenty-five minutes of FMV (Full Motion Video) was included in the 32-bit versions (Sega CD, 3DO, PlayStation, and Sega Saturn) of the game. Road Rash was a very popular game with players and was soon ported to the most popular systems of the time. It also spawned numerous sequels including Road Rash II (1992) and Road Rash 3 (1995).

Sid Meier's Civilization

Date of release: September 1991

Region: USA

Developer: MicroProse

Publisher: MicroProse

Platform: MS-DOS

Designed by Sid Meier and Bruce Shelly, Sid Meier's Civilization, also known as Civilization, Is a single-player, turn-based strategy game. The aim is to build a lasting civilization. The player has the option to customise their game at the start, choosing a small, medium or large landmass, a cool, temperate or warm climate and finally establishing the age of the world at either 3, 4 or 5 billion years old. The player can also choose between five different difficulty levels and select from fourteen different tribes such as the Aztecs, the Romans, the Babylonians, the Egyptians, the Greeks, the Zulus, and the Chinese. The game always begins in 4000 BC. Civilization established what is now referred to as a 4X (explore, expand, exploit, exterminate) strategy game with an emphasis on accordingly exploring the world, expanding your empire, exploiting the land and exterminating your enemies. The player must create and build things, such as cities, settlements, armies, barracks, temples, granaries, marketplaces and walls. Wonders of the World, such as pyramids, hanging gardens or lighthouses, can also be built. Even morale must also be managed. The player must defend against attacking neighbours and conquer their enemies. Diplomacy with other cultures will help with research and technological advancement. As time passes, and the game progresses through the ages, new technologies will open up and your civilization will advance towards the industrial revolution and ends with nuclear power and early space exploration.

Civilization is similar, in some ways, to games like Utopia (1981) and The Ancient Art of War (1984) and would draw influence from Populous (1989) and SimCity (1989), as well as the 1980 Civilization board game yet, would carve out its own particular brand of turn-based strategy games. It was well received by critics and consumers alike, cited for its sheer scope, depth and immersive gameplay. It was soon ported to various home computers and consoles.

Civilization influenced a whole genre of other similar turn-based strategy video games and went on to spawn a whole series of successful sequels and spin-offs. Some of the most notable of these are Sid Meier's Civilization II (1996), Sid Meier's Civilization III (2001), Sid Meier's Civilization IV (2005) and Sid Meier's Civilization V (2010).

Mega Lo Mania/Tyrants: Fight Through Time

Date of release: October 1991

Region: UK

Developer: Sensible Software

Publisher: Image Works

Platform: Amiga

Designed by Sensible Software, Mega Lo Mania, known as Tyrants: Fight Through Time in America, is a single-player, real-time strategy game. You play as one of four gods and must defeat the opposition commanding their followers. Players can order said followers to build, mine, attack, defend, research and procreate. If you defeat your opponents on an island then you progress to the next. Once you have completed three islands then you progress to a new era in time. The game starts in 9500 BC and ends in 2001 AD. There are nine eras in the game, each with its own level of technology for the player to navigate, with a total of twenty-eight islands.

The game was highly praised when it was released, and even though some saw it as inferior to titles such as Populous (1989) and Powermonger (1990), with its technology tree mechanic it would be seen as a stepping stone between those previous god games and future real-time strategy games, such as the ground-breaking Dune II (1992).

Puyo Puyo/Puyo Pop

Date of release: October 1991

Region: Japan

Developer: Compile

Publisher: Compile

Platform: MSX2

Designed by Masamitsu Niitani, Puyo Puyo, also known as Puyo Pop in the West, is a single-player or two-player, falling-block puzzle game. The aim is to link together four or more Puyo together to create a chain, as they drop down from above onto the field. This will then pop, giving the player an amount of points dependent on the amount of Puyo linked if playing in single-player mode, or drop 'Ojama' into your opponent's field if playing two-player. As Ojama cannot be formed into chains with Puyo, this makes it more difficult for your opponent to form chains of their own and clear their field. If the field fills all the way up, the player's game is over. In single-player mode, the game has a narrative where you play as the character Arle Nadja, a 16-year-old female spellcaster who must stop the Dark Prince from taking over the world. Puyo Puyo uses characters from the Japanese dungeon crawl game Mado Monogatari (1990). There are two modes of play: Endless, in which the player plays as long as possible until they are eventually overwhelmed and their field is full, or Mission comprising fifty-two specific missions.

Since Tetris (1984) there had been many similar falling block puzzle games, the year 1990 alone boasting both Columns (1990) and Dr. Mario (1990). Puyo Puyo was the latest and certainly not the last such game in this sub-genre of puzzle games. Puyo Puyo was ported to numerous home computers and consoles, as well as an arcade version, and spawned numerous sequels over the decades, including Dr. Robotnik's Mean Bean Machine (1993), Super Puyo Puyo Tsu Remix (1996), Puyo Puyo~n (1999), Puyo Puyo!! 20th Anniversary (2011) and Puyo Puyo Tetris (2017). The Puyo Puyo series of games has sold more than 27 million units.

Virtuality 1000 series Arcade Games

The Virtuality 1000 series of Virtual Reality Arcade Games was first released in October 1991 by Johnathan Waldern and the Virtuality Group. Since Ivan Sutherland's development of The Sword of Damocles (1968), virtual reality simulation had only been developed in universities, government-funded institutions such as NASA or the military, and a few technology-based businesses. The virtuality 1000 arcade cabinets, or pods as they were also known, featured a rather large, heavy headset and a variety of controllers dependent on the game. Some were stand-up (SU) games while others had the player sat down (SD). The headset displayed two LCD screens with a resolution of 276 x 372 pixels, around a 65-degree field of view, running about twenty frames per second (giving some players motion sickness), four speakers and a microphone. This facilitated multiplayer gaming. Outlets were convinced to sell multiple units so that groups of friends could experience this new and wonderful technology together. While somewhat primitive, haptic feedback gloves were developed, where a user could touch something in the virtual world and feel it with their hands and fingers. The two aforementioned models in the 1000 series: the 1000CS and the 1000SD, both ran on Amiga 3000s.

The Virtuality Group launched a total of nine games with the Virtuality 1000 series: Battlesphere, Dactyl Nightmare, Exorex, Flying Aces, Grid Busters, Grid Warriors, Legend Quest, Total Destruction and VTOL. The games are all a flat-shaded 3D virtual reality reimagining of one game genre or another, and despite what now seems to be very primitive technology were, at the time, rather fun. Indeed, the Virtuality 1000 series of games received a lot of press and was very well received by consumers, reports of motion sickness and uncomfortable apparatus notwithstanding. Many found playing a virtual reality video game a completely new, delightful and immensely enjoyable experience especially when playing multiplayer in a virtual gaming world. For a short time, virtual reality seemed just what was needed in the arcades as home platforms were getting closer to conventional arcade graphics.

Even so, the machines cost around twice to three times as much as most arcade machines and needed a dedicated group of staff to help maintain the pods to supervise and help players. Perhaps this is why virtual reality in the arcades simply wasn't sustainable, the phase lasting only a few years. This factor is exacerbated when players were pumping in coins in PvP fighting games like Street Fighter II (1991) and Mortal Kombat (1992), or co-op games like Teenage Mutant Ninja Turtles (1989) and The Simpsons (1991), which all required minimum staff input. It wouldn't be until 2016 when The Void, a new virtual reality franchise, would be accessible for the public to try.

Alien Breed

Date of release: October 1991

Region: UK

Developer: Team17

Publisher: Team17

Platform: Amiga

Designed by Martyn Brown, Rico Holmes, Andreas Tadic and Peter Tuleby, and with sound and music by Alister Brimble, Alien Breed is a single-player or multiplayer, cooperative run and gun game. The year is 2191 and you have been sent to a distant space research centre to discover why contact with the facility has been lost. The players must shoot their way through hordes of aliens reminiscent of the Xenomorphs in Ridley Scott's Alien movies. The game is played from a top-down perspective as the players search for the lift to reach the floor below. However, you must first find and destroy the reactor, giving the players a 60-second countdown to make it back to the lift and descend to the floor below. The players collects keys, money and ammunition. With the money, you can purchase various items at computer terminals, including maps, ammunition, a first aid kit, a set of six keys, and an extra life. The game features an arsenal of impressive weapons, namely the TS-16 Assault Gun, the Tri-Lazer Gun, the NX-2 Heat sense missiles, the J.A.28 Firewall and the Refraction Lazer, the latter featuring rebounding laser bolts, very handy for shooting around corners. As you descend into the lower levels, the environment changes and the aliens become more dangerous. The players must defeat the queen alien and make it to their escape craft, all the while shooting more aliens who try to hinder your progress before the final countdown reaches zero and the entire research centre explodes.

Alien Breed was very well received and soon became a classic two-player cooperative game for the Amiga, ported to MS-DOS two years later and spawning several sequels. Some of the most notable of these are Alien Breed II: The Horror Continues (1993), Alien Breed: Tower Assault (1994), Alien Breed Evolution (2010) and Alien Breed: Impact (2010).

Super Castlevania IV

Date of release: October 1991

Region: Japan

Developer: Konami

Publisher: Konami

Platform: Super Famicom

Designed by Masahiro Ueno, Kazumi Kitaue, and with music by Masanori Adachi and Taro Kudo, Super Castlevania IV is a single-player, side-scrolling, action platform game. As with the previous two Castlevania games you play as Simon Belmont and must defeat Dracula. The player also confronts a multitude of enemies which they slay with Belmont's signature whip. The whip can be aimed in any one of eight directions and can also be used to swing over large areas by latching onto rings and can even be used to block projectiles. By destroying candles and enemies the player can uncover additional sub-weapons, including the dagger, the axe, the fire bomb and the boomerang. There are also more standard power-ups, including a watch that allows the player to freeze most on-screen enemies, a large heart which gives the player five additional uses per sub-weapon, a cross which destroys all enemies on screen, an invisibility potion which renders the player invulnerable to damage for a few seconds and finally the Morning Star item which increases the power of Belmont's whip. The player starts with five lives. A life is lost if Simon's current health bar is depleted (although the health bar can be replenished with food), if he falls down a pit, or does not finish a level before the timer runs out. Once all lives are lost, the game is over. There are eleven levels in Super Castlevania IV, with a whole host of ghoulish bosses at the end of each, the final boss being Dracula himself. After each boss, the player was given a password to allow them to pick up where they left off at a later date.

Super Famicom and Super Nintendo owners were eager for a 16-bit instalment of the Castlevania series, and Super Castlevania IV did not disappoint with its beautiful graphics and fantastic music. It received high praise from critics and consumers alike. Some have cited Super Castlevania IV as possibly the best Castlevania game and one of the best video games of the nineties.

Catacomb 3-D: The Descent

Date of release: November 1991

Region: USA

Developer: id Software

Publisher: Softdisk

Platform: MS-DOS

Designed by Tom Hall, John Carmack, John Romero and Jason Blochowiak of id Software, Catacomb 3-D is a single-player first-person shooter. The aim of Catacomb 3-D is to defeat Nemesis, the evil lich. You play as the wizard Petton Everhail and must descend into the catacombs and defeat hordes of supernatural and demonic enemies.

Catacomb 3-D is the second game (after Hovertank 3D (1991)) to use John Carmack's 3D game engine. It is a definite improvement over the aforementioned Hovertank 3D with the introduction of texture mapping. Catacomb 3-D also displayed the player's outstretched hand as a way of casting fireballs to vanquish their enemies. This may well be the first time a part of the player's character's body was displayed in a first-person shooter, and this feature would soon become mainstream in later such games. Catacomb 3-D was also the first game to display the current health of the character by showing the character's head as an icon, slowly revealing a skull as the health is depleted, another game mechanic that would also find its way into later games of the genre. Catacomb 3-D featured a freezing time mechanic, almost a decade before being adopted by other games using various methods.

The game spawned several sequels that were developed by Softdisk. These were: Catacomb Abyss 3-D (1992), Catacomb Armageddon (1992) and Catacomb Apocalypse 3D (1993), each of which boasts slight graphical improvements from the original. Catacomb 3-D is id Software's direct predecessor to their landmark first-person shooter, Wolfenstein 3D (1992).

Another World/Out of this World

Date of release: November 1991

Region: France

Developer: Delphine Software

Publisher: Delphine Software

Platform: Amiga and Atari ST

Designed by Éric Chahi with music by Jean-Francois Freitas, Another World, known as Out of this World in North America, is a single-player, side-scrolling cinematic action and adventure platform game. You play as a young scientist called Lester. Whilst working alone one night on Project 23, an accident involving a particle accelerator being struck by lightning transports Lester to an alien world. The aim of the game is initially unclear, but upon exploration, the player subsequently spends the majority of the game attempting to escape a prison with an alien buddy. Lester can run, jump, kick and, once acquired, use a laser pistol. Said pistol has three modes: normal fire, charged shot, and can also create force fields. These can be used to attack and defend against enemies, as well as to break down walls. Lester can perform several other actions during specific circumstances. The game has a one-hit-and-you're-dead game mechanic, but luckily the player has unlimited lives from the most recent checkpoint. This was certainly needed, as some parts of the game are rather difficult. The game ends with Lester and his new friend flying free from the prison on the back of a dragon-like creature.

Except for the music, Éric Chahi developed the game on his own. The themes and look of the game were heavily influenced by science-fiction movies, books and comics of the time. Chahi said the flat-colour animations of the Amiga version of Dragon's Lair also influenced the look of the game. The animations used vector graphics and rotoscoping, reminiscent of games like Karateka (1984) and Prince of Persia (1989).

Another World was highly praised for its flat-colour art style (a style still used in indie games today), smooth animations, clever puzzles, and its perfect mix of plot-driven cutscenes and gameplay. Another World spawned a sequel with Heart of the Alien: Out of This World Parts I and II (1992). Much later, the Another World: 15th Anniversary (2006) edition featured improved graphics with a screen resolution of 1280 x 800 pixels (the original was 320 x 200) and was soon followed by the 20th Anniversary (2011) edition, another remastered release. Another World has been cited as being a strong inspiration for such games as Ico (2001), and Metal Gear Solid (1998).

CD-i

The Phillips CD-i system was released in the USA by Philips and Sony. The concept was to deliver features offered by both consoles and personal computers, which were now utilising new CD-ROM technology, but at a more affordable price than the aforementioned PCs. The CD-i used their own version of CDs which could store 72 minutes of full-motion video (FMV). There were a number of different models offering certain features, including the most versatile 'Intelligent Discman' model. The CD-i could play music, interactive multimedia titles (such as encyclopaedias) and entertainment titles, including games. However, it was music and education that Philips initially focused on, not wanting the CD-i to be seen as a games console. Unfortunately for Phillips, the CD-i never found success against PCs or consoles. It could not compete with the popularity of the SNES or Genesis, and PCs with CD-ROM drives were becoming cheaper every year. The CD-i was a commercial failure and is often cited as one of the worst consoles of all time.

The Legend of Zelda: A Link to the Past/The Legend of Zelda: Triforce of the Gods

Date of release: November 1991/ April 1992

Region: Japan/North America

Developer: Nintendo EAD

Publisher: Nintendo

Platform: Super Famicom/SNES

Designed by Takashi Tezuka, Shigeru Miyamoto and with music by Koji Kondo, The Legend of Zelda: A Link to the Past, known in Japan as The Legend of Zelda: Triforce of the Gods, is a single-player, action-adventure game and the third game in the Legend of Zelda series. The game follows the same narrative beats as the previous games: Link must save Princess Zelda and defeat the dark lord Ganon. Viewed from a pseudo-2D top-down perspective, A Link to the Past used similar gameplay and mechanics as its predecessors, while still introducing several new features, such as moving or attacking in eight directions as opposed to the original four. A further feature was the existence of travel to the Dark World, a parallel world where environments in the everyday world of Hyrule, also referred to as the Light World, are mirrored and given a sombre twist. This new concept was astutely used as a game mechanic to solve certain puzzles.

A Link to the Past also featured beautiful new 16-bit graphics and sound. SNES cartridges typically had 512KB of storage space on them, but A Link to the Past used a 1MB cartridge. Twice the space allowed the developers to create a large and immersive game world. As mentioned above, the original subtitle of the game was to be Triforce of the Gods. However, this and many other elements containing religious references were removed or changed in the game before being released in the West.

A Link to the Past was loved by critics and consumers alike, praised for its art-style, well-designed gameplay, deep game mechanics and sound design. It is considered to be one of the best Legend of Zelda games, which is praise indeed considering the standard in the series is set so high. It is also cited by some to be one of the best video games of all time.

Monkey Island 2: LeChucks's Revenge

Date of release: December 1991

Region: USA

Developer: LucasArts

Publisher: LucasArts

Platform: Amiga, Mac OS and Windows

Designed by Ron Gilbert, Shelley Day, Dave Grossman and Tim Schafer, Monkey Island 2: LeChucks's Revenge is a single-player, graphic adventure game. The aim of the game is to find the legendary treasure of Big Whoop. Once again, you play as Guybrush Threepwood. The sequel uses the same SCUMM engine and interface as the original, these similarities continuing down to the same style of dark humour and narrative structure.

Monkey Island 2: LeChuck's Revenge initially did not sell all that well despite receiving rave reviews from critics. It is a misconception that the first two Monkey Island games were massive hits at the time. Ironically enough, it wasn't until a few years later due to software piracy that the Monkey Island games became so well-renowned, finally receiving the high regard they always deserved. A Special Edition with improved graphics, sound and a new control system was released in 2010.

Mega-CD/Sega CD

The Mega-CD, known as the Sega CD in North America, was released in Japan in December 1991 by Sega. The Mega-CD is a CD-ROM accessory that attaches to the Sega Genesis/Mega Drive. The Mega-CD makes it possible for Genesis owners to play CD-ROM games, as CDs boasted 320 times the storage space compared to a Sega Genesis game cartridge. The Mega-CD also contained a faster CPU.

It was believed that the Mega-CD would be very successful. However, after initially selling 100,000 units, sales began to drop. This plunge is thought to be due to a high price point and only having only two games at launch but is perhaps also due to the Mega-CD's heavy reliance on FMV games. Some publishers and developers were very excited about this technology being brought into home video games, and even some consumers were intrigued to see something different. However, many games focused on this interactive movie genre too much, and the quality of the FMV production, and therefore the games, suffered accordingly. That being said, there were a few good games that took advantage of the larger storage and faster CPU, such as Lunar: The Silver Star (1992), Lunar: Eternal Blue (1994), Final Fight CD (1993), Sonic CD (1993), Popful Mail (1994) and Snatcher (1994).

The Mega-CD was released as the Sega CD in North America in 1992 and in the rest of the world in 1993.

The Shadow of Yserbius

Date of release: 1991

Region: USA

Developer: Ybarra Productions

Publisher: Sierra On-Line

Platform: MS-DOS

The Shadow of Yserbius is a single-player or multiplayer, first-person, graphical Multi-User Dungeon (MUD) role-playing game. The main aim of the game is to enter Mount Yserbius and defeat En-Li-Kil, a powerful elemental, with the promise of finding untold treasures hidden in Yserbius's labyrinthine tunnels. As with other RPGs, the player creates a character before sallying forth. The game screen is split into three: a first-person perspective of your environment including NPCs you interact or battle with, a narrative of what is happening, and another panel that typically displays a paper-doll interface, map or choice of actions during combat. Combat is turn-based and may include multiple enemies or companions if the player decides to join with a party of other players online.

Players could find or join guilds in The Shadow of Yserbius, with some becoming famous or infamous within the community, depending on their reputation. Certain guilds were known to help others, while others were self-proclaimed agents of chaos. This gave the game much more depth, as rather than relying on NPCs to shape the game world, the players themselves were making those decisions and building the narrative themselves. Many people may think of a game such as Eve Online (2003) when considering such a concept in video games, yet this is where it all began.

The Shadow of Yserbius ran online between 1991-96 and gave rise to two sequels with The Fates of Twinion (1993) and The Ruins of Cawdor (1995).

1991 Notable Omissions

Bible Adventures. Big Karnak. Captain America and the Avengers. Captain Commando. Caveman Ninja. Cruise for a Corpse. Cyber Stadium Series: Base Wars. Dragon's Lair II: Time Warp. Eye of the Beholder II. Fatal Fury. First Samurai. Eye of the Beholder II: The Legend of Darkmoon. Geo Storm AKA GunForce. Goblins. Gods. Heimdall. Hero Quest. Jimmy White's Whirlwind Snooker. Joe & Mac. Knights of the Round. LaserScope. Loom. Mega Man 4. Mercs. Metroid II: Return of Samus. Moonstone: A Hard Days Knight. NHL

Hockey. Neutopia II. Prehistorik. Princess Maker. PU-LI-RU-LA. Quackshot Starring Donald Duck. Rainbow Stars: The Story of Bubble Bobble III. Rings of Power. Scorched Earth. SimAnt. Snake Rattle 'n' Roll. Space Quest IV. Spider-Man: The Video Game. Star Control. Steel Gunner. Storm Master. Super Tennis. Super R-Type. Tecmo Super Bowl. Terminator 2: Judgement Day. The Legend of the Mystical Ninja. The Simpson: Bart vs. the Space Mutants. The Terminator. Three Wonders. Tumblepop. Vice: Project Doom. Turrican II: The Final Fight. Yoshi. Wing Commander II: Vengeance of the Kilra.

1992

Dune

Date of release: 1992

Region: Worldwide

Developer: Cryo

Publisher: Virgin Games

Platform: Amiga and MS-DOS

Designed by Remi Herbulot and Stephen Clarke-Wilson, Dune is a single-player, adventure strategy game, based on the novel and movie of the same name. Following a similar narrative, the player plays as Paul Atreides, following him through a tale of intergalactic politics, betrayal and revenge on the planet Arrakis (also known as Dune). The overarching aim of the game is to defeat the games antagonists, House Harkonnen, the antagonists primarily responsible for the orchestrated downfall of House Atreides. For the most part, the game is played from a first-person perspective as the player navigates their environment and interacts with the many varied characters, learning about the world of Dune and carrying out certain tasks in an attempt to persuade the Fremen, the indigenous denizens of Arrakis, to join with Paul and House Atreides. The strategy part of the game comes from balancing between gathering resources, training and deploying military forces, and working on terraforming the planet.

Dune is often overshadowed by its sequel Dune II released at the end of 1992; the latter being often cited as the game which would establish the foundation of almost all real-time strategy games that followed. However, the first Dune game is significant too, for it is not only an accomplished game in its own right but manages to adapt a deep and complex novel and movie into a competent video game, with a unique style and feel. At a time when most movie-to-video game adaptations were nothing short of disastrous, this was no mean feat. It also featured a fantastic original soundtrack by Stéphane Picq.

Dune was ported to the Mega-CD/Sega CD the next year. The CD version included improved 3D graphics and clips from the 1984 movie. The game ended up selling more than its renowned sequel with over 300,000 units.

Desert Strike: Return to the Gulf

Date of release: February 1992

Region: USA

Developer: Electronic Arts

Publisher: Electronic Arts

Platform: Various Computer & Console platforms

Designed by Richard Robbins, Mike Posehn and John Manley, Desert Strike is a single-player, isometric, military shoot 'em up. The aim is to destroy the forces of an insane Middle Eastern dictator named General Kilbaba. Specific objectives vary from mission to mission, yet usually involve destroying enemy installations, capturing the enemy, and saving hostages. The player flies an AH-64 Apache helicopter which is armed with several different weapon systems, including a chain gun, Hydra rockets and Hellfire missiles. The player also gets a choice of co-pilot, each of which has different skills. Friendlies can be rescued by hovering over them, at which point a ladder is dropped and the friendly scurries up the ladder. A similar mechanic is used after destroying specific installations, allowing the player to collect the spoils of war. If the player is hit too many times, the helicopter is destroyed and the player loses one of their three lives. There are only four missions in the game, however, each one can take some time to complete. Players need to be strategic in approaching the enemy and manoeuvre carefully lest they be blown out of the sky.

Desert Strike offers a nice sense of freedom, giving the player a mission to complete yet also allowing them broad latitude as to how they choose to go about doing so. The game also gives you a well-crafted albeit dangerous, isometric world to explore. It is easy to see how Desert Strike was heavily influenced by Choplifter (1982).

The game was highly praised by critics and consumers alike, although there was a degree of controversy from some people who thought its subject matter was in bad taste. The game was successful enough to spawn several sequels, including Jungle Strike (1993), Urban Strike (1994), Soviet Strike (1996) and Nuclear Strike (1997).

Contra III: The Alien Wars/Super Probector: Alien Rebels

Date of release: February 1992

Region: Japan

Developer: Konami

Publisher: Konami

Platform: Super Famicom and SNES

Designed by Nobuya Nakazato and Kazumi Kitaue, Contra III: The Alien Wars also known as Super Probector: Alien Rebels, is a single-player or multiplayer, cooperative (one of the main appeals of the Contra series was to play cooperatively with a friend), run and gun game. It is the fourth game in the popular Contra series. Set in the year 2636, Contra III has similar gameplay and mechanics as its predecessors, yet boasts beautiful 16-bit graphics, bigger and more elaborate enemies, and even more intense action. Players could switch between two weapons, allowing them to use the best tool for the job, and the game featured a new climbing mechanic which allowed the developers to be far more creative with level design. Contra III features six stages, four of which are side-scrolling and two from an overhead perspective.

Contra III received high praise from critics and players alike. As one of the early games for the Super Famicom/SNES, players were rather blown away by its amazing graphics which were a great example of what Nintendo's new system was capable of. It is also considered one of the best Contra games in the series.

Shining Force

Date of release: March 1992

Region: Japan

Developer: Climax Entertainment

Publisher: Sega

Platform: Sega Genesis

Shining Force is a single-player, turn-based, tactical role-playing game and is the sequel to Shining in the Darkness (1991). The aim of the game is to defeat Kane and the armies of the Runefaust nation. You play as Max, and with your allies must prevent the forces of evil from opening the Shining Path which would resurrect the Dark Dragon. The game possesses many of the features found in most Japanese role-playing games or JRPGs. However, whereas the first game in the series was played exclusively from a first-person perspective, Shining Force relies on the more traditional JRPG convention of an overhead perspective as you explore the world and interact with NPCs. While most games of the genre moved to a side-view or first-person perspective during combat, in Shining Force combat is carried out on an isometric grid with characters able to move around and attack their enemies' flanks. Each character moves and attacks in different ways, giving rise to a combat system akin to chess. When a character initiates an attack, the player is shown a third-person pseudo-3D cutscene of the attack. This combat system makes for a unique, immersive and intense experience. The only contemporary game of the time featuring a similar combat system was Fire Emblem: Shadow Dragon and the Blade of Light (1990).

Shining Force received high praise, and its success was enough that many more Shining games were developed in what is now known as the Shining series. Some of these would adopt the turn-based tactical RPG elements of Shining Force. Some in the series made use of real-time combat, such as Shining Resonance (2014), while others were a complete departure from Shining Force. These latter were notably the Shining spin-off fighting games, such as Blade Arcus from Shining (2014). Shining Force was remade for the Game Boy Advance with Shining Force: Resurrection of the Dark Dragon (2004).

Pinball Dreams

Date of release: March 1992

Region: Sweden

Developer: Digital Illusion

Publisher: 21st Century Entertainment

Platform: Amiga

Pinball Dreams is a single-player or multiplayer pinball video game. The aim is to score as many points as possible. Pinball Dreams features real-world physics and four different tables: Ignition is themed around space exploration and a rocket launch, Steam Wheel has an Old West and steam train theme, Beat Box is themed around the music industry, and Nightmare features spooky occurrences in a graveyard.

The game was well-received, selling around 650,000 units. It would also spawn several sequels and spin-offs (not all of which were developed by Digital Illusions) with Pinball Fantasies (1992), Pinball Dreams 2 (1995), Pinball Mania (1995), Pinball Illusions (1995), Absolute Pinball (1996) and True Pinball (1996). While Pinball Dreams was their first game, the Swedish developer Digital Illusions, also known as DICE, would go on to develop the popular Battlefield series (2002-current date).

1991/1992s Golden Joystick Awards

1991/1992s Golden Joystick Awards was hosted in London on the 7th of April.

Heimdall wins Best Graphics of the Year and 16-bit Game of the Year.

The Secret of Monkey Island wins Best Soundtrack of the Year.

Sonic the Hedgehog wins Game of the Year.

Ultima VII: The Black Gate

Date of release: April 1992

Region: Worldwide

Developer: Origin Systems

Publisher: Origin Systems

Platform: MS-DOS

Designed by Richard Garriot, Ken Demarest, Jeff Dee and Raymond Benson, Ultima VII: The Black Gate is a single-player RPG. The game starts with the player, who takes on the role of the Avatar from previous games, attempting to solve a murder mystery and the plot unfolds from there. The game is viewed from a pseudo-3D, top-down perspective as the player explores the game world, interacts with NPCs and battles against different monsters. This instalment of the Ultima series introduced several new features, notably not restricting movement to a grid-based system and different levels of height so players could walk up and down stairs and realistically stack objects without cutting to a new screen. The game could be entirely controlled by a mouse featuring the use of Graphical User Menu Pop-ups, or GUMPS, for containers and player inventories. Combat is in real-time, with party members controlled by the computer. However, the player can set their tactics beforehand and it is possible to pause combat by going into an inventory to give the player time to think or attend to any eventual real-world distractions.

Ultima VII was significant in that many of these features would influence future open-world RPGs, including games like Fallout (1997), Baldur's Gate (1998) and Planescape Torment (1999). The game was ported to the SNES two years later in 1994. Ultima VII: The Black Gate along with Ultima IV: Quest for the Avatar are often cited as two of the best games in the Ultima series.

Kirby's Dream Land

Date of release: April 1992

Region: Japan

Developer: HAL Laboratory

Publisher: Nintendo

Platform: Game Boy

Designed by Masahiro Sakurai and Makoto Kanai of HAL Laboratory, Kirby's Dream Land is a single-player, side-scrolling, action platformer and the first game in the popular Kirby series. The aim of Kirby's Dream Land is to retrieve the food and sparkling stars that have been stolen by gluttonous King Dedede and his rotten band of thieves. You play as Kirby (who is a cutesy blob with blobs for hands and feet) who sets off on his quest towards the dreaded Mount Dedede and must deal with a multitude of enemies, mini-bosses and bosses. Kirby can run, jump, and crouch but his signature game mechanic is the ability to inhale and subsequently spit out enemies, using them as projectiles. Kirby can also inflate himself with air, allowing him to fly through the skies or also attack by shooting air pellets capable of defeating most enemies. There are also other pick-up items along the way which Kirby can use, including the Invincible Candy or Candy Lollipop granting Kirby invincibility and allowing him to defeat most enemies in one hit, bombs to blast enemies, spicy food allowing Kirby to exhale fireballs, mint leaves allowing Kirby to shoot a rapid stream of air pellets, warp stars taking Kirby to the next level or secret areas, and the 1UP which grants Kirby an extra life. More lives can be gained if enough points are accumulated. Kirby's health bar will be reduced to zero if he is hit by enemies too many times, resulting in the loss of one of his lives. Kirby begins the game with three lives. There are five stages in Kirby's Dream Land.

The Kirby character we know today was initially just a placeholder graphic, the intent being to change it in the future. However, the team became rather fond of the placeholder and so decided to keep him on. The name Kirby was chosen in honour of the American attorney John Kirby, who, in 1982, successfully defended Nintendo against a lawsuit by Universal Studios over Nintendo's use of the character Donkey Kong, due to his similarity with King Kong.

Kirby's Dream Land was well received by critics and consumers. While some commented that the game was a little too easy, this could be countered by the fact that players could limit Kirby's health as the game also included an unlockable hard mode. Many praised the unique inhale/exhale game mechanic. It is worth noting that Kirby would spawn many games in the future, and also the fact that it is typically rare for a game originating on a handheld console to go on and establish such a successful series. Most video game franchises up until this point either began in the arcade or on home consoles or a home computer platform. Some of the most notable games in the Kirby series are Kirby Super Star (1996), Kirby's Dream Land 3 (1997), Kirby 64: The Crystal Shards (2000), Kirby's Epic Yarn (2010), Kirby's Return to Dream Land (2011) and Kirby: Planet Robobot (2016). Kirby's Dream Land has sold over 5 million units.

Wolfenstein 3D

Date of release: May 1992

Region: USA

Developer: id Software

Publisher: Apogee Software

Platform: MS-DOS

Designed by Tom Hall, John Romero, John Carmack and Adrian Carmack of id Software, Wolfenstein 3D is a single-player, first-person shooter. Set during World War II, you play as a captured Polish-American spy, William 'B.J.' Blazkowicz, who escapes his prison cell and must subsequently escape from Castle Wolfenstein, shooting any Nazis foolish enough to stand in his way. The tone of the game is set even before the gameplay begins, with the game putting the question of 'how tough are you' to the player by way of difficulty selection. Each of the four options has a corresponding portrait of the player from the easy option entitled 'Can I Play, Daddy?' with Blazkowicz's wearing a baby's outfit with a dummy in his mouth, to 'I am Death incarnate!' with Blazkowicz's eyes glowing red. Enemies come in the form of Guards, Elite Guards, Officers, and dogs. The player will acquire weapons increasing in damage dealt as they progress through the levels and episodes of the games. There are three episodes in the game: Escape from Castle Wolfenstein, Operation: Eisenfaust which deals with the Nazis' efforts to raise an army of the undead, and Die, Führer, Die! in which you must infiltrate a bunker and confront Adolf Hitler wearing a mechanical suit armed with quad chain guns. The player collects food to offset any loss of health and must keep collecting ammo from dead soldiers or hidden caches to better blast their way through the next encounter. New weapons, extra lives and secret passages are cunningly hidden throughout the game. There is even a secret level, based on Pac-Man (1980), with indestructible ghosts who chase you around the level. The HUD at the bottom of the screen depicts the floor you are on, current score, remaining lives and health, ammo counter, keys found, current weapon, and an animated portrait of the head of B.J. Blazkowicz which changes, depending on the circumstances. Picking up a new weapon will cause him to smile while receiving damage causes his face to become bloodied and bruised. This feature was another innovation that would set the trend for future FPSs. The game itself is a mix of 3D environments and 2D scaling-sprites to give the player a fast-paced first-person shooter experience never before seen by gamers.

Wolfenstein 3D is a culmination of over a year's worth of evolution and development in which previous games had acted as stepping stones. John Carmack created a 3D engine, and with the help of the rest of the team, id Software released their first first-person shooter game, Hovertank 3D (1991). The walls of the environment were just plain colours and the enemies were rather forgettable. id Software's second FPS was Catacomb 3D (1991). Catacomb 3D featured texture mapping, making for far more immersive environments, along with the demonic enemies appearing much more intimidating, and the player could actually see their avatar's hand casting fireballs at the monsters. John Romero convinced John Carmack that adapting the previous 2D Castle Wolfenstein (1981), originally a stealth game, into a 3D first-person shooter remake would be a good idea. Wolfenstein 3D was originally released as shareware in the order of the episodes as described above, culminating in all three being released by May 1992. The game makes no apologies for its over-the-top action, violence and at times silliness. Indeed, the sprite of Adolf Hitler in a robot suit with chain guns has become one of video gaming's most well-known and recognisable bosses.

The game received extremely high praise for its graphics and smooth 3D gameplay, selling very well, and it continues to sell even to this day. Wolfenstein 3D is a major milestone in the first-person shooting genre, and in the history of video gaming itself. It is often referred to as the grandfather of 3D shooters. Yet, Wolfenstein would prove to be another stepping-stone towards the daddy of all FPSs: id Software's Doom (1993).

Wolfenstein 3D was ported to a handful of home computers and consoles of the time. id Software also released several other episodes in the Wolfenstein 3D universe, for those who couldn't get enough of William 'B.J.' Blazkowicz's adventures, including The Nocturnal missions, A Dark Secret, Trail of the Madman, Confrontation, Spear of Destiny, Return to Danger, and Ultimate Challenge.

Lunar: The Silver Star

Date of release: June 1992

Region: USA

Developer: Game Arts & Studio Alex

Publisher: Game Arts

Platform: Mega-CD/Sega CD (Genesis/Mega Drive add-on)

With art by Toshiyuki Kubooka and story by Kei Shigema, Lunar: The Silver Star is a single-player RPG. The aim is to become a Dragonmaster, defeat the magic emperor Ghaleon and save the kidnapped Luna. The game features similar gameplay mechanics to most of the JRPGs of the era. The player interacts with NPCs, explores the world, fights monsters and levels-up. However, the developers wanted something rather different with Lunar: The Silver Star. Great emphasis was put on a compelling story that could utilise the CD-ROM format to present gamers with visuals rarely seen before on a console. Even though the majority of the game was played from the traditional 2D top-down perspective, the narrative was interwoven with beautiful anime sequences and high-quality audio.

Lunar: The Silver Star was highly praised. Critics and gamers loved the care and attention that had been put into the narrative, visuals and audio of the game, all the while maintaining the solid gameplay and mechanics expected of RPGs. The game ended up being the second-best-selling game on the Mega-CD/Sega CD, the best-selling game being Sonic the Hedgehog CD (1993). Lunar: The Silver Star received two remakes: one on the Sega Saturn and the other on the PlayStation 1. Each remake was able to add more content compared to the previous incarnation. The original Mega-CD only contained a few minutes of animation, whereas the PlayStation version contained almost an hour. The game also spawned one sequel with Lunar: Eternal Blue (1994), and two spin-offs Lunar: Sanposuru Gakuen (1996), never released outside of Japan, and Lunar: Dragon Song (2005).

Indiana Jones and the Fate of Atlantis

Date of release: June 1992

Region: USA

Developer: LucasArts

Publisher: LucasArts

Platform: 16-bit home computers

Designed by Hal Barwood, Noah Falstein and Shelly Day, Indiana Jones and the Fate of Atlantis is a single-player, point-and-click adventure game. The aim is to find the lost city of Atlantis.

LucasArts would once again use their successful SCUMM engine to develop the game, having previously worked on Indiana Jones and the Last Crusade: The Graphic Adventure (1989). In a similar vein to the previous Indiana Jones game, Fate of Atlantis would use the game mechanic of the IQ score or 'Indy Quotient'. This score could be carried over and continued after completion of one game onto a new game, encouraging players to find the many different possible paths and solutions to confrontations and puzzles through multiple different playthroughs. A particular problem could, for instance, be solved peacefully by searching for clues or by settling things with Indiana Jones' fists.

The game was released two months after The Young Indiana Jones Chronicles TV series aired in America. The CD-ROM version of the game would utilise original voice-over recordings containing around 8000 lines of dialogue.

Indiana Jones and the Fate of Atlantis was well received by critics and consumers alike, selling over a million units. It is considered one of the best games in the point-and-click adventure genre.

Virtua Racing

Date of release: August 1992

Region: Japan

Developer: Sega

Publisher: Sega

Platform: Arcade

Designed by Yu Suzuki, the prolific game designer, engineer, producer and programmer of games such as Hang-On (1985), Space Harrier (1985) and Out Run (1986), Virtua Racing is a single-player or multiplayer, 3D, first-person or third-person, Formula 1 racing game. Virtua Racing was originally only meant to be a proof-of-concept demonstration for Sega's new Sega Model 1 arcade board, which used a cutting-edge microprocessor custom-designed for 3D polygon display. Yet it was apparent that, with a little more development, the game was good enough to be released in the arcades. The game featured three different courses and could be viewed from four different perspectives, depending on the player's preference. By pressing buttons to the left of the steering wheel, the player could change their point of view at any time during gameplay from a third-person view far behind the car to a first-person person perspective from the driving seat. Virtual Racing also featured vibrating force feedback on the steering wheel.

There were a number of different cabinets. One was a single-player version with a seat that the vendors could remove should players prefer to stand. Another was a two-player cabinet allowing people to race each other. One of the game's biggest draws was its incredibly crisp 3D graphics. It ran at an incredible 30 frames per second, which for players in the early 1990s appeared very smooth. Upon release, it quickly became one of the most popular arcade games and was soon ported to the Mega Drive/Genesis. Other games to use the Sega Model 1 Arcade board were Virtua Fighter (1993) and Wing War (1994).

Super Mario Kart

Date of release: August 1992

Region: Japan

Developer: Nintendo EAD

Publisher: Nintendo

Platform: Super Famicom and Super Nintendo Entertainment System

Designed by Tadashi Sugiyama, Hideki Konno and Shigeru Miyamoto, Super Mario Kart is a single-player or multiplayer racing game. In single-player, you race against seven other characters from the popular Mario game franchise, ideal for honing your racing skills. However, it was the multiplayer mode in which friends could race against each other where the real fun and challenge could be found. There are eight drivers to choose from Mario, Luigi, Princess Peach, Yoshi, Donkey Kong, Bowser, Koopa Troopa, and Toad. Some characters' Karts have faster acceleration than those of their competitors, while others boast a better top speed or improved traction. Players could also collect things on the track to gain an advantage. Running over an arrow would boost speed while going over a straight yellow line would make the Kart jump. Hitting a Question Block causes an item box at the top of the screen to spin and gave the player whichever item it stopped at to use. These items are a key component in what makes Super Mario Kart so much fun, namely the Green Shell, Red Shell, Banana Peel, Feather, Mushroom, Star, Lightning Bolt and Boo. The Green Shell can send your competitors into a spin if it hits them, travelling in a straight line and requiring careful aim. The Red Shell acts the same as the Green shell, but homes in on opponents. The Banana Peel will spin a competitor's Kart off the track should they run over it. The Feather allows the player to perform a high jump, typically used for dodging shells or taking a shortcut. The Mushroom gives the player a temporary burst of speed. The Star makes them temporarily invincible, along with giving them a speed boost similar to that of the Mushroom and causes opponents to spin out should they be rammed by the player with the Star active. The Lightning Bolt shrinks and slows all other racers on the track. Finally, Boo makes the player's Kart invisible and invulnerable to harm and steals an opponent's item or weapon.

There are also numerous hazards and obstacles for the player to watch out for on the nineteen tracks in Super Mario Kart, each themed on various levels of the Mario games. As with F-Zero (1990), Super Mario Kart used Mode 7 Scrolling graphics to give the impression of the Karts racing down a 3D track.

The game was a huge hit, becoming an instant classic with players who could not get enough of racing against their friends. Like many successful games, it was easy to learn but difficult to master as there was always another player out there who could beat you. Super Mario Kart ended up being one of the most popular video games for the SNES and has sold almost nine million units to date. It was so popular it spawned its own series of games, some of the most notable of which are: Mario Kart: Double Dash (2003), Mario Kart: Wii (2008), Mario Kart 7 (2011) and Mario Kart 8 Deluxe (2017).

Championship Manager

Date of release: September 1992

Region: UK

Developers: Intelek

Publisher: Domark

Platform: Amiga, Atari ST and MS-DOS

Championship Manager is a single-player, football management simulation game. The game features English football teams all battling their way up from the Fourth to the First Division (now the Premier League). The player begins by choosing their team and the best players. They must manage their team players and their statistics as well as manage team finances and transfers.

The Football Manager series of games had started and carried the torch for football manager games since its inception in 1982 for the 8-bit generation, but now that time was coming to an end. Games like Championship Manager (1992) and Premier Manager

(1992) picked up where Football Manager left off, finally taking the genre into the 16-bit era. Championship Manager was not as popular as its main competitor Premier Manager (1992). However, it did have a strong following and spawned several sequels, most notably Championship Manager '93 (1993) Championship Manager 97/98 (1997) and Championship Manager: Season 01/02 (2001).

Flashback/Flashback: The Quest for Identity

Date of release: 1992

Region: Worldwide

Developer: Delphine Software International

Publisher: U.S. Gold

Platform: Amiga

Designed by Paul Cuisset of Delphine Software International, Flashback, known in the USA as Flashback: The Quest for Identity, is a single-player, 2D, cinematic platformer. The aim of Flashback is to defeat the shapeshifting aliens called 'Morphs' who have infiltrated human society and are intent on conquering the Earth. Set in the year 2140, you play as Conrad B. Hart, suffering from amnesia. The player must first recover his lost memories before carrying on finding out how to stop the Morphs. As Conrad, the player can run, jump, and climb or drop down from ledges. Conrad can also fire his pistol, which has unlimited ammunition, use a force shield, and later a portable teleportation device which the player can throw to reach inaccessible areas, a rather useful gaming mechanic.

Flashback is often compared with Delphine Software International's previous game, Another World/Out of this World (1991). Both feature the use of rotoscoping to create the realistic movement of the characters and have a similar cinematic look and narrative. Although Flashback received some criticism due to its clunky controls, many were entranced by its animations, art-style, intriguing puzzles and narrative with excellent use of cutscenes.

The game sold over 750,000 units by 1995 and became the best-selling French game of all time. It was soon ported to the Acorn Archimedes, Genesis/Mega Drive, MS-DOS and SNES in 1993, followed by the CD-ROM version on various platforms. As with Another World, the CD-ROM version had improved graphics and sound. Flashback spawned a sequel with Fade to Black (1995), and a remake with Flashback: Remastered Edition (2018).

Dragon Quest V: Hand of the Heavenly Bride

Date of release: September 1992

Region: Japan

Developer: Chunsoft

Publisher: Enix

Platform: Super Famicom and Super Nintendo Entertainment System

Known in Japan as 'Doragon Kuesuto Faibu Tenkū no Hanayome,' Dragon Quest V is a single-player RPG and is the second game in the Zenithian trilogy. You play as the hero, whom the player names upon their birth, and the story subsequently follows the protagonist throughout infancy, childhood and adulthood, whereupon the protagonist marries and has a child of their own. Dragon Quest V maintains similar gameplay and many of the same game mechanics as the previous four titles. However, many new features were introduced into the fifth game. It was the first Dragon Quest game to move from the 8-bit Famicom to the 16-bit Super Famicom with improved graphics and sound. Dragon Quest V is also cited as having one of the better narratives when compared with some of the other Dragon Quest games. Finally, it had an improved, turn-based combat system with the opportunity to recruit the creatures you fight against into your party, with each creature boasting a different set of abilities that the player could use. This was not the first time this particular mechanic was used in a video game, with the first occurrence in Digital Devil Story: Megami Tensei (1987), yet it is possible that its addition to Dragon Quest V did inspire such games as the Pokémon (1996-current date) and Digimon series (1999-current date). These are some of the reasons why Dragon Quest V is cited by many to be one of the best games in the series.

The Dragon Quest games were always immensely popular in their country of origin, yet Dragon Quest V was not released outside of Japan, partly due to a lack of sales of previous Dragon Quest games. It didn't receive a remake until over a decade later in 2004 for the PlayStation 2, though once again this was in Japan only. It was not until the game was finally ported to the Nintendo DS in 2008/2009 that Western audiences could play the game. It can also be played on Android and IOS mobile platforms. A computer-animated feature film based on the game titled Dragon Quest: Your Story was released in August 2019.

Super Mario USA

Super Mario USA was released in Japan in September 1992 by Nintendo for the Famicom. In 1988, the Japanese release of Super Mario Bros. 2 was deemed too difficult for Western audiences and so another game, Yume Kōjō: Doki Doki Panic (1987), was taken, altered and changed into Super Mario Bros. 2 and released for the NES in the West, making for a same name but a different game. Now, the Japanese could play this Western version of Super Mario Bros. 2.

Mortal Kombat

Date of release: October 1992

Region: USA

Developer: Midway

Publisher: Midway

Platform: Arcade

Designed by Ed Boon, John Tobias and John Vogel, with music by Dan Forden, Mortal Kombat is a single-player or two-player, fantasy-themed fighting game. The aim of Mortal Kombat is quite simple: defeat your current opponent, be they computer- or player-controlled. Set in 'Earthrealm' on Shang Tsung's Island, the player or players begin by choosing one of seven characters, each of whom can not only perform jumps, punches and kicks but who also have a suite of special moves, combos and a Fatality, also known as a finishing move. The playable characters were the following:

Johnny Cage, whose special moves are firing an Energy Bolt, the Shadow Kick and the self-explanatory Ball Breaker. His finishing move is decapitating his opponent with a single punch.

Kano, whose special moves are a Spin Attack and Knife Throw. His finishing move is ripping out his opponent's heart.

Raiden, whose special moves are his Teleport, Lightning Bolt throw and the Torpedo, a flying tackle. His finishing moves are using his lightning powers to either blow his opponent's head off or to completely disintegrate them.

Liu Kang, whose special moves are the Fireball, the Flying Dragon and Bicycle Kicks. His finishing move is a powerful punch that sends the opponent flying into the air and onto a floor of giant spikes below.

Scorpion, whose special moves are his "Get Over Here!" Grapple Spear and Teleport. His finishing move is to take his mask off, exposing his skull and setting his opponent on fire with his flame breath.

Sub-Zero, whose special moves are his Ice Ball throw and "Slide," a sliding tackle. His finishing move is either to rip his opponent's head off with the spine still attached or to freeze them and then smash them into pieces.

Sonya, whose special moves are the ranged Ring Toss, the Leg Grab and the Square Wave Punch. Her finishing move is to blow a kiss containing a fireball that incinerates her opponent.

Each player has a health bar that if reduced to zero stuns them and leaves them vulnerable, allowing the other player to perform their finishing move and win the round. The first player to win two rounds wins the match.

The arcade cabinet featured a joystick and five buttons for each of the two players. There were two buttons for punching, two buttons for kicking, and a block button, which was a rather unique feature at the time. The game could be played in single-player mode, where the player would have to defeat each character in the roster and two other story-only characters, the first being Goro, a half-human half-dragon beast with four arms and finally Shang Tsung, a powerful and evil sorcerer and the grandmaster of the titular Mortal Kombat tournament.

The game was defined by its characters, whose sprites were digitised actors, and its over-the-top violence. Mortal Kombat became nothing short of a phenomenon, only rivalled by the Street Fighter series. It had a huge following of teenagers and adults who loved the brutal aspect of the game. However, its excessive violence drew the attention of parents and the United States government of the time. Games such as Mortal Kombat, Night Trap (1992) and Doom (1993) resulted in a Bill of Law decreeing that all video games should use a rating system similar to the one used in the film industry, thus the Entertainment Software Rating Board (ESRB) was accordingly established in 1994.

After a huge marketing campaign, Mortal Kombat was ported a year later to most of the popular home consoles in September 1993 on what was dubbed 'Mortal Monday'. However, the SNES version of the game didn't feature some of the game's more violent moves and the blood was replaced with sweat, much to the chagrin of SNES owners. The Sega Mega Drive/Genesis port kept the violence and blood. Owners of this console accordingly viewed it as being the superior port. In its first year, Mortal Kombat on these home systems would sell over three million units. Along with the popularity of the game in the arcade, Mortal Kombat was a true cultural phenomenon. Later, it would be released on the Amiga, Mega CD/Sega CD and MS-DOS. Mortal Kombat has spawned several sequels over time, expanding on the core game mechanics and introducing many more characters to its roster, including some from other franchises. Some notable games of the series are Mortal Kombat II (1993), Ultimate Mortal Kombat 3 (1995),

Mortal Kombat (2011), Mortal Kombat X (2015) and Mortal Kombat 11 (2019).

Alone in the Dark

Date of release: 1992

Region: France

Developer: Infogrames

Publisher: Infogrames

Platform: MS-DOS

Designed by Frédérick Raynal and Bruno Bonnell of Infogrames, Alone in the Dark is a single-player, 3D, third-person, survival-horror game. Set in 1924, you play as either Edward Carnby or Emily Hartwood and must escape from a haunted mansion. The player begins in the attic and must avoid or defeat various supernatural creatures and solve numerous puzzles to fulfil their goal. The game has a compelling Lovecraftian narrative that adds to the whole mythos of the game. The characters and moveable objects are real-time 3D rendered objects and the game features a fixed camera, which meant that the developers could utilise higher quality textures mapped to 3D environments. This technique meant the graphics were a vast improvement on a game such as Hunter (1991), which was also a 3D third-person video game featuring an actual person as the main character (as opposed to a car or spaceship). The only trade-off for this was the fixed camera, though this could be rather beneficial when controlling the aesthetic and mood of a survival-horror game.

Alone in the Dark was one of the few games of the time to elicit a more subtle cocktail of emotions. It focussed on the building of suspense, foreboding, intrigue and fear, not only through visuals but also through its all-important use of sound. It was something new and different from what players usually felt when playing a video game. Almost all modern-day genres of video games were well-established in the early nineties, with the survival-horror genre being one of the few exceptions.

Alone in the Dark is often cited as the precursor to the modern-day survival-horror game, the genre cemented by Resident Evil (1996), a series that would become synonymous and pave the way for many other games in the genre. While a forerunner of survival-horror, Alone in the Dark was highly acclaimed by critics and players. It is believed that it ultimately sold around 2.5 million units, an incredibly impressive feat for a PC game of the time. Alone in the Dark also spawned a series of sequels such as Alone in the Dark 2 (1993), Alone in the Dark 3 (1994), Alone in the Dark: The New Nightmare

(2001) and Alone in the Dark (2008). However, none of these had the same impact as the original.

Night Trap

Date of release: October 1992

Region: USA

Developer: Digital Pictures

Publisher: Sega

Platform: Sega CD

Night Trap is a single-player, interactive, movie video game. The aim of the game is to protect a house full of teenage girls from vampires known as Augers by controlling and triggering traps. The player controls a set of internal CCTV cameras and must use the traps to stop any intruders within the house. The game features full-motion videos (FMVs) of real-life actors.

The game became renowned for its controversy among parents and the United States government, and along with games such as Mortal Kombat (1992) and Doom (1993), as mentioned previously, resulted in a law that all video games utilise a rating system similar to the one used in the film industry. Accordingly, the Entertainment Software Rating Board (ESRB) was established in 1994.

Night Trap was famously accused of 'promoting gratuitous violence and sexual aggression against women' by a United States Senator who had never played the game, never realising that the principal aim of the game was rather to protect the girls in the house from intruders. Nevertheless, this did not stop some retailers from pulling the game from their shelves by Christmas of 1992. In retrospect, the controversy surrounding Night Trap seems ludicrous now to anyone who nowadays might play the game.

Night Trap was ported to several other CD-ROM platforms. If not for initiating a chain of events that would lead to the creation of the ESRB, Night Trap would most likely be regarded as just another corny CD-ROM game using FMVs. Instead, it has become one of the more infamous games in video game history.

Super Star Wars

Date of release: November 1992

Region: USA

Developer: Sculptured Software

Publisher: Nintendo

Platform: Super Nintendo Entertainment System

Super Star Wars is a single-player, run-and-gun video game based on Star Wars: A New Hope (1977). Super Star Wars is a remake of Star Wars (1987), a game only released in Japan for the Famicom, and only loosely following the plot of the movie. The gameplay involves side-scrolling levels where the player initially controls Luke Skywalker. There are also a number of levels that are played from a third-person vehicle perspective with the camera placed behind the vehicle and the game employing Mode 7 graphics to render its scrolling sprites There are fifteen levels in Super Star Wars, starting on the desert planet of Tatooine and ending in the Rebel assault on the Death Star. Han Solo and Chewbacca are also playable characters in the game. Super Star Wars features several power-up items and numerous enemies, several of which were not actually in the original movie.

Super Star Wars was praised for its graphics, sound and smooth gameplay. At the time, it was considered to be the best Star Wars game released for the home market. However, it was also notorious for being extremely difficult. Only the most persistent and skilled players (presumably using something akin to the Force) could hope to complete it. The game spawned two sequels: Super Star Wars: Empire Strikes Back (1993) and Super Star Wars: Return of the Jedi (1994).

Sonic the Hedgehog 2

Date of release: November 1992

Region: Japan/USA

Developer: Sega Technical Institute

Publisher: Sega

Platform: Sega Genesis/Mega Drive

Designed by Masaharu Yoshii, Shinobu Toyoda, Hirokazu Yasuhara and Yuji Naka, and with music by Masato Nakamura, Sonic the Hedgehog 2 is a single-player or two-player, side-scrolling platform game and the sequel to the phenomenally successful Sonic the Hedgehog (1991). The aim of the game is to stop Dr Ivo Robotnik from stealing the seven Chaos Emeralds to power his doomsday machine. As one might expect, Sonic the Hedgehog 2 plays very much like the original, faithfully including all the original game mechanics. However, in the sequel, there are some additional features. This time, two players can work together. One player controls Sonic, while the other controls a new character, Miles 'Tails' Prower, a young fox with two tails. Sonic the Hedgehog 2 also introduced a special stage. If you have fifty rings when you pass through a Star Post checkpoint, you can enter the Special Stage via the Star Circle, with success resulting in the acquisition of one of the Chaos Emeralds. The Special Stage has a 3D, third-person perspective as the camera follows behind Sonic and Tails racing down a linear, tube-like pathway as the player attempts to collect a prerequisite amount of rings and earn the Chaos Emerald. The game also introduced a two-player competitive mode where the screen was split horizontally, and Sonic and Tails had to race to win. This PvP mode could also be played in the Special Stage. There are ten zones in Sonic the Hedgehog 2, each harbouring a host of unique enemies. Sonic and Tails both begin with three lives each but earn a bonus life when they collect 100 and 200 rings. A chance to continue is awarded every time the player scores 100,000 points.

Sonic the Hedgehog 2 is often cited as the best game in the series, primarily due to its level design. It took all the elements from the original and improved them to perfection, in much the same way as Super Mario Bros. 3 (1988). The game went on to sell well over 7.5 million units.

X-Men

Date of release: November 1992

Region: Japan

Developer: Konami

Publisher: Konami

Platform: Arcade

X-Men is a single-player or multiplayer (capable of handling up to six players on some cabinets), side-scrolling beat 'em up, based on the popular Marvel comic book series. The aim of X-Men is to stop the antagonist and master of magnetism, Magneto, from destroying the world. As with many standard beat 'em ups, the player must defeat a multitude of enemies by kicking or punching or using objects in the environment as weapons. The player can also use their mutant's signature ability to take out their foes.

There were some unique features that set X-Men apart from other similar games such as Teenage Mutant Ninja Turtles (1989) and The Simpsons (1991), both also published by Konami. Having a six-player cabinet was unprecedented in the arcade. There were also two-player and four-player versions, but it was the huge six-player cabinet that was a real joy. Inside this cabinet were two screens creating a fantastic widescreen effect. For the first time, six players could work together for a common goal, and for the first time players could play the role of some of Marvel's most popular comic-book super-heroes. Players could choose between Cyclops, Colossus, Wolverine, Storm, Nightcrawler and Dazzler. Unleashing a character's mutant power causes the loss of health points, so the player has to use them judiciously. Items can be picked up to recover health and so allow repeated use of their mutant powers.

For fans of X-Men comic books, the game was a delight. It not only featured the X-Men themselves but many other recognisable characters who acted as bosses, and featured villains such as The Blob, Emma Frost, Pyro, Juggernaut, and the Sentinels. X-Men wasn't ported until 2010 to the PlayStation 3 and Xbox 360.

Ecco the Dolphin

Date of release: December 1992

Region: Worldwide

Developer: Novotrade International

Publisher: Sega

Platform: Sega Genesis/Mega Drive

Designed by László Szenttornyai and Edward Ettore Annunziata of Novotrade International, Ecco the Dolphin is a single-player, action-adventure game, and the first in the Ecco the Dolphin series. The aim of Ecco the Dolphin is to discover the mystery of the giant waterspout which has sucked up all the marine life, including Ecco's pod, from the ocean. The player travels to the Arctic, Atlantis, into Earth's ancient past using a time machine, and finally confronts and does battle with aliens. Ecco can swim underwater and jump into the air. He can attack by swimming quickly towards his foes and bumping into them. Ecco can also 'sing' (via echolocation) which allows him to speak to other underwater creatures or open up new areas. The player must also come up for air every now and then or Ecco will drown, which makes for a particularly nail-biting experience when diving very deep and desperately searching for an air pocket. There are a total of twenty-seven levels.

Ecco the Dolphin became a firm favourite on the Sega Genesis/Mega Drive. Its setting and core gameplay were markedly original and set it apart from most other games of the time. In some ways, it was surprising that when many games were about fighting or shooting, a game about a dolphin became such a success. Yet, the success of Ecco the Dolphin was a testament to its great game design.

After selling well on the Genesis, it was soon ported to the Game Gear, Master System, Microsoft Windows and Sega CD. The game spawned several sequels including Ecco: The Tides of Time (1994) and Ecco the Dolphin: Defender of the Future (2000).

Dune II: The Building of a Dynasty/Dune II: Battle for Arrakis

Date of release: December 1992

Region: Worldwide

Developer: Westwood Studios

Publisher: Virgin Games

Platform: MS-DOS

Dune II: The Building of a Dynasty, also known as Dune II: The Battle of Arrakis, is a single-player, real-time, strategy game based on the novel and movie Dune. The aim of Dune II is to harvest the spice and build up your base and army in an attempt to defeat all the other Houses. The Emperor Frederick IV of House Corrino, a non-canon character only appearing in the games by Westwood Studios, offers the governorship of Arrakis to whichever House can deliver the most spice, prompting the three houses to land on Arrakis and promptly wage war against each other. At the start of the game, the player can choose between House Atreides, House Harkonnen and House Ordos, and must accordingly harvest sufficient spice to placate the Emperor whilst also managing upkeep, development and deployment of their units for attack and defence against the other two houses. If the player progresses far enough in the game they must also contend with the Emperor's deadly and elite force, the feared Sardaukar.

Dune II would become renowned as the game on which almost all real-time strategy games of the future would be based, firmly revitalising and establishing the RTS genre and heavily influencing such popular games as the Warcraft series (1994-current date), the Command & Conquer series (1995-2013), Total Annihilation (1997) and the StarCraft series (1998-2017). Dune II would establish many features used in these games including the fog of war, the use of the mouse to move and instruct units, the upgrading of existing buildings, and the introduction of different factions possessing unique abilities and units.

Even though Dune II may have sold marginally less than its predecessor, it is often considered the superior game and its significance in the evolution of the real-time strategy genre is undisputed. In 1993, Dune II was ported to the Amiga and Sega Genesis/Mega Drive. Dune II: The Building of a Dynasty/The Battle of Arrakis, spawned a partial remake in the form of Dune 2000 (1998) and a sequel with Emperor: Battle for Dune (2001).

Street Fighter II Turbo: Hyper Fighting

Date of release: December 1992

Region: Worldwide

Developer: Capcom Studios

Publisher: Capcom Games

Platform: MS-DOS

Designed by Yoshiki Okamoto, Akira Nishitani and Akira Yasuda of Capcom, Street Fighter II Turbo: Hyper Fighting is a single-player or multiplayer fighting game and is essentially the same game as Street Fighter II: Champion Edition, except that the speed of the game has been increased. Also, each fighter (apart from Guile) has an extra special move, and the character's outfits have had a palette swap. You would think these changes would make little difference to the game. However, in the early nineties, there were many hardcore fans of Street Fighter II. These dedicated players were eager to improve their already lightning-fast reflexes and hone their skills further still with this newer and much faster game.

Bomberman '93

Date of release: December 1992

Region: Japan

Developer: Hudson Soft

Publisher: Hudson Soft

Platform: PC Engine/TurboGrafx- 16

Designed by Shigeki Fujiwara and Tsukasa Kuwahara of Hudson Soft, Bomberman '93 is a single-player or multiplayer puzzle maze game, and the ninth game in the Bomberman series, beginning with the original Bomberman (1983) for Japanese home systems.

The gameplay is similar to the previous Bomberman games where the player or players plant bombs to destroy blocks and kill enemies. Destroying blocks sometimes reveals power-ups such as increasing the blast radius of bombs or replenishing the player's supply. The single-player mode features seven themed game worlds, each containing eight stages and making for an excellent experience in its own right. However, it is in multiplayer mode where the real fun could be found. Bomberman '93 was the first in the series to allow as many as up to five players to play onscreen in a timed death match, using a peripheral device called a multitap. Multiple controllers could be plugged into the multitap, which itself plugged into the console's controller port. This multiplayer experience is why Bomberman '93 is considered to be one of the best in the series.

1992 Notable Omissions

Agony. Aladdin Deck Enhancer. Art of Fighting. Asterix. Axelay. Chakan: The Forever Man. Cho Aniki. Comanche: Maximum Overkill. Crystal Dynamics was founded. Cybernator/Assaults Suits Valken. Dalek Attack. Darklands. Darkseed. Floor 13. Kingdoms of Kingdoms 2 Vikings, Fields of Conquest. Fatal Fury. Gimmick! Mega Man 5. Fatal Fury 2. Fire Emblem Gaiden. Hello Kitty no Hanabatake. Ishar: Legend of the Fortress. Kid Chameleon. King's Quest VI. Landstalker. Legend. Little Samson. Lure of the Temptress. Mario Paint. Otogirisō. Pinball Fantasies. Pocky Rocky. Road Rash 2. Robocop 3D. Sensible Soccer. Sewer Shark. Soulblazer. Star Control II. Star Trek: 25th Anniversary. Streets of Rage 2. Super Mario Land 2: 6 Golden Coins. Super Scope, light gun peripheral. Total Carnage. The Koshan Conspiracy. The Magical Quest Starring Mickey Mouse. Thunder Force IV. Twinkle Tale. Ultima Underworld: The Stygian Abyss. UnReal World. World of Illusion Starring Mickey Mouse and Donald Duck. Zool.

1993

Star Wars: X-Wing

Date of release: February 1993

Region: USA

Developer: LucasArts

Publisher: LucasArts

Platform: Macintosh, MS-DOS and Windows

Designed by Lawrence Holland and Edward Kilham, Star Wars: X-Wing is a single-player, 3D, space-combat simulation game. Set before and during the events of the movie Star Wars Episode IV: A New Hope, the aim of the game is to complete missions against the tyrannical Empire culminating with you playing as Luke Skywalker attempting to successfully destroy the Death Star. The game is viewed from a first-person perspective within the starfighter's cockpit. The player must allocate power between their engines, shields or weapons, dependent on the circumstances, to successfully destroy the enemy and complete a mission. Missions include escorting Rebel ships, disabling enemy vessels and mounting assaults on Imperial convoys or capital ships. Each mission usually involves dogfighting with the Empire's TIE Fighters. Missions can be replayed upon completion, making for good replayability. As well as piloting the X-Wing Starfighter, players also have the chance to fly the A-Wing Interceptor and the Y-Wing Starfighter also featured in the movies.

Star Wars: X-Wing did for the home what Star Wars (1983) did in the arcades ten years previously: it captured the tense excitement of the space battles from the Star Wars movies and put it in a video game. Being one of the first 3D, filled polygon space-combat games for the home market, based on such a successful franchise and accompanied by the film's iconic musical score, Star Wars: X-Wing made for a highly praised and successful video game that sold over 500,000 units by the end of the year. Star Wars fans had been waiting for a game like this for years, the floodgates were open and LucasArts gave gamers several sequels with Star Wars: TIE Fighter (1994), X-Wing vs. TIE Fighter (1997) and Star Wars: X-Wing Alliance (1999).

Star Fox/Starwing

Date of release: February 1993

Region: Japan

Developer: Nintendo EAD

Publisher: Nintendo

Platform: Super Famicom/SNES

Directed by Katsuya Eguchi (Super Mario Bros 3 and Super Mario World) and designed by Shigeru Miyamoto (Donkey Kong, Super Mario Bros and The Legend of Zelda) of Nintendo with programming by Argonaut Software, Star Fox, known as Starwing in Europe, is a single-player, 3D rail shooter. The aim of Star Fox is to defend your homeworld of Corneria against the invading forces of Andross. You play as Fox McCloud, part of the Star Fox team flying the advanced prototype Arwing fighter. In the beginning, the player has a choice of three paths to take on which they will encounter differing planets, sectors of space, asteroid fields or even a space armada. These represent different difficulty levels and also make for great replay value. The game can be viewed from a first-person perspective within the cockpit, a third-person perspective directly behind your ship and another third-person viewpoint situated further behind your ship, as you destroy various enemies with your lasers. You must avoid enemy fire and certain obstacles, or you will take damage to your shields. If your shield is depleted, your ship is destroyed, and you will lose one of your three lives. Power-ups can be collected to help restore your shields, provide temporary invulnerability, grant extra firepower or an extra life (1-up), or allow the use of Nova Bombs which will damage all enemies that are within range of its explosion. At the end of each level, the player must destroy a boss, some of which are huge ships that hove into view before spectacularly breaking apart, to continue to the next level. Fox McCloud flies with three wing-men: Falco Lombardi (an anthropomorphic bird), Peppy Hare (an anthropomorphic hare), and Slippy Toad (an anthropomorphic toad). These will pop up at the bottom of your screen from time to time and talk to you or request assistance.

3D flat-shaded polygonal graphics used in a game like Star Fox were previously thought impossible for the SNES. The first separate Graphics Processing Unit (GPU) called the Super FX was installed into every Star Fox cartridge, which pretty much ran the game itself. In 1993, even though consoles were paving their own way, they were still attempting to emulate the arcade experience, with Star Fox being very similar to arcade games such as the 3D rail shooter Starblade (1991). A game like Star Fox could be seen as the ultimate expression and evolution of Spacewar! (1962) and Space Invaders (1978), the forerunners of the shooter genre. The game was also inspired by co-developers Argonaut Software's previous game Starglider (1986).

Star Fox was highly acclaimed for bringing stunning 3D graphics onto the SNES. It was also praised for its arcade action, interesting characters and its choice of progression through the game. Its graphics simply blew SNES users away, who never thought such a thing was possible. It went on to sell over four million units. It spawned several sequels, namely Star Fox 64 (1997), Star Fox Adventures (2002), Star Fox: Assault (2005), Star Fox: Command (2006), Star Fox 64 3D (2011), Star Fox Zero (2016), Star Fox Guard (2016) and Star Fox 2 (2017).

SimCity 2000

Date of release: 1993

Region: USA

Developer: Maxis

Publisher: Maxis

Platform: Apple Macintosh

Designed by Fred Haslam and Will Wright, SimCity 2000 is a single-player, city-building game and the sequel to SimCity (1989). As with the previous game, there is no specific end goal. The player can either build and maintain an organised, functioning city, or just build one to destroy by triggering one of the many disasters for fun. SimCity 2000 boasts significant graphical improvements from the first game and is now viewed from an isometric view as opposed to the top-down perspective used in the first game. There are several new features such as airports, colleges, hospitals, libraries, marinas, museums, prisons, seaports, subways and zoos. There are also nine different ways to power your city instead of the original two.

A player could build multiple towns and also name places. The game also required careful management of taxes and crime rate. It also featured scenarios and specific events that the player must deal with and recover from. Scenarios include a firestorm, hurricane, flood, recession, and even a giant monster ravaging the city which was a call-back to the original game and is a trademark of the SimCity series. Theoretically, the game can be played indefinitely, as the closest SimCity comes to a goal is if the player can achieve an 'exodus'. This 'exodus' can occur from the year 2051 and involves the player building 300 or more Arcologies to be launched into space in an effort to establish new civilisations on new worlds. It is safe to say that SimCity 2000 was a giant evolutionary leap from the original.

SimCity 2000 was highly praised by critics and was one of the best-selling computer games of the 1990s. It was soon ported to other popular home computers and consoles of the time. It also spawned several expansions and editions, including Scenarios Vol 1: Great Disasters (1994) which included a toolset for players to change assets in the game, SimCity 2000 Special Edition (1995) and SimCity 2000 Network Edition which allowed multiplayer mode across a Local Area Network (or LAN) or over the internet.

PC Gamer

PC Gamer was founded in the UK in 1993 by Future plc. PC Gamer is a monthly magazine devoted to the PC platform. It features news, previews, game and hardware reviews, guides and various tips and tricks.

The US edition of PC Gamer was launched in 1994, with the website going live soon after. Other editions have been launched in countries all over the world, to varying degrees of success. A PC Gamer podcast (UK) was launched in May 2007.

The highest-rated games in PC Gamer's history of reviews are Civilisation II (1996), Quake II (1997), Half-Life (1998), Half-Life 2 (2004), Team Fortress 2 (2007), Spelunky (2008), Minecraft (2009) and Kerbal Space Program (2015), all receiving a score of 96%.

The Lost Vikings

Date of release: April 1993

Region: USA

Developer: Silicon & Synapse

Publisher: Interplay Productions

Platform: SNES

The Lost Vikings is a single-player or multiplayer, side-scrolling, cooperative puzzle platformer. The aim of the game is to defeat Tomator, the alien emperor of the Croutonian Empire. The player or players control one of three Vikings (though originally the game was conceptualised to have around a hundred): Erik the Swift, Baleog the Fierce, and Olaf the Stout, each being kidnapped by the aforementioned antagonist Tomator. Each Viking has different strengths and weaknesses, which when combined with the well-crafted level design makes for enjoyable gameplay. Each level takes place in a different time period. The player can switch between different Vikings but must get each Viking to the level's exit to complete it and continue onwards, requiring the player to use each Viking's respective ability for puzzle-solving and strategy.

The game was praised for its quirky humour, puzzles and graphics. The Lost Vikings was ported to the Amiga, Sega Genesis, and Game Boy Advance. The Sega Mega Drive/Genesis version has forty-two levels, whereas the original SNES version had thirty-seven. It also spawned a sequel with The Lost Vikings 2 (1997).

The Lost Vikings was the first truly well-received game by Silicon & Synapse, which would go on to become one of the most renowned game developers in the world: Blizzard Entertainment.

Nvidia is founded

The Nvidia Corporation was founded in the USA in April 1993 by Jensen Huang, Chris Malachowsky and Curtis Priem. Nvidia was established on the belief that computers of the future would require specialist hardware for specific needs. They researched and developed Graphics Processing Units (GPUs), which are more commonly referred to as graphics cards nowadays, with the intent of pushing the boundaries of graphical performance in video games. The name came about when the company was still nameless but had the convention of naming all their files 'NV', standing for 'Next Version.' Needing to go through incorporation and form the company, the founders supposedly sought out all words containing 'nv', eventually coming across Invidia, the Latin word for envy, and subsequently naming their company Nvidia.

Nvidia's first major release was the RIVA TNT video and 3D graphics accelerator chip in 1998. Their first product in the popular line of GeForce graphics cards was the GeForce 256 in 1999. Nvidia's products (and their competitors) are one of the main reasons why the PC platform is seen as leading the way when it comes to the improvement of graphical performance in video games.

The 7th Guest

Date of release: April 1993

Region: USA

Developer: Trilobyte

Publisher: Virgin Interactive Entertainment

Platform: MS-DOS

The 7th Guest is a single-player, point-and-click, interactive movie video game. The aim of the game is to solve the mystery of the mansion. The player character has amnesia, with no recollection of who they are or how they came to be at the start of the game. The game is set from a first-person perspective, with the player advancing from one room to the next within the haunted mansion. The gameplay almost exclusively involves going from room to room solving puzzles using pre-rendered 2D and 3D imagery and movie sequences also known as Full Motion Video (FMV). The 7th Guest boasts forty minutes of cutscenes, which was an impressive amount for the time.

The game was highly praised for its clever use of puzzles and blend of live-action sequences (corny performances notwithstanding) and 3D pre-rendered environments. It initially sold over 60,000 units, which, considering that the game cost around $100 (an extortionate amount) to buy, is rather impressive. It eventually sold around two million units.

The 7th Guest was the first game to release exclusively on the CD-ROM. It, and games such as Myst (1993) and Star Wars: Rebel Assault (1993), are thought to be the reason why the sales of CD-ROM drives for PCs were reportedly up by 300% for some manufacturers. The game generated so much hype at trade shows that a sequel was in development even before the release of The 7th Guest. It spawned two sequels: The 11th Hour (1995) and The 13th Doll (2019), and a remastered The 7th Guest: 25th Anniversary Edition (2019), which unfortunately looks almost the same as the original.

The 7th Guest and other similar games also inspired many developers into thinking that the future of gaming was to use the CD-ROM format crammed with pre-rendered graphics and FMVs, often with decidedly lacklustre results.

Mortal Kombat II

Date of release: April 1993

Region: USA

Developer: Midway

Publisher: Midway

Platform: Arcade

Mortal Kombat II is a single-player or multiplayer fighting game and the sequel to the immensely popular Mortal Kombat (1992). The aim of the game is simple: defeat your opponent. The game plays very much the same as the original, using digitised characters of real-life actors and featuring copious amounts of blood and violence, which was part of the appeal of the original game. However, Mortal Kombat II also introduced several new features, notably by increasing the roster of playable characters. Both old and new fighters would have a variety of new special moves and fatalities, some of which would use the environment to finish off opponents, such as throwing them into a pool of acid or onto spikes. As with the original game, Mortal Kombat II met with some controversy and was even banned in some countries

Mortal Kombat II was a huge success in the arcades. Acclaim Entertainment, the game's publisher, spent $50 million on a global marketing campaign, which was a great deal of money in 1994 when it was released. Yet it was truly worthwhile. The hype Mortal Kombat II generated when subsequently released for the home market in 1994 made it the most popular game of the time, making $50 million in its first week, the best opening week for a video game ever, at the time. To put this in context, this exceeded the box-office receipts of 1994's biggest movie, The Lion King. Mortal Kombat II is still considered by some as one of the best games in the fighting genre.

NBA Jam

Date of release: May 1993

Region: USA

Developer: Midway

Publisher: Midway

Platform: Arcade

Designed by a team led by Mark Turmell, NBA Jam is a single-player or two-player, side-scrolling basketball game. NBA Jam follows the basic rules of real-life basketball with a little bit of artistic licence here and there. The look and gameplay have both been changed to make for a more exaggerated style better suited for the arcade. The basketball players can jump much higher, there are no fouls and the ball even catches fire with the accompanying commentary of "He's on fire!." Other catchphrases include "Boomshakalaka!" and "He's heating up!." The game also features real teams and digitised player likenesses for fans of the game.

NBA Jam was a huge success. It was the most profitable arcade game of 1993 and one of the most profitable arcade games of all time, boasting a return of over one billion dollars! It paved the way for other arcade sports games in a similar style. It was soon ported to the popular consoles of the day, too.

NBA Jam spawned four sequels by Midway until Acclaim Sports bought out the rights to develop future games. Acclaim published a further eight NBA Jam Games. Some of the most renowned games in the series are NBA Live 2005 (2004), NBA 2K11 (2010) and NBA 2K14 (2013).

Shadowrun

Date of release: May 1993

Region: USA

Developer: Beam Software

Publisher: Data East

Platform: SNES

Shadowrun is a single-player action RPG, based on the popular series of tabletop role-playing games first released in 1989. Shadowrun is set in the mid to late 21st century in an alternate timeline where magic has suddenly returned to the world in an event known as 'The Awakening'. The world is run by mega-corporations, and metahumans analogous to their fantasy equivalents, such as dwarves, elves, orks and trolls, are commonplace. Shadowrun is accordingly a blend of both cyberpunk and fantasy genres. You control the character Jake Armitage, who is suffering from amnesia after an assassination attempt on his life. The initial aim of the game is to discover who ordered the hit on Jake, and the story progresses from there. Shadowrun is played from an isometric perspective, except when conversing with NPCs, when the view switches to talking heads with accompanying text boxes. The combat uses a point-and-click mechanic to target enemies. The player's allies, the titular Shadowrunners, are initially AI-controlled, but the player can take manual control of their actions and issue commands. There are several different types of Shadowrunners: Mercenaries, who specialize in the use of weapons, Deckers, who specialize in hacking into the Matrix, and magic users such as Mages and Shamans. Each Shadowrunner has different levels of an attribute such as Body, Magic, Strength, Charisma, Karma and Armour. Though combat is unavoidable, Shadowrun is essentially a murder-mystery game, where the player must pick up on keywords when conversing with NPCs and solve the mystery of his own identity, why the assassins were sent to kill him and who ordered the attempt on his life. Another intriguing part of the game is hacking into the Matrix, a virtual digital representation of a mega-corporation's computer systems, the defences of which the player must overcome in order to gain access and subsequent control.

Shadowrun was highly acclaimed for being ahead of its time in terms of depth of game mechanics and features, and for being a departure from most RPGs of the time. Another Shadowrun game was released in 1994 for the Sega Mega Drive/Genesis, also based on the tabletop role-playing game. Other notable Shadowrun games are Shadowrun (2007), Shadowrun Returns (2013), Shadowrun: Dragonfall (2014), Shadowrun Chronicles: Boston Lockdown (2015) and Shadowrun: Hong Kong (2015).

Syndicate

Date of release: June 1993

Region: Worldwide

Developer: Bullfrog Productions

Publisher: Electronic Arts

Platform: Amiga and Windows

Syndicate is a single-player, real-time strategy game. The game is set in a cyberpunk dystopian future, where corporations have supplanted governments and run the world. The year is 2096 and the player controls a team of four cybernetically-enhanced characters working for one such corporation in competition with others in a war for global dominance. Viewed from an isometric perspective, the game involves a series of missions, many of which involve an aggressive run-and-gun approach. Other missions involve using the Persuadertron device to coerce NPCs into joining your corporation or becoming part of your four-person team. Your team can receive new and improved cybernetic enhancements and weapons to help ensure the success of further missions. These are developed by the research and development team, requiring funds from the taxation of captured territories from completed missions.

Syndicate spawned two sequels with Syndicate Wars (1996) and a re-imagining of the original with Syndicate (2012).

The Legend of Zelda: Link's Awakening

Date of release: June 1993

Region: Japan

Developer: Nintendo EAD

Publisher: Nintendo

Platform: Nintendo Game Boy

Designed by Takashi Tezuka and Shigeru Miyamoto, The Legend of Zelda: Link's Awakening is a single-player, action-adventure game and the fourth game in the popular The Legend of Zelda series. The Legend of Zelda: Link's Awakening was the first Zelda game that didn't feature the Triforce or the game's namesake, Princess Zelda. It was also the first Zelda game not to take place in Hyrule. Instead, the aim of the game centres on Link searching for eight musical instruments needed to awaken the sleeping Wind Fish. The game is viewed from a top-down perspective and features many of the gameplay elements of its predecessors, such as interactions with NPCs, the exploration of Koholint Island and its dungeons, solving puzzles and defeating a multitude of various enemies. The Legend of Zelda: Link's Awakening was the first Zelda game to introduce fishing and the ocarina instrument, which was later featured in The Legend of Zelda: Ocarina of Time (1998).

The Legend of Zelda: Link's Awakening was also the first Zelda game to be released on a handheld console. Fans of the series were overjoyed to be able to play a Zelda game on a portable device. The game was praised by critics and consumers for bringing the winning Zelda formula to the Game Boy platform, its only drawback being that the game was in monochrome. Thankfully, this changed with the release of The Legend of Zelda: Link's Awakening DX (1998), for the Game Boy Color. The Legend of Zelda: Link's Awakening, along with the DX version, has sold over six million units, and both are often cited as two of the best games for their respective platforms.

Maniac Mansion II: Day of the Tentacle

Date of release: June 1993

Region: USA

Developer: LucasArts

Publisher: LucasArts

Platform: MS-DOS

Designed by Dave Grossman, Tim Schafer, and Ron Gilbert and with art by Peter Chan,

Maniac Mansion II: Day of the Tentacle (often referred to as simply Day of the Tentacle) is a single-player, point-and-click adventure game and sequel to the popular Maniac Mansion. The aim is to stop the evil Purple Tentacle from taking over the world. Set five years after the original game, the player controls one of three characters: Bernard Bernoulli, Laverne and Hoagie. They attempt to time travel into the past in a bid to stop Purple Tentacle from evolving into a tyrannical monster. However, the antagonistic Dr Fred, inventor of the time machine and creator of the Purple Tentacle, has used an imitation diamond instead of a real one for the power source of the time machine, and the three subsequently end up in three different time periods. This is used as a unique game mechanic to solve puzzles. The player can switch between any of the three players, meaning that key objects from one era can be sent back through time using a time machine, or placed somewhere safe in the past to be picked up by another character and used hundreds of years in the future.

LucasArts once again made great use of their SCUMM engine for the game. Similar to other games, players click on a selection of verbs such as 'give,' 'open,' 'close', 'pick', 'look at', 'talk to', 'use', 'push', and 'pull', and then select the elements on the screen or in their inventory to perform the requested actions and accordingly progress through the game.

Day of the Tentacle was praised for its cartoon-style animation, humour and sound design. Curiously, as with the Monkey Island games, Day of the Tentacle would become more popular years after its release and is now considered a cult classic. A remastered version of the game was released in 2016 for iOS, OSX, PlayStation 4, PlayStation Vita and, of course, Windows.

Bill Walsh College Football

Date of release: June 1993

Region: USA

Developer: Visual Concepts

Publisher: Electronic Arts

Platform: Sega Genesis, Sega CD and the SNES

Bill Walsh College Football is a single-player or multiplayer American football game. Bill Walsh College Football featured twenty-four college teams sporting the names of cities, rather than actual college team names, and twenty-four historical teams. It also features a choice of weather conditions, the length of time the game will last and three different gameplay modes.

The name of the game series changed from Bill Walsh College Football to College Football USA in 1995, and then to NCAA Football in 1997, after acquiring the rights to the NCAA name. There are over twenty games in the series at the time of writing. Some of the most notable of these are College Football USA 96 (1995), NCAA Football 99 (1998), NCAA Football 2004 (2003), NCAA Football 06 (2005) and NCAA 14 (2013).

Hi-Ten Bomberman

Date of release: 1993 (not commercially)

Region: Japan

Developer: Hudson Soft

Publisher: Hudson Soft

Platform: Custom-built hardware

Hi-Ten Bomberman was technically released, albeit in a non-commercial fashion, in Japan in 1993 by Hudson Soft. Developed by Katsuhiro Nozawa, Hi-Ten Bomberman is a single-player or multiplayer, action maze game. The aim of the game is the same as other Bomberman games: lay out your bombs within the maze in an attempt to blow up your enemy. Hi-Ten Bomberman has a total of five game modes. The first is Battle Royale, a deathmatch between all ten players on screen at once. Second is 2 Group Battle, a five versus five team deathmatch. Third is the 3 Group Battle, pitting three teams of three players against one another. Fourth is the 5 Group Battle, pitting five teams of two players against one another. Finally, there is the 1 VS 9 Battle, pitting one player against a team of nine other players.

The game ran on custom-designed hardware built by Hudsoft. The idea was to promote awareness of the little-known widescreen HDTV and its 16:9 aspect ratio. Only the high resolution of the high-definition screen made it feasible to have ten players displayed on the screen at once. Hi-Ten Bomberman is the first video game ever to be developed and played on a High-Definition screen.

Hi-Ten Bomberman wasn't released as a commercial product. Instead, it was showcased at the 1993 'Super Caravan' gaming event hosted by Hudson Soft that was shown at forty-four venues across Japan. An upgraded version of Hi-Ten Bomberman made a subsequent appearance at the 1994 'Super Caravan'. This improved version of the game included characters from other video game franchises and was even larger than the event in 1993.

Samurai Shodown

Date of release: July 1993

Region: Worldwide

Developer: SNK

Publisher: SNK

Platform: Neo Geo Arcade, and subsequently Super NES, Game Boy, Sega Mega Drive/Genesis, Game Gear, Sega CD and Sega Saturn

Designed by Eikichi Kawasaki, Tomoaki Fukui and Yasushi Adachi, Samurai Shodown is a single-player or multiplayer fighting game. The aim of the game is to defeat your on-screen opponent. The game attempts to set itself apart from many of the other fighting games of the time by focusing on weapon-based combat set in feudal Japan in the 18th century. It moves from fast-paced action to short moments of calm after a player successfully defends against an enemy's attack. The sound of blade upon blade, with underpinning music reminiscent of traditional Japanese music of the era, made for a very atmospheric game, which is an element missing in most fighting games. Players could also lock swords, where they would have to mash the 'A' button, the loser of the button-mashing content having their character disarmed. If a player was disarmed, they would have to quickly retrieve their sword before being attacked by their opponent. From time to time, the Edo Express delivery man will drop items for players to pick up. The items range from meat that revitalizes your power meter, to gold coins for more points and bombs to throw at the other player. The game featured a choice of twelve playable characters, all with their own style of play and special moves.

Samurai Shodown was yet another game to have some of its content censored on some platforms, due to its liberal amounts of blood and finishing fatalities. Samurai Shodown is considered one of the best games for the Neo Geo platform and has also been adapted into an anime movie.

Seiken Densetsu 2/Secret of Mana

Date of release: August 1993/October 1993

Region: Japan/USA

Developer: Square

Publisher: Square

Platform: Sega Genesis

Seiken Densetsu 2 was released in Japan in August 1993, and as Secret of Mana outside of Japan, in October 1993 by Square for the Super Famicom/SNES. Designed by Koichi Ishi and Hiromichi Tanaka, Secret of Mana is a single-player action RPG and the sequel to Seiken Densetsu: Final Fantasy Gaiden/Final Fantasy Adventure/Mystic Quest (1991). The aim of the game is to restore the legendary Mana Sword's power by finding the eight Mana Seeds in their corresponding Mana Temples and stop the empire ruled by the evil sorcerer Thanatos. The player controls one of three characters and the AI controls the other two, though the player can swap between the characters at any point in the game. Multiplayer involves two players, with the second player controlling any one of the two remaining characters. A third player can also join in the adventure by plugging in another controller, via the Super Multitap peripheral. Combat is in real-time, making Secret of Mana a departure from Square Enix's other RPG series, Final Fantasy, and more akin to the Legend of Zelda games. The only pause in combat comes when the player decides to use items or cast spells. The game also has many other features that one would come to expect of a Japanese RPG of the time, such as buying and selling items, upgrading equipment, levelling up and a rich, extensive story.

Secret of Mana was highly acclaimed for its excellent music, combat mechanics and graphics, the art style of which is a beautiful example of its genre from the 16-bit era, featuring a wide and diverse range of environments. It wasn't until the release of this game that the Seiken Densetsu games would also be referred to as the Mana series. Secret of Mana is often cited as one of the best games for the Super Famicom/SNES.

Sonic CD

Date of release: September 1993

Region: Japan

Developer: Sega

Publisher: Sega

Platform: Sega Genesis' Sega CD

Sonic CD is a single-player, side-scrolling platform game, and the fourth game in the Sonic series. The aim of the game is to stop Dr Robotnik from robotising 'Little Planet' after capturing and chaining it to the ground. The player once again controls Sonic the Hedgehog and must collect Time Stones. The gameplay and mechanics are essentially the same as in previous Sonic games. However, Sonic CD does boast a few new features and characters such as Amy Rose and Metal Sonic, the former Sonic's self-proclaimed girlfriend and the latter an evil robotic version of Sonic whose speed rivals his own, created by Dr Robotnik. The main outstanding feature of the game is its time-travelling aspect, which allows the player to play the same levels in either the past, present or two alternative futures.

Opinion on Sonic CD is rather polarizing. Some people regard it as one of the best games in the series, praising its graphics, music, level design and clever time-travel mechanic, while others don't like it at all. That being said, Sonic CD ended up being the best-selling game for the Sega CD with over 1.5 million units shipped.

Myst

Date of release: September 1993

Region: USA

Developer: Cyan

Publisher: Broderbund

Platform: Macintosh

Designed by brothers Rand and Robyn Miller of Cyan, Inc., Myst is a single-player, first-person, graphic adventure puzzle game. The aim is to explore the island on which the game is set and attempt to find a way off it and back home. The game opens with an atmospheric cinematic, insinuating that the player had stumbled upon the book entitled 'Myst,' whereupon a fissure opened up and into which they fell, finding themselves on a mysterious uninhabited island. The player does not move about the island in real-time but instead moves between predetermined spots. The player can turn the camera at ninety-degree increments around these spots for puzzle-solving or pathfinding. The pay-off to this limited gameplay was that the 3D graphics are all pre-rendered and thus were of a very high quality, never seen in a video game before.

The 2,500 3D graphical renders which make up the game were created using StrataVision 3D and touched up with Photoshop 1.0, with the game itself being made using Apple's HyperCard application. Myst also included over an hour of video, only possible due to the increased storage capacity of the CD-ROM format. Robyn Miller composed 40 minutes of atmospheric and emotive sound and music which play a huge role in immersing the player in the world of Myst.

Myst was highly lauded for its (at the time) incredible graphics, puzzles, sound and the way it immersed players into its world. Myst very much bucked the trend of video games in 1993. In a landscape of fast-paced action as with the Sonic the Hedgehog games or violent games such as Mortal Kombat and Doom, Myst was something entirely different. It also showed that it was possible to make an original and high-quality CD-ROM game, even one containing FMVs. You would think that such a game would only find a niche audience. However, Myst sold over six million units and would become the best-selling PC game for almost a decade.

It was ported to most of the popular platforms of the time, and still is to this day. Myst has had several remakes over the years, such as Myst: Masterpiece Edition (2000) with improved graphics and sound, RealMyst: Interactive 3D Edition (2000) which featured real-time gameplay as opposed to static images, and RealMyst: Masterpiece Edition 2.0 (2015) which is another real-time version of the game. The game spawned several sequels including Riven (1997), Myst III: Exile (2001), Uru: Ages Beyond Myst (2003), Myst IV: Revelation (2004) and Myst V: End of Ages (2005).

Master of Orion

Date of release: September 1993

Region: USA

Developer: Simtex

Publisher: MicroProse

Platform: MS-DOS and Macintosh

Designed by Stephen Barcia and Jeff Johannigman, Master of Orion is a single-player, science-fiction, turn-based strategy game. Often cited as Civilisation (1991) in space, Master of Orion is also a 4X strategy game, where the aim is to explore, expand, exploit and exterminate and ultimately dominate the other factions in the game through military conquest, or through diplomacy to create a peaceful alliance amongst the other, initially hostile, races. Players have the option to choose their Galaxy size: small (24 stars), medium (48 stars), large (72 stars) or huge (96 stars), also difficulty, the number of opponents (1-5) and starting race (ten in total: the Alkari, the Bulrathi, the Darloks, the Klackons, the Melkar, the Mrrshan, the Psilon, the Sakkra, the Silicoids and

Humans), each with different strengths and weaknesses. The game features resource gathering, colonising other worlds, researching technology (the most valuable research site is on the throne-world of the ancients, known as Orion), attacking and defending against the other races, and inter-species diplomacy.

The game met with high praise from almost all critics, being named the best strategy game of 1993 by some. Even though Masters of Orion wasn't the first 4X space strategy game, it has certainly influenced many other such games since, including Stars! (1995), Deadlock: Planetary Conquest (1996), Imperium Galactica (1997) and Sid Meier's Alpha Centauri (1999).

Master of Orion has spawned three sequels: Master of Orion II: Battle at Antares (1996), Master of Orion III (2003), and Master of Orion: Conquer the Stars (2016).

Gunstar Heroes

Date of release: September 1993

Region: Worldwide

Developer: Treasure

Publisher: Sega

Platform: Sega Genesis/ Mega Drive

Gunstar Heroes, originally to be called Lunatic Gunstar, is a single-player or multiplayer, cooperative, side-scrolling run and gun game. The aim of Gunstar Heroes is to retrieve the four mystical gems and defeat Colonel Red. The player or players must fight their way through numerous different enemies to achieve this goal. The player or players can choose to run and fire in the direction they are moving in or stand still and fire in any direction. They can also choose one of four starting weapons: Flamethrower, Homing Shot, Lightning Blaster, or Machine Gun. These choices are dependent on one's play style and they make for good replay value and balance between two players. Guns can be combined to create variations of the aforementioned weapons with a total of fourteen different weapon combinations. Players can also jump, slide, hang and move across wires, grab and throw enemies, and ride in a variety of vehicles. There are seven stages in Gunstar Heroes, the first four of which can be played in any order.

Gunstar Heroes was highly praised for its graphics, animation (especially for the large, elaborate bosses), fast-paced action and innovative game mechanics, such as the gun combinations. Often compared with other very successful run-and-gun games such as

Contra and Metal Slug, Gunstar Heroes is often considered one of the best games for the Sega Mega Drive/Genesis.

Gunstar Heroes was ported to the Game Gear in 1995. It was later released for PlayStation 3, Wii, Windows, and Xbox 360. The game spawned one sequel, namely Gunstar Super Heroes (2005).

Virtua Fighter

Date of release: October 1993

Region: Worldwide

Developer: Sega AM2

Publisher: Sega

Platform: Arcade

Designed by Yu Suzuki, previously mentioned game designer, engineer, producer and programmer of games such as Hang-On (1985), Space Harrier (1985) and Out Run (1986), Virtua Fighter is a single-player or two-player, 3D, fighting game. The aim of Virtua Fighter is to defeat your opponent before the timer runs out. As with most fighting games, each player has a health bar and access to several special moves, some of which are specific to the eight characters available in the game's roster. When a player deals a knockout (KO) to their opponent, they are rewarded with an action replay making full use of the 3D environment using multiple, animated camera angles. A player can also win a round if they have more health than their opponent when the timer runs out or if they can force their opponent out of the ring. Winning three rounds wins the match.

Like Virtua Racing (1992) before it, Virtua Fighter also used the Sega Model 1 system board to render a 3D polygonal fighting game. Virtua Fighter is the first true 3D fighting game since every game preceding it used either traditional sprites, digitised performers or a fixed camera.

Virtua Fighter was ported to the Sega Saturn and the 32X (Sega Genesis/Mega Drive add-on). It also spawned several sequels, some of the most notable of which are Virtua Fighter 2 (1994), Virtua Fighter 4 (1994), and Virtua Fighter 5 (1994).

Ridge Racer

Date of release: October 1993

Region: Japan

Developer: Namco

Publisher: Namco

Platform: Arcade

Ridge Racer is a single-player racing game, the aim being to win each race. At the start of the game, a player chooses a car, track, difficulty level, and automatic or manual transmission. The game is played from a first-person perspective, with courses transitioning between urban and suburban environments. The cars all vary in performance, differing in acceleration, top speed and handling characteristics. Some of the cars were named after old Namco games such as Bosconian (1981), Mappy (1983) and Xevious (1983).

Ridge Racer uses the Namco System 22 arcade system board capable of displaying a high number of 3D polygons with texture mapping. Namco's Ridge Racer was a direct competitor to Sega's Daytona USA (1994), which was released only five months later and led to some contention as to which was the superior game.

The game was highly praised for its 3D graphics and background music, some even going so far as saying it was superior to the aforementioned Daytona USA. Interestingly enough, it is Daytona that seems to have made more of a lasting impact, even having a successful arcade release as recently as 2016, whereas Ridge Racer's last arcade outing was in 1995. Yet Ridge Racer has spawned many sequels, mostly on the home gaming platforms. Some of the most notable of these are Ridge Racer 2 (1994), Ridge Racer (1996), Ridge Racer Revolution (1996), R4: Ridge Racer Type 4 (1998) and Ridge Racer 7 (2006).

Frontier: Elite II

Date of release: October 1993

Region: Worldwide

Developer: David Braben

Publisher: GameTek

Platform: Amiga.

Designed by David Braben (Elite (1984) and Zarch/Virus (1987)), Frontier: Elite II, often referred to as simply Elite II, is a single-player, space trading and combat simulator game, and the sequel to the highly acclaimed and ground-breaking Elite (1984), the game which established the open-world space-trading and combat genre. As with the original Elite, Elite II is a sandbox game in the purest sense of the word. There is no final objective, and the game is never actually finished. This approach appeals to the player's sense of constant self-improvement that exists within so many sandbox or RPG games. You play as a descendent of Commander Jameson, the protagonist from the original Elite game. It is the year 3200 and two major powers control most of the galaxy: the Federation and the Empire. There are, however, lawless parts of the galaxy with danger aplenty. The player can align themselves with either the Federation or the Empire as determined by their actions or be a free agent. It is up to the player whether they stay within the law by trading, ferrying passengers and helping to deal with pirates, or follow a more nefarious path of trading illegal goods and engaging in piracy. There is a range of appealing ships, ordnance and equipment which serve to motivate the player to carry out missions and amass credits in order to purchase them. At some point, the player will be drawn into combat. The player must make effective use of their radar and dogfighting skills to destroy enemy ships. If the player amasses enough kills throughout the game they will be awarded the combat rating of 'Elite'. Players utilise a hyperspace drive to travel between star systems. However, just navigating around a single star system can take several hours due to the realistic vastness and distances required to travel, even with the fastest of ships. As such, Braben introduced a game mechanic that allowed players to accelerate time from between 10 to 10,000 times the normal rate, for the sake of practicality.

The procedurally-generated game world of Elite II was able to accurately represent our own galaxy and run it on the Amiga platform. Players could visit real star systems. The stars of said systems were depicted as they should be, ranging from white dwarfs to red giants. Players could also land on a multitude of planets. These planets, moons and stars were all scaled 1:1, meaning their distances and size were based on real-life measurements. Considering that stars are millions of times larger than planets and the mind-boggling distances involved, this is nothing short of astounding and rather unique for a video game back in 1993.

The original Elite used hidden-line wireframe 3D graphics. Elite II featured flat-shaded and texture-mapped 3D polygons. David Lowe composed the music from the game which uses classical pieces such as Strauss's The Blue Danube, as famously used in the film 2001: A Space Odyssey (1968), as well as some original pieces.

Elite II met with mixed reviews. Some loved it, others not so much. However, no one could argue with its technical achievements. Yet in a time when games like Street

Fighter II and Doom were riding high, Elite II seemed a bit slow for some people's taste. For those who sunk many hours into it, it was still a winner. The game was ported to DOS and the Atari ST. Frontier: Elite II was followed by Frontier: First Encounters (1995) and Elite: Dangerous (2014).

Edge Magazine

Edge was first published in the UK in October of 1993 by Future Publishing. Edge is a monthly publication that features all aspects of video games. Edge has always pursued high quality in everything from its writing and layout to high-end paper and print in an attempt to set itself apart from other games magazines.

Edge not only delves into previews and reviews but also features insights into the making of games, appealing to enthusiasts, the curious and perhaps those looking at getting into the industry. Content from Edge was used for the US publication Next Generation since its inception in 1995.

Edge reviews games with an overall score ranging from 1-10. At this time of writing, only 22 games have been awarded a score of 10, with the first being Super Mario 64 (1996) and the most recent (at the time of writing) being Dreams (2020).

Akumajō Dracula X: Chi no Rondo/Castlevania: Rondo of Blood

Date of release: October 1993

Region: Japan

Developer: Konami

Publisher: Konami

Platform: PC Engine CD

Akumajō Dracula X: Chi no Rondo, known as Castlevania: Rondo of Blood in the West, is a single-player, side-scrolling, action horror-themed platform game. Set 100 years after the events of Castlevania I, II and IV, you play as Richter Belmont, Simon Belmont's direct descendent. You must save your love, Annette, who has been abducted by Dracula. As with other Castlevania games, the player must deal with an army of undead and supernatural enemies and has many weapons at their disposal. Once the player finds Maria Renard, another maiden kidnapped by Dracula and Belmont's distant relative, the player has the option to play as her. Maria is lighter and more agile on her feet and has her own efficient ways of defeating her enemies, but she takes more damage.

Castlevania: Rondo of Blood is often cited as one of the best Castlevania games and one of the best games on the PC Engine. It was highly praised for its beautiful lush 2D graphics, dark atmosphere, smooth gameplay, fantastic level design and incredible music.

It was a great shame that the original was not made available until 2008 on the Wii's Virtual Console. The game was ported to the SNES as Castlevania: Dracula X (1995) and to the PSP as Castlevania: The Dracula X Chronicles (2007). Yet both of these ports were inferior for different reasons compared with the original Akumajō Dracula X: Chi no Rondo released on the PC Engine. A reimagined version has also been released for the PC under the title Castlevania: Dracula X.

3DO Interactive Multiplayer

3DO Interactive Multiplayer was released in North America in October 1993 by The 3DO Company. Conceived by Electronic Arts' founder Trip Hawkins, the 3DO line of consoles is, in fact, a series of hardware specifications to which electronic manufacturers could develop their own version of the 3DO. The first of these was Panasonic with their FZ-1 model.

The 3DO is a fourth-generation, 32-bit console and sold for $699.99 when released. The controller featured a D-pad and three buttons, but only had only one controller port. However, the controllers could daisy chain by plugging into one another. There were also other controllers available with six buttons. At the time, the 3DO was the most powerful console on the market and was advertised with cool-looking 3D games that had visuals way ahead of their time in terms of graphics capabilities. Yet apart from looking rather nice (the FZ–1 model in particular) compared to some other CD-ROM-based consoles of the time, the 3DO was not that successful. Every electronics manufacturer was attempting to capitalise on the new multimedia CD-ROM format at the time, and games consoles were just another facet of this craze. Not only were there different versions of the 3DO, but there were also many other unsuccessful CD-ROM-based consoles, resulting in the market becoming too saturated. There was also a serious lack of quality control when it came to the games and anyone could just throw a bunch of B-Movie quality FMVs together and call it a game. Perhaps the most infamous of these slapdash games was Plumbers Don't Wear Ties (1993), often regarded as being so bad that it was almost good.

Originally, the 3DO was supposed to have several launch titles yet ended up only having one: Crash 'n Burn (1993), the name not being the best of omens. However, despite being renowned for some terrible titles and bad ports, the 3DO did have a few playable titles from its library of over 280 games. Most notable are Road Rash (1994), Star Control II (1994), Super Street Fighter II Turbo (1994), The Need for Speed (1994), Gex (1995), Lucienne's Quest (1995), Return Fire (1995), and Samurai Shodown (1995).

Sam & Max Hit the Road

Date of release: November 1993

Region: USA

Developer: LucasArts

Publisher: LucasArts

Platform: MS-DOS

Designed by Sean Clark and Mike Stemmle, Sam & Max Hit the Road is a single-player, 2D, point-and-click graphic adventure game based on the titular anthropomorphic comic book characters created by Steve Purcell. Sam is a dog, Max is a rabbit, and both work as private detectives in New York City. The aim of the game is to solve the mystery behind the missing bigfoots, who were until recently frozen in blocks of ice but have now mysteriously disappeared. As with other games developed by LucasArts, Sam and Max Hit the Road uses the SCUMM engine to create another game that has a well-rounded narrative, a good sense of humour and plenty of puzzles, although some of the puzzles are a little obscure. That being said, Sam and Max Hit the Road is rather significant as it was one of the first games to be completely voice-acted from start to finish.

Sam & Max Hit the Road spawned three sequels: Sam & Max Save the World (2006), Sam & Max Beyond Space and Time (2007), and Sam & Max: The Devil's Playhouse (2010).

Gaia Gensoki/Illusion of Gaia/Illusion of Time

Date of release: November 1993

Region: Japan

Developer: Quintet

Publisher: Enix

Platform: SNES

Designed by Masaya Hashimoto, Yasuyuki Sone and Tomoyoshi Miyazaki, Gaia Gensoki [The Gaia Fantasy Chronicle], known as Illusion of Gaia in the USA and Illusion of Time in the EU, is a single-player JRPG. The aim of the game is to collect as many ancient artefacts as possible and stop the evil which is coming to Earth as heralded by a comet. Set around what is known as the Age of Exploration (roughly around the 16th century), you play as an explorer named Will. The player travels to places such as Angkor Wat, the Pyramids of Giza, the Great Wall of China, Machu Picchu, and The Nazca Lines in South America. After encountering the metaphysical being known as Gaia, Will can change into two other forms, each with different abilities. The player can play as the Dark Knight named Freedan, or later in the game as a being of solid energy called Shadow. Changing forms allows the player to reach previously inaccessible parts of the game world, with each form also having different strengths and weaknesses. Combat in Illusion of Gaia takes place in real-time. When enemies are defeated, they will drop jewels, which can be spent to boost a player's attack, defence or health.

The well-known Japanese manga artist Moto Hagio worked on the character design, and the music was composed by Yasuhiro Kawasaki. The science-fiction author Mariko Ōhara also contributed to the story.

Illusion of Gaia was fairly well received. Praised for its graphics, puzzle-solving and music, it sold around 650,000 units in total.

Atari Jaguar

The Atari Jaguar was released in North America in November 1993 by IBM. Developed by the Atari Corporation, the Atari Jaguar is a fifth-generation, cartridge-based console, and the first 64-bit home console (although this has been a matter of debate for some time), initially selling for $249.99. Yet partially due to its internal architecture, developers found it hard to utilise its full potential. None of the Jaguar's games looked as if they were from a technically superior system as compared to a typical SNES or Genesis/Mega Drive game.

A lack of games for the system generated little interest from gamers and developers alike. Also, the Sega Saturn and Sony PlayStation were set to release the following year and were already generating a lot of buzz and excitement, to say nothing of the rumours of Nintendo's 'Project Reality', which would turn out to be the Nintendo 64. Sadly, the

Atari Jaguar would be the last console to use the Atari brand name. When you consider that it was Atari Incorporated which originally coined the phrase 'video game' back in the early 1970s, started the coin-operated arcade industry with Pong (1972), and defined the second generation of video game consoles with the legendary Atari VCS/2600 (1977), it seems a shame that this would be the end of the line for Atari consoles. Indeed, it would herald a greater changing of the guard throughout the next decade. Both Atari and later Sega would bow out from making consoles, while Sony's PlayStation (1994) and Microsoft's Xbox (2001) would take their place.

In 1996, Atari released a CD-ROM add-on for the machine and even a virtual reality headset, the Jaguar VR. However, with the release of the aforementioned Saturn and the PlayStation, both of them rapidly out-selling the Jaguar, its fate was sealed.

The Atari Jaguar was not without good or well-regarded games, however. It boasted titles such as Alien Vs Predator (1994), Iron Soldier (1994), Raiden (1994), Tempest 2000 (1994), Rayman (1995) and Iron Soldier II (1997).

Disney's Aladdin (Super Famicom and SNES)

Date of release: November 1993

Region: Japan/USA

Developer: Capcom

Publisher: Capcom

Platform: Super Famicom and SNES

Disney's Aladdin is a 2D, single-player, side-scrolling platform game based on the popular Disney animated movie of the same name. The game follows the same narrative as the movie and features broadly similar game mechanics to the Sega Mega Drive/Genesis version of the same game. The major difference is that Aladdin defeats enemies by jumping on them or throwing apples to disorientate them in the SNES version, whereas in the Sega Genesis game Aladdin has a scimitar to deal with his foes.

The game was highly praised for its quality of graphics and animation, its fluid gameplay and adaptation of sound and music from the movie. It ended up being Capcom's second-best-selling game for the SNES with 1.8 million units sold.

Disney's Aladdin (Genesis/Mega Drive)

Date of release: November 1993

Region: Worldwide

Developer: Virgin Games

Publisher: Sega and Disney Software

Platform: Sega Genesis/Mega Drive

Disney's Aladdin is a 2D, single-player, side-scrolling platform game based on the popular Disney animated movie of the same name. As with the SNES version of the game, this also follows the narrative of the movie and behaves as a standard platform game would. However, it is this version of the game that affords Aladdin the use of a scimitar to defeat his enemies, as opposed to just jumping on them or pelting them with apples as with the SNES version.

Despite the fact the aforementioned SNES version is a very accomplished video game adaptation of the movie, it is the Genesis/Mega Drive game that is often cited as having superior graphics, animation and gameplay. However, there are diehard fans of both versions of these games who will swear blind that their preferred choice is indeed the best. As a matter of fact, the overall quality of animation at the time for a video game for both platforms was so good that the two games were seen as a benchmark for other similar games to strive towards. The popularity of Disney's Aladdin at the time was indeed great with the sales speaking for themselves. Aladdin would be the Genesis/Mega Drive's third-best-selling video game of all time with four million units sold, over twice that of its SNES counterpart.

FIFA International Soccer

Date of release: December 1993

Region: Worldwide

Developer: Extended Play Productions

Publisher: EA Sports NK

Platform: Sega Genesis/Mega Drive

FIFA International Soccer is a single-player or multiplayer soccer game and was intended as a tie-in with the 1994 FIFA World Cup. Played from an isometric viewpoint, the game features forty-eight national teams, though the players themselves are fictional. Players can choose team formations and strategies. The game features four play modes: Exhibition, League, Playoffs and Tournament, which is analogous to the FIFA World Cup.

FIFA International Soccer was praised for its presentation and animation; however, the gameplay was a little clunky and it is notoriously difficult to play.

FIFA International Soccer was the first game in the FIFA series which continues to this day. The game would introduce new features throughout the years, including real-life players' names and likenesses. The most notable releases of its many sequels are FIFA World Cup 98 (1998), FIFA 07 (2006), FIFA 09 (2008), FIFA 11 (2010), FIFA 12 (2011), FIFA 13 (2012) and FIFA 14 (2013). The fact that Electronic Arts has not published a game to surpass FIFA 14 since 2013 is a matter of concern for some fans of the series.

Gabriel Knight: Sins of the Father

Date of release: December 1993

Region: USA

Developer: Sierra On-Line

Publisher: Sierra On-Line

Platform: MS-DOS and Macintosh

Developed by novelist and video game author Jane Jensen and Bill Crow, and produced by Robert Holmes and John E. Grayson, Gabriel Knight: Sins of the Father is a single-player, supernatural detective, point-and-click adventure game. Set in New Orleans, you play as Gabriel Knight, an aspiring novelist and bookshop owner who is a bit of a ladies' man. The aim of the game is to solve the mystery behind a series of killings known as the 'Voodoo Murders'. The game uses familiar mechanics of the point and click genre to explore, interact and use objects in the environment. Beautifully illustrated scenes are viewed from a variety of camera angles to better advance the narrative, from high-angle to eye-level and talking head shots, and even using a graphic novel style for cutscenes. Later in the game, the story takes a supernatural turn, involving possession and human sacrifice.

The game is certainly intended for a more mature audience, not just because of its adult imagery, but rather for its darker narrative. The game features real places in New Orleans and oozes the feel and culture of America's Deep South. Sierra On-Line managed to get some great voice actors for the game, including Tim Curry and Mark Hamill. Their performances certainly increased the game's production value and overall appeal.

Gabriel Knight: Sins of the Father did not sell as well as Jensen had hoped. Yet, it still sold well over 100,000 units and did generate enough interest to warrant two sequels with The Beast Within: A Gabriel Knight Mystery (1995), and Gabriel Knight 3: Blood of the Sacred, Blood of the Damned (1999).

Cannon Fodder

Date of release: December 1993

Region: UK

Developer: Sensible Software

Publisher: Virgin Interactive Entertainment

Platform: Amiga

Cannon Fodder is a single-player, multi-scrolling, military action shoot 'em up. The aim of Cannon Fodder is to carry out the mission objective set out at the beginning, which usually revolves around killing a variety of enemies. Other missions include destroying key enemy buildings or factories, rescuing hostages, kidnapping an enemy leader, protecting civilians, and getting the civilians home alive. The game is viewed from a top-down perspective. The character sprites are small, giving the developers more room for the player to view the surrounding environment, similar to a game like Dune II (1992) and Warcraft: Orcs & Humans (1994). Indeed, the game shares many gameplay elements with an RTS game. The player must be tactical as well as aggressive, lest they meet a quick death. The player is given control of a small squad of troops with which they must shoot enemy soldiers and destroy installations. The squad can be split up into smaller fireteams or even a single trooper to better preform reconnaissance or to execute a pincer movement. However, smaller numbers are more vulnerable to being overwhelmed by enemy troops. The player also has access to grenades and bazookas. These more powerful weapons are limited in supply, but more ammunition can be found in crates. Players can also control vehicles such as tanks, helicopters, jeeps and even an armoured snow vehicle called a Skidooz. Each vehicle can hold up to eight soldiers. Cannon Fodder also features power-up items dropping from time to time and giving troops extra range, more ammo, improved defences, and even invincibility. The game has a nice variety of environments and maps, ranging from the jungle, Arctic wastes, deserts, moorlands, and an underground base. Certain terrain can slow both the player's troops and enemies alike or make it impossible to shoot, so the player must be tactical in their approach. There are twenty-three missions in Cannon Fodder, with each mission divided into a number of levels, of which there are seventy-two in total.

Cannon Fodder was well received, often cited as one of the best games of 1993 and beloved by fans of the Amiga platform. Praised for its graphics, gameplay and music, the game also garnered a degree of controversy, with some finding its use of poppy iconography and general depiction of war as offensive. However, others, including Sensible Software themselves, said that the game was supposed to have an ironic and anti-war message overall. The game was ported to many of the popular home computers and consoles of the time and spawned two sequels with Cannon Fodder 2 (1994) and Cannon Fodder 3 (2011).

Doom

Date of release: December 1993

Region: USA

Developer: Id Software

Publisher: Virgin Id Software

Platform: MS-DOS

Designed by John Romero, John Carmack, Tom Hall, Adrian Carmack and with music and sound by Bobby Prince, Doom is a single-player or multiplayer, first-person 3D shooter. The aim of Doom is to kill the hordes of demons that are pouring out through an inter-dimensional portal to Hell on Mars' moon of Phobos. You play as a lone marine, who became unofficially known as the 'Doom marine' or 'Doomguy.' The player must deal with all manner of possessed humans, demons and twisted, horrific cyborg-demon enemies. Fortunately, the game boasts a plethora of weapons to obliterate them, from the marine's Fists to the Pistol, Chainsaw, Shotgun, Chain gun, Rocket Launcher, Plasma Rifle, and the iconic BFG9000, all of which turn your enemies into a bloody mess. Items are scattered around the game world, including but not limited to Medi kits and Health Bonuses, different kinds of armour, colour-coded keys, a radiation suit to protect the marine from radioactive waste and other floor hazards, and Light Amplification Goggles, which allow the player to see the skulking demons in Doom's terrifying dark rooms.

John Carmack was able to develop his 3D engine even further since Wolfenstein 3D (1992). id Software's new game would now have multiple levels, incorporating elevators, platforms, stairs and windows. It could even handle the use of animated textures, which were perfect for depicting pools of toxic waste or lava. Walls were no longer set at 90 degrees to one another but now could be at any angle, and entire sections of walls and floors would move to significantly change the configuration of a level. All this meant a revolutionary leap forward. It allowed a more varied and ambitious freeform-level design beyond anything that had preceded it. The game maintains the HUD at the bottom of the screen from the aforementioned Wolfenstein 3D so that the player can keep a track of their health, armour and ammo, along with collected keys and weapons.

The game's multiplayer mode helped put the term deathmatch firmly into the video game culture lexicon. Initially only available over a Local-Area Network, or LAN, two to four players could go head-to-head against each other, with the deathmatch being expanded into an online multiplayer mode in 1994.

Doom was also one of the first games to be heavily modded. Modding is a process whereby home developers could change the asset files that made up the game, modifying them to give the game a fresh perspective or put a new twist on things. This was due to id Software allowing public access to the game's code and the in-house tools, allowing the players to do anything from making small tweaks to making their own levels or even completely remake and remodel the game. Again, it was Doom that would popularise and define the concept of modding for future games.

id Software had been spearheading the first-person shooter genre almost single-handedly for the last two years, tentatively at first with Hovertank 3D (1991) and Catacomb 3D (1991). Reaching full recognition and success with Wolfenstein 3D (1992), they knew they were onto a winning formula and stayed true to making a game that they themselves would want to play. If Wolfenstein 3D is considered the grandfather of the FPS genre, then Doom is surely the father.

Doom was initially released as a shareware game in episodes. The first episode entitled 'Knee Deep in the Dead' was released for free in December 1993. The hype for the game had been building for some time, and when it was finally released networks crashed due to the number of people attempting to download it at once. It is believed that by 1995 more people had installed Doom than the Windows 95 operating system! To say that it was a success would be an understatement. Episode 2 'Shores of Hell' takes the player to Mars' other moon of Deimos, which has been transported to Hell. Episode 3 'Inferno' takes the player to Hell itself where the player must defeat the final boss and mastermind behind the whole demonic invasion. Ultimate Doom was released in 1995, containing all the original three episodes, plus an additional episode, 'Thy Flesh Consumed', all in one retail package.

This was yet another game that triggered controversy. Some did not like the game's occult and satanic imagery, not to mention its profuse amounts of unfettered and bloody violence.

Doom was nothing short of a phenomenon, with a player base in the tens of millions. Highly praised for its graphics, mechanics, addictive gameplay and music, it is cited by some as the most significant game of all time. Doom was a watershed moment in the first-person genre and video games as a whole, heavily influencing many FPS games that would come after, known as Doom clones. Any kind of visceral FPS owes its existence to the ground laid out by Doom, for it is this giant's shoulders upon which they all stand. Game franchises such as Battlefield, Borderlands, Bioshock, Call of Duty, Counter-Strike, Destiny, Far Cry, F.E.A.R., Half-Life, Halo, and Medal of Honor can all trace their roots to Doom. Even popular 3D third-person games such as Mario 64 (1996) and Tomb Raider (1996) owe their creative level design to the ground-breaking, multi-dimensional 3D level design of Doom. Its importance is hard to overstate and is why Doom is often cited as one of the greatest and most significant games in video game history.

Doom was soon ported to most of the popular gaming platforms of the time and has spawned a whole series of sequels, the most notable of which are Doom II: Hell on Earth (1994), Doom 64 (1997), DOOM (2016) and DOOM Eternal (2020).

1993 Notable Omissions

Alien Breed II: The Horror Continues. Alone in the Dark 2. Amiga CD32. Batsugun. Battletoads & Double Dragon. Battletoads in Battlemaniac. Breath of Fire. Busbsy in Claws of Encounters of the Furred Kind. Cadillacs and dinosaurs. Championship Manager '93. Clayfighter. Croteam is founded. Dr. Robotnik's Mean Bean Machine. Eternal Champions. Eye of the Beholder III: Assault on Myth Drannor. Fighters History. Final Fight CD. FM Towns Marty. In the Hunt. Jungle Strike. Kirby's Adventure. Lemmings 2: The Tribes. Link: The Faces of Evil & Zelda: The Wand of Gamelon. Mega Man 6. Mega Man X. Microcosm. Monster Bash. NES- 101. Ninja Baseball Bat Man. Phantasy Star IV. Pioneer's LaserActive console. Plok. Plumbers Don't Wear Ties. Premier Manager. Privateer. Raiden II. Return to Zork (original Zork remake). Sega VR. ShadowCaster. Shining Force II. Soccer Kid. Star Wars: Rebel Assault. Stronghold. Sonic The Hedgehog Spinball. The Incredible Machine. The Settlers. ToeJam & Earl in Panic on Funkotron. Super Mario All-Stars. The Chaos Engine. The Fates of Twinion. Transarctica. Ultima Underworld II: Labyrinth of Worlds. VictorMaxx Stuntmaster Headmaster from Future Vision Technologies. Warlords II. Zombies Ate My Neighbors.

1994

First DreamHack conference

The first official DreamHack gaming event is held in a school cafeteria in Malung, Sweden in 1994. The event has since grown to be one of the largest computer festivals in the world with over 27,000 participants and holds the world record for the largest LAN party. Along with said LAN party, DreamHack also boasts one of the fastest internet connections in the world (1.6 Terabytes per second as of the time of writing), with every event also featuring gaming competitions, digital art competitions, live concerts and an Expo.

Sonic the Hedgehog 3

Date of release: February 1994

Region: North America and Europe

Developer: Sega Technical Institute

Publisher: Sega

Platform: Sega Mega Drive/Genesis

Sonic the Hedgehog 3 is a single-player or two-player, side-scrolling, 2D platform game. The aim of Sonic the Hedgehog 3 is to collect all the Chaos Emeralds, preventing Doctor Robotnik from using them to relaunch his crashed 'Death Egg' space station. Sonic the Hedgehog 3 expanded on every aspect of the previous Sonic games with more extensive and varied levels, new power-ups including bubble shields of various kinds, one of which allows Sonic to breathe underwater, another which attracts nearby rings and yet another that protects him from level hazards and enemy fire. The shields allow for a smoother flow of gameplay rather than the stop-start of getting hit and losing rings too often. In this latest Sonic game, Tails can fly for longer periods of time. Sonic the Hedgehog 3 also introduced a new special stage, which requires the player to run around a 3D chequerboard environment collecting all the blue spheres to retrieve a Chaos Emerald.

What was known as Sonic the Hedgehog 3 and Sonic & Knuckles (released October 1994) were both originally developed as one game. They were finally released as two separate titles due to costs and time constraints. As with Sonic the Hedgehog 1, Sonic the Hedgehog 3 was an unmitigated success and one of the best-selling games for the Sega Mega-Genesis/Mega Drive console.

Daytona USA

Date of release: March 1994

Region: Japan

Developer: Sega AM2

Publisher: Sega

Platform: Arcade

Designed by Toshihiro Nagoshi of Virtua Racing (1992) and Yu Suzuki (Hang-On (1985), Space Harrier (1985) and Out Run (1986)), Daytona USA is a single-player or multiplayer, stock car racing game. The aim of the game is to finish the race before the timer runs out, and in multiplayer, the aim is to finish ahead of your opponents. The game featured a realistic experience for the player with driving mechanics such as power slides and drifting. Players could choose between four different camera angles, ranging from first-person to third-person perspective. There are three tracks to race on in Daytona USA.

Sega's mission was to create a racing game that would be superior to its direct competitor, Namco's Ridge Racer (1993). As with Out Run, the game's developers chose to design another themed racing experience, this time taking inspiration from the races of the National Association for Stock Car Auto Racing, otherwise known as NASCAR. The initial standard cabinet was made for two players to race next to one another. Four of these could be linked together to allow for eight players to race together. The developers used satellite imagery to map the famous Daytona International Speedway in Florida, USA. Daytona USA was the first game to utilise Sega's new Model 2 board (the previous Model 1 was used in Virtua Racing (1992) and Virtua Fighter (1993) to great effect). The Model 2 featured 3D texture filtering and texture anti-aliasing and was capable of handling 300,000 polygons running at a frame rate of 60 frames per second.

Daytona USA was praised for its (at the time) incredible 3D graphics and is cited as one of the most successful arcade games of all time. It is regarded by some as the best arcade racing game of all time. It seemed that, as far as some were concerned, arcades were still holding their own against the home systems, at least in the racing genre. The game was released on the Sega Saturn in 1995, on Windows in 1996, and on the PlayStation and Xbox platforms in 2011. Daytona spawned several sequels including

Daytona USA: Championship Circuit Edition (1996), Daytona USA 2: Battle on the Edge (1998), and Daytona Championship USA (2016). The fact that Sega was able to release a successful arcade cabinet (which still allows for up to eight players) in 2016 is a testament to the enduring legacy of the Daytona brand.

The Elder Scrolls: Arena

Date of release: March 1994

Region: USA

Developer: Bethesda Softworks

Publisher: Bethesda Softworks

Platform: MS-DOS

Designed by Vijay Lakshman, Christopher Weaver and Ted Peterson, The Elder Scrolls: Arena is a single-player, first-person, action role-playing game and the first game in the hugely popular Elder Scrolls series. Set on the continent of Tamriel during the 389th year of the Third Era, the aim of the game is to collect the fragments that make up the Staff of Chaos, which holds the key to defeating the Imperial Battlemage Jagar Tharn, who has usurped the throne of Emperor Uriel Septim VII.

The developers of The Elder Scrolls: Arena were greatly inspired by Ultima Underworld: The Stygian Abyss (1992) and Legends of Valour (1992). The Elder Scrolls: Arena is very similar in terms of character creation, stats, levelling-up, exploration and the other staple features of a typical fantasy RPG.

The game shipped with eight floppy disks, a hint book and a game manual. A deluxe version was also released on CD-ROM with additional and improved graphics and sound in 1994. The original floppy disk game was released as freeware in 2004. The Elder Scrolls: Arena was greeted with mixed opinions. Some loved the epic scale of the game, featuring an entire continent of towns and dungeons to explore with a multitude of quests. However, others found the size of the game world a little overwhelming. It has also been criticised for its clunky controls. Despite this, The Elder Scrolls: Arena had a lot of fans and has since become a cult classic, perhaps due in part to its rather more famous sequels The Elder Scrolls II: Daggerfall (1996), The Elder Scrolls III: Morrowind (2002), The Elder Scrolls IV: Oblivion (2006), The Elder Scrolls V: Skyrim (2011), The Elder Scrolls Online (2014) and The Elder Scrolls VI (TBA).

X-COM: UFO Defense/UFO: Enemy Unknown

Date of release: March 1994

Region: North America and Europe

Developer: Mythos Games

Publisher: MicroProse

Platform: Amiga and MS-DOS

Designed by Tim Roberts, Julian Gollop of Rebel Star Raiders (1984) and Laser Squad (1988), and Nick Gollop, UFO: Enemy Unknown (known as X-COM: UFO Defense in the United States) is a single-player, turn-based strategy game and the first in the XCOM series. Set in 1998, the aim of the game is to defeat the aliens who are invading the Earth. You play as the commander of the newly-formed albeit clandestine Extra-terrestrial Combat (X-COM) force. UFO: Enemy Unknown is comprised of two markedly different modes, named the Geoscape and the Battlescape. The Geoscape is played in a 2D user interface view and involves base building, research and development, personnel management, resource and financial management, monitoring and responding to alien activity. The Battlescape is played from an isometric view and is invariably in response to alien activity on the ground, taking the form of various missions. These missions are tactical, turn-based combat of the deployed X-COM squad on a trooper-by-trooper basis against their extra-terrestrial foes. As the game progresses, the player can enhance their troops' combat potential via the reverse-engineering of captured alien technology and the development of an arsenal of advanced weaponry to use against the alien forces. This more advanced weaponry is certainly needed as the various Alien enemies you encounter become stronger and more difficult to kill. It is eventually discovered that the leader race of aliens, known as the Ethereals, has established the main base on Mars. The endgame of X-COM is a final assault on said alien base to try and end the extra-terrestrial threat once and for all. UFO: Enemy Unknown has several endings depending on whether the player is victorious in their final assault, whether they have successfully managed finances and resources, or whether they have accrued enough success in their overall performance against the aliens.

The game was highly praised for its challenging and immersive gameplay and its in-depth mechanics. Players found, like in any good game, that they could become completely immersed for many hours. It popularized the turn-based strategy genre on the PC and was soon ported to the PlayStation and Windows.

UFO: Enemy Unknown has spawned many sequels, some of the most notable of which are X-COM: Terror from the Deep (1995), XCOM: Enemy Unknown (2012) and XCOM 2 (2016). Even though there had been many turn-based strategy games in the past, these sequels would establish not only the XCOM brand but what has been described by some as an actual XCOM genre, with a set and well-defined style of gameplay and underpinning mechanics similar to those of the XCOM series of games. Examples of such XCOM-like games are UFO: Aftermath (2003), Xenonauts (2014) Phantom Doctrine (2018) and Phoenix Point (2019), the latter of which happens to be designed by Julian Gallop. UFO: Enemy Unknown is often cited as one of the best video games of all time.

Beneath a Steel Sky

Date of release: March 1994

Region: UK

Developer: Revolution Software

Publisher: Virgin Interactive Entertainment

Platform: Amiga and MS-DOS

Beneath a Steel Sky is a single-player, point-and-click adventure game set in a dystopian future. The aim of the game is to discover your past and defeat the LINC (Logical Inter-Neural Connection) supercomputer. You play as Robert Foster, a man brought up in 'The Gap' (the name given to Australia's Outback in the game) after being the sole survivor of a helicopter crash as a child. The game begins after Foster is kidnapped and forcibly taken to Union City. As with other point-and-click adventure games, the player must explore their environment, interact with NPCs and make use of various items to solve puzzles in order to progress.

The game's chief designer, Charles Cecil, wanted to create something akin to a mature comic book in a video game format and so contacted Dave Gibbons (of 2000AD and Watchmen) to help with the development of Beneath a Steel Sky. Like Revolution Software's first game, Lure of the Temptress (1992), Beneath a Steel Sky used the Virtual Theatre Engine. Beneath a Steel Sky was very highly praised across the board for its graphics, dialogue (the humour of which can be a bit hit or miss), story, atmosphere and puzzles. It also won the 1995 Golden Joystick Award for 'Best Adventure Game'.

Super Metroid

Date of release: March 1994

Region: Japan

Developer: Nintendo R&D1

Publisher: Nintendo

Platform: Super Famicom

Designed by Yoshio Sakamoto, Gunpei Yokoi who worked on the original Metroid in 1986, and Makoto Kano who worked on Metroid II (1991), Super Metroid is a single-player, action-adventure, science-fiction themed vertical & horizontal scrolling platform game and the third game in the Metroid series. Once again, you play the role of the spacesuit-clad female bounty hunter, Samus Aran. The aim of the game is to retrieve the infant Metroid organism stolen by space pirates. Super Metroid sees the return of the tried-and-tested gameplay of the original, with the player finding power-ups, armour enhancements and weapon upgrades as they explore, along with unlocking new abilities for Samus which allows the player to explore previously inaccessible parts of the game. This latter in particular is the signature mechanic for which the Metroid series is known. As well as beautiful 16-bit graphics and larger levels, new features included being able to aim and fire in all directions, a mini-map and an inventory screen. Like the first game, this one also has multiple endings based on how long it takes to complete.

Super Metroid was highly praised for its graphics, gameplay and its incredibly atmospheric music composed by Kenji Yamamoto. It is often cited as one of the best video games of all time.

Final Fantasy VI/Final Fantasy III

Date of release: April 1994

Region: Japan

Developer: Square

Publisher: Square

Platform: Super Famicom

Designed by Yoshinori Kitase and Hiroyuki Ito, Final Fantasy VI, known as Final Fantasy III in the West, is a single-player, 2D JRPG and the sixth in the main series of the popular Final Fantasy games. Set in a world that mixes technology with magic, Final Fantasy VI was unlike any of its predecessors in terms of world-building. The aim of Final Fantasy VI is to overthrow the oppressive Gestahl Empire, although this being a Final Fantasy game there are many interconnecting subplots and therefore other goals to accomplish during the game. Final Fantasy VI has fourteen playable characters; each is introduced with their own engaging backstory and each with a different skill set. Some boast higher stamina while other characters will have higher magic power. In levelling up, it is best to focus on boosting a character's aptitude. For example, even though any character can learn magic it is best for the character or characters with the highest Magic Power to specialise in magic and thus inflict the most damage with their magic skills. The turn-based combat system is pretty much the same as in previous Final Fantasy games.

Final Fantasy VI would be the last Final Fantasy game to feature 2D sprites before making the transition to 3D in Final Fantasy VII (1997). The game was highly praised for its beautiful 16-bit graphics, its roster of characters with whom it was very easy for the player to become emotionally invested, the sheer scope of the story which was unprecedented at the time, and its music by Nobuo Uematsu. A culmination of everything that made the Final Fantasy series a success in the past, Final Fantasy VI is considered one of the best, if not the best Final Fantasy game and RPGs of all time.

Final Fantasy VI was released as Final Fantasy III in the US in October 1994 on the SNES. It was ported to the PlayStation in 1999 and the Game Boy Advance in 2006.

1994 Golden Joystick Awards

1994s Golden Joystick Awards is hosted in London on 16th May.

Super Mario All-Stars wins Console Game of the Year.

The Legend of Zelda: Link's Awakening wins Handheld Game of the Year.

Cannon Fodder wins Best Original Game of the Year.

Theme Park

Date of release: June 1994

Region: Europe and North America

Developer: Bullfrog Productions

Publisher: Bullfrog Productions & Electronic Arts

Platform: 3DO, Amiga and MS-DOS

Developed by Peter Molyneux and Demis Hassabis, Theme Park is a single-player construction and management simulator. The aim is to run a successful theme park. The endgame is the choice to either auction your theme park off for as much money as possible or keep it for yourself. If you sell, then you can start afresh in another part of the world. There are two modes in Theme Park: sandbox mode and business mode. In sandbox mode, the player can build whatever they want with no constraints whereas in business mode, the player has to micromanage every aspect of the theme park they are currently running, from finances to maintenance to customer and staff satisfaction. Theme Park features over thirty attractions and facilities including rollercoaster rides, Ferris wheels, bouncy castles, treehouses, shows, coconut shies, arcades, shops, food stalls, and toilets. The game is broadly similar to SimCity (1989), and like SimCity, the player can also choose to sabotage their creations just for the fun of it.

The game was highly praised for its graphics, addictive gameplay and sense of humour and was soon ported to most of the popular home consoles of the time. Theme Park was incredibly successful, selling fifteen million units. It spawned two sequels with Theme Park Work/Sim Theme Park (1999) and Theme Park Inc/SimCoaster (1999).

Puzzle Bobble/Bust-a-Move

Date of release: June 1994

Region: Japan

Developer: Taito

Publisher: Taito

Platform: Arcade

Puzzle Bobble is a single-player or two-player puzzle game. Based on the Bubble Bobble franchise, the aim of Puzzle Bobble is to clear all the different coloured bubbles (or balls as they are sometimes referred to) that are currently on-screen in each of the thirty-two levels. The player does this by using a mechanical device called a pointer to fire a bubble at the pre-established mass of bubbles above. Bubbles can be bounced off the side of the arena walls to get to difficult-to-reach areas, and if the player can create a connection of three or more bubbles of the same colour, they will fall away and award points for being cleared. Every now and then the mass of bubbles will move down closer to the pointer, with the tempo of the music increasing the closer the bubbles are to the bottom of the screen. If the mass of bubbles crosses the line at the bottom of the play area, then it is game over. In two-player mode, players compete side by side. If a player creates a connection of four or more bubbles, then some of those bubbles are put onto their competitor's screen, meaning that players must not only attempt to clear their own screen but also seek to hamper their opponent's efforts.

The basic game mechanic of Puzzle Bobble is very addictive and is immense fun when playing against a friend. As well as being ported to a multitude of platforms at the time and for many years after, it has also inspired many clones such as the popular Snood (1996) and Worms Blast (2002).

Star Wars: TIE Fighter

Date of release: July 1994

Region: USA

Developer: Totally Games

Publisher: LucasArts

Platform: MS-DOS

Designed by Totally Games, Star Wars: TIE Fighter is a single-player, 3D, space combat and simulation game, and the second game in the Star Wars: X-Wing series, even though you fly a TIE Fighter. Set after the events of Star Wars Episode V: The Empire Strikes Back, you play as a TIE Fighter pilot and must carry out missions ranging from escort runs, rescue attempts and raids on Rebel ships. The game also contains a narrative where you help prevent a coup against Emperor Palpatine. Star Wars: TIE Fighter is a game with surprising depth, expanding on the Star Wars Expanded Universe (or Legends, as it is known since the franchise's acquisition by Disney) and its lore, taking place and accordingly filling in the background of many different locales, all knitted together with a diverse array of cutscenes and gameplay. While flying your TIE (Twin Ion Engine) Fighter, the player must carefully route and reroute the energy of the ship to its various systems, prioritising shields, weapons or speed depending on the situation. The game also features hotkeys allowing you to give commands to your wingmen and allows the player to set the priority of repair for different damaged systems should their TIE Fighter take a hit or two.

Star Wars: TIE Fighter rides the line between a simple space combat game and a more in-depth simulation. Almost every key on the keyboard has a function, yet the game is quite simple in its gameplay. The player does not need to have all the keys written down or memorised to enjoy themselves as an in-game prompt at the bottom of the screen will appear to help the player, making the game so much more accessible and fun. Star Wars: TIE Fighter is both an arcade game and a simulator, its depth and associated skill ceiling drawing the player in and immersing them further with each mission. Games like Star Wars: TIE Fighter can be played with the keyboard and mouse but are so much better when played using a joystick, giving a more visceral feel when dogfighting. At times, there are twenty or thirty ships flying in all directions, making the player feel like they are in the centre of the action, all scored with the familiar Star Wars music of John Williams.

The game was highly praised for its graphics, sound and enemy AI and is often cited as one of the greatest video games of all time. Star Wars: TIE Fighter was subject to several releases where both graphics and sound were correspondingly enhanced, culminating in the Collector's CD-ROM version. Star Wars: TIE Fighter was later released for Macintosh, Linux and Windows.

The King of Fighters '94

Date of release: August 1994

Region: Worldwide

Developer: SNK

Publisher: SNK

Platform: Arcade Neo Geo

The King of Fighters '94 is a one-player or two-player fighting game. The aim is to defeat all of your opponents. The King of Fighters '94 was the first fighting game where you choose a team of three rather than just one character. Each team represents a specific country, and the player chooses said country and the order in which the three characters will fight. This means that competent players have to master multiple characters, as opposed to just one along with said characters' strengths and weaknesses when matched against certain other characters. These characters were taken from some of SNK's previous titles such as Ikari Warriors (1986), Psycho Soldier (1987), Art of Fighting (1992) and Fatal Fury (1993). There are a total of eight teams of three fighters in The King of Fighters '94.

The game was praised for introducing the team mechanic into fighting games, although it is worth noting that players wished they could make up their own teams rather than having to settle for the preset ones that came with the game, but this feature would be introduced in later games. A remake of the game was released only in Japan in 2004 for the PlayStation 2. The King of Fighters '94 spawned multiple sequels, some of the most notable being The King of Fighters '95 (1995), The King of Fighters '98 (1998), The King of

Fighters 2002 (2002), The King of Fighters XIII (2010) and The King of Fighters XIV (2016).

Mother 2: Giygas Strikes Back/Earthbound

Date of release: August 1994

Region: Japan

Developer: Ape

Publisher: Nintendo

Platform: Super Famicom

Designed by Shigesato Itoi and Satoru Iwata, Mother 2 is a single-player JRPG and the sequel to Mother (1989). Set in the year 199X, a meteorite crashes on the outskirts of a small town. A mysterious alien force named Giygas has consumed everything that is good in the world, leaving most of its inhabitants twisted and hostile. The aim of the game is to collect the eight melodies that will make a song and save the world. The player controls a boy called Ness and a party of up to four of his friends who live in Eagleland, a spoof of the United States. While 2D, the game is portrayed through oblique projection to give the impression of being 3D, as opposed to the top-down or isometric perspectives used by other contemporary RPGs. As with many JRPGs, combat is turn-based and takes place from a first-person viewpoint, with the player fighting enemies ranging from Annoying Old Man, New Age Retro Hippie and Unassuming Local Guy. The real emphasis in Mother 2 is on the narrative of the game, and this means talking to NPCs a lot more than in other JRPGs. This is necessary to not only understand what is going on but to also progress through the game. Luckily, the dialogue in Mother 2 is genuinely funny and each NPC has a wealth of different responses.

The Mother series was a huge departure from the mainstream RPGs of the day, which it parodies. There was nothing quite like it at the time. Music was also a huge part of the game. Composed by Keiichi Suzuki and Hirokazu Tanaka, Mother 2 contains a staggering amount of different musical styles from all over the world that were integrated into the game.

Mother 2 was released in North America in June 1995 for the SNES as Earthbound, renamed as such to avoid confusion as the original Mother was never released in the US. At the time, Earthbound did not receive as much praise as it did in Japan and sales were fairly poor. However, over time it has become a cult classic and is now highly regarded. Ironically, it is now often cited as one of the greatest video games of all time and has influenced such games as South Park: The Stick of Truth (2014) and Undertale

(2015).

The Need for Speed

Date of release: August 1994

Region: Canada

Developer: EA Canada

Publisher: Electronic Arts

Platform: 3DO

The Need for Speed is a single-player or multiplayer racing game, with the main goal being to finish first across the various tracks and courses. The Need for Speed places the player's view inside one of various sports cars with an emphasis on realistic handling and audio. It also features Full Motion Video (FMV) commentary on all cars included in the game. As well as racing other cars, players have to outrun the police from time to time. There are a total of three courses in The Need for Speed, with that number being brought up to six with the later ports of the game.

The Need for Speed is the first in The Need for Speed series. Some of the most notable of these are Need for Speed: Underground (2003), Need for Speed: Underground 2 (2004), Need for Speed: Most Wanted (2005), and Need for Speed: Hot Pursuit (2010).

Virtua Cop

Date of release: September 1994

Region: Worldwide

Developer: Sega AM2

Publisher: Sega

Platform: Arcade

Designed by Jun'etsu Kakuta, Toshinori Asai and Yu Suzuki (Hang-On (1985), Space Harrier (1985), Out Run (1986), Virtua Racing (1992) and Virtua Fighter (1993)), Virtua Cop is a single-player or multiplayer, 3D, first-person, light gun rail shooter. The aim of the game is to take out the antagonistic crime boss and his multitude of henchmen. The player reloads their gun by pointing away from the screen and pulling the trigger on the plastic gun. They must also be careful not to shoot any innocent bystanders, accidentally or otherwise. The game also features automatic weapons, exploding barrels and bosses. The game was thrilling and tremendous fun to play, even more so if the player had the money to play as both player one and two, affording them the use of both pistols to be used akimbo, but equally as enjoyable (and less expensive) when played with a friend.

Virtua Cop was highly praised for its fluid 3D graphics (which used the same Sega Model 2 arcade system board like many other Sega 3D arcade games of the time), its fast-paced action and multiplayer aspect which allowed two players to work together toward a common goal. Virtua Cop was the first real big hit in the on-rail shooter genre of games, where you play as a character, since the Operation Wolf series of arcade games in the late eighties. It would inspire other similar arcade light gun rail shooters, such as the Time Crisis series (1995-2015) and The House of the Dead series (1996-2018). It was ported to the Sega Saturn, Windows, and PlayStation 2 in 2002. Virtua Cop spawned two sequels with Virtua Cop 2 (1995), and Virtua Cop 3 (2003).

System Shock

Date of release: September 1994

Region: USA

Developer: LookingGlass Technologies

Publisher: Origin Systems

Platform: MS-DOS

Designed by Doug Church and Warren Spector, System Shock is a single-player first-person action-adventure game. Set in the year 2072 aboard a space station, you play as a hacker who has been captured by the TriOptimum Corporation. They offer you a deal of dropping all charges against you if you agree to work for them, promising lucrative cybernetic enhancements to sweeten the deal. The aim of the game is to hack into the space station's rogue AI, SHODAN. The player is allowed to set four different difficulty categories of the game on a scale from 0-3. The categories are Combat, Puzzle, Mission and Cyber. This allows the player unprecedented control over the gameplay never before seen in the genre.

System Shock sits between twitch shooters like Doom (1992) and more adventure-oriented first-person games such as Ultima Underworld: The Stygian Abyss (1992), which Church and Spector both worked on. The player switches between two different modes to interact with the environment in first-person: a mode to aim and shoot enemies and a mode allowing for point-and-click interaction with the environment and its objects. This can be a little tricky sometimes, however, and is one of the few weak points of the game. There are sixteen weapons in System Shock, along with secondary weapons such as frag grenades, gas grenades and mines. The player can also collect and use different stimulants or drugs to help them, depending on the situation. The player will need all these to deal with enemies such as mutants, killer cyborgs and robots that SHODAN has let loose on the station. The game featured various dialogue from the station logs and SHODAN, which enhances the already tense atmosphere of the game as she gloats, goads and threatens you. One of the game's most innovative ideas is the ability to hack into cyberspace, a 3D wireframe environment where the player can fly around collecting data, interacting with nodes and shooting down enemy programs.

The game shipped with nine floppy discs, or a single CD-ROM version with enhanced graphics, sound and spoken dialogue. System Shock was a game way ahead of its time. Many first-person games since, which involve a competent amount of narrative and a multitude of game mechanics allowing you to interact with your environment, can trace their roots back to System Shock. Yet, for some, its control scheme was a little contrived and difficult to use.

System Shock spawned a more popular sequel with System Shock 2 (1999). The Deus Ex series (2000-2017) and the Bioshock series (2007-2013) are seen as spiritual successors to System Shock. The game was ported to the Mac OS in December 1994, and an enhanced edition was released on Windows in 2015.A remake was also released in 2023.

Entertainment Software Rating Board (ESRB) is established

The Entertainment Software Rating Board (ESRB) was established in the USA in September 1994. The ESRBs mandate is to assign age ratings to video games dependent on their content. This came about due to the 1993 congressional hearings concerning games such as Night Trap (1992) and Mortal Kombat (1992) and how they were supposedly affecting America's children. Ratings include Everyone (E), suitable for all ages; Everyone 10+ (E10+), suitable for 10 years and older; Teen (T), suitable for 13 years and older; Mature (M), suitable for 17 years and older; and finally Adults Only (AO), suitable for 18 years and older. The enforcement of ratings is lackadaisical, to say the least, and it is common for most children to circumvent the system and play games with any rating. Indeed, this has been the case throughout the entire history of video games. However, the rating system does act as a useful guide for those parents who are mindful of such things. After the establishment of the ESRB, many other countries followed suit with their own rating system. Ironically, the establishment of the ESRB allowed the proliferation of even more violent games throughout the 1990s and beyond, now that they could comfortably adhere to the ratings board.

Of late, the ESRB has come under criticism for its lack of action involving the restriction of age and microtransactions. The ESRB maintains that the microtransaction, or the loot box model where a player pays real money for a chance to win something of great value within the game, is not gambling. Other countries strongly disagree and some have even prohibited the use of such practices.

Little Big Adventure/Relentless: Twinsen's Adventure

Date of release: October 1994

Region: France

Developer: Adeline Software International

Publisher: Electronic Arts

Platform: MS-DOS

Little Big Adventure, known as Relentless: Twinsen's Adventure in every other part of the world apart from Europe, is a single-player action-adventure game. The aim of Little Big Adventure is to defeat the game's main antagonist Dr FunFrock, who tyrannically rules over the planet of Twinsun. This is no mean feat to accomplish, for Dr FunFrock has the ability to clone an inexhaustible supply of soldiers to enforce his will and possesses teleportation devices to dispatch them instantly anywhere on the planet. You play as Twinsen, who has been imprisoned for having prophetic dreams of a coming disaster. You must escape the prison, stop Dr FunFrock and avert a global disaster.

The game is played from an isometric point-of-view with characters and some interactive game assets modelled as 3D objects. During gameplay, the player can choose between four different modes: normal, athletic, aggressive, and discreet. The mode selected determines whether the player wishes to fight their way out of a particular situation or instead opt for a more diplomatic or circumspect approach.

Little Big Adventure sold over 500,000 units. It was praised for its well-crafted graphics, world-building and voice acting. It certainly found a following with players who loved this kind of isometric action-adventure genre, with puzzle elements. The game was ported to PC-98, FM Towns and PlayStation, and spawned one sequel with Little Big

Adventure 2/Twinsen's Odyssey (1997).

Sonic & Knuckles

Date of release: October 1994

Region: Worldwide

Developer: Sega Technical Institute

Publisher: Sega

Platform: Sega Genesis/Mega Drive

Designed by Hirokazu Yasuhara and Yuji Naka of the Sega Technical Institute, Sonic & Knuckles is a single-player or two-player, side-scrolling, 2D platform game. The aim of Sonic and Knuckles is to save Angel Island by preventing Dr Robotnik from relaunching his crashed Death Egg space station. Seeing as how Sonic & Knuckles and Sonic the Hedgehog 3 were originally developed as one game, Sonic & Knuckles plays very similarly to the aforementioned Sonic the Hedgehog 3 and the same features, such as shields and the 3D special stage, are present in the game. One of the main differences is that the player chooses either to play as Sonic or Knuckles at the beginning of the game. Knuckles the Echidna is a character first introduced in Sonic the Hedgehog 3. He can climb walls, glide and use his signature spiked knuckles to punch things, hence the name.

Sonic & Knuckles was well received, and despite Sonic & Knuckles being a spin-off from the main series of Sonic games, it actually sold more units than Sonic the Hedgehog 3 (1994) and is also one of the best-selling games for the Sega Genesis/Mega Drive console.

Killer Instinct

Date of release: October 1994

Region: USA & Europe

Developer: Rare & Nintendo

Publisher: Midway

Platform: Arcade

Killer Instinct was released in North America in October 1994 by Midway for the arcade. Developed by Rare, and in collaboration with Nintendo, Killer Instinct is a single-player or two-player fighting game. The aim of the game is to defeat your opponent in a best-out-of-three-rounds bout. Killer Instinct takes its inspiration from Street Fighter II and Mortal Kombat, the two most popular fighting games on the block at the time. It features combos, finishing moves (of which each character has two along with a humiliation finishing move which forces your opponent to dance) and copious amounts of blood. Many other features served to set Killer Instinct apart from its contemporaries, however. It featured two health bars rather than one, ultra-combos which allowed a player to string a massive amount of hits upon an opponent, and a combo breaker which allowed a player on the receiving end of a combo to break out of said combo. The game also featured ten playable fighters, the roster being remarkably diverse for a fighting game and including, amongst others, a werewolf, a cyborg, a velociraptor, a skeleton, and an alien made of ice. Each had a backstory and motivation for fighting in the Killer Instinct tournament.

What also set Killer Instinct apart from other fighting games, and indeed other arcade games, was that it was the first arcade cabinet to incorporate a hard drive. Before this, all arcade machines would store the game on a series of ROM chips. Having a hard drive meant that the game could store more data, meaning more detailed 3D models and graphics, including very detailed backgrounds and better overall sound quality. As with the upcoming Donkey Kong Country (1994), Rare used renders of high polygon 3D models created in Alias (which developed in Autodesk Maya) and on Silicon Graphics (SGI) workstations to create the backgrounds and character models that would then be converted into highly detailed sprites. This all ran at a beautifully fluid 60 frames per second.

Upon release, Killer Instinct was a big hit, its diverse range of characters and incredible graphics being highly praised. It was ported to the SNES and Gameboy in the following year, yet unfortunately, these versions could not attain the graphical heights of the arcade. Killer Instinct has had two sequels to date with Killer Instinct 2 (1996) and Killer Instinct (2013).

Earthworm Jim

Date of release: October 1994

Region: USA & Europe

Developer: Shiny Entertainment

Publisher: Playmates Interactive and Virgin Interactive Entertainment

Platform: Sega Mega Drive/Genesis, subsequently the SNES. Earthworm Jim is a single-player, side-scrolling, run-and-gun platform game. The aim of the game is to rescue Princess What's-Her-Name from the numerous enemies whom the player must defeat. You play as Earthworm Jim, who finds and is able to use a super-space-cyber-suit that enables him to run, jump, fire his gun and head whip his enemies. Jim's head whip is also used to interact with the environment, such as being used to swing from hooks or hover down to lower levels. Each level has an end-of-level boss, which must be defeated before Jim can progress onwards. Players will also play a third-person racing game between levels, involving Jim racing his single-seat spaceship, called the Pocket Rocket, against Psy-Crow the bounty hunter, avoiding asteroids and collecting blue orbs and speed boosts. If Jim wins the race he will progress to the next level. If he doesn't, he must fight Psy-Crow to continue. Other levels feature gameplay ranging from riding on the back of a giant hamster to controlling a submarine.

Earthworm Jim was well received and praised for its animation, over-the-top cartoon style and surreal sense of humour. It was ported to most of the popular platforms over the next two years. It has also spawned several sequels with Earthworm Jim 2 (1995), the disappointing Earthworm Jim 3D (1999), Earthworm Jim: Menace 2 the Galaxy (1999), and Earthworm Jim HD (2009), a remake of the original game.

Doom II: Hell on Earth

Date of release: October 1994

Region: Worldwide

Developer: id Software

Publisher: GT Interactive Software

Platform: MS-DOS

Doom II: Hell on Earth is a single-player or multiplayer, first-person shooter and the sequel to the immensely successful Doom (1993). The aim of Doom II is to battle through hordes of demons, who have invaded Earth, deactivate a force field so that the few remaining humans can escape from the last remaining spaceport, and then follow the demons back to Hell and try and deal with them once and for all. Doom II uses the same gameplay and mechanics as the first Doom, giving players more of what they wanted. The level design is a little more elaborate. The player now has access to the Super Shotgun and the Megasphere power-up that boosts health and combat armour up to the maximum possible level. Doom II also increases the number of enemies, and bosses from the original game turn up as regular enemies. There are thirty levels in Doom II, along with two secret levels. Multiplayer involved cooperative play or deathmatch on a Local Area Network (LAN) or by using a third-party, online dial-up service to play against other players on the internet. These services were refined over the years providing a more immersive online gaming experience as time went on.

Doom II sold out within a month and went on to become the best-selling computer game of 1994. It was soon ported to the Mac OS.

Game Zero launches

Game Zero was launched as the first regular online website dedicated to video games in November 1994. Initially, a bi-monthly print magazine based in Ohio, USA, Game Zero had a circulation of 1500 before moving to a CD-ROM-based magazine. The Game Zero website was only active between 1994 and 1996.

Warcraft: Orcs & Humans

Date of release: November 1994

Region: USA

Developer: Blizzard Entertainment

Publisher: Blizzard Entertainment

Platform: MS-DOS

Designed by Bill Roper and Patrick Wyatt, Warcraft: Orcs & Humans is a single-player or multiplayer real-time strategy (RTS) game and the first in the incredibly successful Warcraft franchise. In the single-player mode, the player can either play the Human campaign or the Orc campaign and after playing through as one race, the player can proceed to play the other. The aim of the game is dependent on each mission and associated objectives, though most consist of building your base by mining gold and cutting lumber, building up an army (which means developing more advanced buildings for stronger, more varied units), and finally destroying the current opponent's army and base. In the multiplayer mode, the player's aim is very much the same, playing against other human adversaries across a Local Area Network (LAN) or Dial-up modem. The narrative framing of Warcraft: Orcs & Humans is that the Orcs have come through a portal from their dying world of Draenor to the world of Azeroth, inhabited by humans. Having been repelled once in the past by the humans, the Orcs have returned with a vengeance. Warcraft: Orcs & Humans' strong back story and narrative resulted in a very compelling game. The play area is split up into two parts. On the right, and taking up most of the screen, is a top-down perspective view of the map showing troops and buildings. Areas not yet explored are covered in darkness in what is known as the 'fog of war' and must be explored to be revealed. On the left is an overview of the current map, any troops or buildings selected and possible commands that can be given to said troops or buildings. Warcraft: Orcs & Humans featured melee and ranged units, siege units and magic users who can use a multitude of spells. This varied range of units gave rise to a myriad of different strategies and approaches.

Warcraft: Orcs & Humans was a huge success and highly praised for setting a new standard, picking up where Dune II (1992) left off in terms of defining real-time strategy games. It would set the standard for all such games to come, and along with its sequel Warcraft II: Tides of Darkness popularised the RTS genre. It was later ported to Mac OS. The game was the beginning of a huge video game franchise with each subsequent game larger and more elaborate than the last. These games include Warcraft II: Tides of Darkness (1995), Warcraft III: Reign of Chaos (1999), World of Warcraft (2004-current date) with its numerous expansion sets, and Hearthstone (2014). The Warcraft brand has also branched out to include novels, comic books, manga, tabletop games and the feature film Warcraft (2016).

Genesis 32X/Super 32X/ 32X

Released in North America in November 1994, the Genesis32X (known as the Super 32X in Japan and the 32X in Europe) is a fifth-generation add-on for the Sega Genesis/Mega Drive console. Developed as a means to give owners of the aforementioned consoles access to 32-bit games, the 32X slots into the console's cartridge port, and a 32X game cartridge then slots into the top of the 32X.

The 32X was meant to keep up with the times before the launch of the Sega Saturn, yet the Saturn was launched within months of the 32X. This confused consumers and led to a lack of confidence in Sega's overall direction. With Nintendo and Sony waiting in the wings, this was something they couldn't afford. The 32X also had a small and unimpressive games library. Despite its attractively low price point, consumers were far more willing to wait and invest their money on a more promising, true fifth-generation console, rather than this strange and limited hybrid.

Donkey Kong Country

Date of release: November 1994

Region: Worldwide

Developer: Rare

Publisher: Nintendo

Platform: Super Famicom/SNES

Donkey Kong Country is a single-player or multiplayer, side-scrolling platform game. The aim of the game is to retrieve Kong's horde of bananas stolen by the Kremlings. Donkey Kong Country features Donkey Kong and his nephew Diddy Kong, running, jumping, and defeating enemies by jumping on them and collecting items. The player can acquire an extra life by either collecting 100 bananas, collecting the letters which make up the word KONG or by collecting extra life balloons. Other mechanics in the game include throwing barrels at enemies, barrel cannons which launch Donkey and Diddy Kong along a set trajectory, riding different animals, and hidden rooms which can be discovered by destroying specific walls. There are forty levels in Donkey Kong Country.

Tim and Chris Stamper (who in the past had founded the 'Ultimate Play the Game' game publishing company) Jetpac (1983), Sabre Wulf (1984) and Knight Lore (1984) used renders of high polygon 3D models using Alias (which developed into Autodesk Maya) and Silicon Graphics workstations (SGI) to create the sprite animation giving Donkey Kong Country its unique look. This effective technique would have a great influence on other developers who would utilise it in their games. With each SGI workstation costing £80,000 each and necessitating lengthy rending times, Rare took an enormous risk. Yet the pay-off was to have the look of a highly-detailed 3D game, the likes of which had not been seen before on home consoles, without any of the processing cost during gameplay.

The game was marketed as 'The world's first fully rendered video game', and footage of the game spoke for itself. Upon release, Donkey Kong Country was regarded as ground-breaking for its graphics, although it did receive some criticism for its somewhat average gameplay. Yet one cannot argue with the game's success, as it would go on to sell over nine million units. The game was ported to the Game Boy Color and Game Boy Advance in 2000 and 2003, respectively. Donkey Kong Country, being a spin-off of the original Donkey Kong series, has spawned a number of its own sequels. Some of the most notable of these are Donkey Kong Country 2: Diddy's Kong Quest (1995), Donkey Kong Country Returns (2010) and Donkey Kong Country: Tropical Freeze (2014).

Sensible World of Soccer

Date of release: November 1994

Region: UK

Developer: Sensible Software

Publisher: Renegade GT Interactive

Platform: Amiga

Designed by Jon Hare and Chris Chapman, Sensible World of Soccer is a single-player or multiplayer soccer and soccer management game. The game offered not only a top-down virtual game of soccer to play but a career mode spanning over twenty seasons where you play as a manager throughout. This could lead players through all kinds of interesting and emergent narratives, such as a rags-to-riches career or running the team of your dreams and taking them to FA Cup or even World Cup victory. The game also featured team editing, in-depth formations and the buying and selling of players.

Sensible World of Soccer accomplished something incredible and logistically mind-boggling. It not only included every international team around the world, but also every professional club in the entire world! If this was not enough, the developers of Sensible World of Soccer also included actual real-life players for these thousands of teams and attempted to include accurate real-world statistics for every player. Previous soccer games had around 100-150 teams, while more modern games have about 300. Sensible World of Soccer had about 1,500 teams, with over 20,000 individual players. Each of the teams and even players perform how you might expect them to in real life, for example it is highly unlikely that an obscure club from halfway around the world is going to beat a Premier League team from England.

The initial game was rushed and included a host of bugs that Sensible Software attempted to fix with the release of an update on a free floppy disk. The game received very high praise for its technical achievement along with its playability and management system. Sensible World of Soccer was followed by several editions over the next few years which would enhance and update pretty much every feature of the original game. Sensible World of Soccer has been cited by some as one of the most significant video games of all time.

Sega Saturn

Released in Japan in November 1994, the Sega Saturn is a 32-bit, CD-ROM-based, fifth-generation video game console. It can display 16.7 million colours at a resolution of 704x224 pixels. The Sega Saturn was the successor to the Sega Genesis/Mega Drive and was set to compete with Sony's upcoming PlayStation and the Nintendo 64 (known then only as 'Ultra 64'). Even though the Saturn boasted dual-CPU architecture making it technically more powerful than the PlayStation, it was built partly with 2D graphics in mind. This, coupled with a lack of support, made it difficult for developers to take advantage of its raw processing power and were often only able to utilise one of the CPUs resulting in no significant difference in graphics to the aforementioned PlayStation. Sony also undercut the price of the Saturn, making the PlayStation yet again the more appealing of the two consoles.

By the time Nintendo launched their 32-bit console in 1996, the Saturn was already struggling against the PlayStation. It soon found the N64 was also surpassing it in sales, cornering a neat portion of the console market for Nintendo. The Sega Saturn sold over 9 million units but compared with 33 million units for the N64 and an astounding 102 million units for the PlayStation, it was considered a failure. This is perhaps due to the difficulty developers found with the platform and the fact that Sega never released a Sonic the Hedgehog flagship game for the console, its most successful title from the previous generation. However, there were (and still are) many fans of the console and it is seen by some as an underappreciated and unsung hero of the 32-bit era. Even though it didn't fulfil its potential, there are still some great games for the Sega Saturn. Some of the most notable of these are Sega Rally Championship (1995), Virtua Cop (1995), Virtual Fighter 2 (1996), Dragon Force (1996), Night into Dreams (1996), Guardian Heroes (1996), Saturn Bomberman (1997), Die Hard Trilogy/Arcade (1997), Shining Force III (1997), X-Men Vs Street Fighter (1997), Panzer Dragoon Saga (1998), Radiant Silvergun (1998) and Street Fighter Zero 3 (1999).

Sega Channel

The Sega Channel was launched in North America in December 1994. Provided by Tele-Communications, Inc. (TCI) and Time Warner Cable, the Sega Channel was a video game streaming service and the first in video game history. Customers paid for an adaptor that would be inserted into the cartridge slot of the Genesis, which would then be plugged into the cable TV socket.

The Sega Channel offered fifty games a month, demos, online cheat codes, help and even hosted competitions for a subscription of $15 a month. Games would take a few minutes to download but would sometimes fail due to the noise in the cable. Noise, being unwanted random disturbances or errors of an otherwise wanted information signal, was not a big problem when watching TV, but was disastrous when attempting to download game data. Furthermore, the games were only loaded onto the console's

RAM, meaning that once the console was switched off, the game and all associated progress were lost. The Sega Channel was also only offered by some cable operators.

The service ran from 1994 to 1998 and had up to 250,000 subscribers. The Sega Channel received praise for its innovation and is now seen as a precursor of many concepts we now see as commonplace today, such as the digital downloading of games and game streaming services.

PlayStation

The Sony PlayStation, also referred to as the PS1 or the PSX (Sony's original codename for the console), was released in Japan in December 1994. The Sony PlayStation is a fifth-generation, 32-bit CD-ROM-based video game console. It can display 16.7 million colours and 180,000 textured polygons per second at a resolution of 640x480 pixels. What would one day become the PlayStation was initially conceptualised as a CD-ROM-based console, designed and developed in collaboration between Sony and Nintendo back in 1989 and called the Nintendo SNES-CD or PlayStation. However, Nintendo was not happy with the contract and proceeded to talk with Philips concerning a similar deal. Subsequently, Nintendo announced they would be dropping Sony and instead partnering with Phillips on a similar project, the day after Sony had just announced their deal with Nintendo. Furious at being stabbed in the back and humiliated by Nintendo, Sony decided to go it alone and develop their own console. Hype soon began on what sounded to be a very powerful and capable games console, built to handle the next generation of games, especially 3D games, which would become the main focus of the console's architecture.

Released in Japan only a week after its closest competitor the Sega Saturn, the Sony PlayStation was a huge success and was soon outselling its rival. The console was released in the rest of the world later the next year, in 1995, and met with similar success with many retailers quickly selling out of their stock.

The Sony PlayStation was a watershed moment in video game history and would change the landscape of gaming culture forever. For the last several years, the console market had been dominated by Nintendo and Sega. Over the coming years, a huge variety of games would be released for the PlayStation, coupled with Sony's unique marketing strategy aimed at young adults with high disposable incomes, which soon made playing games officially cool. The PlayStation would decimate all competition. In the 1990s, high-profile personalities would openly talk about the PlayStation and the games they were playing. Video games in the late nineties were everywhere and becoming accepted in mainstream culture by those who had previously shunned them. Behind this phenomenon was the PlayStation, which had almost single-handedly redefined video games forever.

By the end of the decade, the PlayStation would become the best-selling home video game console of all time with around 103 million units sold, outselling its nearest competitor, the Nintendo 64 (1996), by 69 million units. It is currently the sixth best-selling video games console at the time of writing. From out of nowhere, Sony's console dominated the fifth generation of game consoles. A slim version of the console named the PS One was released in July 2000. Around 2400 games were released for the original PlayStation. Some of the most notable of these are Wipeout XL (1996), PaRappa the Rapper (1996), Castlevania: Symphony of the Night (1997), Tomb Raider (1997), Final Fantasy VII (1997), Metal Gear Solid (1998), Resident Evil 2 (1998), Tekken 3 (1998), Crash Bandicoot: Warped (1998), Street Fighter Alpha 3 (1999), Medal of Honor (1999) and Tony Hawk's Pro Skater 2 (2001).

Tekken

Date of release: December 1994

Region: Worldwide

Developer: Namco

Publisher: Namco

Platform: Arcade

Designed by Seiichi Ishii and Hajime Nakatani, Tekken is a single-player or two-player 3D fighting game, and the first in the Tekken series. The aim of Tekken is to beat your opponent. A variation on this genre-codified theme is that the number of rounds and their time limit could be set by the player or players within certain parameters. Tekken also featured eleven locations, these being the Acropolis (Greece), Angkor Wat (Cambodia), Chiba Marine Stadium & Kyoto (Japan), Chicago & Monument Valley (USA), King George Island (Antarctica), Fiji, Szechwan (China), Venezia (Venice, Italy), and Windermere (UK). There are eight playable characters in the arcade version and seventeen in the PlayStation port.

The game was highly praised when released for the arcade and perhaps even more so when released in 1995 for the PlayStation. A 3D texture-mapped fighting game when released in 1995 on a console was very impressive for the time, and it was a big improvement on the flat-shaded models of Virtua Fighter (1993). These character models were also more rounded out, making them look a little more like real people, and even though the controls and gameplay were a little clunky, it didn't seem to matter as the players could adapt. In the mid-nineties, gamers were hungry for 3D and Tekken was a 3D fighting game on the home console. Tekken would become part of the gaming culture where for the first-time console games could be found in bars, pubs and nightclubs being played casually alongside games like Wipeout (1995) and Gran Turismo (1997). Tekken would go on to be the first PlayStation game to sell over a million units and spawned several sequels, some of the most notable of these being Tekken 3 (1998), Tekken Tag Tournament (1999) and Tekken 5 (2005).

Marathon

Date of release: December 1994

Region: USA

Developer: Bungie

Publisher: Bungie

Platform: Macintosh

Designed by Jason Jones and Alex Seropian, Marathon is a single-player and multiplayer first-person shooter and the first game in the Marathon trilogy. The game is set in the year 2794 AD on the titular UESC Marathon, a massive colony ship built from the Martian moon Deimos and which is travelling to the Tau Ceti solar system. With a population of thousands of colonists, the Marathon has been in deep space for hundreds of years when it finally reaches the planet Tau-Ceti 4. Aliens subsequently attack the Marathon, and Durandal, one of Marathon's three AIs, goes rampant – a form of AI self-awareness which typically results in destructive impulses. It is the player's aim to defeat the aliens swarming inside the Marathon and stop Durandal. The player is assisted in their task by Leela, one of Marathon's other and still-benevolent AIs.

Marathon was quite different from what was referred to as Doom clones in that it had a strong narrative often derived from interacting with computer terminals. It was also the first first-person shooter to allow the player to look and shoot up and down, rather than having this axis locked. This feature became a prerequisite for all first-person shooters to come. The game also featured texture mapping and dynamic lighting. In multiplayer mode, Marathon can host a deathmatch of up to eight players via a Local Area Network (LAN). Marathon was also one of the first video games to feature live audio chat.

The game was highly lauded for its graphics, fast-paced gameplay and narrative. Even though Marathon was not Bungie's (the developer who would later be synonymous with their ground-breaking Halo: Combat Evolved (2001) game) first successful game, it certainly earned the company a lot of recognition. It is interesting to note that Marathon had many similarities to the aforementioned Halo: Combat Evolved (2001). Both are sci-fi FPS, the interior of the UESC Marathon feels akin to the interior of the UNSC Pillar of Autumn in which the first and last missions of Halo take place, and the AI Leela could be compared to Halo's Cortana. Marathon spawned two sequels in what is now known as the Marathon trilogy with Marathon 2: Durandal (1995) and Marathon Infinity (1996). Marathon was eventually ported to Windows in 2011.

1994 Notable Omissions

3dfx founded. Alien Breed: Tower Assault, Alien Vs Predator. All New World of Lemmings. Alone in the Dark 3. Alpine Racer. Battle Isle 2. Battletoads (arcade version). Blackthorne. Breath of Fire II. Brian Lara Cricket. Busby II. Crusader of Centy. Cannon Fodder 2. Darkstalkers: The Night Walkers. Demon's Crest. Doctor Hauzer. Donkey Kong 94. Ecco: The Tides of Time. Game Developer Magazine. Gravity Power. Heretic. Jagged Alliances. Jazz Jackrabbit. King's Field. King's Quest VII: The Princeless Bride. Iron Soldier. Liberation. Lunar: Eternal Blue. Lufia & the Fortress of Doom. Magic Carpet. Master of Magic. Mega Man 6. Mega Man X2. Mega Turrican. Metal Marines. Micro Machines 2: Turbo Tournament. Monster Max. Neo Geo CD. Nintendo PowerFest '94. Outpost. PC-FX. Policenauts. Quadrax. Raiden DX. Point Blank. Rise of the Robots. Popful Mail. Ravenloft: Strahd's Possession. Reunion. Ridge Racer 2. Samurai Showdown II. Scorched Tanks. Shining Force CD. Snatcher. Sparkster. Spider-man and Venom: Maximum Carnage. Star Crusader. Streets of Rage 3. Sub-Terrania. Subwar 2050. Super Star Wars: Return of the Jedi. Super Game Boy. Super Punch-Out!! Tempest 2000. The Lion King. Tiger Games. Tokimeki Memorial. Total Eclipse. Under a Killing Moon. Uniracers. Urban Strike. Virtuality 2000 series. Wario's Woods. Wing Commander III Heart of the Tiger. Zoda's Revenge: StarTropics II.

1995

Bioware founded

The video game developer Bioware was founded in Alberta, Canada in February 1995 by Ray Muzyka and Greg Zeschuk. Their first game was Shattered Steel (1996), a mech simulation game released on MS-DOS. The company's second game, Baldur's Gate (1998), was a licensed Dungeons and Dragons game and a huge success with sales in excess of two million units. Bioware is best known for its D&D series (1998-2002), Star Wars: Knights of The Old Republic series (2003- 2011), Mass Effect series (2007-2017) and Dragon Age series (2009-current date). Bioware was bought by Electronic Arts in 2007.

Star Wars: Dark Forces

Date of release: February 1995

Region: USA

Developer: LucasArts

Publisher: LucasArts

Platform: MS-DOS

Designed by Daron Stinnet, Ray Gresko and Justin Chin of LucasArts, Star Wars: Dark Forces is a single-player, 3D, first-person shooter. You play as mercenary Kyle Katarn, whose services are hired by the Rebel Alliance. The game is comprised of a series of missions, the first of which involves recovering the plans for the Death Star. The rest of the game's missions involve the discovery and subsequent foiling of the Empire's Dark Trooper Project. The Dark Troopers are an experimental and highly lethal super Stormtrooper (although they are surprisingly easy to kill) which pose a serious threat to the Rebels. Dark Forces' gameplay consists of similar elements to other FPS games of the time. The player faces familiar villains from the Star Wars universe, such as Stormtroopers, different kinds of Imperial droids, Gamorrean Guards, and bounty hunters including Boba Fett. To deal with these enemies, the player has access to a number of offensive weapons as well as other items to help in a wide variety of environments. Ammunition and power-ups are scattered throughout each mission. Star

Wars: Dark Forces contains fourteen missions overall.

After Doom (1993) there was a whole slew of first-person shooter games, and it was seen as being only a matter of time until a Star Wars FPS game was developed. Star Wars: Dark Forces was praised for its graphics and level design. It featured more freedom of movement than some of its FPS predecessors, boasting multiple floor levels and graphical innovations such as animated textures and haze. However, some were disappointed with the marked absence of a useable and iconic lightsaber and the game not having multiplayer capability. Star Wars: Dark Forces was ported to the PlayStation in 1996 and has sold almost a million units. It became the first game in the Star Wars Jedi Knight series (games in which the player would get to wield a lightsaber) which include: Star Wars Jedi Knight: Dark Forces II (1997), Star Wars Jedi Knight: Mysteries of the Sith (1998), Star Wars Jedi Knight II: Jedi Outcast (2002) and Star Wars Jedi Knight: Jedi Academy (2003).

Magical Pop'n

Date of release: March 1995

Region: Japan

Developer: Polestar

Publisher: Pack-in-Video

Platform: Super Famicom

Magical Pop'n is a single-player, side-scrolling, action-platform game. The aim is to recover a Magic Jewel stolen from the kingdom of To'ahl by the Demon King, who seeks to use it to control the world. You play as the Princess of To'ahl and must battle numerous foes to complete your quest. The player can use their standard sword attack to defeat the variety of enemies pitted against them or use certain spells, each of which has a standard casting mode and can also be overcharged. These spells include Energy Beam, Exploding Wand (which acts like a bomb), Magic Chain (the basic version acts as a grappling hook allowing you to swing across pits, while the overcharged version fires lethal chains in every direction), Ice Blast, Fire Blast, and Inner Sonic (a dash attack). Each time you use one of these spells it costs the player a number of stars, ranging from two to twenty. Therefore, it is paramount to collect as many stars as possible and use them wisely. There are six stages in Magical Pop'n, each laid out in a non-linear fashion. Players can attempt to finish the stage as quickly as possible or take their time and explore. However, Magical Pop'n does not feature any 'save game' utility and so the player must complete the game in one sitting, which did not go down well with some.

Magical Pop'n was praised for its graphics, animation, game mechanics (in particular its control system) and music. Since its release, Magical Pop'n has garnered a cult following and is one of the rarest Super Famicom titles; an average copy is thought to be worth around £1,500 or $1900.

Descent

Date of release: March 1995

Region: Worldwide

Developer: Parallax Software

Publisher: Interplay Productions

Platform: MS-DOS

Designed by Mike Kulas and Matt Toschlog, Descent is a single-player or multiplayer, first-person shooter. The aim of Descent is to destroy several mines located on numerous planets and moons in the solar system by destroying each mine's reactor. The player must deal out death and destruction to the multitude of robots (which have been infected by a virus) that attempt to stand in your way. You must also try and rescue hostages within the mine. Colour-coded keys must be obtained to progress further into the mine to reach and subsequently destroy the current mine's reactor. Shield orbs and ammunition are scattered throughout the levels to help the player survive. The mine's layouts can be rather complex, though luckily the player can view a 3D wireframe map of it in its entirety. Multiplayer involves either cooperative play of up to four players, with the aim of destroying the mine and earning the prestige of the highest score, or three deathmatch modes of up to eight players in total.

Descent was highly praised for its graphics and arcade action and, in particular, was noted for its six degrees of movement that offered freedom of movement rarely experienced before on a home system. It also had a 640 x 480 resolution, which was the gold standard for FPSs in the mid-nineties. Its only criticism was that some players experienced motion sickness while playing.

Taking its inspiration from the developers of Doom (with which it was often compared), Descent was released as shareware, with seven levels available to try out and twenty levels in the full retail version. This model was becoming more common in this decade, the idea being that players would get a taste of the game and, if the game were good enough, couldn't resist purchasing the full product. It was soon ported to the Macintosh, PlayStation and much later to Windows. Like Doom, Descent was opened up for modding. In 1997, its source code was made available for anyone to create their own version of the game. Barring expansion packs, Descent has spawned two sequels: Descent II (1996) and Descent 3 (1999). Descent is often credited as being the first free-roaming fully-3D First Person Shooter (where everything in the game, not just the environments but the character as well, are 3D models), a full year before the highly acclaimed Quake (1996).

Panzer Dragoon

Date of release: March 1995

Region: Japan

Developer: Sega, Team Andromeda

Publisher: Sega

Platform: Sega Saturn

Directed by Yukio Futatsugi, Team Andromeda, Panzer Dragoon is a single-player, 3D, third-person, rail shooter. Set thousands of years in the future, the aim of Panzer Dragoon is to stop the Black Dragon from reaching the black tower. You play as Keil Fluge who must ride the Blue Dragon, with which he has acquired a psychic connection after the death of the Blue Dragon's previous rider. The player must fly through several different environments on their quest, avoiding obstacles and defeating a multitude of enemies. The player uses Keil's gun to shoot down incoming enemy projectiles (which is imperative for survival), and the dragon's lasers to destroy enemies. There are six levels in Panzer Dragoon. One major aspect that set Panzer Dragoon apart from others in its genre was that the player, while flying in one direction, could still turn and shoot a full 360 degrees around themselves, allowing for a greater degree of freedom than in previous rail shooters.

The game received high praise for this game mechanic as well as its music and amazing 3D graphics, which were some of the best on any home console at the time. It also had a good story, told between gameplay via several cutscenes. This elevated it to more than just another arcade shooter. Panzer Dragoon didn't sell as many units as it deserved to, perhaps due in part to the Saturn's relatively meagre sales in comparison to the PlayStation. It wasn't until word of mouth and other means that the game received the accolade it deserved, and later cult status. It is often cited as one of the best games for the Sega Saturn. Panzer Dragoon spawned a number of sequels with Panzer Dragoon II Zwei (1996), Panzer Dragoon Saga (1998) and Panzer Dragoon Orta (2002). The game received a remake in 2020.

Chrono Trigger

Date of release: March 1995

Region: Japan

Developer: Square

Publisher: Square

Platform: Super Famicom (SNES)

Designed by Takashi Tokita, Yoshinori Kitase, Akihiko Matsui and Hironobu Sakaguchi (who all worked on the Final Fantasy series of games), Yuji Horii and Akira Toriyama (Dragon Quest), and with music by Yasunori Mitsuda and Nobuo Uematsu (Final Fantasy), Chrono Trigger is a single-player or multiplayer RPG. You play as Chrono, who must travel 400 years into the past to save Princess Nadia and then subsequently travel to the future to defeat Lavos before the giant creature can destroy the planet. However, as with many JRPGs, Chrono Trigger's plot is extremely intricate with a narrative that involves a multitude of characters, along with time-travelling into several eras from the ancient past to the far future. Yet at no point does the story feel convoluted: rather, it serves to engage the player and draw them in. Chrono Trigger possesses many of the established elements found in a JRPG, but there are also a number of unique features. Instead of gaining experience as in a typical RPG, in Chrono Trigger characters gain new attacks and combo attacks. Characters can combine their attack with up to two other characters' attacks to create a multi-character combo attack. These attacks range from imaginative and varied to powerful and downright strange at times. The game also coined the option of New Game Plus, which allows the player to play the game again with their previous stats and abilities intact from their previous playthrough. Playing in the New Game Plus option gives the player additional material to keep the game fresh and offer more playability. There are also eleven different endings.

Chrono Trigger was highly praised for its beautiful graphics, well-balanced gameplay, story, sound design, humour and high replay value. It would be one of the last classic games to be developed for the SNES, representing a perfect ending to the 16-bit era as 3D seemed to be the future of gaming. It was ported to the PlayStation in 1999 and much later to the Nintendo DS (adding a multiplayer companion mode), mobile platforms and Windows.

The game spawned a sequel with Chrono Cross (1999). There have been other Chrono games to reach different stages of development, but nothing was ever released. Chrono Trigger is often cited as one of the best games for the Super Famicom/SNES as well as one of the best video games of all time, and it is no wonder when you consider the amount of talented people who worked on it.

D/D's Diner

Date of release: April 1995

Region: Japan

Developer: Warp

Publisher: Panasonic

Platform: 3DO

Designed by Kenji Eno, D (also known as D's Diner) is a 3D, first-person horror-themed interactive movie adventure. You play as Laura Harris and must explore a creepy hospital, which strangely and immediately turns into a castle upon Laura's arrival, and wherein her father has apparently gone on an insane killing spree. Gameplay consists of exploration and solving puzzles, but the core of the game's appeal is its disturbing narrative, compounded further by the fact that the player cannot pause or save the game and has only two hours in which to complete it. There are two different endings dependent on the player's actions at the end of the game.

D was another evolution of games such as Myst (1993) and The 7th Guest (1993), where highly detailed 3D models (for the time) were prerendered, in this case on Amiga 4000s, into Computer-Generated Full-Motion Videos (CG FMVs), with the corresponding FMV being played back depending on the player's input.

Kenji Eno originally submitted a version of D which was far more censored than the original cut of the game for fear that it would not be published. After receiving a rating suitable for teenagers, Eno then submitted the original and uncut version to the publisher. At a time when there were few video games with mature content, D stood apart. Perhaps this is why it quickly garnered a cult following. The game was highly praised for its 3D graphics, story and horror elements, and went on to sell over a million units. It was later released for the Sega Saturn, PlayStation and MS-DOS. D has spawned two sequels with Enemy Zero (1996) and D2 (1999).

Electronic Entertainment Expo (E3)

The first Electronic Entertainment Expo, more commonly referred to as E3, was first held in Los Angeles, California, USA on May 11-13, 1995. E3 came about due to a lack of promotion and visibility of video games at the other computer and electronic expos held at the time. The video game industry was now huge, and had been for some time worth more than the music and movie industry combined. This new trade show would be solely dedicated to the video game industry, its publishers and developers.

E3 became the largest video game expo in the world. However, it was only limited to those with professional connections within the industry. In 2017, attendance was opened up to the general public due to the amount of video game influencers on platforms such as YouTube.

Sid Meier's CivNet

Date of release: 1995

Region: USA

Developer: MicroProse

Publisher: MicroProse

Platform: MS-DOS

Developed by Sid Meier and Bruce Shelly, CivNet is a multiplayer version of Civilization (1991). Up to seven people could play together using either a Local Area Network (LAN) or via a dial-up modem across the internet. Players either took turns in a specific order or all at the same time, meaning the game would only progress once all players had completed their turn. The game also supported a chat mode, allowing for player-to-player communication ranging from negotiation to taunting. Players could also design their own maps using a map editor and customize or personalise the game's assets, allowing for a high degree of creativity.

CivNet didn't change much from the original Civilization, and some fans of the original were more interested in the upcoming Civilization II (1996). However, CivNet had been four years in the waiting for other Civilization players and they loved it.

Phantasmagoria

Date of release: August 1995

Region: USA

Developer: Sierra On-Line

Publisher: Sierra On-Line

Platform: MS-DOS and Microsoft Windows

Designed by Roberta Williams and directed by Peter Maris, Phantasmagoria is a single-player, horror-themed, point-and-click interactive movie. You control Adrienne Williams, a writer who moves into a mansion previously owned by notorious illusionist Zoltan Carnovasch. He was rumoured to have murdered a number of his wives. The aim of the game is to survive the horrors unleashed by the mansion. The game is played from fixed-camera perspectives using live actors originally shot against a bluescreen and then substituted for 3D computer-generated backdrops. Players click on areas of the screen and on objects to move the character and manipulate objects, similar to Myst (1993) or The 7th Guest (1993).

Unlike Myst and The 7th Guest, however, Phantasmagoria had the added complexity of being a third-person game, with a cast of twenty-five actors, over a thousand backgrounds, and a score featuring a 135-voice choir. The cost of development would come to around $4.5 million when it was originally set to be $800,000. There is evidence that Williams went in this direction due to the popularity of violent games such as Doom (1993) and Mortal Kombat (1992).

The pacing of the game can be a little slow and the script and acting are decidedly corny. However, Phantasmagoria's technical achievement at the time cannot be denied, and a lot of thought and hard work went into the production of this game. Phantasmagoria was very successful, despite its many shortcomings. The mild sex, violence and gore, which provoked much controversy upon the game's release, did not hamper its overall popularity. Quite the opposite: it proved to make the game even more alluring, and Phantasmagoria ended up grossing $12 million in its opening weekend, making it one of the best-selling games of 1995 and Sierra's best-selling game to date. Phantasmagoria spawned one sequel with Phantasmagoria: A Puzzle of Flesh (1996).

Super Mario World 2: Yoshi's Island

Date of release: August 1995

Region: Japan

Developer: Nintendo EAD

Publisher: Nintendo

Platform: Super Famicom

Designed by Takashi Tezuka and Shigeru Miyamoto, and with music by Koji Kondo, Super Mario World 2: Yoshi's Island is a single-player or multiplayer, side-scrolling platform game. The aim of Yoshi's Island is to reunite Baby Mario with Baby Luigi. The player controls Yoshi, the friendly dinosaur, and their friends, who all form a relay to carry Baby Mario on their backs across the various levels. Yoshi can run, jump, use a flutter jump to stay in the air longer, and use their long tongue to gobble up an enemy and subsequently spit them out to take out other enemies. Another way they can destroy enemies and otherwise interact with the environment is by aiming and throwing eggs. Yoshi can carry up to six eggs at a time, which can be seen trailing behind him as he moves. There are several power-up items available in-game for Yoshi to use. These include extra life (1-Up Mock Up balloons, with an extra life also gained by collecting the 5 Flowers and 20 Red Coins found scattered around each level), Green Watermelons (allowing Yoshi to spit up to 30 seeds), Red Watermelons (allowing Yoshi to spit fire) and Blue Watermelons (allowing Yoshi to freeze enemies solid). Yoshi can also transform into either a Helicopter, Mole Tank, Submarine, Train or Car for a limited amount of time when collecting the appropriate morph bubbles. If Yoshi is hit by an enemy, Baby Mario is knocked off his back and begins to float away in a bubble as a countdown begins. Yoshi must regain Baby Mario before the timer reaches zero or Baby Mario will be taken away. The game also features bonus challenge minigames, multiple puzzles and boss fights. There are forty-eight levels in Super Mario World 2: Yoshi's Island, spread out across six different and visually distinct worlds.

The stand-out feature of Super Mario World 2: Yoshi's Island is its stylised and hand-drawn graphics, a complete departure from almost all video games of the time, especially as 3D graphics were all the rage. Over a decade later, many games would adopt graphics that would mimic real-world art media such as pastels or watercolours. However, Super Mario World 2: Yoshi's Island with its colouring-book look is perhaps the first game to do so. This unique look was achieved by first drawing everything by hand, then scanning the artwork, and finally touching up these digitised images on the computer. Super Mario World 2: Yoshi's Island has significantly influenced the art style of many future video games.

Super Mario World 2: Yoshi's Island was released on the Game Boy Advance in 2002. Yoshi also featured as the main character in their own series of spin-off games, some of the most notable of these being Yoshi's Island DS (2006), Yoshi's Woolly World (2015) and Yoshi's Crafted World (2019). These Yoshi games would always pay particular attention to alternative art styles. Super Mario World 2: Yoshi's Island is cited by some as one of the best video games of all time.

Wipeout

Date of release: September 1995

Region: UK

Developer: Psygnosis

Publisher: Psygnosis

Platform: PlayStation

Designed by John White, Dominic Mallinson, and Nick Burcome, and with music by Tim Wright, Wipeout is a single-player or multiplayer, 3D, futuristic racing game. Set in the year 2052, the player controls one of the eight selectable high-speed, anti-gravity craft in the four teams comprising the F36000 racing league, with each craft boasting different handling characteristics, top speed and acceleration. On the tracks are power boosts and power-ups that the player can collect. These include mines, missiles, rockets, shields and shockwaves. There are seven tracks total in Wipeout, situated in cities all over the world. If the player can complete all six then the seventh track is unlocked, called Firestar and set on the planet Mars.

The game featured a memorable techno soundtrack featuring music from CoLD StoRAGE, Leftfield, Orbital and The Chemical Brothers. The music was a key component during gameplay, changing tempo dependent on the player's speed, creating a perfect synergy between gameplay, visuals and sound. This music was released on both vinyl and CD in 1996, and once more served to highlight just how important music was to video games.

Wipeout was highly praised for its graphics and music, though some did feel that the difficulty was rather high. Technically, it was far superior to any other racing game on the market and underlined the power of the PlayStation platform. Wipeout was part of a new wave of video games that were perceived as not being just for children or adolescents. With its unique and slick design, presentation (as designed by British graphic design studio The Designers Republic) and music, Wipeout appeared to transcend being more than just a video game, earning cult status almost overnight. Wipeout was yet another game that became part of a new wave of gaming culture where, for the first time, console games could be found in bars, pubs and nightclubs, being played casually alongside other PlayStation games like Tekken (1994) and Gran Turismo (1997).

A PlayStation Link Cable could be used to connect two consoles and facilitate multiplayer, but each player still needed their own television. The game was soon ported to Windows and the Sega Saturn. Wipeout also spawned several sequels, some of the most notable of which are Wipeout 2097 (known as Wipeout XL in North America) (1996), Wipeout 3 (1999) and Wipeout HD (2008).

Rayman

Date of release: September 1995

Region: Europe and North America

Developer: Ubi Studios

Publisher: Ubi Soft Entertainment

Platform: Atari Jaguar and PlayStation

Designed by Gerard Guillemot and Michel Ancel, Rayman is a single-player, 2D, side-scrolling platformer. The aim of Rayman is to retrieve the Protoon which has been taken by Mr. Dark, recover the scattered Electoons and restore balance to the world. The gameplay consists of running, jumping, climbing, avoiding hazards and collecting Electoons. Rayman can take out various enemies with either a quick jab or a much stronger windup punch. He can also use his ears as a helicopter to float to the ground. There are also several power-ups for Rayman to collect. These can provide extra lives, increased speed and more powerful punches. The game features eighteen levels set across six worlds.

Rayman himself is rather an interesting character, as his hands and feet are not visibly attached to his body, but otherwise act as if they are. Michel Ancel originally created the character when he was a teenager, citing influences from various fairy tales. While the original design did indeed have limbs, they had to be removed due to graphical processing issues and technical limitations. Rayman was highly praised for its graphics, especially its quality of animation and music. It is also noted for its difficulty.

The game has been ported to various popular platforms over the years. Rayman is also the best-selling PlayStation 1 game of all time in the UK, illustrating that even though it seemed that everything was 3D, a 2D platform game could still prove very popular. However, the sequel would end up becoming a 3D game. Rayman is the first game in the Rayman franchise, consisting of almost fifty games. Some of the most notable of these games are Rayman 2: The Great Escape (1999), Rayman 3: Hoodlum Havoc (2003), Rayman Origins (2011) and Rayman Legends (2013).

Command and Conquer

Date of release: September 1995

Region: Europe and North America

Developer: Westwood Studios

Publisher: Virgin Interactive Entertainment

Platform: MS-DOS and Mac OS

Command and Conquer is a single-player and multiplayer real-time strategy (RTS) game. Set in an alternate 1990s, the Global Defense Initiative of the United Nations squares up against the cult-like Brotherhood of Nod and their charismatic leader, Kane, as two forces fight over a new resource called Tiberium, spread out across the Earth after a recent meteorite impact in Italy. The player can choose to play either as the GDI or the Brotherhood of Nod, the goal being the destruction of the opposing forces. As with other, similar RTS games, players must gather resources (in this case, Tiberium), to build their base facilities and armies, which they will need to beat the opposing force. A tech tree underpins the mechanics of the game, where the more advanced structures must be researched and built to unlock more powerful units in the game. It is imperative that players explore new areas to discover much-needed resources and protect their base while still keeping up the pressure against enemy units and their base. The game also featured Full Motion Videos (FMVs) to progress the narrative of the campaign. The acting in these sequences was notably cheesy, but at the time became just another part of the game's appeal. Multiplayer presented the opportunity for up to four players to compete against one another using a LAN or a dial-up modem over the internet.

Command and Conquer was a huge success when released and would go on to sell over three million units. It was highly praised for its intuitive control system, the depth of strategy it offered and its music. It was soon ported to a multitude of popular platforms of the time. Westwood Studios had previously established the foundations of the modern RTS genre with Dune II (1992). Blizzard's Warcraft series and what would become the Command and Conquer series would together define the future of RTS games.

The massively popular Command and Conquer series includes many games, some of the most notable of these being Command and Conquer: Tiberium Sun (1999), Command and Conquer: Red Alert 2 (2000), Command and Conquer: Renegade (2002), Command and Conquer: Generals (2003), Command and Conquer 3: Tiberium Wars (2007) and Command and Conquer: Red Alert 3 (2008).

Tactics Ogre: Let Us Cling Together

Date of release: October 1995

Region: Japan

Developer: Quest Corporation

Publisher: Quest Corporation

Platform: Super Famicom

Designed by Yasumi Matsuno, Tactics Ogre: Let Us Cling Together is a single-player, tactical RPG and the sequel to Ogre Battle: The March of the Black Queen (1993). You play as Denim who, with your sister, seeks retribution against the Dark Knights who burned your hometown to the ground, massacred its citizens and kidnapped your father. The story takes place in the land of Valeria where three different ethnic groups are at war.

The game is played from a series of isometric grid-based maps during both combat and the narrative parts of the game, which gives the player options on how they wish to proceed at certain points, changing the direction of the story. The combat is the real meat and potatoes of the game, expanding on turn-based combat in a regular RPG and designed similarly to games such as Fire Emblem: Ankoku Ryu to Hikari No Tsurugi. There are number of different classes in the game, all with different abilities and attributes which level-up after gaining experience on the battlefield. Specific classes have better match-ups against other classes while being weaker against others.

Tactics Ogre: Let Us Cling Together is often cited as helping to establish the gameplay and mechanics of future tactical RPGs. It is often compared with Final Fantasy Tactics (1997), which was released two years after. It cannot be denied that Final Fantasy Tactics has a very similar look, animations and design to Let Us Cling Together. This is due to ex-employees of Quest Corporation working on Square Soft's Final Fantasy Tactics. Let Us Cling Together was also ported to the Sega Saturn and Sony PlayStation. Other games in the Tactics Ogre series include Ogre Battle: Person of Lordly Caliber (1999) and Tactics Ogre: The Knight of Lodis (2001).

Worms

Date of release: October 1995

Region: UK

Developer: Team 17

Publisher: Ocean Software

Platform: Amiga and Amiga CD32

Designed by Andy Davidson of Team 17, Worms is a single-player or multiplayer, 2D, turn-based artillery game. The aim of Worms is to destroy all the other teams' worms. There are a number of options for the player to change when setting up a match, which can result in a wide variety of gameplay experiences, including the move timer (ranging from ten seconds to unlimited, dictating how long a player had to select, move and attack with one of their worms), number of rounds required to win, round time, worm placement, number of land mines per map, action replay, stockpiling (allowing the player to carry over acquired weapons to next round), and much more. The game is played on a 2D landscape. Larger than the screen size and will scroll and zoom to focus on the current player's elected worm. On each turn, a player can move and then take an action with their selected worm. Tools are used to traverse or dig through the landscape, ranging from blow-torches to bungee cords. Weapons vary from melee to ranged and explosives. These weapons vary in the amount of damage they cause to an enemy worm, if indeed they can hit it at all The landscape plays a key role in a player's strategy, as an enemy can be in cover or totally exposed, dependent on the current circumstances. Wind speed and direction must also be considered when using trajectory-based weapons. There are over fifty weapons and tools available in Worms, with the game also featuring ten different landscapes to fight over. The game also came with a Random Landscape Generator. The player could type in a word (such as their own name) or a number, and a landscape would be generated based on that name or number. Landscapes could also be created by players creating their own 960 x 350 8-colour images. Popular landscapes could be downloaded from the World Wide Worm website. All this gave fans of the game plenty to play with. Up to sixteen players could participate in multiplayer games of Worms using the hotseat method, meaning each player jumps on to take their turn at the computer.

Davidson was inspired by Lemmings (1991) and previous artillery games such as Scorched Earth (1991), both of which had cult status on the Amiga platform. Worms was met with mixed reviews, but it cannot be denied that it did have widespread appeal and it ended up selling over five million units across various platforms. The success of Worms spawned several sequels, some of the most notable of which are Worms Armageddon (1999), Worms World Party (2001) and Worms W.M.D. (2016).

Twisted Metal

Date of release: November 1995

Region: USA

Developer: SingleTrac

Publisher: Sony Interactive Entertainment

Platform: PlayStation

Designed by Mike Jackson and Scott Campbell, Twisted Metal is a single-player or multiplayer, 3D, vehicular combat game. Taking place on Christmas Eve of 2005, the aim of Twisted Metal is to destroy all the other competitors in the tenth Twisted Metal competition. Calypso, the organizer of the competition, will grant the winner any one wish, with no limits on the extent, cost or consequences thereof. The player can choose from one of twelve possible colourful combatants. The player can damage other vehicles by ramming or shooting them. However, the player's health is depleted when ramming, so it is safer to shoot them. All vehicles have a pair of machine guns with unlimited ammo, which can overheat. There are also various offensive items scattered around the arena for players to pick up, including missiles, mines, tyre spikes, rearward-firing flame vents, oil slicks and turbo boosts. The standard machine guns on the vehicles are relatively weak, so these pick-ups play a vital role in the player's success. A player can restore some health by driving through 'Health Stations' which take the form of blue ramps. If the player's health is reduced to zero, they lose a life, with a player only having three lives. There are six combat arenas in Twisted Metal, each one larger and featuring more combatants and thus higher difficulty than the last. The game has multiple FMV end cutscenes dependent on who the character plays as.

The game was fairly well received. Players loved the violent, chaotic gameplay and the variety of vehicles and their drivers. While Twisted Metal did receive criticism for its below-average graphics, it could not be denied that many people loved the game and had a lot of fun. The game was ported to Windows in 1996. Twisted Metal spawned several sequels, some of the most notable of which are Twisted Metal 2: World Tour (1996), Twisted Metal III (1998), Twisted Metal 4 (1999), Twisted Metal: Black (2001) and Twisted Metal: Head-On (2005).

GameFAQs

The GameFAQs website was launched in November 1995 by Jeff Veasey. GameFAQs (Frequently Asked Questions) was developed in an effort to collate a number of online video game guides in one place. The site started with ten pages and hundreds of FAQs, and it now hosts thousands of pages and has around eighteen million visitors per month, making it one of the most successful video game websites. GameFAQs content also includes news, reviews, walkthroughs, cheats and discussion boards.

Donkey Kong Country 2: Diddy's Kong Quest

Date of release: November 1995

Region: Japan

Developer: Rare

Publisher: Nintendo

Platform: Super Famicom (SNES)

Donkey Kong Country 2: Diddy's Kong Quest is a single-player or multiplayer, side-scrolling platform game and the sequel to the successful Donkey Kong Country (1994). You play as either Diddy Kong or his girlfriend Dixie Kong, the latter's first appearance in the Donkey Kong series. The aim of the game is to rescue Donkey Kong who has been abducted by King K.Rool. This sequel features similar gameplay and mechanics to the original, although in this game you play as Diddy and Dixie, between whom the player can switch. Because each character has different abilities, certain sections of the game lend themselves to using one character more than the other. The player typically starts as Diddy. If he is hit by an enemy then control switches to Dixie and vice versa. The player can retrieve their lost character from barrels scattered across the levels marked 'DK'. If their last character is hit, then the player loses a life. If all lives are lost, the game subsequently ends. There are fifty-two levels spread across eight worlds in Donkey Kong Country 2: Diddy Kong's Quest.

Rare used the same pre-rendered 3D imagery technique for their sprites as they had in Donkey Kong Country, giving it a unique look among other 2D platformers. Donkey Kong Country 2: Diddy Kong's Quest was highly praised for its graphics and gameplay. Many welcomed its higher difficulty and said that it improved on the original in every way. The game is often cited as one of the best platformers of all time and was ported to the Game Boy Advance in 2004.

Suikoden

Date of release: December 1995

Region: Japan

Developer: Konami

Publisher: Konami

Platform: PlayStation

Suikoden is a single-player, 2D JRPG. The aim is to overthrow the Scarlet Moon Empire, by collecting all 108 warriors, referred to in-game as the Stars of Destiny who are recruitable characters. However, things are not that straightforward. You play as Tir fighting for the rebels against General Teo McDohl of the Empire, who unfortunately is your father. Suikoden is like other JRPGs of the time in that the player explores the world, interacting with NPCs and levelling through fighting a variety of enemies. Battles are random and combat is turn-based, either taking place against a single or small group of foes or on a much larger scale with two armies. The first instance is seen from an isometric view, the mechanics of which are similar to other turn-based RPGs of the day. The military battles are portrayed from a side view with many more characters on a large battlefield. The player can choose to use charge, bow or magic against the enemy in the large-scale battles, analogous to the game of Rock, Paper, Scissors: charge attacks, for instance, beat bow attacks but lose to magic attacks

The game was praised for its story, which was quite different from the usual 'saving the world' narrative of most other RPGs and was mainly focused on character development and the corrupt Empire, and the 107 (as Tir is the 108th) other recruitable characters, most of whom are playable.

The game was ported to the Sega Saturn and Microsoft Windows in 1998. Suikoden also had a feature where the player could import their save file into the sequel, Suikoden II (1998). Suikoden also spawned other sequels and spin-off games. Some of the most notable are the aforementioned Suikoden II (1998), Suikoden III (2002) and Suikoden V (2006). The Suikoden games have garnered a strong cult following since their inception.

Warcraft II: Tides of Darkness

Date of release: December 1995

Region: North America

Developer: Blizzard Entertainment

Publisher: Davidson & Associates

Platform: Mac OS and Windows

Developed by Sam Didier, Michael Morhaime, Patrick Wyatt and Ron Miller, Warcraft II: Tides of Darkness is a single-player or multiplayer RTS and the sequel to Warcraft: Orcs & Humans. Set six years after the first game, the aim of Warcraft II depends on the chosen campaign. The player can choose to play either the Orc campaign or the Human campaign. Once completed, they can choose to play the other, with the scenarios getting more difficult as the player progresses through the narrative of the game. The User Interface is split up into two parts. On the right and taking up most of the screen is a top-down perspective view of the game world, showing troops, buildings and the surrounding environment. Areas not explored are covered in the now-familiar darkness of the fog of war as established in Warcraft: Orcs & Humans and must be explored to be revealed. On the left is an overview of the current map as well as any troops or buildings selected and the possible commands that can be given to said troops or buildings. Resources comprise of gold, lumber and oil are displayed at the top of the screen. There is an elaborate tech tree that underpins the mechanics of the game, where players must build and research to unlock more advanced buildings, units and unit abilities. Units consist of resource gatherers, melee, ranged, siege, spellcaster (who have some spectacular abilities like summoning a destructive blizzard, turning another unit into a sheep or raising the dead), aerial, demolition and sea units. Some of these units featured other races such as Elves, Gnomes, Dwarves, Ogres and Goblins.

Warcraft II saw some vast improvements from the first game. As well as graphics and sound, there were now far more units. Players could select larger groups of units, originally only four but now nine. Players were also no longer forced to build alongside roads, as was the case in the first game. Warcraft II also introduced naval combat. The game also had plenty of humour. Clicking on units multiple times would reveal a vast array of hidden and humorous responses, of which there are hundreds in total. Multiplayer involved using a LAN or dial-up modem and could cater for up to eight players.

The game was a huge success and was highly praised for its graphics, strategy elements, range of units and sound. It firmly established the Warcraft franchise and paved the way for future Blizzard games including StarCraft (1998). Blizzard released an official expansion pack in Warcraft II: Beyond the Dark Portal (1996). Many players were still hungry for more and Blizzard allowed third-party developers to release their own expansion packs, meaning that there were hundreds of levels available for fans to play. Blizzard also released the Battle.net edition (1999) allowing players to play online with greater ease than before.

Warcraft II was the best-selling computer game of 1995, has sold over three million units since its release and has won multiple awards. It is often cited as one of the best video games of all time.

Virtual Boy

The Virtual Boy (originally dubbed the VR32) was released in Japan in December 1995. Developed by Nintendo, the Virtual Boy is a 32-bit, fifth-generation, cartridge-based mobile games console.

Using parallax scrolling effects, the Virtual Boy was able to give games a sense of depth: not really virtual reality but stereoscopic 3D graphics. The console itself was a large head-mounted display on a stand. The player had to position their eyes up to the lenses to view the games, with the games themselves displayed in red monochrome, of which there were only twenty-two released.

The Virtual Boy is regarded as a huge failure for Nintendo with its unimpressive 3D (which often gave players headaches), its monochrome graphics, high price, lack of good games and lack of portability. It would appear that this time, the available technology was just not yet able to reach what Nintendo was hoping for.

Time Crisis

Date of release: December 1995

Region: Japan

Developer: Namco

Publisher: Namco

Platform: Arcade

Time Crisis is a single-player, first-person, 3D, light gun rail shooter. The aim of Time Crisis is to save President MacPherson's daughter, who has been captured by Sherudo Garo. You play as agent Richard Miller and must deal with a multitude of enemies to achieve your goal. Time Crisis was Namco's answer to Sega's Virtua Cop (1994). It differentiated itself from its competition in that it had a cover system. The player could press and release a foot pedal on the arcade cabinet to toggle ducking behind cover and reloading their weapon. However, there was a timer to dissuade players from staying in cover for too long. The timer can be extended by dispatching specific enemies quickly and finishing each area. There are three stages in Time Crisis, with each stage comprising three areas.

The game was generally well received, though comparisons were inevitably made with Virtua Cop. Some people preferred Time Crisis for its cover system, while others thought Virtua Cop was the better game as Time Crisis lacked power-ups, innocent bystanders (to avoid shooting), and multiplayer. This would be rectified in later games.

The game was ported to the PlayStation and later to the PlayStation 2. Time Crisis spawned several sequels, some of the most notable of which are Time Crisis II (1998), Time Crisis 3 (2002) and Time Crisis 4 (2006).

Lego Fun to Build

Date of release: December 1995

Region: Japan

Developer: The Lego Group

Publisher: Sega

Platform: Sega Pico/Kids Computer Pico

Lego Fun to Build is a single-player, multi-genre game. Gameplay involves a number of mini-games, such as building Lego models with a scoring element, a racing game, an underwater side-scrolling game, an air hockey game and a 3D Lego free building game.

Apart from the 3D aspect, the game played and sounded like something from a decade earlier. However, this is perhaps to be expected when considering it was developed for an educational platform. The game itself was never released outside of Japan, and even though there is nothing remarkable about the game, it is significant in that it is the first Lego video game, of which there have since been a great many. It may be worth noting here some of the best: Lego Star Wars: The Complete Saga (2007), Lego Batman 2: DC Super Heroes (2012), Lego Marvel Super Heroes (2013), Lego Dimensions (2015) and Lego Star Wars: The Force Awakens (2016).

Tales of Phantasia

Date of release: December 1995

Region: Japan

Developer: Wolf Team

Publisher: Namco

Platform: Super Famicom (SNES)

Tales of Phantasia is a single-player RPG and the first in the 'Tales of' series, also known as Tales of series. The aim of Tales of Phantasia is to travel through time in an attempt to defeat Dhaos, the evil sorcerer king. You play as Cress Albane, a young swordsman, who is accompanied by his ever-expanding group of comrades. Combat itself is in real-time using the Linear Motion Battle System (LMBS). All combatants are lined up on the ground facing off on a 2D plane. The player controls Cress while the AI controls the other two characters in the currently-selected party, though the player can choose how aggressive these players fight and if they want to take manual control to cast a spell, for instance. Characters can also combine attacks to devastating effect. Such confrontations are random happenstance in the game, in the same manner as the Final Fantasy games.

Tales of Phantasia was praised for its graphics and sound and is often cited as one of the best RPGs for the Super Famicom. It was ported to PlayStation as a Japanese-exclusive game in 1998. It was not released in the West until 2006 and then only on the Game Boy Advance. The game has inspired the publishing of a series of seven novels, a manga first published in 2008 and a four-episode anime series. However, the most significant result of Tales of Phantasia is the many other video games and spin-off titles it has spawned. Some of the most notable of these games are Tales of Symphonia (2003), Tales of the Abyss (2005), Tales of Vesperia (2008), Tales of Xillia (2011), Tales of Berseria (2016) and Tales of Arise (2021).

1995 Notable Omissions

3D Lemmings. Air Combat. Alblon. Alien Soldier. Anvil of Dawn. Ascendancy. Battle Arena Toshinden. Battle Arena Toshinden 2. BioForge. Brain Dead 13. Castlevania: Dracula X. Chop Suey. Clock Tower. College Football USA 96. Comix Zone. Destruction Derby. DonPachi. Discworld. Dogz: Your Computer Pet. Dragon Quest VI: Realms of Revelation. Earthworm Jim 2. Ein no Filena/Eternal Filena. Eternal Champions: Challenge from the Dark Side. Fade to Black. Final Fight 3. Flight Unlimited. Full Throttle. Front Mission. Gex. Heroes of Might and Magic: A Strategic Quest. Hexen. Hyper Iria. I Have No Mouth and I Must Scream. immercenary/Perfect World. Jagged Alliance. Jumping Flash!. King Arthur & the Knights of Justice. King's Field II. Kirby's Dream Land 2. Legend of Illusion Starring Mickey Mouse. Light Crusader. Lucienne's Quest. Marathon 2: Durandal. Mario's Picross. Master of Magic. Mechwarrior 2: 31st Century Combat. Mega

Man 7. Mega Man X3. Monster Max. Mortal Kombat 3. Panel de Pon. Police Quest: SWAT. Quest for Fame. Return Fire. Ristar. Road Rash 3. RPG Maker 95. R-Zone. Satellaview. Secret of Evermore. Seiken Densetsu 3/Trials of Mana. Sid Meier's Colonization. Souls Edge (first Soulcalibur game). Star Trek: The Next Generation – A Final Unity. Star Wars: Rebel Assault II. Steel Panthers. Street Fighter: The Movie. Super Bomberman 3. Super Mario World 2: Yoshi's Island. Sylvan Tale. Tekken 2. Terranigma. The 11thHour. The Beast Within: A Gabriel Knight Mystery. The Dig. The King of Fighters '95. The Orion Conspiracy. The Ruins of Cawdor. Tokimeki Memorial: Forever With You. Torin's Passage. Undercover Cops. VFX1 Headgear. Virtua Cop 2. Wing Commander IV: The Price of Freedom. X-COM: Terror from the Deep. Zeewolf.

1996

Guardian Heroes

Date of release: January 1996

Region: Japan

Developer: Treasure

Publisher: Sega

Platform: Sega Saturn

Designed by Tetsuhiko Kikuchi and Masaki Ukyo, Guardian Heroes is a single-player or multiplayer, side-scrolling, 2D, hack and slash RPG. The aim of Guardian Heroes is to defeat the wizard-king Kanon. The game can be played in either Story Mode or Versus Mode. Versus Mode allows up to six players to fight one another, choosing which character to fight as. The player can also choose from four different characters in the Story Mode. Defeating the multitude of enemies sent to stop them earns experience points that can be used to improve the character's many stats, notably Strength, Vitality, Intelligence, Mentality, Agility and Luck. Players can move and fight in the foreground, mid-ground or background plane, enabling them to evade attacks and engage different enemies situated across these various planes. The game also features branching paths between levels, facilitating alternate playthroughs against different bosses and featuring differing endings. This gives the game immense replayability.

At a time when many game developers were making the transition to 3D, Guardian Heroes was a love letter to the 2D, side-scrolling, hack and slash or beat 'em up genre. It brought arcade-style action into the home with a new IP. The game was highly praised for its anime-style cutscenes, characters, gameplay, multiple paths, three-plane mechanic, and music. It is often cited as one of the best games for the Sega Saturn platform. Guardian heroes spawned one sequel with Advance Guardian Heroes (2004).

Duke Nukem 3D

Date of release: January 1996 shareware version first episode, April 1996 full version

Region: USA

Developer: 3D Realms

Publisher: FormGen

Platform: MS-DOS

Duke Nukem 3D is a single-player or multiplayer, first-person shooter and the third game in the Duke Nukem series. It is the first Duke Nukem game to make the transition to 3D. The aim of the game is simple: stop the alien invasion. You play as the titular hero and, as with many games that took their inspiration from Doom (1993), must dispatch a host of enemies using an array of weapons and excessive violence. However, Duke Nukem had a lot of new features not found in Doom and many of its other clones. As well as the usual weapons of FPSs of the day, Duke Nukem 3D featured several unique ones such as the Pipe Bomb or the Laser Tripbomb, which could be thrown or placed and subsequently activated. The game also featured the Shrinker, which shrinks the enemy down allowing Duke to then crush them underfoot, and the Freezethrower, which freezes an enemy that Duke can then shoot or kick shattering them to pieces.

The game also saw an evolution in control from its predecessors. This was the first time that a player could crouch (and thus duck into cover), jump and sprint in a first-person shooter, allowing for a much greater degree of freedom of movement and making for a true milestone in the genre. The environments were far more destructible than in previous FPS games: barrels could explode, windows shatter, and holes could be blown into walls. The game's graphics were also a huge improvement. Duke Nukem 3D could be played at a whopping 800 x 600 pixels whereas Doom was played at 320 x 200. The difference was immense.

What else set Duke Nukem apart from other FPS games was the emphasis on his character and one-liners. Duke is a satirical portrayal of the Hollywood action heroes of the 1980s and 1990s. The game had some critics, citing its protagonist as vulgar, and that the game itself was promoting sex and violence. However, most critics and players loved the game. Duke Nukem 3D was a perfect sign of the times in the video game zeitgeist. It seemed to embody that rebellious punk rock era of gaming.

Multiple versions of the game would be released over the years, each adding new levels, enemies, weapons and overall improvements in graphics and sound. It was also ported to many different platforms. With the arrival of Quake later this same year, moving the first-person shooter completely over to 3D, Duke Nukem 3D would be one of the last in this era of 3D environments mixed with 2D character sprite FPS games.

Pokémon Red and Green/Red and Blue

Date of release: February 1996

Region: Japan

Developers: Game Freak

Publisher: Nintendo

Platform: Game Boy

Directed by Satoshi Tajiri and produced by Shigeru Miyamoto (of the Donkey Kong, Mario and The Legend of Zelda franchises), Pokémon Red and Green (originally called Pocket Monsters: Red and Green when released in Japan) is a single-player or multiplayer RPG. The aim of Pokémon Red and Green is to become the best Pokémon trainer there ever was, by collecting all eight Gym Badges from their respective Gym Leaders by beating them in a Pokémon battle, resulting in access to the Indigo Plateau and permitting the player to subsequently and consecutively challenge the Elite Four and the reigning Pokémon Champion. An optional goal of the game is to collect all 151 Pokémon. However, each of the two editions has Pokémon unique to only that version of the game, requiring external Pokémon trading. Similar to other RPGs of the time, the players are viewed from a top-down perspective where they can explore the Kanto region and interact with various NPCs. When entering into turn-based combat against an opponent or a wild Pokémon, the view changes to a third-person perspective (similar to Shining Force (1992)) and the player's character uses their Pokémon creatures to fight on their behalf. Each Pokémon has different attacks and abilities to use in battle to weaken the opposing Pokémon, successful attacks reducing its HP. When a Pokémon's HP drops to zero, it faints. Pokémon gain XP per opponent defeated, levelling up and even evolving after the battle is over should their level be sufficient, gaining higher stats and new attacks.

One of the mechanics of the game that set it apart from other games was the ability to capture wild Pokémon using a Poké Ball. This was an idea inspired by Satoshi Tajiri's childhood obsession with studying insects near his family home. The capture of a wild Pokémon was not a sure thing, however, as the success of the attempt was determined by the strength of the Poké Ball chosen for the capture attempt, and the current HP of the Pokémon the player was attempting to capture, plus any potential status conditions the Pokémon was afflicted with. When using the Game Boy Link Cable, players of Red and Blue could go head-to-head and battle it out with their team of six Pokémon or trade, with some Pokémon being game-exclusive as mentioned beforehand, while others required trading to evolve. For some, collecting all 151 Pokémon was the true lure of the game.

The games were soon released as Pokémon Red and Blue in the West in 1998. Initial sales were slow, as the Game Boy was at the end of its life and this new game didn't look like anything special. However, appearances can be deceiving, and Pokémon would only grow in popularity. With the allure of trading necessary to find the hidden and elusive 151st Pokémon and thus fill the Pokédex, the thrill of Pokémon battles and the collecting and raising of the perfect team, the game would go on to become a worldwide cultural phenomenon.

Pokémon Red and Green/Pokémon Red and Blue is often cited as one of the best video games of all time and is the most successful video game of the 1990s, selling more than 47 million units since its initial release. This is incredible when considering the evolution of video game graphics and the consumer's eagerness for 3D games. It is a testament to Pokémon Red and Green/Pokémon Red and Blue gameplay and mechanics that this simple-looking monochrome game was so astoundingly popular.

Pokémon Red and Green/Pokémon Red and Blue was the first game in the Pokémon series, which would lead to the most successful video game franchise of all time spawning merchandise, trading card games, and an equally long-running series of multiple anime series and films. Since their release, these games have had subsequent remakes on more recent platforms. Of the many much-loved Pokémon games, some of the most notable are Pokémon Gold and Silver (1999), Pokémon Ruby and Sapphire (2002), Pokémon X and Y (2013), Pokémon Sun and Moon (2016), and Pokémon Sword and Shield (2019). Pokémon has also spawned many spin-off Pokémon games, such as the Pokémon Ranger and Pokémon Mystery Dungeon series.

Resident Evil/Bio Hazard

Date of release: March 1996

Region: Japan

Developers: Capcom

Publisher: Capcom

Platform: PlayStation

Originally conceptualised as a remake of Sweet Home (1989) and designed by Shinji Mikami and Tokuro Fujiwara (of Ghost 'n Goblins (1985) & Sweet Home (1989)), Resident Evil, known as Bio Hazard in Japan, is a single-player, third-person, survival horror game and the first in the highly successful Resident Evil series. The aim of Resident Evil is to discover what happened to your fellow STARS (Special Tactics And Rescue Service) elite task force members, who were investigating a bizarre series of mass murders in Raccoon City, and to subsequently survive and escape alive. The game begins with the 'so bad it's good,' FMV cutscene of the STARS team investigating the outskirts of the city, before being attacked by some unknown creature. Once the team reaches a nearby mansion, the game switches to the traditional 3D graphics of the time. The player starts the game by choosing to play as either Chris Redfield or Jill Valentine and can walk, run, explore, stab and shoot to defeat a multitude of zombies and other monsters throughout the game. To progress through to other areas of the mansion, the player must solve puzzles for which the series would become well known. Typical puzzles would involve finding the pieces to subsequently place in a statue and opening a new room or passageway. The game placed high emphasis on inventory management and conservation of ammunition, the latter of which is severely limited. The limited aspect also extends to the sparse placement of healing items such as First Aid Sprays or herbs (which can be mixed to combine their effects, ranging from healing to curing poison). Progress can only be saved in specific rooms using a typewriter and an acquired ink ribbon, with these also being found in limited quantities.

Resident Evil is played through a series of fixed camera views. The characters are rendered in real-time, however, the majority of the environment is pre-rendered allowing for a more realistic look with higher quality textures and crisper shadows. These were rendered on Silicon Graphics workstations using Soft Image. The game had four different endings depending on which character you played as and whether you were able to rescue any other STARS members.

Resident Evil is regarded as the father of modern-day survival horror games, a genre that had not quite been fully codified until the tenets introduced by this game. Jump scares, the feeling of omnipresent dread and trepidation and limited resources essential to survival would become synonymous with the genre, spawning a whole series of Resident Evil games that would not only influence other video games but also revitalise interest in zombies across all media. It was a huge success and sold over five million units, making it the best-selling PlayStation game at the time. It is often cited as one of the greatest video games of all time (despite the corny voice acting) and is Capcom's most successful video game franchise.

Resident Evil was soon ported to Windows, the Sega Saturn and much later to the Nintendo DS. A Resident Evil remastered remake was also released in 2002. Some of the most notable Resident Evil games are Resident Evil 2 (1998), Resident Evil (remake) (2002), Resident Evil Zero (2002), Resident Evil 4 (2005), Resident Evil 7: Biohazard (2017) and the remake of Resident Evil 2 (2019).

Super Mario RPG: Legend of the Seven Stars

Date of release: March 1996

Region: Japan

Developer: Square

Publisher: Nintendo

Platform: Super Famicom/ Super Nintendo Entertainment System

Directed by Yoshihiko Maekawa and Chihiro Fujioka, and produced by Shigeru Miyamoto, Super Mario RPG: Legend of the Seven Stars is a single-player, isometric RPG. The game begins with Bowser kidnapping Princess Toadstool. Usually, the aim of the game would be to rescue her. However, the goal of this game changes when a giant sword falls from the sky, breaking the Star Road and scattering the seven stars that antagonist Smithy and his gang are after. The actual aim of the game is to find the seven stars and defeat Smithy and his cronies. Bowser, amongst several others, becomes a controllable character in this party-based RPG. Super Mario RPG: Legend of the Seven Stars features all the usual game mechanics of a JRPG incorporating Mario and his supporting characters. However, as well as being isometric, Legend of the Seven Stars boasts several unique features. Foremost among these is a timing element, used during the turn-based combat part of the game. A well-timed button press during an attack or when being attacked significantly increases your hit points or defence, thus maximising or limiting damage, respectively. There are also various mini-games and a substantial amount of platform gameplay, with coin collecting. All in all, these features help make it feel more like a typical Mario game, rather than a generic RPG with a Mario skin on it.

Originally Super Mario RPG: Legend of the Seven Stars was going to be a top-down RPG, but upon considering the success of the pre-rendered backgrounds and sprites of Donkey Kong Country (1994), the development team decided to use Silicon Graphics workstations to pre-render a 3D world with an isometric view instead with fantastic results.

Super Mario RPG: Legend of the Seven Stars was highly acclaimed by critics and consumers alike, praising its graphics, humour, gameplay, and beautiful music by Yoko Shimomura. Even the most cynical were blown away by how well Mario and his friends had been translated into the RPG genre. The game is often cited as one of the best games for the SNES and one of the best video games of all time. It never saw a true sequel due to Square working with Sony's PlayStation and wanting to focus on CD-ROM media as opposed to cartridge-based games. However, Nintendo did use similar RPG elements in Paper Mario (2000) and other Mario games since.

Dragon Force

Date of release: March 1996

Region: Japan

Developer: J-Force

Publisher: Sega

Platform: Sega Saturn

Dragon Force is a single-player, real-time strategy RPG. Set in the fantasy world of Legendra, the aim of the game is to unite the warring nations of Legendra and battle against the armies of the evil god Madruk. The game consists of narrative (some of which takes the form of cutscenes) and administrative sections (such as making selections between various generals and troop choices), an overview of the map and, naturally, the all-important combat. The combat takes part in a large, pseudo-3D side-scrolling area where the camera can either automatically follow the action or be player-controlled. The player can also control what kind of troops they want as well as their formation, pausing the action and issuing commands at any time to any number of their army, which can be up to one hundred soldiers strong. The player can also use their officer's special (often magical) attack, and terrain also plays a role in how successful you are. These combat rounds last for 90 seconds. If all the troops are wiped out in battle, then the two remaining generals can enter a duel to decide the outcome. The RPG elements of the game involve improving your stats and gaining new abilities the more battles are won.

Dragon Force was highly acclaimed for its story, characters, RPG elements and combat. With up to two hundred soldiers fighting it out in a pitched battle, nothing quite like it had been seen before and it made for quite the immersive spectacle. Dragon Force is often considered one of the best games for the Sega Saturn. The game was released worldwide later that year and ported to the PlayStation 2 in 2005 as a Japanese exclusive. It has spawned one sequel with Dragon Force II: Kamisarishi Daichi ni (1998), also released only in Japan.

Metal Slug

Date of release: April 1996

Region: Worldwide

Developer: Nazca Corporation

Publisher: SNK (Shin Nihon Kikaku)

Platform: Arcade (Neo Geo)

Produced by Takashi Nishiyama and designed by Kazuma Kujo Meeher, Metal Slug is a single-player or multiplayer, side-scrolling run and gun game, and the first in the popular Metal Slug series. Set in the year 2028, the aim of Metal Slug is to prevent evil General Morden from taking over the world. You play as Captain Marco Rossi or Lieutenant Tarma Roving and must dispatch a multitude of enemies as well as bosses. The player has the use of various weapons and power-ups throughout the game. Said weapons and power-ups are gained by freeing the POWs encountered, who are depicted as chained and bearded men in rags. From time to time, the player can jump into one of the titular Metal Slug SV-0001 tanks, greatly increasing their offensive and defensive capabilities. There are six missions in Metal Slug, featuring stunningly beautiful environments such as the jungle, a train station, harbour, a snowy mountain, war-torn urban areas, forests and mines. The environment is highly destructible, adding to the chaotic action around the player.

It is easy to see how Metal Slug came about when following Kazuma Kujo Meeher's career as a playtester for R-Type II (1989). He then worked on Geo Storm AKA GunForce (1991), then as lead designer for In the Hunt (1993). They, and Metal Slug, all possess beautiful 2D graphics and excellent gameplay. Because the evolution of 3D graphics moved so quickly, many of the 3D games released around this time would soon show their age. Yet a game like Metal Slug used all that available processing power and used it to polish the graphical potential of a 2D game until it shone. This is why Metal slug looks great and runs so smoothly, even to this day. Those who go back yet again to Metal Slug will discover small, and at times humorous, details in the characters' reactions.

Perhaps its only shortcoming is its notorious difficulty. As an arcade game, this caused many to disengage after a short time. However, in every other department, it excels, and the Metal Slug series could be viewed as the very pinnacle of the run-and-gun genre in the nineties.

Metal Slug spawned numerous sequels, remakes and spin-off games. Some of the most notable is the remake of Metal Slug 2 (1998), Metal Slug X (1999), Metal Slug 3 (2000), and Metal Slug 5 (2003). The original game has been released on multiple platforms over the years with incremental refinements.

Gamespot

Gamespot was founded in the USA in May 1996 by Pete Deemer, Vince Broady and Jon Epstein. Along with the expected fare of a video game-centric website, Gamespot also allowed visitors to contribute their own material in the form of blogs and reviews.

Today, Gamespot is one of the most popular gaming websites on the net with an estimated fifteen million unique monthly visitors.

Quake

Date of release: June 1996

Region: USA

Developer: id Software

Publisher: GT Interactive

Platform: MS-DOS and Microsoft Windows

Developed by John Romero and John Carmack, Quake is a single-player or multiplayer, first-person shooter and the first in the Quake series. The main aim of the game is to enter through portals called Slipgates into the different dimensions of Quake and collect magical runes to prevent the invasion of Earth by the creatures of Quake, and ultimately defeat Shub-Niggurath, the game's final boss. The player can play any episode, known as dimensions, in any order (although some episodes are much more difficult than others), dealing out bloody death to your Doom-Esque and Lovecraftian enemies with a satisfying array of weapons such as the Double-Barrelled Shotgun, the Nailgun, the Super Nailgun, the Grenade Launcher, the Rocket Launcher, and the Thunderbolt. Quake has many similarities with id Software's previous FPS series Doom (1993), offering ammo, health and armour pick-ups. It also features power-ups for invisibility, invulnerability and damage multiplication. Around the levels of Quake, you will discover such things as teleporters, secret areas, elevators, lava, water, extendable bridges and wind tunnels. The dark world of Quake is a blend of gothic sci-fi, with a horror theme permeating every corner. The lighting and sound are used to perfection. Lights flicker on and off, revealing or hiding enemies. The foul creatures of Quake can often be heard but not always seen, having the player on their toes and constantly searching the area around them, expecting an attack from anywhere at any time. Similar to Doom, the level design is also excellent.

Unlike Duke Nukem 3D (1996), the player could not crouch or deploy explosives and the environments were not destructible. However, Quake did offer the first, fully real-time, 3D rendered first-person shooter experience with texture-mapped polygons and real-time lighting, fully utilising OpenGL and the new dedicated GPUs (Graphics Processors Units, known more colloquially nowadays as graphics cards). This made for very smooth gameplay, heightening the immersion and facilitating a fast-paced and responsive multiplayer experience. Multiplayer in Quake consisted of six maps involving

Cooperative, Deathmatch and Team Deathmatch game modes.

Perhaps even more significant was the fact that Quake was the game to spearhead a new type of control system. Instead of implementing a gamepad (controller) or joystick, players began using the W A S D keys for movement, with the mouse used for aiming. There was resistance by some to the implementation of this new control system, which seems strange now, considering it would become the standard control method for FPS games on the PC. In short, Quake represented what would become the future of the first-person shooter.

As with Doom, Quake received many updates, new maps, mods and innovations for its multiplayer elements over the years from id Software, third-party developers and the wider community in general. Indeed, Team Fortress Classic (1999) by Valve is an original Quake mod. Quake is often viewed as one of the most significant and also one of the greatest video games of all time. It was ported to most of the popular computer platforms and consoles of the time and spawned several sequels, the main games in the series being Quake II (1997), Quake III Arena (1999), and Quake 4 (2005).

Nintendo 64

Released in Japan in June 1996, the Nintendo 64 (originally called the Ultra Famicom and the Nintendo Ultra 64), often referred to as the N64, is a 64-bit, cartridge-based, fifth-generation video game console and supports 16.8 million colours, with a maximum screen resolution of 640 x 480 pixels.

What would become the N64 first came about when Silicon Graphics Inc. approached Nintendo, offering a partnership to use their 64-bit chip in Nintendo's next generation of consoles. An agreement was reached and in 1993 work began on 'Project Reality'. While the new console was shrouded in secrecy, the nature of the console's controller was even more secretive. The controller in question would be revolutionary, offering a newly conceived analogue joystick. The analogue joystick would soon be picked up by the competition and has since become an essential part of the game controller. The console itself featured four controller ports on the front to easily facilitate a four-player split-screen.

The N64 launched with three available games: Super Mario 64, Pilotwings 64 and Saikyō Habu Shōgi, the latter only being released in Japan. Super Mario 64 would go on to become the console's best-selling game. Nintendo decided to price their new console to match that of the Sega Saturn and Sony PlayStation, who had both recently dropped their prices. Such a choice made the N64 very reasonably priced for such a new console. Nintendo's console went on to sell 33 million units by the end of its generation and despite being a fraction of the market leader, the Sony PlayStation, with 103 million unit is still considered a great success.

The N64 was very popular and had some of the most genre-defining releases of the decade. Most notable of these are Super Mario 64 (1996), Mario Kart 64 (1996), Star Fox 64 (1997), GoldenEye 007 (1997), The Legend of Zelda: Ocarina of Time (1998), Banjo-Kazooie (1998), Super Smash Bros. (1999), Perfect Dark (2000), Paper Mario (2000) and The Legend of Zelda: Majora's Mask (2000).

Super Mario 64

Date of release: June 1996

Region: Japan

Developer: Nintendo EAD (Entertainment Analysis & Development Division)

Publisher: Nintendo

Platform: Nintendo 64

Directed and produced by Shigeru Miyamoto and with music by Koji Kondo, Super Mario 64 is a single-player, third-person, 3D platform game. The aim of Super Mario 64, as with most Mario games, is to rescue Princess Peach from Bowser's clutches. To do so, Mario must collect the 120 Power Stars found within the Princess's castle to unlock new areas, reach Bowser and defeat him. Stars are acquired by gathering coins, completing mini-games, solving puzzles, finding secret areas and defeating bosses in each level. Different levels can be accessed through paintings within the castle, which acts as the game's hub. These levels, also known as courses, are all substantially different from one another, ranging from floating islands and underground caverns to snow-covered mountains and water, desert and lava areas. As well as some familiar enemies and power-ups, Super Mario 64 introduces three caps that Mario can utilise by activating specific switches. The Wing Cap allows Mario to fly. The Metal Cap grants immunity from fire and poison damage along with preventing drowning, at the cost of Mario sinking like a stone should he set foot in the water. The Vanish Cap allows Mario to pass through wire meshes and enemies alike without taking damage. The player had a degree of control and freedom not seen before in any other platform game. Not only could Mario move in any direction, but the speed of movement was determined by how far the player pushed the analogue control on the gamepad: push it a little and Mario would walk, while pushing it all the way would send Mario running. Mario could also crouch, crouch and slide, crawl, wall jump, triple jump, backflip, cartwheel, punch, kick, jump kick, preform leg sweeps and slide kicks, slide attack, climb, and swim.

The beauty of Super Mario 64 was not just all the amazing ideas that were crammed into it, but the degree of freedom the player had. Many of the courses had an open-world approach where, even though the end goal was the same, there was an almost infinite way to approach it with the degree of control afforded to the player. Nintendo had established a gold standard for 2D platform games with its Super Mario Bros. series on the NES and SNES, and now it seemed to have once again set that standard within the 3D realm.

Super Mario 64 was the foundation for future 3D Mario games, such as Super Mario Sunshine (2002), Super Mario Galaxy (2007), Super Mario Galaxy 2 (2010), Super Mario 3D Land (2011), Super Mario 3D World (2013) and Super Mario Odyssey (2017). It may have not been the first example of a character-based third-person 3D game, that accolade perhaps going to Hunter (1991). However, Super Mario 64 is responsible for refining mechanics and gameplay enough to inspire the many third-person video games of the future. Super Mario 64 became the best-selling game for the Nintendo 64 with over eleven million units sold and is often cited as one of the greatest and most significant video games of all time.

Nights into Dreams

Date of release: July 1996

Region: Japan

Developer: Sonic Team

Publisher: Sega

Platform: Sega Saturn

Directed by Naoto Ohshima, produced by Yuji Naka and designed by Takashi Iizuka, Nights into Dreams is a single-player or multiplayer, 3D action game. The aim of the game is to collect enough energy to defeat Wizezman, the evil ruler of Nightopia, who is capturing the dream energy of humans in an effort to rise from the subconscious and rule the real world. You control a character called Nights, a Nightmaren who lives in Nightopia (the world of human dreams), and must work together with Elliot and Claris, two human children, to stop Wizeman. Nights can fly in any direction, perform loop-the-loops and, to attack, can grab and throw enemies or pull off his signature Drill Dash. The player must collect twenty blue chips and take them to the Ideya Capture machines to overload them and thus release the stolen dream energy. They must then return to the Ideya Palace to deposit the dream energy before proceeding to the next stage. Points are awarded for collecting stars and flying through rings and power loops. The more rings you successively fly through without interruption, the more points the player scores.

A standard Saturn control pad could be used with a D-Pad for controlling Night's flight through the air, yet a far more enjoyable gaming experience could be had using the Saturn 3D Control Pad, which had been developed alongside Nights into Dreams.

Soon after its release, Nights into Dreams was highly regarded for its graphics and the freedom that Nights' flight offered during gameplay. It is considered by some to be one of the best games for the Sega Saturn and one of the best video games of all time. Nights into Dreams remained an exclusive title for over a decade, not being ported to another platform, the PlayStation 2, until 2008. The game spawned one sequel with Nights: Journey of Dreams (2007).

Star Ocean

Date of release: July 1996

Region: Japan

Developer: tri-Ace

Publisher: Enix

Platform: Super Famicom

Directed by Joe Asanuma, produced by Yoshinori Yamagishi and designed by Masaki Norimoto, Star Ocean is a single-player, third-person, action RPG and the first in the Star Ocean series. The aim of Star Ocean is to cure a deadly disease spreading across the population of the planet Roak. To accomplish this, our heroes must travel 300 years into the past and seek out Asmodeus, King of the Demon World, who is the key to developing a vaccine. As with many JRPGs, Star Ocean is played from a top-down perspective as the player directs the game's main protagonist, Roddick Farrence, and his accompanying party, of which there could be a maximum of eight members. The game has everything you would expect to find in a 16-bit JRPG for the Super Famicom, yet also boasted some more unique features. Unlike many other JRPGs of the time, combat is real-time rather than turn-based. The player controls one character in the party while the others are controlled by the AI. The player can set up battlefield formations ahead of time to give them a degree of control and a say in the strategy of upcoming battles. Characters also have special attacks, differing depending on their current distance from the enemy. When levelling up, party members receive skill points that they can assign to a wide array of different abilities. There is also a crafting system allowing players to craft items, such as weapons, armour, potions and food. In short, this made for quite the departure from the usual JRPGs.

The game cartridge featured the S-DD1 compression chip due to help store the vast amount of graphical data Star Ocean needed. As a result, Star Ocean is one of the best-looking games for the Super Famicom platform.

It was never released outside of Japan until 2008 for the PlayStation Portable (PSP) under the title Star Ocean: First Departure. Some of the other most notable games in the Star Ocean series are Star Ocean: The Second Story (1998), Star Ocean: Till the End of Time (2003), and Star Ocean: The Last Hope (2009). A remastered version of The Last Hope was released in 2017.

Tecmo's Deception: Invitation to Darkness

Date of release: July 1996

Region: Japan and North America

Developer: Tecmo

Publisher: Tecmo

Platform: PlayStation

Tecmo's Deception: Invitation to Darkness (often referred to as simply 'Deception'), known in Japan as Kokumeikan and in Europe as Devil's Deception, is a single-player, first-person, action role-playing game and the first game in the Deception series. The game's plot centres around a prince framed for the murder of his father, the king of Zemekia, by the prince's younger brother, Yurias. At his execution, the eldest prince and player character swears vengeance and makes a pact with Satan. The aim of the game is to kill or capture the various NPCs within the Castle of the Damned, with each level introducing new visitors to the Castle. Gameplay is composed of two main elements. The first part involves the player planning out where to lay a multitude of traps and even creating new rooms with a set amount of Magic Points and Gold on a 2D map. The second part of the game takes place from a first-person viewpoint within the castle. The player must lure or chase the level's NPC characters into the various traps, accordingly, killing or capturing the intruders and earning more Magic Points and Gold to use for the next levels. There are six different endings in Deception, dependent on the player's choices.

Deception was highly praised for its graphics and innovative gameplay. Its concept of setting the player up as a bitter villain rather than as the stereotypical noble hero of most RPGs was lauded for being very unique. The setting up and successful initiation of traps was also noted as being a very different and rewarding game mechanic.

The other games in the Deception series are Kagero: Deception II (1998), Deception III: Dark Delusion (1999), Trapt AKA Kagero II: Dark Illusion (2005), Deception IV: Blood Ties AKA Kagero: Dark Side Princess (2014) and an expanded version of Deception IV titled Deception IV: The Nightmare Princess (2015).

Tokyo Game Show

The Tokyo Game Show, or TGS, was first held in Japan in August 1996. Held twice a year in the spring and the autumn from 1996 to 2002 and subsequently taking place only once a year, the TGS attracts hundreds of thousands of visitors. The show focuses on Japanese game developers presenting new games, with said games available for hands-on demos and displays, along with merchandise sales and hardware, mobile gaming, PC gaming and educational games showcases. Competitions and tournaments can also be found at the TGS, the largest of which is the Street Fighter tournament which is part of Capcom's official Pro Tour circuit.

Cosplay has also played a larger part of the show over the years. People come from all over the world to take part in the Cosplay Collection Night, where participants parade on stage in hand-crafted outfits of their favourite characters. These costumes have become steadily more elaborate and impressive over the years, some on par with what one might expect to find in the television or movie industry.

Harvest Moon

Date of release: August 1996

Region: Japan

Developer: Amccus

Publisher: Pack-In-Video

Platform: SNES

Harvest Moon is a single-player, 2D, farming simulation game. Viewed from a top-down perspective, the aim of Harvest Moon is to maintain the farm that the player inherits from their grandfather. To accomplish this goal, you must prepare the land for crops and tend to the animals on a regular basis. The young man you play as can interact with the local villagers and may even marry one of the eligible bachelorettes.

The game was a curiosity, for it was so very different from anything else, even when compared to other simulation games. Many did not know quite what to make of it, and it seemed to some that looking after a farm was a tedious idea for a game. However, others found the game relaxing, immersive and rather addictive.

Harvest Moon is perhaps the first-ever farming simulation game, beginning a whole new sub-genre. This sub-genre has since become incredibly popular and is one in which players spend hundreds or even thousands of hours of their leisure time happily tending to their virtual estates. Perhaps some of the most notable farming simulation games are Stardew Valley (2016), Farmer's Dynasty (2017), Staxel (2018), My Time at Portia (2018) and Farm Simulator 19 (2018).

Harvest Moon was the first game in the Harvest Moon series, or what is now known as the Story of Seasons series of games. Some of the most notable of these games are Harvest Moon 64 (1999), Harvest Moon: Back to Nature (1999), Harvest Moon: Friends of Mineral Town (2003), Harvest Moon: A Wonderful Life (2004), Harvest Moon: Animal Parade (2009) and Story of Seasons: Trio of Towns (2017).

Valve Corporation

The Valve Corporation, often referred to as just Valve, was founded in the USA in August 1996 by Gabe Newell and Mike Harrington. Valve's first game, Half-Life, was released in 1998 and quickly became cited as being not only the best FPS of its day but the best PC game of its time. Valve is known for its very popular and successful games such as the aforementioned Half-Life series (1998-2020), Team Fortress 1 & 2 (1999 and 2007), Counter-Strike series (1999-2014), Defense of the Ancients (DOTA) (2003-20), Left for Dead series (2008-12) and Portal series (2007-11). Even more lucrative than these games was the release of Steam, a video game digital distribution service, launched in 2002. Originally a way to distribute their own games, Valve soon opened this up to other games developers and the platform exploded in popularity, size and scope. It wasn't long until the majority of digital sales of video games for the PC were conducted through Steam. This is still the case today with Steam known for its famous seasonal sales. Valve recently released its own virtual reality headset, the Valve Index, in 2019.

Crash Bandicoot

Date of release: September 1996

Region: North America and Europe

Developer: Naughty Dog

Publisher: Sony Computer Entertainment

Platform: PlayStation

Developed by Jason Rubin, David Siller and Andy Gavin, Crash Bandicoot is a single-player, third-person, 3D platformer and the first game in the Crash Bandicoot series. Set on three little islands located south-east of Australia, you play as Crash, the titular bandicoot, whose genes have been modified by the mad Doctor Neo Cortex. The aim of the game is to overcome various obstacles and enemies to stop Cortex from conquering the world and to reunite Crash with his girlfriend, Tawna Bandicoot. The game is played from a variety of camera angles, with some levels being played with the camera behind Crash as he moves away, or with the camera in front of him as he flees toward it. Bonus levels are more traditional in that they are, for the most part, 3D side-scrolling platformer affairs. Crash can run, jump or spin to attack enemies. Crates scattered about each level can be smashed with a spin attack, potentially revealing some of the many power-up items. These can vary from Wumpa Fruit (collecting 100 pieces of which will grant an extra life) to the Aku-Aku, a magical witch doctor mask, who takes one hit for Crash in his stead, thus protecting the bandicoot, whilst collecting three of them without getting hit grants temporary invulnerability. Some crates indicate what they contain, such as the Arrow Crate or Bounce Crates, which grant multiple items. TNT Crates will explode after three seconds if jumped on but detonate immediately if Crash inadvertently spin attacks them. If the player is hit by an enemy or succumbs to one of the many hazards in the game, such as deep pits, rolling boulders or spikes, then a life is lost. If all lives are lost, then the game is over.

Rather than using specialised PCs for development, the team used Silicon Graphics workstations worth $100,000 apiece. The result was a game that, some believed, had the best graphics, and animation of the time. The gameplay and music were also highly praised. Crash Bandicoot sold over six million units and is the eighth best-selling PlayStation One game.

There are several Crash sequels, some of the most notable being Crash Bandicoot 2: Cortex Strikes Back (1997), Crash Bandicoot: Warped (1998), Crash Team Racing (1999) and Crash Bandicoot 4: It's About Time (2020). A remake of the Crash Bandicoot was released as part of the Crash Bandicoot N. Sane Trilogy (2017) which was a remaster of the first three games in the series.

Imagine Games Network (IGN)

The Imagine Games Network, more commonly referred to as IGN, was founded in the USA in September 1996 by Chris Anderson and Jonathan Simpson Bint. IGN is a video games website originally made up of five different websites: N64.com, Next-Generation.com, PSXPower, Saturnworld and Ultra Game Players Online. Soon after, many other sites (known as channels at the time) became accessible on IGN. IGN features game news, previews, reviews, walkthroughs, and tips and tricks. Though keeping the IGN brand name, the site has branched out to include and cover many other forms of pop culture. It has also opened up a multitude of offices in countries all over the world. Today, IGN is one of the most popular gaming websites in the world, with an estimated 20 million unique monthly visitors.

The Elder Scrolls II: Daggerfall

Date of release: September 1996

Region: North America and Europe

Developer: Bethesda Softworks

Publisher: Bethesda Softworks

Platform: MS-DOS

Developed by Julian Lefay and Christopher Weaver, The Elder Scrolls II: Daggerfall is a single-player, first-person, action RPG and the sequel to The Elder Scrolls: Arena (1994). The two major aims of the Daggerfall are set by the personal request of the Emperor, Uriel Septim VII. First, the player must free the ghost of King Lysandus. The second and more significant is to locate the Mantella, the key to resurrecting Numidium, a colossal brass golem. The game has six different endings depending on whether the player or one of the Emperor's enemies can free and control the golem and thus defeat their enemies.

Daggerfall's game world was and still is astoundingly large at 62,394 square miles, with over 15,000 villages, towns, cities and, of course, dungeons, all populated with around 750,000 NPCs. Players could choose between eighteen different classes or create a custom-made one. The game also featured guilds, knightly orders and religions that the player could join, a spell-creation system, the ability to enchant weapons, and the possibility to become a vampire, a werewolf or a wereboar. Daggerfall also introduced the concept of levelling-up abilities that were used the most. Use a sword to strike down your enemies and your skill with a sword would accordingly improve. Using magic would accordingly result in your magic ability increasing instead. This was far more organic than assigning skill points and was so intuitive that it was carried over to all future Elder Scrolls games. Daggerfall was truly open-world, allowing the player to go anywhere and do anything in a world that was, for some, overwhelmingly large, yet for others, it was a role-playing dream come true.

Daggerfall was praised by critics and consumers alike, with the initial release of the game selling out within days. Despite its many bugs, Daggerfall still excelled when it came to immersing the player in a fantasy world, winning several gaming awards for best role-playing game.

The House of the Dead

Date of release: September 1996

Region: Japan

Developer: Sega AM Research & Development No.1

Publisher: Sega

Platform: Arcade

The House of the Dead Is a single-player or two-player, horror-themed, rail shooter. The aim of the game is to stop Dr Roy Curien from creating and releasing his undead army across the country. To this end, the player must deal with hordes of undead enemies. You play as AMS agents Thomas Rogan and his partner, known as 'G.'Enemies' limbs are blown off in a bloody mess as they shamble towards you, a headshot being the only sure way of taking down some of the undead creatures in one shot or inflicting the maximum possible damage. The horror aspect of The House of the Dead was very popular and set it apart from other similar games of the time. Like many other light gun shooters, the player shoots off screen with their plastic gun to reload. Each stage has a boss at the end, with the game informing the player of the boss's weak spots. If a player shoots a hostage or is hit by an enemy, they will lose a life point. If a player is able to save all the hostages in the game, they will subsequently find a secret room containing extra lives and bonuses: very handy, especially near the end of the game before the final boss. Life points can be restored by finding first-aid packs, and naturally, when all life points are lost, the game is over. The player can choose different paths to take, meaning that, unlike other on-rail shooters, the game is not linear and has several endings dependent on the player's actions.

The House of the Dead series, along with the Resident Evil games, would not only influence other horror-themed video games but revitalise interest in zombies across all media. House of the Dead in particular has been credited for popularising the fast-moving zombies seen in multiple films since.

The game was ported to the Sega Saturn and Windows PC. The House of the Dead spawned several sequels and spin-off games, with some of the most notable of these being The House of the Dead 2 (2000), The House of the Dead III (2002), and The House of the Dead 4 (2005).

Revelations Persona

Date of release: September 1996

Region: Japan

Developer: Atlus

Publisher: Atlus

Platform: PlayStation

Directed by Kouji Okada, Revelations Persona, known in Japan as Megami Ibunroku Persona, is a single-player RPG. It is the first game in the Shin Megami Tensei: Persona series, often shortened to the Persona series. The Persona series itself is a spin-off of the Megami Tensei franchise (with the Megami Tensei series beginning at first as a series of novels), the first game of which was Digital Devil Story: Megami Tensei (1987). Persona is set in the modern-day, centred on a group of high school students. The initial aim of the game is to help the silent protagonist's friend Maki and stop the villain Takahisa Kandori from using his reality-altering device. The game's story is of epic proportions, taking many twists and turns and involving parallel worlds and multiple selves. The concept of the game is that the player and party members can call upon their Personas to assist them in battle.

The concept of what exactly defines or constitutes a Persona varies from game to game within the series, but broadly speaking a Persona is an external manifestation of an element of the user's personality or psyche. Personas are invariably associated with the Arcana of the Tarot for general ease of classification as regards shared characteristics, and usually appear as demons, gods or other mythological figures. Revelations: Persona has twenty-one different classes of Persona, and with the ability to capture any of the hundred-plus enemies and subsequently fuse them to create new Personas, the player does not want for choice. Every Persona was beautifully designed by artist Kazuma Kaneko and the Persona series would become accordingly renowned for its art style. In-game navigation is displayed through an overhead map or from a first-person viewpoint when walking through the school or a dungeon. Cutscenes and combat are seen from an isometric viewpoint which is turn-based. Players can use melee weapons, guns, items and of course summon their Personas to fight for them.

Revelations: Persona (and the other games in the series) deal with many deep and thought-provoking themes centred around the self and existence. The player can gain appropriate revelations about themselves, others and indeed life in general, elevating Revelations: Persona to more than just a game. Revelations: Persona was praised for its departure from most RPGs of the time, with special note paid to its compelling story, deep mechanics, and gameplay. Furthermore, it quickly became notorious for its difficulty, demanding dedication on a god-like level to complete.

It was ported to Windows in 1999, and a remake of Revelations: Persona was released for the PSP in 2009. The original game was released in the West in 2018 for the PlayStation Classic. Some of the most notable games in the Persona series are Persona 2: Eternal Punishment (2000), Persona 3: FES (2007), Persona 4: Golden (2012) and Persona 5: Royal (2019).

Meridian 59

Date of release: December 1995 (launched) September 1996 (commercial launch)

Region: USA

Developer: Archetype Interactive

Publisher: The 3DO Company

Platform: Windows

Designed by brothers Andrew and Chris Kirmse, and produced by John Hanke, Meridian 59 is a Massive Multiplayer Online Role-Playing Game (MMORPG). Hundreds of years ago, a great empire used a portal to establish multiple colonies on other worlds. However, at some point preceding the game, something went wrong and the 59th provincial colony was cut-off. The aim of Meridian 59 is rather open in that the player can explore, fight monsters and, in later updates of the game, join guilds and schools. The schools teach different skills for use in combat, with there being no limit to the number of schools a player could join.

Meridian 59 (also known as M59) holds the accolade of being the first 3D graphical, massively multiplayer online role-playing game (MMORPG) and also one of the longest-running. At the time, though, this concept was so new that it was referred to as a Graphical Multi-User Dungeon (GMUD) and was seen as just an evolution of the text MUDs of the 1970s and 1980s and the 2D isometric graphical MUDs of the 1980s and 1990s. It is also maybe the first game to update local files on a user's computer, thus auto-patching the game, which in 1995 was rather a novel concept. The game could accommodate a few hundred players in one world. When the user base rose into the thousands, multiple game worlds were launched to meet the demand.

The game's graphics were rather poor even for the time, and it lacked a great many features. However, it was the first first-person, 3D MMORPG. The novelty of being able to meet up with friends or make new ones with hundreds of other players online and share adventures in a fully-realised 3D world was a great allure for some.

The Neverhood

Date of release: October 1996

Region: North America

Developer: The Neverhood, Inc.

Publisher: DreamWorks Interactive

Platform: Windows

Designed by Doug TenNapel and Mark Lorenzen, The Neverhood (also known as The Neverhood Chronicles or Klaymen: The Mystery of Neverhood in Japan), is a single-player, third-person (and at times first-person), point-and-click adventure. The aim of the game is for Klaymen, the player character, to discover his origins and purpose in the world, solving puzzles and progressing the narrative. The Neverhood is markedly unique in that Klaymen and the deserted surreal world he inhabits are both entirely constituted of claymation. The gameplay and underlying mechanics of the game are rather simple compared to others in the genre. There is no inventory and therefore no mechanics involving the combining of various items to solve puzzles, no alternative options to interacting with the environment and only one way to do anything, making the game completely linear. All interaction is performed by utilising the on-screen mouse pointer, which rather appropriately is also made of clay, and clicking on the environment.

The Neverhood is possibly the first game to use stop-motion clay animation. Because of its use of real-world lighting and objects, The Neverhood has a degree of realism never before seen in a video game, making it rather unique.

The Neverhood was highly praised for its art style yet criticised for its difficult puzzles and lack of depth when it came to gameplay or mechanics. One sequel, Skullmonkeys (1998), was developed for the PlayStation.

Tomb Raider

Date of release: October 1996

Region: UK

Developer: Core Design

Publisher: Eidos Interactive

Platform: Sega Saturn, PlayStation and MS-DOS

Programmed by Paul Douglas, written by Vicky Arnold, with art by Toby Gard (the creator of Lara) and music by Nathan McCree, Tomb Raider is a single-player, third-person, action-adventure game. You play as Lara Croft, a wealthy archaeologist and adventurer. The initial aim of the game is to find an artefact called the Scion of Atlantis for powerful businesswoman Jacqueline Natla. Tomb Raider's gameplay consists of exploring levels, progressing via solving elaborate environmental puzzles with the various switches, levers and pressure pads scattered throughout. Lara must also deal with various enemies found within the tombs such as wolves, bats, bears, crocodiles, Velociraptors, a Tyrannosaurus Rex and (later in the game) skinless guardians of Atlantis. Luckily, Lara has her iconic twin pistols to deal with these enemies and later gains access to a shotgun, dual magnums and dual Uzis. Lara can walk, run, climb by pulling herself up or dropping down, sidestep, roll, swim, and perform impressively acrobatic forward and sideways jumps along with a backwards somersault. She is also able to shoot at any assailant whilst in the air, thus avoiding their attacks. These controls gave the player an enormous amount of freedom. The roll, for instance, could be used when running from an enemy and, subsequently, rolling and attacking, as the roll served to turn Lara 180° in a very short amount of time. The roll could also be used to break Lara's fall, mitigating some of the damage received from falling above a certain height. Players could also perform more complex moves such as a graceful handstand whilst Lara pulls herself onto a ledge, or a swan dive when jumping into a body of water. Items to collect included ammunition for guns, a small or large medi-pack and objects necessary for puzzle-solving, ranging from keys to missing fuses. There are four areas to explore in the game: Peru, Greece, Egypt and Atlantis. The environments were spectacular in their scope and diversity, spanning as they did across the entire globe. There is also a training level at the Croft manor, accessible from the main menu and intended for the player to familiarise themselves with the controls. In the Playstation and Saturn versions of the game, players could only save the game at certain points within a level as marked by a floating blue crystal. While this restriction did not apply to PC and Mac players, the existence of secrets consisting of caches of ammunition and medi-packs meant it was of utmost importance to explore every nook and cranny of the game.

After its initial release on the Sega Saturn, Tomb Raider was soon ported to the PlayStation and MS-DOS. It was with the PlayStation's burgeoning user base that Tomb Raider's popularity would explode. The game was highly praised for its graphics, gameplay, mechanics, level design, puzzle-solving, narrative, the character of Lara Croft herself, and the incredible music used to perfection in evoking an atmospheric and mysterious sense of wonder and excitement. In short, it got everything right for a game of this genre. Tomb Raider by itself boosted the sales of the PlayStation. It won multiple awards and is often cited as one of the most significant and best video games of all time.

Lara Croft's debut in Tomb Raider shook the gaming world and beyond. She, and as a consequence, the game was embraced by the mainstream media. She became an icon and could be seen everywhere: in magazines such as The Face, Newsweek, Rolling Stone and even Time. She was the star of a series of Lucozade adverts and modelled a dress by Gucci. She was nothing short of a cultural phenomenon. Lara Croft helped to make gaming more accepted by mainstream culture and appear much cooler. She is now recognised as the most successful video game heroine of all time.

It was not surprising that one of the most successful, best-selling and impactful games of its time would give rise to many sequels. Some of the most notable of these are Tomb Raider II (1997), Tomb Raider: Legend (2006), Tomb Raider: Underworld (2008), Tomb Raider (2013) and Tomb Raider: Rise of the Tomb Raider (2015).

Tamagotchi

The Tamagotchi was released in Japan in November 1996 by Bandai. Created by Akihiro Yokoi and Aki Maita. The Tamagotchi is a very small, digital, handheld game, often in the shape of an egg, on a key chain with three buttons and a 32 pixel LCD screen. This kind of device would become known as a digital pet. The concept of a Tamagotchi is that it is a small alien species left on Earth and it is up to the owner of the Tamagotchi to nurture the pet. Pets hatch from an egg and grow over time. The player must feed, toilet train, play with and nurse the pet back to health should it fall ill. If the pet is neglected for too long, it would eventually die. Later models facilitated the option to link to your friends' pets, allowing the pets to become friends as well and even get married. With these later models, players could also earn Gotchi Points and subsequently use them to buy more elaborate foods, accessories, toys and decorations for their pet's rooms.

From 1996 to the current day, the Tamagotchi brand has released over twenty different games on numerous platforms and its highly original concept of the digital pet has been copied by numerous other companies. It seemed that everything from Pokémon to Barbie was at one point or another selling their own version of the Tamagotchi.

The impact on children of what became the Tamagotchi craze of the late nineties cannot be understated. Some children seemed addicted to them. Others were traumatised after their pet died, with some schools resorting to banning them. It is believed that over 82 million Tamagotchis have been sold worldwide.

Dead or Alive

Date of release: November 1996

Region: Worldwide

Developer: Team Ninja

Publisher: Tecmo

Platform: Arcade

Created by Tomonobu Itagaki, Dead or Alive is a single-player or multiplayer, 3D fighting game, and the first in the Dead or Alive series. The games takes place in what is known as the Dead or Alive World Championship. The player can choose from one of eight characters, with the aim being to beat your current opponent by successfully knocking them out (KO) twice. Dead or Alive set itself apart from other 3D fighting games with an easy-to-use but a markedly elaborate grappling system, whereby players could guard and counter their opponent's grabs and throws, mixing martial arts with wrestling. The results made for some very satisfying animations and bouts. A player could also hurt their opponent by forcing them to the edge of the fighting area and onto the waiting explosives.

Dead or Alive was very provocative for the time. The female characters tended to be markedly voluptuous and replete with bouncing breasts, with there also being the flashing of underwear. Obviously, this appealed to hormonal teenage boys who were the largest demographic for this genre of game. The series has unashamedly carried on these concepts and is well-known for it to this day.

After the success of the arcade release, the game was ported to the Sega Saturn and PlayStation. The most notable games in the Dead or Alive series are Dead or Alive 3 (2001), Dead or Alive 2 Ultimate (2004), and Dead or Alive 5 Last Round (2015).

Tekken 3

Date of release: November 1996

Region: Japan

Developer: Namco

Publisher: Namco

Platform: Arcade

Set fifteen years after the previous game, Tekken 3 is a single-player or two-player, 3D fighting game, and the third in the Tekken series. The aim is to defeat your opponent. Several new characters were introduced in the game, including Bryan Fury, Eddy Gordo, Hwoarang, Jin Kazama, and Ling Xiaoyu. Some of these new characters would become firm favourites and mainstays of the Tekken series. The game made significant progress in terms of graphics from the first two games, as now that characters could properly circle one another rather than just sidestep, creating a more immersive 3D environment.

Tekken 3 was highly acclaimed by critics at the time and is often cited as one of the best video games of all time. The game was ported to the PlayStation in 1998, where it became immensely successful. It is considered one of the best fighting games for the PlayStation 1 and was the fourth best-selling game on the platform.

Parappa the Rapper

Date of release: December 1996

Region: Japan

Developer: NanaOn-Sha

Publisher: Sony Computer Entertainment

Platform: PlayStation

Produced and directed by Masaya Matsuura, Parappa the Rapper is a single-player rhythm game. You play as the titular Parappa, who wants to gain the affection of Sunny Funny, the daisy girl. To accomplish this goal, Parappa must hone his rapping prowess and acquire several skills throughout a series of scenarios. Each stage has a different setting and teacher. When the music starts, an icon corresponding to either the player or the teacher will move across a bar, with one or more of the action buttons of the PlayStation controller also appearing at some point along the bar. The player must press the same action button on their controller when their icon moves across it. Feedback on a player's performance is given on the right of the screen as either Awful, Bad, Good or Cool during gameplay. If the player finishes the rap on Awful or Bad, then they cannot move on to the next stage. If the player is successful, they can then attempt to achieve a Cool ranking by playing the stage again and freestyling to impress their current trainer. There are six stages overall in Parappa the Rapper.

Parappa the Rapper is quite a departure from many games around at the time. It has distinctive, brightly coloured, flat-shaded 3D environments while the characters are intentionally paper-thin. As a matter of fact, Parappa is a play on words in Japanese meaning 'paper-thin'.

The game was highly praised for its memorable characters and catchy music. It is also a rhythm game, cited by some as the first rhythm video game, and is certainly responsible for influencing the genre in the arcades and people's homes. Parappa the Rapper was just another example of how diverse the PlayStation platform was, challenging the norms of what video games were considered to be, branching out to new concepts and different ways of playing.

Parappa the Rapper spawned a spin-off game with Um Jammer Lammy (1999) and a sequel with Parappa the Rapper 2 (2001). The original game was remastered for the PlayStation 4 in 2017.

Mario Kart 64

Date of release: December 1996

Region: Japan

Developer: Nintendo EAD

Publisher: Nintendo

Platform: Nintendo 64

Directed by Hideki Konno and Produced by Shigeru Miyamoto, Mario Kart 64 is a single-player or multiplayer, third-person, 3D, kart racing game and the second in the popular Mario Kart series and the first one to be in 3D. In single-player, there are two game modes to choose from, the first being Mario GP where eight racers compete for points on a series of tracks categorised into Cups, and the second being Time Trial, where the player drives solo to set and subsequently improve on their best time around a course. In Time Trial, the player can select to 'save ghost' after finishing a race. The next time they race in that mode, a ghostly image of another Kart appears and races to the player's current best time on the track, giving the player something to race against. Up to four players can play in multiplayer mode, thanks to the Nintendo 64's four controller ports. Multiplayer mode featured the new battle mode, which took place in an arena and where players had three balloons attached to their kart. If a kart was damaged, a balloon was lost. Should a player lose all their balloons, then they were out of the game, with the winner being the last player standing. The screen was split into two, three or four depending on the number of players, which was all very novel for a 3D game in 1996. In multiplayer and single-player both, players could choose between three difficulty levels as measured by engine sizes (50cc, 100cc or 150cc), eight drivers of varying weight categories and vehicle handling characteristics (Mario, Luigi, Peach, Toad, Yoshi, Donkey Kong, Wario and Bowser), and a single track or Cup to race on. There are four Cups to compete in, each composed of four very different tracks. When running over item boxes scattered about the course, random power-ups could be obtained. Tried and true from the previous entry in the series, these power-ups were the Green Shell, Red Shell, Banana Peel, Mushroom, Star, Lightning Bolt and Boo, with the Feather being cut from Mario Kart 64. New additions were the Triple Mushrooms (allowing for three speed boosts), the Super Mushroom (allowing for a technically unlimited amount of speed boosts albeit over a limited time), the Banana Bunch, Triple Green Shell and Triple Red Shell (multiples of the power-ups of the same name), the Fake Item (when thrown, it mimics an item box and stuns karts that drive into it) and finally, the dreaded Spiny Shell (also known as the Blue Shell, it automatically and unerringly homes in on the player in 1st place, inflicting more damage and a longer stun than the Red Shell upon impact). Mario Kart 64 also featured the addition of being able to carry multiple items and slipstream behind other karts.

Despite being the first Mario Kart game in 3D, the players, karts and items were still 2D sprites. Their 3D look is due to the tried and tested formula of pre-rendering 3D computer models and displaying them as a series of animated sprites, depending on user input.

Mario Kart 64 was deemed not as impactful as the original Mario Kart on the SNES, yet it was still an incredibly popular game and the second-best-selling game for the N64, shipping almost ten million units in its lifetime. It certainly acted as a healthy springboard for some of the fantastic 3D Mario Kart games to come.

1996 Notable Omissions

Absolute Pinball. Apple Bandai Pippin. Bahamut Lagoon. Beyond the Beyond. Brian Lara Cricket. Blood Omen: Legacy of Kain. Broken Sword: The Shadow of the Templars. Bubble Trouble. Busby 3D. Civilization II. Command and Conquer: Red Alert. Cool Boarders. Daytona USA: Championship Circuit Edition. Death Rally. DeathDrome. Donkey Kong Country 3. Drowned God. Final Doom. Firaxis Games was founded. Fire Emblem: Seisen no Keifu. Escape Velocity. Front Mission: Gun Hazard. GTI Club Rally Cote d'Azur. GunGriffon. Indiana Jones and His Desktop Adventures. International Track & Field. Killer Instinct 2. King's Field III. Kirby Super Star. Lunar: Sanposuru Gakuen. Marathon Infinity. Masters of Orion II. Mega Man 8. Micro Machines Military. Mystaria: The Realms of Lore. Panzer Dragoon II: Zwei. Phantasmagoria: A Puzzle of Flesh. Pilot Wings 64. Ridge Racer. Ridge Racer Revolution. Ripper. Rise 2: Resurrection. Shattered Steel. Shining Wisdom. Silent Hunter. SimCopter. Snood. Soviet Strike. Star Control 3. Star Wars: Shadows of the Empire. Street Fighter Alpha 2. Super Puyo Puyo Tsu Remix. Syndicate Wars. Tekken 2. Terra Nova: Strike Force Centauri. The Kingdom of the Winds/Barum Eui Nara. The Logical Journey of the Zoombinis. The Legend of Oasis. Tokyo Wars. True Pinball. Twisted Metal 2. Urban Runner. Vectorman 2. Virtua Cop 2. Virtua Fighter 2. Virtual On: Cyber Troopers, Wave Race 64. Wipeout 2097 and Wipeout XL. Wild Arms. Wing Commander IV: The Price of Freedom. World Soccer: Winning Eleven '97/Goal Storm '97/International Superstar Soccer Pro. WWF In Your House. Z. Zork: Nemesis.

1997

Diablo

Date of release: January 1997

Region: North America

Developer: Blizzard North

Publisher: Blizzard Entertainment

Platform: Windows

Developed by Bill Roper and David Brevik, Diablo is a single-player or multiplayer, action RPG. The aim of the game is to defeat Diablo, The Dark Lord. To do so, the player must delve into several dungeons beneath the cathedral in the town of Tristram, dispatching hordes of foul enemies along the way. Diablo is viewed from an isometric perspective, shrewdly making walls semi-transparent depending on the angle that they are viewed from, to more easily see your character and enemies. An overlay map of the dungeon can be activated, also semi-transparent, to help the player orientate themselves. An ornate stone bar at the bottom of the screen provides information and forms the user interface. A red orb of liquid life on the left displays current health and a blue orb represents the character's current amount of mana. Between the two orbs are the quick access objects, such as life potions that may need to be taken quickly in a fight. Buttons on the information bar include access to your character's stats and an inventory screen that uses the tried and tested paper doll interface. The player can choose from three different classes: Warrior, Rogue and Sorcerer, each class with its varying strengths and weaknesses. When your character levels up you can distribute experience points to improve your character's attributes. New skills or spells can be learnt when a character levels up. As combat is real-time every conceivable advantage needs to be taken given the general difficulty level; players could assign hotkeys for their spells to fight more efficiently. Diablo features legions of enemies, including monsters such as skeletons, zombies, Magma Demons, Goatmen, Horned Demons, Winged Fiends and many others. These creatures drop loot when killed, allowing the player to purchase weapons, armour and items to help them in their quest. There are also numerous other items and loot to be found in crates and barrels scattered about the dungeon. There are sixteen dungeon levels in Diablo. Each dungeon is procedurally generated, meaning that when a player enters a dungeon for the first time, it is created based on an algorithm with a certain amount of set pieces, but also with a certain degree of randomness, making for a unique dungeon delve with every playthrough. Multiplayer involved playing with friends over either a LAN (Local Area Network) or dial-up internet connection.

Diablo brought deep lore and game mechanics coupled with an emphasis on looting along with stylish fast-paced action, reminiscent of hack and slash games, to the RPG genre in what would subsequently become known as a hack and slash action RPG. It was highly praised for its randomly generated dungeons, impressive graphics and atmosphere due in no small part to its sound design and music. Although there had been many hack and slash games over the years, Diablo set itself apart with the weight the game placed on action and looting, which would go on to influence later games such as Dungeon Siege (2002), Torchlight (2009), Path of Exile (2013) and Grim Dawn (2016).

Later in the same year, Synergistic Software developed an expansion pack titled Diablo: Hellfire, most notable for adding the Monk class to the roster of playable characters. The original game was ported to the PlayStation and Mac OS in 1998. Diablo has spawned several sequels with Diablo II (2000), Diablo III (2012) and Diablo IV (2023). Diablo is often cited as one of the best video games of 1997 as well as one of the best video games of all time.

Final Fantasy VII

Date of release: January 1997

Region: Japan

Developer: Square

Publisher: Square and Sony Computer Entertainment

Platform: PlayStation

Directed by Yoshinori Kitase, produced by Hironobu Sakaguchi and written by Kazushige Nojima, Final Fantasy VII is a single-player RPG. The aim of Final Fantasy VII is to stop the forces of Shinra Inc., an evil militant megacorporation, the mad super-soldier Sephiroth and later, as if that weren't enough (this being a game in the Final Fantasy series, after all), the unleashing of the ultimate destructive spell known as Meteor, the impact of which threatens all life on the planet. You play as Cloud Strife, an ex-SOLDIER (the elite fighting forces of SHINRA, typically boasting superhuman combat prowess), now working with Avalanche. Avalanche is an eco-terrorist group seeking to save the planet from Shinra's unthinking plundering of natural resources, most notably Mako. Avalanche is seeking to destroy the Mako reactors which they believe are destroying the planet. (Mako is the liquid form of the planet's lifestream, the lifestream being a tangible river of spiritual energy and the sum of all things both living and dead in Final Fantasy VII). Cloud is joined throughout the game by an array of other memorable playable characters, namely Aerith Gainsborough, Tifa Lockheart, Barret Wallace, Red XIII, Cid Highwind, Yuffie Kisaragi, Cait Sith and Vincent Valentine, all with fully fleshed-out backstories, evolving and interconnecting storylines and a unique range of abilities. While Final Fantasy VII featured cinematic 3D cutscenes, which were very advanced for the time, the majority of gameplay consisted of moving Cloud around and interacting with the world and its many NPCs using 3D character models on top of pre-rendered backgrounds. Character models sported a very low polygon in this mode. In the randomly encountered combats, however, both the characters and their enemies were portrayed in much greater detail. Combat takes place in an Active Time Battle (or ATB) system. Each character has a time gauge, which, when full, allows them to act, with the player being able to choose between attacking, using magic or items or, if available, summoning monsters to attack their foe. These summons play a short 3D sequence upon being selected, lending the battle a real cinematic feel. Summons, along with Materia, can be found and awarded throughout the game, and bequeath various benefits and drawbacks when attached to weapons and armour, aiding the player to tailor the party members around their preferred playstyle. The game world of Final Fantasy VII is vast, and the player has access to the Chocobos (large flightless birds, and the broad equivalent of horses in the Final Fantasy universe), the Highwind airship and Shinra submarines to better explore. The game also features vehicular combat modes and several mini-games.

The game would deal with many adult and complex themes, ranging from life, birth and death to loss and identity. Avalanche is portrayed both as saving the planet yet also destroying people's lives, due to the overall dependency on Mako energy. This and other themes served to illustrate how games were maturing, presenting their worlds in shades of grey and thus open to interpretation and debate rather than an overly simplified portrayal of good versus evil.

Square decided to move from Nintendo (home of the first six Final Fantasy games) to the PlayStation when they realised that this new instalment using 3D graphics would not fit onto an N64 cartridge. Only the CD-ROM format could provide the raw storage required for this epic game, and even then the game shipped on three discs.

Upon release, Final Fantasy VII took the gaming world by storm. The game's level of epic cinematic presentation had never been seen before. The 3D cutscenes were way ahead of anything else around at the time and were considered a landmark in video game storytelling. The poignant death of one of Final Fantasy VII's main characters is often cited to this day as the most shocking in video game history. The highest praise was also lavished upon its stunning graphics, robust battle system and what has become its iconic music and score by Nobuo Uematsu, which elevates the cutscenes, gameplay and battles to a new level. The PlayStation's huge user base made it the most successful Final Fantasy game to date and one of the best-selling PlayStation games with over twelve million units having been sold. Final Fantasy VII has also won several prestigious awards over the years and is often cited as one of the greatest video games of all time and is arguably the most influential in the long series of Final Fantasy games. Various Final Fantasy merchandise and cosplay centres more around Final Fantasy VII than any other game in the series. This seventh instalment was so popular that in spawned its own subseries beginning with the computer animated film Final Fantasy VII: Advent Children (2005), and two video games Dirge of Cerberus: Final Fantasy VII (2006) and Crisis Core: Final Fantasy VII (2007). Remakes of the original games have been released in 'episodes' with Final Fantasy VII Remake (2020) and Crisis Core: Final Fantasy VII – Reunion (2022).

Sangokumusou/Dynasty Warriors

Date of release: February 1997

Region: Japan

Developer: Omega Force

Publisher: Koei

Platform: PlayStation

Dynasty Warriors is a 3D, single-player or two-player, weapon-based fighting game and the first in the Dynasty Warriors series. The aim of the game is to successfully land enough hits on your opponent to deplete their health. The roster features ten playable characters, with a further six to unlock, and each one has a unique weapon to use against their opponents. The gameplay is slow-paced and involves precise and carefully-timed parries and ripostes rather than the lightning-fast button combinations of other fighting games of the time.

Even though reviews of the game were fair to good, there was nothing exceptional about Dynasty Warriors. The most significant factor about it was that it gave rise to the Dynasty Warriors series. The original is also very different from the other games in the series, which are well known for the player fighting a huge number of opponents all at once, as opposed to the one-on-one fighting of the first game. Because of this difference in gameplay in the next instalment, the second game is called Shin Sangokumusou (the first game in the Shin Sangokumusou series) in Japan and Dynasty Warriors 2 in the West. The third game is accordingly Shin Sangokumusou 2 in Japan and Dynasty Warriors 3 in the West, a discrepancy in naming convention that would continue through the years.

There are many sequels and spin-off games in the Dynasty Warriors series, some of the most notable sequels being Dynasty Warriors 4 (2003), Dynasty Warriors 5 (2005) and Dynasty Warriors 8 (2013).

Turok: Dinosaur Hunter

Date of release: March 1997

Region: USA

Developer: Iguana Entertainment

Publisher: Acclaim Entertainment

Platform: Nintendo 64

Developed by David Dienstbier, Turok: Dinosaur Hunter is a single-player, first-person shooter based on the titular character and associated comics first established in the 1950s and is the first game in the Turok series. You play as the time-travelling Native American warrior Tal'Set and current bearer of the mantle of Turok. You must find the eight pieces of the Chronoscepter, a powerful artefact sought by the Campaigner, antagonist and evil overlord of the Lost Land. The player explores the jungle of the Lost Land in search of keys that open up new levels. The player can run, jump, climb and swim. Turok also plays like a standard FPS of its time and features a multitude of both weapons and enemies, including other humans, dinosaurs and even demons.

Even though the N64 had the 3D capabilities to handle a first-person shooter, a lot of the game's content had to be severely compressed to fit onto the 8MB of storage space available in its cartridge, with the concurrent CD-ROM as used by both PCs and PlayStations able to store around 650MB of data.

Nevertheless, Turok was highly praised for its graphics and gameplay, although there was some criticism of the noticeable slowdown when there was an abundance of enemies displayed. The game was a big success, selling 1.5 million units and illustrating that the N64 also had some decent third-party games in its library. The game spawned several sequels, most notably Turok 2: Seeds of Evil (1998), Turok 3: Shadow of Oblivion (2000) and Turok: Evolution (2002). The game was remastered in 2015.

Bushido Blade

Date of release: March 1997

Region: Japan

Developer: Light Weight

Publisher: Square

Platform: PlayStation

Bushido Blade is a 3D, single-player or two-player fighting game, with the aim varying depending on the choices made. Story Mode showcases a narrative whereby the player must fight several opponents whilst also following the Bushidō warrior code. This means that the player cannot engage in any actions which would be seen as being dishonourable, such as stabbing enemies in the back or attacking an enemy who hasn't drawn their weapon. Should they do so, progress in the campaign will be frozen after a certain point, and the player must subsequently restart from the very beginning after being rebuked for their dishonourable conduct. Vs. Mode is the game's two-player versus mode, allowing two players to fight head-to-head. In Slash Mode, the player must defeat 100 opponents who appear one after another. Bushido Blade also features a Training Mode, along with P.O.V. Mode, whereby the player can choose to play from a first-person perspective. Even farther removed than Dynasty Warriors and the slew of fast-paced, action-packed fighting games of the time, Bushido Blade introduces the single deathblow system, where just one strike from a weapon can kill an opponent, although sometimes a blow can severely wound instead. There are no health bars, special meters, timers or rounds in Bushido Blade, only the player and their opponent. There are six playable characters, each with their own strengths and weaknesses, and eight different weapons, each with different weights and lengths and, accordingly, different striking speed, power and ability to block. Players can run around, jump, and climb on certain parts of the environment, taking the fight elsewhere. While players can block, it is not something to be relied upon, given the extreme lethality of the game, with the mastery of parrying proving far more valuable a skill to acquire.

For the time, the environments were remarkably picturesque, offering atmospheric lighting and weather effects: for instance, a moment of stillness in between bouts in the Cherry Blossom garden or as the snow falls in the forest, the player contemplating whether the next moment will bring them death or glory. The game also had great sound design and nice attention to detail, like being able to slice through bamboo and watch it fall between the player and their opponent. The unique concept of the game's high lethality served to heighten tension and made players feel as if they were living on a knife edge. Players could not just wade in and leave themselves wide open, but instead, wait and try to find the perfect moment to strike. This gave Bushido Blade a pure and unique experience rarely found amongst its fellow fighting games, and indeed other games in general.

Bushido Blade gave rise to one sequel with Bushido Blade 2 (1998). The Kengo series (2000-2006) is considered the spiritual successor to the Bushido Blade series.

Castlevania: Symphony of the Night

Date of release: March 1997

Region: Japan

Developer: Konami Computer Entertainment Tokyo

Publisher: Konami

Platform: PlayStation

Directed, Produced and programmed by Toru Hagihara, with art by Ayami Kojima and music by Michiru Yamane, Castlevania: Symphony of the Night, known as Akumajō Dracula X: Gekka no Yasōkyoku in its native Japan, is a single-player, 2D, side-scrolling, horror-themed action platformer. The game begins in the final stage of Castlevania: Rondo of Blood (1993), where, playing as Richter Belmont, the player defeats Dracula. Four years later, evil once more stirs in the castle and Dracula must once again be defeated. This time, you play as Alucard, Dracula's son, rather than a scion of the Belmont family and must defeat a multitude of undead creatures throughout the game. The discovery of ancient relics enables Alucard to access new areas of the castle by granting him extra powers, such as a double jump, and the ability to shapeshift into a bat, a wolf, and even into a mist. Should he have the magic points, Alucard can also cast spells, of which there are eight in total, ranging from Summon Spirit to Hellfire, to better fight the foul denizens of Dracula's castle. Hidden weapons and sub-weapons can also be found throughout the levels to help overcome the more powerful enemies. Some of these sub-weapons include the Holy Water which bursts into sacred flames, the Cross which hits every enemy currently on screen, the Stopwatch which freezes most enemies, and the Agunea which strikes enemies with lightning. Alucard gains experience by defeating enemies and bosses, and upon levelling up increases his four main attributes, namely Strength, Constitution, Luck and Intelligence, along with his Hit Points and Magic Points. As well as collecting hearts, which are consumed upon using sub-weapons, the player can also collect gold, typically found by destroying candles but also dropped by enemies. Gold can be spent in the Long Library, where Alucard can sell gems, buy items, purchase tutorial videos detailing how to beat certain bosses, study the statistics of enemies that the player has already fought and even listen to the game's haunting choral music. The player can only save the game in Save rooms, and the fact that the castle turns upside down partway through the game and is still playable, with the save rooms remaining accessible, is a testament to the game's excellent level design.

Castlevania: Symphony of the night was highly acclaimed at the time of its release. It is often cited as one of the best, if not the best, of the Castlevania series and one of the best video games of all time, and it is easy to understand why. Even though there is not a huge jump in graphics from the previous generation, the game is nevertheless beautiful. Packed with features and with the additional RPG element, Castlevania: Symphony of the Night was a joy to play. The music by Ayami Kojima, too, is incredible. At a time when most games were 3D, it was nice to see that well-made 2D games were definitely still worth playing.

Castlevania: Symphony of the Night was ported to the Sega Saturn and much later to many other different platforms.

Star Fox 64/Lylat Wars

Date of release: April 1997

Region: Japan

Developer: Nintendo EAD

Publisher: Nintendo

Platform: Nintendo 64

Directed by Takao Shimizu, produced and designed by Shigeru Miyamoto, Star Fox 64, known as Lylat Wars in the PAL Region, is a single-player or multiplayer rail shooter. While Star Fox 64 is essentially a remake of the original Star Fox game, there are enough differences and additional content to make it distinctive. Again, the player character is Fox McCloud, part of the Star Fox team, piloting the advanced prototype Arwing fighter and must fight back against the invading forces of Andross. As per the original, you can choose your path throughout the game giving the player a chance to try different destinations on a new playthrough. The gameplay consists primarily of one of two modes. The 3D Scroll Mode is similar to the original game where the player generally flies in one direction, shooting down enemies until reaching their goal at the end. All-Range mode involves flying around in a large square-shaped area, where your ultimate goal is located somewhere within said area. Players of the original game will be familiar with the graphical overlay displaying useful information such as your shield gauge, boost gauge, remaining Arwings, remaining Smart Bombs, enemy shield gauge and aiming reticule. Destroyed enemies will sometimes drop helpful items, which can boost firepower or recover shields, repair the Arwing (if damaged) or grant an additional Smart Bomb. The player must also be on the lookout to help any teammates in trouble. A portrait of them requiring help and an arrow on the screen indicates where you need to go to save them. Useful dogfighting manoeuvres in Star Fox 64 tied to specific controller input include the Arwing's boost and airbrake, braking and barrel rolling to avoid enemy fire, the Somersault (a Kulbit manoeuvre) to cause pursuing enemies to overshoot, and the U-turn, reminiscent of an Immelmann turn, to bring the Arwing's guns to bear on an enemy attacking from behind, although they can only be used in All-Range mode. A new feature of the game was the introduction of the Landmaster, a tank that the player controls in two of the game's missions and the Blue-Marine submarine which is available in one of the missions.

Star Fox 64 was the first game to make use of the Rumble Pak, a small device that fixes onto the N64 controller and vibrates during certain points in the game, for example when the player's Arwing is hit. This was a first for home console game controllers and made for a more immersive experience. The vibration feature in a controller would become a standard feature for many years to come. The game's music and score by Koji Kondo and the huge amount of voice-over and chatter from the different characters throughout the game took up a whole third of the memory of the entire game.

Despite being criticized by some for its short campaign and its disappointing multiplayer mode, Star Fox 64 was highly acclaimed for its 3D graphics, gameplay, audio and integration of the Rumble Pak. Star Fox 64 sold over four million units, making it one of the best-selling games for the N64. A remake of the game was released in 2011 for the Nintendo 3DS. Star Fox 64 is often considered the best of the Star Fox games and one of the best video games of all time.

Atelier Marie: The Alchemist of Salburg

Date of release: May 1997

Region: Japan

Developer: Gust Co. Ltd.

Publisher: Gust Co. Ltd.

Platform: PlayStation

Atelier Marie: The Alchemist of Salburg is a single-player RPG and the first in the Atelier series of games. The aim of the game is to create something outstanding enough to prevent the player character's expulsion from their alchemy class. Said player character is Marie, a 19-year-old student gifted at alchemy but terrible at concentrating in classes. To fulfil the aim of the game, Marie must collect ingredients from around the game world and subsequently prepare these ingredients in her atelier, or workshop. As with other traditional JRPGs, there is a world map, a first-person viewpoint when you are interacting with NPCs, and the traditional isometric view when in towns, in the workshop or combat. Combat is the tried and tested turn-based variety taking place on a grid, where the player can choose between several different methods of attack, or alternatively heal and use items. The player can have a maximum of three characters in their party, including the titular Marie.

The game was later ported to the Sega Saturn, Microsoft Windows, Dreamcast and PlayStation 2. Unfortunately, Atelier Marie: The Alchemist of Salburg was never officially released in the West. However, a fan-made translation of the PS2 version became available in 2018. To date, there have been well over twenty games in the main Atelier series. Some of the most notable of these are Atelier Iris: Eternal Mana (2004), Mana Khemia: Alchemist of Al-Revis (2007), Atelier Shallie: Alchemists of the Dusk Sea (2014), Atelier Ayesha: The Alchemist of Dusk (2012) and Atelier Ryza: Ever Darkness & the Secret Hideout (2019).

Dungeon Keeper

Date of release: June 1997

Region: UK

Developer: Bullfrog Productions

Publisher: Electronic Arts

Platform: MS-DOS & Windows

Designed by Peter Molyneux, Mark Healy and Simon Carter, Dungeon Keeper is a single-player or multiplayer, real-time strategy and dungeon management/god game. The aim of the game varies depending on the scenario, yet a key aspect is to build and maintain a dungeon and repel any invaders or interlopers. The isometric view can be rotated and zoomed in or out as the player controls their minions. Or, more accurately, attempts to control them, as they have their own AI and must be persuaded into performing the player's bidding, even if this means picking them up with your giant hand (which acts as the game's cursor), dropping them where they are needed and perhaps even slapping them around a bit until they behave. The player will need to use their minions to dig out new areas from the hub of the dungeon, known as the Dungeon Heart. These areas are where minions can rest, eat, train, study new technology and store any acquired treasure which is subsequently distributed as wages for the player's minions. There are a multitude of minions to choose from, and the player can possess their minions and control them from a first-person perspective. However, this serves as more of a novelty than a recommended approach. The way the game is meant to be played is from the isometric view with the player performing the necessary macro- and micro-management of minions, traps and dungeon upkeep. Combat involves any adventurers foolish enough to enter your dungeon being dealt with by the player's minions and any traps prepared for them ahead of time. Dungeon Keeper sports a rather hands-off approach during combat, though the player can join the fray with the odd thunderbolt cast here and there; the whole experience is devilishly fun.

Even though Dungeon Keeper was not the first game where you play as the villain, Tecmo's Deception: Invitation into Darkness (1996) being one such game predating it, it was still a rare novelty, making it stand out from other games of the time. Dungeon Keeper was highly acclaimed for its departure from most other video games in its concept, as well as its fiendishly funny, dark sense of humour.

Later that year The Deeper Dungeons was released, an expansion pack featuring fifteen new levels. Dungeon Keeper spawned one sequel with Dungeon Keeper 2 (1999). In 2010 a fan-made game called KeeperFX was released, which was an updated version of the base game.

Digimon

With the immense success of the Tamagotchi, released in November 1996, it was a reasonable assumption that others would try and emulate such a concept. Created by Akiyoshi Hongo and released by Bandai in June 1997, Digimon (a portmanteau of Digital Monster) was a similar key chain digital game device able to fit into the palm of your hand. Whereas the Tamagotchi was essentially aimed at girls, the Digimon was decidedly more masculine in scope, being that the Digimon were meant for combat. Similar to other virtual pets, the player must nurture their pet by feeding, cleaning, training, healing and helping it get to sleep. Once the Digimon reaches a certain level of evolution, they can battle other Digimons by linking to a friend's device.

The Digimon was incredibly successful with initial sales of fourteen million units, thirteen million of which were in Japan alone. Several different models were launched to the market over the years, each introducing new elements and features. To date, it is believed that over twenty-four million Digimon devices have been sold. Digimon exploded into a highly successful franchise which includes anime, films, manga and of course the many video games, the first of which was Digimon World (1999).

Final Fantasy Tactics

Date of release: June 1997

Region: Japan

Developer: Square

Publisher: Square

Platform: PlayStation

Final Fantasy Tactics is a single-player, isometric, turn-based, tactical RPG, the aim of which is to meet the objectives of each battle, which often means defeating the enemy. The game is set in the medieval land of Ivalice. Still recovering from the Fifty Year War against the eastern kingdom of Ordalia, Ivalice is plunged further into chaos after the death of the reigning King Ondoria Atkascha III. There are two heirs to the throne, both subject to various schemes and skulduggery, and a power vacuum quickly forms as two regents rise to oppose each other: Duke Larg of Gallione and Duke Goltana of Zeltennia. Through behind-the-scenes political machinations, the situation quickly sours as the War of the Lions breaks out, so called due to the forces of Duke Larg marching under the banner of the White Lion against the forces of Duke Goltana under their respective banner of the Black Lion. You play as Ramza Beolve, thrust into a preeminent role in the War of the Lions by his association with a mercenary group charged with guarding the kidnapped princess Ovelia. His story is interwoven throughout the narrative of the game and highlighted by the game's combat: the meat and potatoes of Final Fantasy Tactics. The combat is turn-based and takes place on a rotatable isometric grid of varying heights and landscape features including water, hills and assorted man-made structures. The player's attack team is made up of up to five units. Each unit can be placed to create their own formation on the field before combat begins. A status screen is provided at the bottom of the screen displaying the current player's portrait, Experience Points (Exp), Hit Points (HP), Magic Points (MP) and Charge Time (CT), which is the bar that must be filled before the unit can perform their next action. Final Fantasy Tactics operates off the job system, meaning that each character has a job, essentially their class (ranging from Archer to Geomancer to Dark Knight) and a zodiac sign which can deal increased damage to enemies if the character's zodiac sign and job are compatible. Other qualities a unit possesses are how far they can move, how high or far they can jump, their associated speed stat (which affects how fast or slow their CT is) and the base power of their attacks. Spells can be used by specific units, although some of these can take time to charge. These spells can be anything from direct attacks, debuff spells, recovery spells, or defensive spells. Some units can even summon powerful monsters to fight on their allies' behalf. There are dozens of spells in Final Fantasy Tactics, making for a very deep and rich experience. Units can also be equipped with weapons, armour and other helpful items. The overall lay of the land can greatly affect the player's strategy: for instance, it is a good idea to have ranged units placed on higher topography as they cause higher damage when attacking enemies situated below them. Mobility is also affected by the topography, weather and even what type of weapons and armour the units are carrying.

The game was directed by Yasumi Matsuno, creator of Tactics Ogre: Let Us Cling Together (1995), a similar turn-based tactical RPB. In fact, many of the development team who worked on Tactics Ogre also worked on Final Fantasy Tactics.

Final Fantasy Tactics was highly praised at the time. Its popularity has only increased over time, garnering it a cult game status. It is now considered by some to be one of the best video games of all time Final Fantasy Tactics is the first game in the Final Fantasy Tactics series. Perhaps the most notable of this series are Final Fantasy Tactics Advance (2003) and Final Fantasy Tactics: The War of the Lions (2007). As well as this, other games, such as Vagrant Story (2000) and Final Fantasy XII (2006), have been set in the land of Ivalice.

Carmageddon

Date of release: June 1997

Region: UK

Developer: Stainless Games

Publisher: Sales Curve Interactive

Platform: MS-DOS, Windows & Mac OS

Designed by Mark Teal, Neil Barnden and Patrick Buckland, Carmageddon is a single-player or multiplayer, third-person, 3D, vehicular combat racing game. It is a free-for-all race where the only aim is to complete all the laps in the time provided. Extra time is awarded for running over pedestrians (who are zombies in some versions of the game and real people in others) and bashing into other cars. Destroying all opposing cars or killing all the pedestrians is also another way to win the race in Carmageddon. The other aim of the game, apart from causing as much death and destruction as possible, is to increase your ranking and earn money. This can be done by fulfilling the set goals of the race, which subsequently awards money which the player can then spend on upgrading and repairing their vehicle. The game featured eleven locations, thirty-six tracks, and realistic vehicle deformation. Apart from the unfettered violence of the game, the music and the digitised animated portraits of real actors were seen as nice touches and greatly added to the game's character and overall experience.

Initially, Carmageddon was originally developed as a Mad Max game, but after the deal fell through Stainless Games sought inspiration from the film Death Race 2000 (1975). Of course, Carmageddon followed a long ancestry in this particular sub-genre of the vehicular combat game that all began with Death Race (1976), itself drawing inspiration from Death Race 2000. Other such visceral and violent games in a similar vein were Road Rash (1991) and Twisted Metal (1995).

Carmageddon initially failed to meet rating standards in several countries, including the UK, it's country of origin. Pedestrians had to be replaced with zombies, along with other changes aimed at turning down the violence to secure the game's rating and subsequent release, the process taking almost an entire year. Stainless Games attempted to make the game as controversial as possible to drum up interest, and it worked. The game was notorious for its violence, and the infamy of it initially being banned (along with some countries choosing to maintain said ban) made it even more appealing for some players.

Carmageddon spawned an expansion pack, the Splat Pack, and gave rise to four sequels with Carmageddon II: Carpocalypse Now (1998), Carmageddon TDR 2000 (2000), Carmageddon: Reincarnation (2015) and Carmageddon: Max Damage (2016).

GoldenEye 007

Date of release: August 1997

Region: Worldwide

Developer: Rare

Publisher: Nintendo

Platform: Nintendo 64

Directed and produced by Martin Hollis and designed by Duncan Botwood, GoldenEye 007 is a single-player or multiplayer, first-person shooter, based on the James Bond film GoldenEye (1995). The single-player campaign closely follows the plot of the film. As MI6 secret agent James Bond, the player must stop a criminal syndicate from using an electromagnetic pulse satellite weapon, codenamed 'GoldenEye'. The game features a multitude of weapons based on their real-world counterparts but sporting slightly different names with which to take out your enemies, including knives, the PP7 Special Issue (based on James Bond's signature suppressed Walther PPK), assault rifles, submachine guns, PDWs, sniper rifles, and a whole slew of explosives ranging from mines to rocket launchers. Of course, as James Bond, the player has access to several gadgets, ranging from the Watch Laser to the data thief. A great deal of emphasis is placed on stealth during certain parts of the game, as triggering alarms or the sound of loud gunfire can bring down a veritable swarm of enemies. Other parts of the game eschew the need for subtlety and demand the player cause as much chaos and mayhem as possible. The player can pick up armour vests to help take on the multitude of enemies when the bullets start flying. GoldenEye would prove to be one of those rare games where it excelled both with its single-player campaign and its multiplayer in equal measure. Up to four players can shoot it out in split-screen death matches. Players can set the rules of the game beforehand, choosing their map, character, weapons and game length. There are also eight different modes or game scenarios available in multiplayer, and aside from Normal mode, 2 Vs 2, 3 Vs 1, and 2 Vs 1, each is named after other films in the James Bond series reflecting the twist on the gameplay: You Only Live Twice where players have two lives; The Living Daylights, where whoever holds the flag the longest wins; The Man With the Golden Gun where players scramble to find the Golden Gun placed on the map which kills in one shot; and finally Licensed to Kill, where every shot or hit is lethal.

Rare took photographs of the actual film sets to more accurately portray the in-game environments and better immerse players in that world. As with some other N64 games which used 3D graphics, Rare used an SGI Onyx workstation to build the environments and characters of GoldenEye 007.

The game sold over eight million units, making it the third best-selling game for the N64. GoldenEye was a watershed moment for the first-person shooter genre on home consoles and paved the way for subsequent games, such as Medal of Honor (1999), Perfect Dark (2000) and Call of Duty (2003). GoldenEye was one of the most beloved games for the N64.. Being a more mature and gritty game, it was a welcome departure for the platform as opposed to the child-friendly intellectual properties that Nintendo was known for. Many cite GoldenEye as one of the best video game adaptations based on a film, if not the best. Furthermore, not only is it ranked as one of the best games for the N64, but also one of the greatest video games of all time. A reimagining of the game GoldenEye 007 was released in 2010 for the Nintendo Wii and DS, along with the Xbox 360 and PlayStation 3.

Game.com

The Game.com (pronounced "game com") was an 8-bit, fifth-generation, cartridge-based handheld console released in August 1997 in the USA by Tiger Electronics. Priced at $69.95, the Game.com featured a black and white (with 4 grey levels) 200 x 160 LCD screen. It also included a phone directory, calendar and calculator applications. The Game.com was significant as it was the first handheld games console to include a touchscreen and the first which could connect to the internet through a 14.4 kilobit per second modem. Players could also connect consoles with a cable for multiplayer games.

The Game.com was supposed to compete with the Nintendo Gameboy, and even though it was marginally superior in graphics (although the screen was rather blurry) and sound quality, it suffered from slow frame rates, unreliable internet connectivity and a lack of games; only twenty-one games were released for the system. Added to that the fact that the Gameboy Color (1998) was looming large on the horizon, there are quite a few factors as to why the Game.com was a failure.

Bomberman 64

Date of release: September 1997

Region: Japan

Developer: Hudson Soft

Publisher: Hudson Soft

Platform: Nintendo 64

Bomberman 64 is a single-player and multiplayer, 3D, puzzle platform game and the first Bomberman game for the N64. The aim of the game is to stop Altair, one of the main villains of the series, who has stolen the Omni Cube to use for his own evil ends. Bomberman must destroy the enemy bases and deal with multiple enemies, including a boss, on each world in his quest to ultimately stop Altair. There are five different worlds to clear in Bomberman 64. The five worlds are Green Garden, Blue Resort, Red Mountain, White Glacier and Black Fortress. As with other Bomberman games, gameplay revolves around destroying all enemies with Bomberman's bombs. Bombs can be dropped or kicked to damage and destroy enemies. Bombs can also boost Bomberman up to a higher level if stood upon. They can also be pumped-up while held to make their detonations more powerful. Bomberman can also pick up certain items which can give him more powerful bombs, remote-controlled bombs or allow him to place more bombs. Other items give Bomberman more health or allow the player to make aesthetic changes to Bomberman. Bomberman64 also introduced the Skull item to the series, which can cause several adverse effects on an opponent if thrown at them.

Also new to the series in this game is the Evil power-up, which affects all enemies on-screen when picked up. The effects caused by the Skull and Evil range from everyone getting bigger, to slower movement, players' positions changing at random, to all bombs suddenly exploding with maximum power. Luckily, Evil in particular only appears once every battle in multiplayer mode.

The multiplayer mode was not as good as some previous Bomberman games, though it was still eminently playable, fun and easily accessible on the N64 platform with its four controller ports. There are six different maps to enjoy in Bomberman 64 multiplayer. Players choose to play in either Single Battle mode or Team Battle mode. The main attraction of the game was the single-player story mode, which was a departure from most Bomberman games where multiplayer was the sole reason to play.

This was not the first 3D Bomberman game to be released, despite what some may believe. The first 3D game of the series was the somewhat lesser-known, first-person 3-D Bomberman (1984). However, Bomberman 64 was far more advanced with textured 3D polygons shown from a third-person perspective and a player-controlled movable camera.

Ultima Online

Date of release: September 1997

Region: Worldwide

Developer: Origin Systems

Publisher: Electronic Arts

Platform: Microsoft Windows

Directed by Starr Long, produced by Richard Garriot (AKA Lord British, who originally coined the term MMORPG, or massively multiplayer online role-playing game) and designed by Raphael Koster, Ultima Online is an isometric MMORPG. The game was advertised as 'more than fantasy because it really exists and more than a game because it never ends and a giant leap beyond anything you've ever seen,' and it was no marketing hyperbole. Ultima Online was both graphically and technically the most advanced MMORPG to have been released, able to cater for several thousand players.

Nowadays, it is a common occurrence that the course of MMORPGs narrative can be shaped by the players themselves such as in Eve Online (2003). However, in 1997 such a thing hadn't happened before, until one fateful day when such an event took place and a player was able to attack and kill Lord British's' Avatar, the man behind Ultima since its inception in 1979 and usually invulnerable to any form of attack apart from that one moment when he was addressing a host of players. An impossible event had been brought about by one single player, demonstrating how MMORPGs were set apart from all other genres of games in that the players could sculpt the future of the game. Furthermore, Ultima Online would spearhead the concept of world events where the developers would, without warning, activate an event such as unleashing hordes of undead upon a city. The way the world evolved and changed alongside the players, coupled with the players evolving and changing relationships and interactions with each other, made Ultima Online feel like a living, breathing world. The game offered blissful escapism upon which players would spend hundreds, even thousands, of hours of their lives.

Ultima Online would also introduce a new phenomenon in video games, namely that of selling virtual items such as weapons, houses or even characters for real-world money. Some of the most prized of these could go for thousands of dollars. A contemporary MMORPG of the time, Meridian 59 (1995), used a subscription service based around an hourly fee of $15, which was definitely not cheap. Ultima Online instead opted for a fixed monthly subscription fee, which proved far more popular, and it wasn't too long before the game had over 100,000 subscriptions, far exceeding that of any other MMORPG and reaching its peak in 2003 with around 250,000 subscriptions. Indeed, soon after the release of additional servers had to be opened up all over the world to accommodate the demand for the game.

Ultima Online became the undisputed king of the MMORPG genre and would go on to release eight expansions, adding new territories and new worlds to explore. A new game engine with improved graphics was also released under the name of Ultima Online: Kingdom Reborn (2007). As Ultima Online evolved over the next several years, it would set the standard and lay the foundation for all MMORPGs to come, such as Lineage (1998), Everquest (1999), RuneScape (2001), the aforementioned Eve Online (2003), World of Warcraft (2004), Guild Wars 2 (2012), Final Fantasy XIV Online (2013), and The Elder Scrolls Online (2014).

Oddworld: Abe's Oddysee

Date of release: September 1997

Region: USA

Developer: Oddworld Inhabitants

Publisher: GT Interactive Software

Platform: PlayStation

Oddworld: Abe's Oddysee is a single-player, flip screen, cinematic platform game. Playing as Abe, the aim of the game is to save your fellow Mudokons from becoming slaughtered for their meat at the RuptureFarms meat processing factory. Abe's Oddysee is reminiscent of other cinematic platformers, including Prince of Persia (1989), Another World (1991) and Flashback (1992), in its gameplay and mechanics. Involving elements of stealth, timing and puzzle-solving, the game was notoriously challenging and could be off-putting for some. However, it could also be very rewarding the further the player progresses as Abe gains new abilities. Furthermore, the player had infinite lives and could save at any point to mitigate the high difficulty of the game. Abe's Oddysee features different endings depending on how many Mudokons you save.

Oddworld: Abe's Oddysee was highly praised for the quality of its 3D cinematics and how they interwove with the narrative. The gameplay was a mix of high-quality 3D and 2D imagery, giving rise to graphics and animation that amazed many consumers. The game certainly looked next-generation. The game also benefitted from a $10 million marketing campaign, bringing huge awareness to this new IP.

Oddworld: Abe's Oddysee was a big hit and has spawned a series of Oddworld games. Some of the most notable of these are Oddworld: Abe's Exodus (1998), Oddworld: Much's Oddysee (2001) and Oddworld: Stranger's Wrath (2005). A remake of the original game was released in 2014 called Oddworld: New 'n' Tasty!

Postal

Date of release: September 1997

Region: USA

Developer: Running with Scissors

Publisher: Ripcord Games

Platform: Microsoft Windows

Postal is a single-player, isometric shooter. The premise is simple, as the player character is a man who has been evicted from his home and believes that the world is evil and full of people out to get him, and so he subsequently goes on an unending killing spree. The broad goal for progression is to kill the required number of law enforcement officers to proceed to the next level. Dead officers drop weapons, ammunition and health packs. Along with an assortment of guns available to them, the player can also throw grenades and Molotov cocktails. Killing civilians has no in-game benefit, yet players would happily indulge in this action, leaving dozens of bloody corpses strewn about the place.

Postal would become the latest in a line of ultra-violent video games for which the nineties would become infamous, and which certain members of the gaming community seemed to crave. The fact that the video game violence in this instance was played out in an everyday urban environment was a little too close for comfort for some, and the game was banned in Australia and Brazil. It is easy to get hung up on the violence in Postal and consider little else regarding the game. However, Postal has an interesting tone moving from very dark to comical, as improbable as that may sound. Also, the art style of the environments, while not the most beautiful, was in fact just one, huge, hand-drawn image, rather than an environment made up of generic repeating tiles. This feature was rather unique for the time.

The game was re-released as Postal Plus in 2001 and spawned two sequels, namely Postal 2 (2003) and Postal 3 (2011). A remaster of the original game, Postal Redux, was released in 2016. The game is now freeware.

Total Annihilation

Date of release: September 1997

Region: North America

Developer: Cavedog Entertainment

Publisher: Cavedog Entertainment

Platform: Windows

Developed by Ron Gilbert (of Maniac Mansion (1987) and The Secret of Monkey Island (1990) fame), Chris Taylor and Clayton Kauzlaric, Total Annihilation is a single-player or multiplayer, real-time strategy game. As with other RTS games of the time, the aim is to gather resources (in this case, metal and energy), and build a self-sufficient defensive base and offensive force, underpinned by a standard tech tree, in an effort to destroy enemy forces. To this end, players are given access to a veritable arsenal of units suited for naval, aerial and ground combat. Total Annihilation also has several features that distinguished it from its RTS contemporaries. Firstly, resources are gathered in a constant stream rather than being delivered in batches by miners. Secondly, the game features an element of electronic warfare, with all enemy units displayed on radar should they be within the detection radius. Players and AI alike can construct mobile radar jammers to prevent their units from showing up and thus be able to launch surprise attacks. Thirdly, the game is also capable of displaying hundreds, and in a later patch thousands, of separate units making for huge battles on an epic scale. Finally, Total Annihilation places particular importance on a unit called the Commander, a powerful and irreplaceable mech that is the only initial unit the player starts the game with. The Commander is crucial for base construction at the outset of the game, and a lynchpin for leading and beating back assaults past a certain point in the game.

With the success of Command and Conquer (1995) and the first two Warcraft games (1994 and 1995), and the release of Age of Empires a month after Total Annihilation's release, RTS games had truly entered their golden era. Even though it never garnered as much of a following as the aforementioned games, this one nevertheless won several awards. However, the game did have a marked imbalance between the two playable factions and several broken game mechanics that a player could exploit and use to gain an unfair advantage over their opponents.

Total Annihilation's popularity at the time is due to being developed at that perfect time for RTS games, and the fact that it was one of few such games that took place in a science-fiction setting and allowed players the satisfaction of nuking their enemies. The game spawned two expansion packs and inspired two spiritual successors: Supreme Commander (2007) and Planetary Annihilation (2014).

Age of Empires

Date of release: October 1997

Region: North America

Developer: Ensemble Studios

Publisher: Microsoft

Platform: Windows

Developed by Bruce Shelly (Railroad Tycoon (1990) and Civilization (1991)), Brian Sullivan, Rick Goodman, and with music by Stephen Rippy, Age of Empires is a single-player or multiplayer, isometric RTS game. The aim is decidedly variable, based on the current victory conditions. These vary between controlling all Artifacts or Ruins on the map for 2000 years (roughly five minutes of real-time), building and successfully defending a Wonder of the World for 200 years, or through military conquest. Players can also tweak, select or define their own victory conditions. In multiplayer mode, players can choose to play against the computer, against other players, or play cooperatively against the computer. Up to eight could play together, either online or over a LAN. The single-player campaign gives you the opportunity to play through twelve different scenarios centred around some of history's greatest civilisations, including the Ancient Egyptians, the Greeks, the Assyrians, the Persians, the Shang, and the Yamato. Each campaign plays as a series of missions, each with a specific goal to achieve. Each mission begins by explaining what the civilization has achieved thus far, and the challenges that must be overcome both on the map and in the narrative, fully immersing the player in their role of guiding their chosen civilization over time, from humble beginnings to great empires. As well as the standard gaming mechanics in an RTS, Age of Empires also included trading and diplomacy between civilisations. Researching technology was also key to progress in the game, giving players a chance to see how civilisations of the past developed. Paying tribute to other civilisations helped to maintain alliances. There were also opportunities to convert enemy units to the player's side using a priest.

Age of Empires set itself apart from many other RTS games of the time in that it was based on real-life historical events. Spanning over 12,000 years (12,000 BC to 500 AD), it served to reignite interest in history, ranging as it did from the Stone Age to the beginning of the Middle Ages. With a plethora of different campaigns, rather than the usual one or two, and coupled with the game's multiplayer aspect, Age of Empires had a huge amount of solid content for the RTS enthusiast and became a staple of the genre, much loved by many PC gamers.

As well as an expansion pack entitled Rise of Rome (1998), Age of Empires spawned many sequels, most notably Age of Empires II: The Age of Kings (1999), Age of Empires II: The Conquerors (2000) (often cited as one of the greatest PC games of all time), Age of Mythology (2002) and Age of Empires III (2005). A remastered version of the original, Age of Empires: Definitive Edition, was released in 2018.

Fallout

Date of release: October 1997

Region: USA

Developer: Black Isle Studios

Publisher: Interplay Productions

Platform: MS-DOS, Windows, Mac

Developed by Tim Cain and Christopher Taylor, Fallout is a single-player, isometric, retro-futuristic, post-apocalyptic, turn-based RPG and the first game in the popular Fallout series. Set in 2161 in an alternate and post-apocalyptic future after the global nuclear war of 2077, you play as the Vault Dweller, a resident of a pre-war underground fallout shelter designated Vault 13. The initial aim of the game is to save Vault 13 by exploring the Wasteland and finding a replacement Computer Chip before the Vault's water reserves run dry. If the player accomplishes this they must then subsequently find the source of the unnatural mutations in the Wasteland that are giving rise to the Super Mutants, a source of great concern to Vault 13's Overseer. The player visits a vast array of locations, interacting with NPCs, which more often than not are part of a faction or group, ranging from militant human gangs, Ghouls, dangerous Super Mutants to the technologically advanced, power-armour-clad Brotherhood of Steel.

The game has multiple endings depending on the choices made by the player. They can accomplish the goals set out for them or refuse completely and wipe out the Vault entirely. With the use of their Pip-Boy 2000, a wristwatch-Esque computer, to aid in orientation, objective-tracking and inventory management, the Vault Dweller sets off into the Wasteland. At character creation, the player can choose to 'tag' three skills out of a possible eighteen. Tagged skills level up at twice the normal rate and serve as lynchpins to a particular character build, pushing the Vault Dweller into a certain playstyle that can range from stealthy to diplomatic to brute force.

The player can also choose up to two traits which help greatly in solidifying the given playstyle of a build and are almost impossible to change once chosen. As a result of the in-depth character creation system, the game can be played in a variety of different styles. However, the Wasteland is a dangerous place and even the most charismatic Vault Dweller has to resort to violence from time to time. Combat in Fallout is turn-based, where the player can spend a varying amount of Action Points to move, attack or perform specific actions, the effectiveness of which is determined by the points spent on the Vault Dweller's seven primary different statistics, decided by character creation. Called the S.P.E.C.I.A.L. (standing for Strength, Perception, Endurance, Charisma, Intelligence, Agility and Luck) system, these statistics govern the Vault Dweller's prowess in certain skills and influence the choice of weapon and combat style: the Small Guns skill keying off Agility as compared to the Unarmed Skill, which is determined by the total of Agility and Strength divided by two. As your character progresses, the player can put more points into their S.P.E.C.I.A.L. stats, further sculpting and customising their Vault Dweller's given play style. Furthermore, adding points to one of the S.P.E.C.I.A.L. stats affects derived statistics, which include total Hit Points, Armour Class, Action Points, Carry Weight, Melee Damage, Damage Resistance, Poison Resistance, Radiation Resistance, Healing Rate and Critical Chance. Players can recruit NPCs who accompany the Vault Dweller and fight alongside them in combat. These companions range from human to canine, the latter invariably called Dogmeat and who would go on to be a mainstay in the Fallout series.

Originally called Vault 13, Fallout is considered the spiritual successor to Wasteland (1988), also from Interplay Productions. The X-COM games (1994 onwards) were also cited by the developers as being a major influence. The style of Fallout is reminiscent of the retro-futurism associated with the Atomic Age called Atompunk featuring such cultural references as Buck Rogers-inspired ray guns while also heavily featuring musical, stylistic and aesthetic elements of 1950s culture. Even though the game is isometric, certain 3D elements were used in Fallout, such as the talking heads for NPCs, created using Lightwave 3D and Photoshop.

Fallout was well received by critics and consumers alike, widely praised for its writing, characters, humour and game mechanics. It is often cited as one of the best and most significant video games of its time, redefining the RPG genre. Its success has perpetuated the popular Fallout series, most notably Fallout 2 (1998), Fallout 3 (2008) and Fallout 4 (2015).

1996/1997s Golden Joystick Awards

1996/1997s Golden Joystick Awards is hosted in London in November 1997.

Parappa the Rapper wins Most Original Game.

Super Mario 64 wins Best Looking Game.

Wipeout 2097 wins Best Sounding Game.

Super Mario 64 wins Game of the Year.

Tomb Raider II

Date of release: November 1997

Region: UK

Developer: Core Design

Publisher: Eidos Interactive

Platform: Windows, Mac, and PlayStation

Tomb Raider II is a single-player, third-person, action-adventure game and the sequel to the ground-breaking Tomb Raider (1996). The aim of Tomb Raider II is to find the Dagger of Xian, an artefact that has the power to turn the wielder into a powerful dragon. Once more, the player character is the intrepid adventurer Lara Croft, globe-trotting around the world in seventeen different locations, including the Great Wall of China, Venice, a sunken shipwreck, a Tibetan Monastery, and ancient catacombs. Tomb Raider II includes new weapons, such as the M16 assault rifle and Harpoon Gun, as well as dynamic lighting, allowing Lara to hold and throw Flares to light up dark areas of the environment. There are also sections where Lara can drive vehicles to better explore the various level. These range from a speedboat to explore the canals of Venice to two different types of snowmobiles in Tibet. Another great improvement was with the player being able to save their game at any point on all systems, rather than having to laboriously find a blue save crystal.

With Lara having since become such an iconic character, she too received some improvements in the form of a more streamlined model with a realistic moving ponytail. Lara also wore different outfits depending on her environment, ranging from a brown leather jacket in the Tibetan levels to a wetsuit.

The popularity of both Lara Croft and the Tomb Raider franchise in the late 1990s cannot be understated. This sequel not only became one of the best-selling video games for both the PlayStation and the Tomb Raider series overall but was also one of the most commercially successful games at the time, selling over eight million units.

Despite PlayStation being perceived as the exclusive platform for the Tomb Raider games, an expansion pack including four bonus levels was released as a PC exclusive in 1999 called Tomb Raider II: Golden Mask.

Grand Theft Auto

Date of release: November 1997

Region: UK

Developer: DMA Design Limited

Publisher: Microsoft

Platform: MS-DOS, Windows, PlayStation, Game Boy Color

Grand Theft Auto (originally conceptualised as Race'n'Chase) is a single-player or multiplayer, action-adventure game and the first in the popular Grand Theft Auto series. The aim of the game is to earn enough points to advance to the next level. The game is viewed from a top-down perspective and is set across several fictional cities in the

United States of America, the first being Liberty City. To earn points, the player must take on criminal jobs and missions as distributed from phone booths. More points can be earned by carjacking and running into other vehicles. Numerous weapons can be found in crates scattered across the map, for use against anyone unwise enough to get in your way, along with body armour for when the police come after the player. Despite having specific jobs and missions to accomplish, players tended to just steal cars and generally cause mayhem by themselves. Even though Grand Theft Auto was not the first sandbox game by any stretch of the imagination, its sequels would become the gold standard for the genre.

The design of the game was inspired by the Miami Vice (1986) video game which uses a similar top-down view. Elite (1984) and Frontier: Elite II (1993) are also cited as inspiring Grand Theft Auto with their non-linear gameplay. Even Pac-Man (1980) has been cited as an influence on Grand Theft Auto, with the roads being the maze, the police playing the part of the ghosts, and running pedestrians over akin to eating Power Pellets.

Grand Theft Auto was not highly regarded by critics at the time. However, consumers loved it and it thrived in particular on the PlayStation. The significance of its legacy cannot be denied as it spawned some of the most commercially successful video games of all time, the most notable being Grand Theft Auto: Vice City (2002), Grand Theft Auto IV (2008), and Grand Theft Auto V (2013).

Quake II

Date of release: December 1997

Region: USA

Developer: id Software

Publisher: Activision

Platform: Windows

Developed by Kevin Cloud, American McGee, John Carmack and Adrian Carmack, and with music by Sonic Mayhem, Quake II is a single-player or multiplayer, first-person shooter. Whilst the game is called Quake II, it is not an official sequel to Quake (1996) since it does not continue the story of the original. However, id Software and their genre-defining FPS games are held in high regard for their adrenaline-inducing, action-packed gameplay and excellent level design as opposed to their high-brow narrative. The aim of Quake II is simple: mow down hordes of the grotesque cybernetic aliens known as the Strogg and ultimately kill the Strogg leader. Along the way, the player must fulfil other mission objectives, such as shutting down the alien defence system or stealing a tank commander's head to gain access to and subsequently call down an airstrike to progress to the next level.

Fulfilling these objectives to form a narrative was the shape of things to come, as future FPS games such as Half-Life (1998) and Medal of Honor (1999) also relied more heavily on objectives to emphasise and give direction to the narrative of the game as opposed to simply killing the enemy with little other context given.

There were also additional features to Quake II, such as improved enemy AI and four new weapons, including the Railgun and the BFG10K. Nevertheless, Quake II is broadly similar to Quake. The most noticeable difference between the two games is primarily aesthetic, with the gothic theme of Quake as opposed to Quake II's science-fiction.

Quake II was well-received. It never had quite the same impact as the first Quake, though it was always going to be difficult to accomplish that when Quake was so revolutionary. The game was ported to the PlayStation and the N64. However, it was on PC where the game was at its best and where the multiplayer version thrived.

Sega Bass Fishing/Get Bass

Date of release: December 1997

Region: Japan

Developer: AM1

Publisher: Sega

Platform: Arcade

Sega Bass Fishing is a single-player fishing game, first released for the arcade. The player uses a fishing rod controller, the line of which is connected to the cabinet. Using different lures, the aim is to catch a specific weight of fish within the time limit across the four stages of the game.

Sega Bass Fishing was launched for the Sega Dreamcast in 1999, which included more stages and features, and used the bespoke Sega Fishing Controller. Later still, it was ported to several other consoles, ranging from the Wii to the Xbox 360.

Sega Bass Fishing was a very successful Dreamcast game due to its unique and fun gameplay.

Gran Turismo

Date of release: December 1997

Region: Japan

Developer: Polys Entertainment

Publisher: Sony Computer Entertainment

Platform: PlayStation

Developed by Kazunori Yamauchi, Takeshi Yokouchi and Hirotaka Komiyama, Gran Turismo is a single-player or multiplayer racing game. The aim of the game is to win races that earn different levels of driver's licences, unlocking access to events, new tracks to race and new cars to drive. There are eleven tracks and roughly 240 licenced cars in the game, the total varying depending on which regional version of the game is being played. The range of cars includes models from Aston Martin, Chevrolet, Honda, Mazda, Mitsubishi, Nissan, and Toyota. Gran Turismo was one of the first games to use real brands for advertising banners alongside the tracks and was also one of the first games to use the DualShock controller, which used analogue controllers and featured vibrational feedback.

At the time, the realism of the cars in the cutscenes and the game was incredible. Consumers were excited about how realistic and beautiful the reflections on the cars looked. Furthermore, the game was not just aesthetically pleasing but also featured solid gameplay. The only drawback was that the cars never received any damage, no matter the severity of the collision. This was a stipulation from the car manufacturers themselves: they did not want to see their beloved cars damaged in any way, not even virtually. Necessitating five years to develop, Gran Turismo Touted itself as 'the Real Driving Simulator,' redefining the racing game genre. The game was yet another perfect example of the PlayStation's target audience: young adults with a high level of disposable income.

The game was highly praised for its graphics, in particular its reflection-mapping, gameplay, ground-breaking physics engine and soundtrack. It became the definitive racing simulator, setting the gold standard for other games to aspire to. It has spawned several sequels and spin-off games, some of the most notable of which are Gran Turismo 2 (1999), Gran Turismo 3 (2001) and Gran Turismo 4 (2004). Gran Turismo was the number one best-selling game for the original PlayStation and is often cited as one of the best video games of all time. At the time of writing, such is the precision of Gran Turismo that the games in the series have and are being used to train the next generation of professional racing car drivers. Making it not only a game but a very realistic driving simulator.

1997 Notable Omissions

Air Warrior III. Beatmania. Bladerunner. Blast Corps. Blood. Breath of Fire III. Broken Sword II: The Smoking Mirror. Championship Manager 97/98. Close Combat: A Bridge Too Far. Colony Wars. Crash Bandicoot 2: Cortex Strikes Back. Blast Corps. Croc: Legend of the Gobbos. Culdcept. Derby Stallion. Diddy Kong Racing. Die Hard Trilogy. DoDonPachi. Doom 64. Einhänder. Everybody's Golf. Fighters Megamix. Final Furlong. Formula 1 97. G1 Jockey. Game Boy Color. Grandia. Hexen II. Imperialism. Independence Day. Independence War. Intelligent Qube. Interstate '76. Herc's Adventures. Jane's 688(I) Hunter Killer. Klonoa: Door to Phantomile. Little Big Adventure 2/Twinsen's Odyssey. MDK. Mega Man Legends. Mega Man 8. Mega Man X4. Micro Machines V3. MLB 98 (first MLB game). Mortal Kombat 4. Myth: The Fallen Lords. Need for Speed II. Neo Geo 64. Nuclear Strike. Outlaws. Overboard!/ Shipwreckers! Panzer General II. PlayStation: The Official Magazine. Poy Poy. Riven. SaGa Frontier. Shadow Warrior. Shock Troopers. Shining Force III. Sid Meier's Gettysburg!. Silhouette Mirage. Sonic Jam. Sonic R. Spellcross. Star Wars Jedi Knight: Dark Forces II. Star Wars: X-Wing vs TIE Fighter. Steep Slope Sliders. Street Fighter Collection. Tengai Makyō: Daiyon no Mokushiroku. Tetrisphere. The Curse of Monkey Island. The King of Fighters '97. The Last Blade. The Last Express. The Lost Vikings 2. Theme Hospital. Vandal Hearts. Warlords III: Reign of Heroes. WCW vs now: World Tour. Wing Commander: Prophecy. Worms 2. Kirby's Dream Land 3. X-COM: Apocalypse. X-Men Vs Street Fighter. Yoshi's Story. Zork: Grand Inquisitor.

1998

Resident Evil 2

Date of release: January 1998

Region: Worldwide

Developer: Capcom

Publisher: Capcom

Platform: PlayStation

Directed by Hideki Kamiya and produced by Shinji Mikami, Resident Evil 2 is a single-player, survival horror game and the sequel to the genre defining Resident Evil/Bio Hazard (1996). Set two months after the first game, Resident Evil 2 finds rookie police officer Leon S. Kennedy and Claire Redfield (younger sister of Chris Redfield from the first game) amidst a zombie-infested Raccoon City. Players get to play through the game from one character's point of view, then subsequently the other as they attempt to uncover just what happened in Raccoon City and try to escape alive. Both Leon and Claire traverse the same buildings and areas, but at different times (although they do bump into one another occasionally). The second playthrough will allow access to areas previously inaccessible and permit the player to piece together the entire story upon completion. There are four different endings in Resident Evil 2, depending on specific decisions made during the game. As with the first game, Resident Evil 2 uses a fixed camera system in a 3D environment, the pre-baked textures making for some beautiful-looking backdrops. The video of real actors from Resident Evil has since been discarded for some awesome-looking, 3D, pre-rendered sequences, at least by the standards of the time. Resident Evil 2's gameplay and mechanics are similar to its predecessor. Players have limited ammunition for their various weapons, items are scarce and carrying capacity is limited. Save points are only found in safe rooms where players must use their limited ink ribbons on the typewriters to save their progress. First Aid Sprays or the green, red and blue herbs provide healing or cure poison to a greater or lesser extent, depending on how they are combined. Inventory management and the scarcity of valuable resources form the core of what makes the game such an intense and exciting experience. Resident Evil 2 also carried over the puzzles from the first game, often requiring players to find pieces of a puzzle and place them at another specific point to progress further in the game. The areas Resident Evil 2 takes place in include the streets of Raccoon City, the Police Station, the sewers and the Umbrella Corporation

Underground Laboratory.

Resident Evil 2 was highly praised for its graphics, gameplay, story, atmosphere and sound design. Its only criticism was its clunky and tank-like control scheme for the player characters. In 1998, Resident Evil 2 became the fastest-selling game in North America, breaking the records previously held by Super Mario 64 (1996) and Final Fantasy VII (1997): its popularity at the time cannot be understated. This highly anticipated sequel cemented Resident Evil as the foremost series in the survival horror genre. It exceeded its predecessor in every aspect and is often considered the best of the Resident Evil games that were released for the fifth-generation consoles. It is also considered one of the greatest video games of all time.

Resident Evil 2 was ported to Windows, the N64, Dreamcast, GameCube and the Game.com. A remake was released in 2019, which also received extremely high praise.

Bust a Move: Dance & Rhythm Action/Bust a Groove

Date of release: January 1998

Region: Japan

Developer: Metro Graphics

Publisher: Enix

Platform: PlayStation

Bust a Move: Dance & Rhythm Action, known as Bust a Groove outside of Japan, is a single-player or multiplayer, music rhythm game. The aim is to beat your opponent by out-dancing them using your mysterious jive power and harness the power of the Groovetron. As with other rhythm games, the player must press specific button inputs in time with the music to outperform and outdance their opponent. The key to success in single-player mode would be to keep in sync with the music and build up the Enthusiasm Gauge to perform more difficult dance moves and thus win over the crowd. In multiplayer, the aim is to build up combo moves and attack your opponent with a player-character-specific 'Jammer' move, interfering with their dance. Players can avoid attacks by pressing the square button at the right time to perform a somersault and dodge the attack. Bust a Move features a roster of ten colourful characters to choose from, with another four hidden characters to unlock.

The game was highly praised for its gameplay and music, and for setting itself apart from most other games of the time. Bust a Move's huge popularity came off the back of the success of the PlayStation's other rhythm game, PaRappa the Rapper (1996), and the upcoming arcade hit, Dance Dance Revolution (1998). Bust a Move spawned an arcade version and a sequel with Bust a Move 2: Dance Tengoku Mix/Bust a Groove 2 (1999).

Panzer Dragoon Saga

Date of release: January 1998

Region: Japan

Developer: Team Andromeda

Publisher: Sega

Platform: Sega Saturn

Directed by Yukio Futatsugi and designed by Manabu Kusunoki, Panzer Dragoon Saga is a single-player, action-adventure RPG and Sega's answer to PlayStation's hugely successful Final Fantasy VII (1997). You play as Edge, who has sworn to stop Craymen and his Black Fleet after they killed Edge's companions and left him for dead. Unlike the other games in the Panzer Dragoon series, which are on-rail shooters, Panzer Dragoon Saga mixes real-time and turn-based combat in the form of random encounter battles as the player flies about atop their dragon. The player can also explore large areas of the game world on the dragon and smaller areas on foot, similarly interacting with NPCs to other RPGs. The playable sections of the game are interspersed with voice-acted cinematics, giving much more depth to the story compared with other Panzer Dragoon games.

Panzer Dragoon Saga is spread across four CDs, with the first released as a demo in the Sega Saturn Magazine. Despite being a great game, it failed to compete with Final Fantasy VII, possibly due in part to PlayStation's unrivalled dominance over the market. Panzer Dragoon Saga just didn't get the attention it deserved, even though critics and consumers fawned over it, praising its graphics, gameplay, cinematics and sound design. The game soon achieved cult status, seen as a hidden gem that most gamers of the time had never played.

Panzer Dragoon Saga is often cited as the best game for the Sega Saturn and one of the greatest video games of all time. At the time of writing, it is highly sought after and copies of it are rare, making it rather valuable. The fact that it has never been available on any other platform and has never been remade only adds to its value.

Xenogears

Date of release: February

Region: Japan

Developer: Square

Publisher: Squaresoft

Platform: PlayStation

Xenogears is a science-fiction, single-player or multiplayer RPG and the first in what some refer to as the Xeno series. You play as Fei Fong Wong, who ends up fighting in a war against the powerful Solaris Empire. The story of Xenogears is truly epic in scope, covering many psychological and religious themes. The backstory and world-building are not found in the game, instead covered in Xenogears PERFECT WORKS: The Real Thing, a prestigious book which sells for well over £100. Xenogears' thought-provoking themes are intended to have the player wonder what they would do in such circumstances as the story unfolds before them. The narrative is played out in either beautiful anime cinematics, in-game cutscenes or overlaid in text on the current isometric game screen. Combat is turn-based with an Active Time Battle System, which had become standard for Square JRPG games of the time, using physical and magical attacks (even though the game is decidedly sci-fi in scope), and casting buffs and debuffs. Xenogears was a little different from other JRPGs of the time in that it used an action point system that players could use to string together specific combos known as Deathblows, some of which could be very innovative, markedly lethal and a real thrill to unleash upon your on-screen adversaries. Characters in the player's party will at times fight with their giant Mecha known as Gears, adding another interesting and satisfying element to the combat. Being able to orbit the camera (as opposed to being constrained to a fixed camera) whilst exploring these environments was another feature that set Xenogears apart from games like Final Fantasy VII (1998). The rest of the gameplay is exactly what one would expect from a standard JRPG, featuring a world map filled with intriguing locales, interactions and conversations with the game's many NPCs and the buying and selling of weapons and equipment.

What eventually became Xenogears was originally going to be a sequel to the highly-acclaimed Chrono Trigger (1995) but was later changed due to its sci-fi elements being too dissimilar. It was even conceived of as being what would become Final Fantasy VII (1997), but again development took it away from that path.

Xenogears does have its flaws. It is often criticised for its pacing and lack of gameplay during the second half of the game. However, its ambition, imagination and uniqueness have earned it a cult status that few games of the time have attained, and it is also often cited as one of the best RPGs of the time. Xenogears was only ported to systems in North America. The other games in the Xeno series consist of the Xenosaga games, of which there are six, and the Xenoblade Chronicles, of which there are also six games. Some of the most notable games in the Xeno series are Xenosaga Episode I (2002), Xenosaga Episode III (2006), Xenoblade Chronicles (2010), Xenoblade Chronicles 2 (2017) and Xenoblade Chronicles 3 (2022).

Tenchu: Stealth Assassins

Date of release: February 1998

Region: Japan

Developer: Acquire

Publisher: Sony Music Entertainment Japan (Activision in other parts of the world)

Platform: PlayStation

Directed by Takuma Endo and with incredible music by Noriyuki Asakura, Tenchu: Stealth Assassins is a single-player, third-person stealth game. Set in sixteenth-century Japan, the game begins with the player choosing between two characters. The first of these options is the male ninja Rikimaru, who is stronger but slower and uses a ninjatō sword. The second possibility is the female ninja Ayame, who is not as strong but moves faster and performs more combos with her two kodachi short swords. Each is the sworn protector of Lord Ghoda and young Princess Kiku. Tenchu: Stealth Assassins comprises ten missions. Most of these missions are made up of assassinations, though others involve delivering a message or gathering a rare herb at the top of a mountain to save Princess Kiku's life. The player must finally defeat Lord Mei-Oh and his servant Onikage who have the Princess held captive and opened a portal to the demonic underworld. The game has huge replayability. Once the player has finished the game with one character, there is of course the subsequent playthrough with the second. At the end of each mission, the player receives a performance-based rank ranging from Thug up to Grand Master, depending on how often they were spotted and how their kills were performed. The player can attempt any previous mission as many times as they wish. Before each mission, the player can choose to equip their ninja from a limited amount of items, including the obligatory Grappling Hook, shuriken or crimson blades (the naming thereof being region-dependant), Caltrops, Poison Rice, Mines, Coloured Rice, Grenades, Smoke Bombs and Healing Potions. Of particular importance in Tenchu is the Ki meter, situated at the bottom left of the screen and which indicates the proximity of enemies and how alert they are to the player's presence with a ?, !, !! or !? symbol, with a numerical value between 0-100 indicating how close an enemy is. The player can crouch amongst bushes, press flat against walls or evade detection through judicious use of the Grappling Hook to zip up to the rooftops or rafters above. In-game cutscenes throughout the game flesh out the narrative and give more depth to the characters.

Tenchu has been cited as one of the most influential games in the stealth genre. It added the element of verticality never before seen in the genre, making it possible to drop down and instantly kill an enemy from above. Players could reap huge rewards by taking their time, performing stealthy kills from behind and then disappearing back into the shadows, in their quest to seek perfection and earn the ever-elusive rank of Grand Master. The soundtrack is beautiful yet highly underrated and features an opening theme, ten mission tracks and an ending theme. Each is distinct and fit each aspect of the narrative perfectly.

The game was re-released in 1999 with a level editor allowing players to create their own levels. Acquire released an expansion pack entitled Tenchu: Shinobi Hyakusen (1999) containing 100 levels made by users using the level editor. There were also secret missions to unlock, with the expansion pack featuring 122 levels in all. Tenchu also spawned several sequels, the most notable of which are Tenchu 2: Birth of the Stealth Assassins (2000), Tenchu: Wrath of Heaven (2003) and Tenchu: Fatal Shadows (2004).

StarCraft

Date of release: March 1998

Region: USA

Developer: Blizzard Entertainment

Publisher: Blizzard Entertainment

Platform: Windows

Designed by Chris Metzen and James Phinney, StarCraft is a single-player or multiplayer, isometric RTS game. Set around the end of the 25th century, the game is made up of three parts and follows several different protagonists, whom the player controls, along with their associated forces. In the first part of the game, the player controls Jim Raynor, together with the forces of the Terran Confederacy or the Sons of Korhal led by Arcturus Mengsk and elite Ghost operative Sarah Kerrigan. Mengsk betrays and sacrifices Kerrigan to the Zerg so that he can fulfil his ambitions of overthrowing the Confederacy and becoming emperor of the new Terran Dominion. Disgusted by this, Jim Raynor breaks away from Mengsk, taking with him a small rebel force which would become known as Raynor's Raiders. In the second part of the game, the player controls the Zerg forces along with Kerrigan who was captured and changed into a Zerg/Human hybrid with formidable psionic powers, calling herself the "Queen of Blades." The end goal of the second part is for the Zerg to invade and defeat the Protoss on their home planet of Aiur at the behest of the Zerg Overmind. The third and final part of the game gives the player control over the Protoss, who end up joining forces with Jim Raynor and his Raiders to defeat the Zerg Overmind and its forces on Aiur.

Plot exposition would take place within pre-rendered cutscenes, or via talking heads on video screens and during gameplay. Despite being similar to Blizzard's previous RTS game, Warcraft II: Tides of Darkness (1996), and other games of the genre which feature resource gathering, base building and strategic macro- and micro-management of units, StarCraft differed vastly in many ways. Perhaps some of the most obvious is the stark differences in gameplay between the Terrans, the Protoss and the Zerg. The Terrans (humans) have some interesting technology such as Seige tanks and Ghost operatives that can cloak and 'paint' a target, allowing the player to launch a nuclear strike to devastating effect. The insectoid Zerg propagate and move quickly and can have the advantage of numbers, and what the Protoss lack in numbers they make up for in having the most advanced technology. The huge differences between these species, the dynamics during gameplay between them and the number of unique strategies it allows for players, makes for an RTS game with a skill ceiling never before seen by gamers before.

The game's compelling story was another feature that set it apart from its peers. Mengsk's betrayal of Kerrigan would become one of the most powerful moments in video game storytelling when StarCraft's sequel, Starcraft II: Wings of Liberty (2010) was released, again illustrating how the narrative was intensifying the immersion of video games and how it could endure across the decades.

Other evolutions from previous Blizzard RTS games included the use of pre-rendered sprites using 3D Studio Max, along with an isometric view of the battlefield to accommodate the 3D look of the game. StarCraft also necessitated a thorough redesign of the Warcraft II game engine. Furthermore, the game also featured an exceptional multiplayer option, which included several game modes and could accommodate up to eight players using the Battle.net internet service. Multiplayer games could be extremely competitive, and nowhere in the world was this truer than in South Korea, where the game became a national sport broadcast on dedicated TV channels. Matches were watched by hundreds of thousands of people and the game was officially recognized as a sport by the South Korean government. StarCraft had not only revolutionised the RTS genre but video games as a whole, and the vast majority of people in the world weren't even aware of that fact yet. Even to this day, many governments and branches of the mainstream media find it difficult to embrace and accept video games, which are far more popular than most sports, and would never dream of giving them the kind of exposure and recognition that South Korea did and still does to this day.

StarCraft sold over 11 million units, with almost half of these sales coming from South Korea alone, making it one of the best-selling PC games of the time. It is often cited as one of the most significant RTS games of all time, as well as one of the best video games of all time. It has inspired multiple novels, spawned one expansion pack with StarCraft: Brood War (1998), two add-ons entitled Starcraft: Insurrection (1998) and Starcraft: Retribution (1998), and perhaps most notably the highly acclaimed StarCraft II trilogy of games comprised of StarCraft II: Wings of Liberty (2010), StarCraft II: Heart of the Swarm (2013) and StarCraft II: Legacy of the Void (2015). A remastered edition of the original was released in 2017.

Parasite Eve

Date of release: March 1998

Region: Japan

Developer: Square

Publisher: Square

Platform: PlayStation

Directed by Takashi Tokita and produced by Hironobu Sakaguchi, and featuring music by Yoko Shimomura, Parasite Eve is a single-player, action RPG with survival horror elements. It is recognised as a sequel to the Japanese science fiction horror novel of the same name by Hideaki Sena and is the first game in the Parasite Eve series. The aim of the game is to stop the seemingly supernatural being known as Eve from killing the citizens of New York via spontaneous human combustion and to prevent the birth of a malevolent Ultimate Being. You play as police officer Aya Brea, who is the only person who is immune to the outbreaks of spontaneous human combustion. The game is played using a blend of set camera angles or panning cameras in 3D environments, very much akin to the formula used in Resident Evil 2. Combat is real-time as you wait for your attack gauge to fill, at which point the player can pause the game and attack using a variety of weapons and supernatural attacks which use Parasite Energy (similar to magical attacks and magic points or mana usage in a traditional RPG). The player can see the given area of effect of their chosen attack, allowing for optimal placement and target coverage.

Set against the backdrop of a snowy New York City on Christmas Eve and with its foreboding cinematics and haunting music, Parasite Eve makes for an excellent atmospheric survival horror game, although the gameplay can be a bit clunky at times. It was also Square's first M-rated game.

Parasite Eve was very well-received in Japan and managed to sell almost two million units. The game spawned two sequels with Parasite Eve II (1999), often cited as the best game in the series, and The 3rd Birthday (2010).

Spec Ops: Rangers Lead the Way

Date of release: April 1998

Region: USA

Developer: Zombie Studios

Publisher: Ripcord Games

Platform: Windows

Spec Ops: Rangers Lead the Way, also known as Spec Ops: Ranger Assault, is a third-person, single-player or multiplayer, tactical shooter game. The player can switch between controlling each soldier in turn or delegate control of squad mates to the AI and issue orders instead. Owing to the game being a military simulation, there is a broad range of real-world weapons and grenades at the player's disposal. Spec Ops: Rangers Lead the Way features five missions, set in different parts of the world.

The game received fair to good reviews. An expansion pack, Spec Ops: Ranger Team Bravo, was released later the same year. Spec Ops: Rangers Lead the Way is significant as not only was it the first in the Spec Ops series but was also one of the first in a new wave of realistic military simulation wargames, such as Operation Flashpoint: Cold War Crisis (2001) and ARMA (2006). Apart from this first instalment, most of the games in the Spec Ops series were not very highly rated, the one exception being the excellent Spec Ops: The Line (2012).

Radiant Silvergun

Date of release: May 1998

Region: Japan

Developer: Treasure

Publisher: Treasure

Platform: Arcade

Radiant Silvergun is a single-player or cooperative play shoot 'em up. Playing as fighter pilots, the aim of the game is to destroy wave after wave of oncoming enemies. Differing from traditional games of this genre, in Radiant Silvergun players have access to all sorts of power-ups from the very start. The game has three primary weapons whose firing modes can be combined into three new types of shooting, as well as a laser sword to hit nearby enemies. The trick is using the most efficient weapon for each situation, disposing of enemies as quickly and as efficiently as possible.

Radiant Silvergun served to illustrate that even though everyone seemed to want to play 3D games, there were still those in Japan who loved to play old school shoot 'em ups. Indeed, there is an argument to be made that the genre was always prominent there, and still is to this day. It would be no exaggeration to say that it is in part due to games like Radiant Silvergun that in modern-day Japan rows of shoot 'em ups, typically bullet hell games, are still eagerly being played, the country being far less affected by the decline of the West's arcades in the nineties.

Radiant Silvergun has often been cited as one of the greatest and most significant shoot 'em ups of all time. The game was ported to the Sega Saturn in July 1998 and received a spiritual sequel with Ikaruga (2001).

Unreal

Date of release: May 1998

Region: USA

Developer: Epic MegaGames

Publisher: GT Interactive

Platform: Windows

Unreal is a single-player or multiplayer, first-person shooter and the first instalment in the Unreal series. The aim of the game is to discover a way off the hostile planet of Na Pali. Playing as Prisoner 849, the narrative follows the player escaping the crashed prisoner transport ship, through the landscape of Na Pali and delving into the many internal structures of the native Nali, including the Nali Castle, which is featured in the beautiful cinematic menu screen. Throughout the game, you must kill or be killed by the many forms of Skaarj, a race of reptilian aliens. There are over twenty different enemies in the game, some attacking with claws, rocks or by spitting acid, while others are armed with a variety of weapons. However, Prisoner 849 is far from defenceless, acquiring several weapons throughout the game, ranging from kinetic to energy to explosive similar to other FPS games. In fact, it went an extra step further in terms of inspiration, as seen with guns like the Razorjack which fires ricocheting, spinning, serrated blades and the Eightball Launcher which could fire up to six heat-seeking rockets, or fire rockets one at a time and even featured an alternate fire mode which turned the rocket into a bouncing grenade instead. The game also features power-ups, such as the Amplifier which can dramatically increase the power of your energy weapons by a factor of four for a set amount of shots. Unreal also features many other items collected through the course of play to help defeat the Skaarj. The Universal Translator acquired at the beginning of the game can analyse and interpret messages, providing the narrative for the game as well as giving hints and clues as to how to progress. There are several different Suits which nullify damage from a certain type of hazard, Armour which offers general damage mitigation to better protect the player, Jump Boots affording higher jumps and Scuba Gear which facilitates underwater exploration. Health can be replenished with bandages, the Super Health Pack which can over-heal the player past their initial maximum of 100, and the curious Nali Healing Fruit, which is a seed that, once planted, quickly grows fruit which also boosts health. Unreal also features Flares, a Flashlight and a Searchlight which all help light up the game's many dark areas and serve to showcase Unreal's fantastic dynamic lighting. The game reaches its climax as you teleport from the Nali Castle to the Skaarj mothership and confront the Skaarj queen.

Unreal was developed with the first iteration of the now-legendary Unreal Engine. Tim Sweeny began creating the Unreal Engine (written in C++) in 1995. By the time it was finished and used for Unreal, it was ready to take full advantage of the power of the graphics cards of the time with cutting-edge features such as volumetric fog and the previously mentioned dynamic lighting. The Unreal Engine has also been adopted by the film and television industry and is arguably the most widely used and prolific gaming engine in the industry, often setting the gold standard for other game engines to aim for. The most current iteration of the engine at the time of writing is the Unreal Engine 5.

The game was highly praised for its graphics, gameplay and enemy behaviour, as well as its narrative. It was often compared to and quoted as being superior to Quake II in many ways. An expansion was soon released in the form of Unreal Mission Pack I: Return to Na Pali (1999) and was followed by numerous Unreal games. Some of the most notable of these are Unreal Tournament (1999), Unreal Tournament 2004 (2004) and Unreal Tournament 3 (2007).

Descent: FreeSpace – The Great War

Date of release: June 1998

Region: USA

Developer: Volition

Publisher: Interplay Productions

Platform: Windows

Designed by Adam Pletcher, Descent: FreeSpace – The Great War, more often referred to as simply FreeSpace or FreeSpace 1, is a single-player or multiplayer, first-person, space combat simulator. Set in the 24th century, you play as a starfighter pilot as part of the Galactic Terran Alliance (GTA) set in a war that has been raging for fourteen years against the alien Vasudans. The initial missions of the game pit you against the Vasudan forces, but the plot takes a dramatic twist when the even more deadly Shivans surge into the conflict. With their far more advanced technology, they can not only cloak their ships, making them to all intents and purposes invisible, but their fighters seem invulnerable to the GTA's weapons. In desperation, the Terran and their hitherto Vasudan foes join forces to find a way to battle this new menace. Between missions, each major plot point is played out in elaborate 3D cinematics. The gameplay is viewed from a first-person perspective from within the cockpit of one of the many fighters the player pilots throughout the game. Different craft are designed for each particular mission, of which there is a huge variety throughout the story. Players begin with a series of tutorials. This reveals the depth of game mechanics as you are taught about energy management between shields, a variety of weapons and engines. The HUD is a thing of beauty, displaying every necessary readout from radar, shields, energy management and enemy status. Each HUD display can be set to on, off or 'popup,' meaning the HUD only appears when specific statuses change. It is also possible to change the HUD's colour and relative brightness for ease of readability.

Multiplayer could be played via Cooperative missions PvP matches as individuals or in teams by way of LAN or over the internet using Parallax servers.

For fans of the genre, FreeSpace was an incredible game, easily standing shoulder to shoulder with games like the Star Wars: X-Wing series that ran from 1993 to 1999, Colony Wars (1997) and Wing Commander: Prophecy (1997). There was genuine suspense and drama in its story and gameplay. Often, a mission would drastically change when giant enemy battleships would suddenly emerge from wormholes, making players feel as if they were part of an exciting space adventure.

FreeSpace is a great example of how PC games were beginning to offer a variety of graphical detail depending on the capabilities of the computer, including varying texture quality, particle effects and lighting effects, something unheard of in the previous decade. This would become even more prevalent by the turn of the millennium.

FreeSpace spawned one expansion with Silent Threat (1998) and a full sequel with FreeSpace 2 (1999), which became even more highly acclaimed than the original.

Commandos: Behind Enemy Lines

Date of release: June 1998

Region: Europe

Developer: Pyro Studios

Publisher: Eidos Interactive

Platform: Windows

Designed by Gonzalo Suárez and Ignacio Pérez Dolset, Commandos: Behind Enemy Lines, often just referred to as Commandos, is a single-player, isometric, real-time tactics game. On the face of it, Commandos strongly resembled a shoot 'em up like the classic Cannon Fodder (1993). Nothing, however, could be further from the truth. Players had to think about exactly what they needed to do and plan exactly how they would do it. Members of the player's squad can easily be killed if spotted, and the game placed a great emphasis on stealth. Each enemy has a Vision Cone, a visual representation of their visual range, to help the player know how to circumvent the enemy or engage them in the most advantageous way. Footprints in the snow could also give away squad members' positions. For the most part, enemies would shoot on sight. However, if the squad mate stayed still, the enemy would take them away and lock them up in their camp, giving the player a chance at rescuing them. It was often critical that the player did just that, as every character had their own area of expertise and associated skillsets, such as the Sapper (explosives export) or Sniper and were oftentimes needed to complete the mission. There were a variety of missions including sabotage, rescue missions and assassination. There are twenty missions to play through in Commandos.

Commandos: Behind Enemy Lines became enormously popular in Europe and was highly praised for its graphics, difficulty and unique gameplay, which set it apart from many other games of the time. Along with its expansion pack, it went on to sell over a million units. Together with games like Myth. The Fallen Lords (1997) and Sid Meier's Gettysburg! (1997), Commandos would help establish the emerging real-time tactics genre, which differentiated itself from RTS games by focusing less (or, in a lot of cases, not at all) on resource gathering and base building and more on battlefield tactics and unit micromanagement.

The game spawned three sequels with Commandos 2: Men of Courage (2001), Commandos 3: Destination Berlin (2003) and Commandos: Strike Force (2006).

Banjo-Kazooie

Date of release: June 1998

Region: USA

Developer: Rare

Publisher: Nintendo

Platform: Nintendo 64

Banjo-Kazooie is a single-player platform game. The main characters are the titular Banjo, the easy-going honey bear, and his feathered breegull friend, Kazooie. The premise of the game is that Banjo and Kazooie are called to action and must rescue Banjo's sister, Tooty, from the evil witch Gruntilda. As Banjo, the player can run, jump, climb, swim and perform a forward roll attack, but can also switch to controlling Kazooie, who can fly, climb steep slopes and pull off several special attacks.

Banjo-Kazooie is an all-singing, all-dancing, platforming and collectathon game. The player must collect a certain number of Jigsaw pieces to proceed to other game worlds, each of which is based around a particular theme, ranging from swamp to frozen peak and even haunted house. Musical Notes need to be collected to open the Note Doors barring progress through Gruntilda's lair. Collecting five Jinjos (little dragon-like creatures awards more Jigsaw pieces. Eggs can be used as ammunition to shoot at enemies. Red feathers are consumables to be used to fly. A Golden feather grants Banjo and Kazooie temporary invulnerability. The skull-shaped Mumbo tokens can be used by the shaman Mumbo Jumbo to transform Banjo into different forms. Golden Banjo Statuettes give Banjo and Kazooie an extra life. Honeycomb pick-ups heal for one unit of Banjo and Kazooie's health bar. Kazooie will also be able to use the Wading Boots and Running Shoes to traverse certain environmental hazards. Other gameplay elements involve solving puzzles and defeating bosses. There are ten areas in total to explore in Banjo-Kazooie, including Gruntilda's Lair.

The game was a commercial success, selling over two million units and becoming a firm favourite with N64 owners. Produced by Rare, of GoldenEye (1997), Banjo-Kazooie helped to cement its reputation as one of the best developers for the N64 platform. Many said it was easily comparable with the much-lauded Super Mario 64 (1996), praising its graphics, smooth gameplay, level design, music and the sheer number of great ideas crammed into this one game. Banjo-Kazooie has spawned four more games in the series, these being Banjo-Tooie (2000), Banjo-Kazooie: Grunty's Revenge (2003), Banjo-Pilot (2005) and Banjo-Kazooie: Nuts & Bolts (2008).

Snake

Date of release: 1998

Region: Worldwide

Developer: Nokia

Publisher: Nokia

Platform: Nokia 6110

Programmed by Taneli Armanto for the Nokia 6110 mobile phone, Snake is a single player 2D monochrome clone of the arcade game Blockade (1976). The aim of the game is to collect as many of the blocks as possible, and in turn, earn the highest score possible. The player can turn the snake in any one of four directions. Whenever a block is collected/consumed, the player-controlled snake gets longer, making it more and more difficult to manoeuvre around the limited gameplay area until the snake invariably crashes into itself, ending the game.

Snake was one of a handful of games which came pre-installed on the Nokia 6110 and was by far the most successful. In the late 1990s, the mobile phone industry exploded, going from only a few people owning a mobile to almost everyone owning one in the span of a few short years. Snake was the first truly popular mobile phone game, akin to Pong (1972) for the arcades.

Mobile video games would evolve concurrently along with mobile phone hardware over the years. Mobile games now amount to over half of the digital video games market, valued at around $180 billion a year at the time of writing. This growth is only expected to rise.

Colin McRae Rally

Date of release: July 1998

Region: Europe

Developer: Codemasters

Publisher: Codemasters

Platform: PlayStation

Colin McRae Rally is a single-player or multiplayer, third-person racing game. Based on the 1998 World Rally Championship, the game features in-game models based on real-life cars and actual drivers of the event. However, the American version of the game did not feature real-life drivers except for Colin McRae. Options for a player's choice of the car were dependent on the chosen difficulty level. The player could hone their driving skills in the game's tutorial mode, called Rally School, or practise getting the fastest time in a single-player Time Trial. Rally mode offered a two-player split-screen on the PlayStation, and on PC it was possible to have up to eight players race against each other using a LAN. Championship mode offered the player a whole season of rallying across eight different countries.

The game featured real-world physics and damage to the player's car, which could hamper performance and even prevent the player from finishing the game if it was too severe. The game also had varying times of day and weather conditions, like rain, snow and fog, significantly affecting driving conditions. As in real rally racing, the player has a co-driver who can be heard giving crucial information about corners ahead, and understanding such prompts was crucial to success during a race. The game features the voices of both Colin McRae and his co-driver Nicky Grist, who also acted as technical consultants for the game.

Although not the first rally game, Colin McRae Rally was the first off-road rally simulation game to popularise the genre. The game became a firm favourite with players and went on to sell four million units. The sequel Colin McRae 2.0 was an even more refined game and was arguably more popular than the original. There are over a dozen games in the Colin McRae Rally and Dirt series, which is what it subsequently became known as. Some of the most notable are Colin McRae: Dirt 2 (2009), Dirt 3 (2011) and Dirt Rally (2015).

Soulcalibur

Date of release: July 1998

Region: Worldwide

Developer: Project Soul

Publisher: Namco

Platform: Arcade

Soulcalibur is a single-player or two-player, weapon-based fighting game. Even though it is the first game to be named Soulcalibur, it is in fact the second in the Soulcalibur series after Soul Edge (1995). The aim of the game, as in most fighting games, is to defeat your current opponent. Soulcalibur is perhaps the first fighting game to introduce a full 3D eight-way movement system. All previous games only had minimal movement towards and away from their opponent, whereas Soulcalibur allowed complete freedom of movement around its beautiful-looking arenas, something never experienced before.

Another feature that made Soulcalibur a milestone in this genre was that it ran at a smooth 60 frames per second (fps) as opposed to the 30 fps of the aforementioned Soul Edge, which was more typical for the genre. Furthermore, players could input combo commands before their character had finished their current action or combo, allowing them to queue combo after combo. Known as buffering, this technique was possible in other games of the genre, particularly Tekken, but demanded almost millisecond-precise timing. Soulcalibur, by comparison, was far more forgiving. Soulcalibur also featured a charged attack which, while very powerful, left the player vulnerable for a moment, and the Guard Impact, which could parry or redirect incoming attacks.

Soulcalibur was soon ported to the Dreamcast in 1999 and became a popular game to play, especially if the player was lucky enough to own a Dreamcast Arcade Stick that comprised a joystick and six buttons for a quasi-arcade experience. In practice, the Dreamcast version was undoubtedly superior to the original arcade version and showed off the true capabilities of the console. Soulcalibur on the Dreamcast looked so good and played so well that it was a true milestone in video game history. The day had finally arrived when an arcade conversion surpassed the original. For so long now, home ports had been reaching for that arcade-perfect experience. With Soulcalibur on the Dreamcast, the time had come when it was possible to develop a superior conversion of a 3D game for the home. The Dreamcast's competition was also found wanting, there simply wasn't a fighting game on the PlayStation or N64 that could come close to it.

Soulcalibur is often cited as one of the best games for the Dreamcast, one of the best fighting games of all time and one of the best video games of all time. Soulcalibur spawned several sequels, some of the most notable being Soulcalibur II (2002), Soulcalibur IV (2008) and Soulcalibur VI (2018).

Wargaming is founded

Wargaming was founded in August 1998 in Minsk, Belarus, by Victor Kislyi. The company began developing strategy video games, its first games being DBA Online (2000) and the Massive Assault series (2003-2006). Wargaming now has twenty offices globally and is best known for its free-to-play massively-multiplayer online games World of Tanks (2010), World of Warplanes (2013) and World of Warships (2015).

Tom Clancy's Rainbow Six

Date of release: August 1998

Region: USA

Developer: Red Storm Entertainment

Publisher: Red Storm Entertainment

Platform: Windows

Tom Clancy's Rainbow Six is a single-player and multiplayer, first-person tactical shooter and the first game in the Rainbow Six series. The game follows the same narrative as the Tom Clancy novel of the same name. Through a series of missions, the aim of the game is to stop the Phoenix Group eco-terrorist group from releasing a deadly strain of the Ebola virus at the 2000 Summer Olympics. Each mission begins with a briefing and a planning stage. The player kits their team out with the best equipment for the job splits them into smaller fire teams and then uses a map and interface to plan what actions each team will perform, and when. There was nothing like this in the FPS genre, and if the player could take the time to perform a perfectly coordinated and executed attack, it could feel incredibly rewarding. Emphasis during gameplay is on stealth and tactics since both Rainbow operatives and the enemy could be killed with one or two shots. This gives rise to a lot of suspense and a high degree of immersion. The player can control any one of a possible six teammates. To help better complete a mission, certain tools of the trade are available, ranging from the Heartbeat Sensor, which can track human heartbeats through walls and determine whether they are terrorists or hostages, to door charges, demolition kit, lockpick kit and flashbangs.

Rainbow Six was another example of a different breed of FPS game, forming the third distinct genre of First Person Shooters. The first was derived from and inspired by Doom (1993) and Quake (1996). Half-Life (1998) set the foundation for the second, that of the narrative FPS, while games like Spec Ops: Rangers Lead the Way (1998) and Rainbow Six carved out their own niche and codified the third genre, that of the more life-like military first-person tactical shooter. Like the newly evolving stealth genre, Rainbow Six was a difficult game but could be a very rewarding and immersive experience for those who exercised patience and used well thought out strategy for breaching and entry.

Rainbow Six was soon ported to the Dreamcast, Game Boy Color, Mac OS, N64 and PlayStation. Some of these ports were not as good as the original PC version, which is widely considered the best. The game spawned an expansion pack with Tom Clancy's Rainbow Six Mission Pack: Eagle Watch (1999). There are many games in the Rainbow Six series, some of the most notable being Rainbow Six: Rogue Spear (1999), Rainbow Six: Vegas (2006), Rainbow Six: Vegas 2 (2008) and Rainbow Six: Siege (2015).

Metal Gear Solid

Date of release: September 1998

Region: Japan

Developer: Konami Computer Entertainment Japan

Publisher: Konami

Platform: PlayStation

Directed and produced by Hideo Kojima, Metal Gear Solid is a single-player, action-adventure stealth game. It is the third game in the highly acclaimed Metal Gear series, but the first to be in 3D. Playing as Solid Snake, the player must infiltrate the codenamed "Shadow Moses" island off Alaska, which houses a nuclear weapons disposal facility and has been taken over by ex-special forces unit FOXHOUND, a unit Snake was formerly a part of. Throughout the game, the seemingly straightforward mission spirals into rescuing hostages, unravelling the secrets of Shadow Moses and FOXHOUND, and gaining and losing allies and enemies through double and triple-crosses, with the game culminating in a final confrontation against the nuclear-missile-armed bipedal mecha Metal Gear REX.

The majority of the game is played from an elevated camera angle, with a mini-map on display in the top right of the screen. Known as radar in the game, this helps identify enemies and displays their vision cones, allowing the player to better sneak past the guards or CCTV cameras. Alternatively, the player can lure out guards by making some noise like knocking against a surface, and subsequently sneaking up behind them and incapacitating the guard investigating the source of the sound. In certain outdoor areas, Snake will leave footprints in the snow, which the guards will also investigate. Snake can also use his iconic cardboard box to hide inside, but this ploy doesn't always fool the guards, depending on the circumstances. Alerting the guards will bring them homing in onto Snake's position, and though it is possible to fight them with a variety of weapons the game provides, it is easy to be overrun and killed. The player must also defeat several unique and iconic bosses who make up FOXHOUND, most of which have attained memetic status amongst the video game community. MGS bosses include formidable gunfighter Revolver Ocelot, the massive Native-American shaman Vulcan Raven, expert markswoman Sniper Wolf, mysterious Decoy Octopus and Psycho Mantis, capable of using telekinesis and mid-reading abilities. The only way to defeat Mantis is to unplug your controller from port 1 and plug it into port 2 in an inspired use of game mechanics). Finally, the mastermind of it all and FOXHOUND's leader is none other than Liquid Snake, who as the name suggests shares more than just a passing connection with Solid Snake. These bosses would go on to become legendary video game characters. Each one was superbly voice-acted and depicted with a fascinating design and backstory, requiring radically different approaches to defeat. They weren't just generically evil and two-dimensional characters but felt like real people, some with tragic narratives explaining the reasons they had gone down such a dark path. It was Metal Gear Solid's in-game cinematic narrative intertwined with its gameplay which elevated it to a place previously unexplored by video games before. The game also featured a host of supportive and fully-fleshed-out characters whom the player can contact, or be contacted by, using certain frequencies on their Codec.

An expanded version of the game was released for PlayStation and Windows as Metal Gear: Integral (1999) and a remake was also released for the Nintendo GameCube with Metal Gear Solid: The Twin Snakes (2004). Metal Gear Solid and its subsequent games are thought to have influenced other stealth games such as Tom Clancy's Splinter Cell (2002), Assassin's Creed (2007), and even Dishonoured (2012).

Metal Gear Solid sold over seven million units, quickly earning cult status as a must-play PlayStation game. Winning multiple awards, it has received many perfect to near-perfect scores from a multitude of publications. It is often regarded as the game to popularize the stealth genre and is often cited as one of the best and most significant video games of all time.

Spyro the Dragon

Date of release: September 1998

Region: USA

Developer: Insomniac Games

Publisher: Sony Computer Entertainment

Platform: PlayStation

Spyro the Dragon is a single-player, third-person, 3D platform game. The aim of is to defeat the evil Gnasty Gnorc, who has turned all the other dragons into crystalised statues. To accomplish this, Spyro must collect the jewels either lying around or in chests which must be broken into, find the dragon eggs and free the dragons from their crystal prisons by stepping on their pedestal. There are five dragon worlds in Spyro the Dragon, excluding Gnasty's Industrial World. Furthermore, the game is entirely open-world so the player can travel to any dragon world in any order and at any time they want. Spyro, the titular character of the series, is a small but feisty purple dragon, who can run in any direction and jump to varying heights, depending on how long the jump button is held, breathe fire and charge. He can also glide and evade left and right. Sparx the Dragonfly accompanies Spyro, providing useful information.

The PlayStation was generally known for games aimed at teenagers and young adults, while Nintendo was aimed more at kids and families. Spyro, along with games like Crash Bandicoot (1996), was PlayStation's answer to the new wave of 3D cutesy platformers, popularised by the very well-received Mario 64 (1996), and Sony's attempt to branch out to a younger demographic. Although sales were slow to start, word of mouth soon made Spyro incredibly successful, with sales eventually reaching almost five million units. This spawned several sequels, namely Spyro 2: Ripto's Rage (1999) and Spyro: Year of the Dragon (2000). All three Spyro games were remastered with Spyro Reignited Trilogy (2018). Even though the originals looked great in their day, there is no denying the huge leaps in graphic fidelity since, leading to the new, stunning look of the remastered version. Insomniac games would go on to develop other similar 3D Platformers with their popular Ratchet & Clank series of games.

Lineage

Date of release: September 1998

Region: South Korea and the USA

Developer: NCSoft

Publisher: NCSoft

Platform: Windows

Designed by Jake Song, Lineage is an isometric MMORPG and was the most successful video game to come out of South Korea, which is no mean feat given the country's prolific gaming culture. Inspired by Ultima Online (1997) and with game mechanics borrowed from NetHack (1987), Lineage is a typical online medieval fantasy RPG, where players choose their character, fight both monsters (PvE) and one another (PvP), complete quests and interact with the environment in a multitude of other ways, for example buying and selling items at in-game stores.

Soon after release, Lineage amassed over 500,000 subscribers and became the most successful online RPG in the world. By 2003, this number had reached three million. To put this in perspective, the incredibly popular Ultima Online had around 225,000 subscribers in 2003. Like Ultima, Lineage saw numerous examples of another rather new phenomenon, namely the selling of virtual items such as weapons, houses or even characters for real-world money. Some of the most prized of these could go for tens of thousands of dollars.

The game spawned one sequel, Lineage II (2003), which is a prequel. Lineage II would go on to attract over fourteen million players. A mobile port of Lineage was released in 2017 called Lineage M which has grossed over $4 billion at the time of writing, making it one of the most successful mobile games of all time.

Dance Dance Revolution

Date of release: September 1998

Region: Japan

Developer: Konami

Publisher: Konami

Platform: Arcade

Inspired by rhythm games like Parappa the Rapper (1996) and Bust a Move: Dance & Rhythm Action/Bust a Groove (1998), Dance Dance Revolution is a single-player or two-player, musical rhythm and dance game. The premise of the game is simple: hit the corresponding arrow button (up, down, left or right) located on the dance platform at your feet to the directional arrow displayed on the screen to earn points and receive feedback from the game, varying from 'Miss' to 'Good' to 'Great' to 'Perfect.' If the player can hit four sequential Greats or Perfects, then a combo gauge builds. However, hitting Good or below breaks the combo chain. If the player garners too many misses, the game ends. There are a vast array of tunes to choose from with differing levels of difficulty. Dance Dance Revolution featured 3D dancing characters in the background as the arrows scrolled by and featured a total of fifty-two songs.

Easy to learn but difficult to master, Dance Dance Revolution had a broad appeal, pulling in both the more traditional gaming crowd and also those with an inclination more to music or dance without necessarily being avid gamers themselves. With a lot of practice, it wasn't long before the impressive spectacle of two players dancing in perfect unison was drawing crowds and served to make the game even more popular. Competitions were held and videos were released of the many stunning dance performances and high scores on Dance Dance Revolution.

By the end of 1998, Dance Dance Revolution was the most successful arcade machine in Japan. The PlayStation version, which included a plastic dance mat, was released a year later. There are many iterations and sequels to Dance Dance Revolution, some of the most notable being Dance Dance Revolution 5thMix (2001), Dance Dance Revolution Extreme (2002), Dance Dance Revolution SuperNova (2006), Dance Dance Revolution (2014) and Dance Dance Revolution A (2016). Dance Dance Revolution is arguably the most significant rhythm and dance game, serving to firmly establish the genre.

Game Boy Color

The Game Boy Color was released in Japan in October 1998 by Nintendo. The Game Boy Color is an 8-bit, cartridge-based, fifth-generation handheld games console, capable of displaying 56 different colours simultaneously on screen from a total palette of 32,768. It uses a 160 x 144 pixel colour Liquid Crystal Display, measuring 47 x 41 mm. The overall dimensions, button layout and screen dimensions are almost identical to those of the original Game Boy.

While the Game Boy Color had no backlight it was backwards compatible with every Game Boy game, a first for a handheld console. Appropriately enough, the word "color" in the Game Boy Color's logo uses the five colours that the console was initially released in pinkish-red for the letter C (known as Berry), purple for O (Grape), lime-green for L (Kiwi), yellow for the second O (Dandelion) and finally teal for L (Teal).

Like its predecessor, it easily outsold the other handhelds of the time. The Game Boy Color is often seen as an upgraded iteration of the Game Boy and so their sales are often combined to a total of 118 million units between the two. Some of the most notable games for the Game Boy Color are The Legend of Zelda: Link's Awakening DX (1998), Super Mario Bros DX (1999), Tetris DX (1999), Metal Gear Solid (2000), Wario Land 3 (2000), Dragon Warrior (2000), Pokémon Gold/Silver (2001) and The Legend of Zelda: Oracle of Seasons/Ages (2001).

Grim Fandango

Date of release: October 1998

Region: USA

Developer: LucasArts

Publisher: LucasArts

Platform: Windows

Directed by Tim Schafer (previously of The Secret of Monkey Island (1990) and Day of the Tentacle (1993)), Grim Fandango is a single-player, graphic adventure game. Set in the Land of the Dead, you play as Manuel 'Manny' Calavera, whose goal is to assist Mercedes 'Meche' Colomar to the Land of Eternal Rest. The player moves through the narrative of the game by conversing with a huge variety of colourful characters and by solving puzzles. If the player is stuck or unsure as to how to progress, they can wander around the game environment and Manny will eventually home in on important areas nearby and prompt the player to assist.

Similar to Resident Evil (1996), each environment is based on a pre-rendered 3D model with a fixed camera view. This technique was chosen because the necessary graphics do not have to be rendered in real-time and as such can be of much higher quality. Of particular note in Grim Fandango is its lighting, owing to the heavy aesthetic influence of both film noir and the Mexican holiday of Día de Muertos, or Day of the Dead. Further adding to the game's flair is its setting in a city akin to New York, featuring many characters with varying New York accents as thick as they come.

The game was highly praised for its unique art style, witty script and excellent voice acting, cinematography and music, along with a narrative that was unprecedented in video games. It received multiple awards and is often cited as the best graphic adventure game ever developed and one of the best video games of all time and.

Yet, at the time it was a commercial failure for LucasArts. Interest in graphic adventure games still had a healthy following, typically garnering sales into the hundreds of thousands of copies. However, the industry had grown so much that the other genres of games, particularly those rendered in real-time 3D worlds, were shifting millions of units. Furthermore, 1998 wasn't the best year for Grim Fandango to release. Some of the most significant games in video games history were released that same year, including Baldur's Gate, Resident Evil 2, The Legend of Zelda: Ocarina of Time, Metal Gear Solid, StarCraft, Unreal and Half-Life. Amongst this stellar release schedule of massively influential and genre-defining games, it was easy for even a gem like Grim Fandango to be overshadowed and go underappreciated. Since then, however, Grim

Fandango has become accepted as a critically acclaimed cult masterpiece.

Dreamcast

The Sega Dreamcast was released in Japan in November 1998 and was the successor to the Sega Saturn (1995). The first sixth-generation video game console, the Dreamcast is a 128-bit GD-ROM (Gigabyte Disc Read-Only Memory, a propriety optical disc format of Sega's capable of storing up to around 1GB of data) based machine sporting 16MB of RAM and 8MB of VRAM. It also had a built-in modem and web browser, a first for a home console. It represented not only the next step in the next generation of 3D games but heralded the arrival of online gaming on consoles.

The Dreamcast did see early success, being the only sixth-generation console on the block. Unfortunately, with the release of the PlayStation 2 looming large in early 2000, which boasted not only its own next-gen graphics but also a DVD player and backward compatibility, the Dreamcast's sales soon began to drop. The Nintendo GameCube and Microsoft's Xbox further added to the lacklustre sales of the Dreamcast. Sadly, this would be Sega's last console, with the company deciding instead to focus on software development announced in 2000. This was a far cry from the glory days of the Sega Mega-Genesis/Mega Drive (1988) when the company held its own against the market leader of the time that was Nintendo.

The Sega Dreamcast would go on to sell just over 9 million units, less than half the Nintendo GameCube (22 million) and far less than the PS2 (155 million).

However, to disregard the console would be to do it an injustice. There are many fans of the Dreamcast, and it gave the public a taste of the next generation of 3D graphics. Its hardware, too, was certainly cutting edge at the time, which made it very exciting. There are many great and unique titles for the Dreamcast, with some of the most notable being Sonic Adventure (1998), Shenmue (1999), Soulcalibur (1999), Crazy Taxi (2000), Marvel Vs Capcom 2: New Age of Heroes (2000), Phantasy Star Online (2000), Jet Set Radio/Jet Grind Radio (2000), Skies of Arcadia (2000), Rez (2001) and Ikaruga (2002).

Half-Life

Date of release: November 1998

Region: USA

Developer: Valve

Publisher: Sierra Studios

Platform: Windows

Developed by Mike Harrington, Gabe Newell and Marc Laidlaw, Half-Life is a single-player, first-person shooter. The aim of Half-Life is to defeat the extra-dimensional Xen who have overrun the Black Mesa Research Facility. Playing as Dr Gordon Freeman, the player must defeat the many alien and human enemies as well as solve various puzzles to accomplish this task.

Unlike many FPS games of the time, Half-Life has a slow and story-driven beginning, introducing the player to various characters as they speak to Gordon throughout the facility, building intrigue and suspense until the moment the infamous resonance cascade occurs. The player starts their fight against the aliens with Gordon's now-iconic crowbar, before getting their hands on such weapons as the 9mm Pistol, Submachine Gun, Shotgun, laser-guided Rocket-Propelled Grenade Launcher, Fragmentation Grenades and Laser Trip Mines. The player also acquires a Hazardous Environment (HEV) suit which provides a degree of protection against attacks and environmental hazards ranging from poison, fire, electricity, acid or radiation, which the suit can detect with its in-built Geiger counter. The HEV also has a flashlight and provides the game's HUD. Players will need all these tools to traverse the dangerous environment and defeat the many enemies, including the fast-moving parasitic Headcrabs, mindless Zombies (created by a Headcrab attaching to the victim's face and taking control over their body), the intelligent Vortigaunts which can shoot electricity, and the heavily-armoured Alien Grunts.

The game is a departure from the norm of the time in that it has no cutscenes. Instead, NPCs speak to the player and events will occur when scripted, and during these events, the player retains full control and has free movement so as to not break immersion. The game is always seen through Gordon's eyes, who remains a stoic and silent protagonist throughout.

The release of Half-Life was a watershed moment for the first-person shooter genre, redefining what an FPS game could be. The game featured excellent narrative, pacing, level design (Valve used a heavily modified version of id Software's Quake engine called GoldSrc) and memorable set-pieces, the likes of which had never been seen before. The environments were particularly unique. Half-Life was one of the first 3D games which featured an abundance of destructible objects, which was a feature that would become more and more popular with gamers. The environments also played a key part in defeating some of the game's larger, more difficult creatures which were otherwise unfazed by Gordon's more conventional weapons.

The use of set-pieces in Half-Life would also cement another precedent for future video games. Before Half-life, aspects of an FPS were pretty basic. The story was set and it was a case of a non-stop killing spree until the player defeated the final boss. If not for Half-Life introducing compelling characters and interwoven narratives, the FPS genre would have perhaps become stagnant with unending Doom and Quake clones. Instead, the FPS landscape would forever change, and what Half-life wrought in 1998 can be seen echoed and influencing some of the most significant FPS games that were yet to come, moulding games such as Halo: Combat Evolved (2001), Medal of Honor: Allied Assault (2002), Far Cry (2004), F.E.A.R. (2005) and Bioshock (2007), all of which included a strong emphasis on narrative and featured cleverly designed and memorable set-pieces.

Third-party developer Gearbox Software released three expansion packs with Half-Life: Opposing Force (1999), Half-Life: Blue Shift (2001) and Half-Life: Decay (2001). Valve has subsequently released episodic sequels with Half-Life 2 (2004), Half-Life 2: Episode 1 (2006), Half-Life 2: Episode 2 (2007) and Half-Life: Alyx (2020). The original Half-Life was remade as Black Mesa in 2020. Half-Life received numerous awards, and for years after its release was cited by many as the best video game for the PC platform. It is also considered one of the best and most significant video games of all time.

Tencent is founded

Pony Ma, Zhang Zhidong, Xu Chenye, Chen Yidan and Zeng Liqing founded Tencent in November 1998. Tencent is a Chinese technology conglomerate, and although it did not acquire any developers or publishers until 2011, it has since become the biggest company in the video game industry. Just a few of the games Tencent owns are mobile games such as Crossfire (2007), Clash of Clans (2012), Clash Royale (2016), PlayerUnknown's Battlegrounds Mobile (2018) and Honor of Kings/Arena of Valor (2015), the latter boasting a total revenue of $10 billion. Tencent also owns Riot Games, developer and publisher of League of Legends (2009), at the time of writing has a stake of 40% of Epic Games (the developers and publishers of the wildly successful Fortnite (2017)), and also possesses holdings in Activision Blizzard and Ubisoft Entertainment. All told, these games and acquisitions have brought in about $50 billion in revenue and only makeup only a fraction of the Tencent conglomerate.

The Legend of Zelda: Ocarina of Time

Date of release: November 1998

Region: Japan & North America

Developer: Nintendo EAD

Publisher: Nintendo

Platform: Nintendo 64

Produced by Shigeru Miyamoto and directed by Toru Osawa, Yoichi Yamada, Eiji Aonuma, Yoshiaki Koizumi and Toshio Iwawaki, and featuring music by Koji Kondo, The Legend of Zelda: Ocarina of Time, often referred to as simply Ocarina of Time, is a single-player, third-person, action-adventure game. It is the fifth game in the Zelda series and the first game of the series in 3D. Once more, and playing as Link, the player must stop the evil sorcerer, King Ganondorf, from attaining the Triforce which has the ability to grant him godlike power. The player begins the game as young Link. After finding the three Spiritual Stones, Link can enter the Sacred Realm and claim both the Master Sword, which is sorely needed to fulfil his quest. However, in going for the Master Sword, Ganondorf is able get to the Triforce first. Link suddenly awakens seven years in the future, where Ganondorf's evil has spread across all of Hyrule. Approached by Rauru, one of the seven Sages, Link is thrust into a quest where he must battle numerous foes and travel to the five temples under Ganondorf's sway to free them and awaken five of the remaining sages who are unaware of their identity as such. Each of these areas is geographically and aesthetically distinct from the others and presents its own set of challenges. Link battles his enemies primarily using a sword and shield, but has access to other gadgets and weapons, from bombs to magic spells. Link's Fairy Bow can also be used to shoot three different types of magic arrows (Fire, Ice and eventually Light), for use both in combat and to hit specific switches. There is also a hookshot that can grab onto certain objects and pull them towards Link or instead have Link grapple towards said objects, depending on their weight. There are also numerous other items that Link can use to help him against enemies or traverse his environment. The game also features hidden treasure, puzzles aplenty, stores and Link's trusty horse Epona, allowing the player to travel a lot quicker around the expansive fantasy world of Hyrule. Link is also accompanied by a tiny guardian fairy called Navi. She assists him throughout his adventure, typically by giving hints on what to do and highlighting potential enemy weaknesses. The Ocarina of Time, a musical instrument that, if played at a specific time and place with a specific song, affords Link access to new areas of the game world.

The Legend of Zelda: Ocarina of Time includes ninety minutes of in-game cutscenes which are extremely cinematic itself is to give a feeling of continuity within the game and gameplay. Ocarina of Time is also renowned for its intuitive targeting system, known as Z-targeting. This would set a precedence for future action-adventure games, as it would for all games featuring context-specific actions. Z-targeting allowed for context-specific actions to be performed by locking on to the point of interaction and pressing the Z button. Whether underwater or climbing, the same button may be used, with only the action undertaken changing depending on the circumstances. Even though this had been done in other games before, Ocarina of Time served to popularise this idea with its excellent implementation.

Fans of the Zelda series had been waiting for this since the launch of the N64 in 1996. At the time, there was a distinct lack of first-party games for the N64, and so the highly anticipated Ocarina of Time arrived at a much-needed time for the platform. The game was cited by many as a perfect game, exceeding expectations in every department. It won numerous awards, and for years it was often referred to as the best video game ever made. Even though The Legend of Zelda: Ocarina of Time was not the first 3D action-adventure game (that accolade perhaps goes back to Activision's Hunter on the Amiga and Atari ST in 1991), Ocarina of Time and Tomb Raider (1996) would help the industry realise the potential of the third-person action-adventure genre on both fifth-generation consoles and for the future thereafter. Nintendo released one direct sequel to Ocarina of Time with The Legend of Zelda: Majora's Mask (2000) and a remake entitled The Legend of Zelda: Ocarina of Time 3D (2011) for the Nintendo 3DS.

Thief: The Dark Project

Date of release: December 1998

Region: USA

Developer: Looking Glass Studios

Publisher: Eidos Interactive

Platform: Windows

Thief: The Dark Project is a single-player, first-person, stealth game and the first in the Thief series. The aim of Thief is played out in a series of missions that involve either stealing a valuable object or releasing a prisoner, ultimately leading through a narrative that has the player confront the Trickster god who, for all intents and purposes, is akin to the devil. The player character is Garrett, a freelance thief. Sneak... Stalk... Steal... and Survive is the tagline for Thief: The Dark Project, and also neatly sums up the gameplay experience. Staying undetected means staying in the shadows and not making too much noise when moving, which varies depending on movement speed and even what kind of surface Garrett is currently moving across. The visibility gem on the player's HUD indicates how close they are to being detected.

Garrett's blackjack can be used to knock out guards from behind, and it is also possible to pick up bodies and hide them. Garrett also has a sword which can be used to kill enemies, but the sound and commotion of a sword fight can alert other guards and result in being overwhelmed. Players also have access to a bow, which comes with an array of different arrows. Normal arrows can be used to hit faraway buttons and switches or kill weaker guards silently with one well-placed shot, though they can only injure tougher guards, thus alerting them to Garrett's presence. Fire arrows can set things alight in a particular situation, while water arrows are very handy for dowsing torches in well-lit areas, plunging the area into darkness. They are also perfect for taking down the undead when infused with holy water. Moss arrows are used to coat noisy surfaces with a carpet of moss, creating areas where no sound is made at all when traversed. Noise-maker arrows will draw guards to the location targeted, and rope arrows allow the player to climb up to higher levels when fired at a wooden surface. The bow with its vast array of arrows was one of Thief's defining game mechanics. The game also featured other useful items such as lockpicks, speed potions, flash bombs and mines.

Though the level design could be a bit haphazard, the gameplay with its haunting atmosphere and tense ambient sound design throughout served to immerse the player and draw them in. The world of Thief, too, was markedly unique, where medieval aesthetics are mixed with aspects of the Industrial Revolution. It is indeed strange and grows even stranger still when the supernatural is thrown into the mix, electricity and magic both commingling. However, the blend of wildly different themes served only to highlight the game's uniqueness.

Thief is also arguably the first first-person stealth game. With Metal Gear Solid, Tenchu: Stealth Assassins and now Thief: The Dark Project all being released in 1998, it made for a watershed year for the nascent stealth genre. While the aforementioned games are very accomplished in their own right, Thief carved its own niche, with a heavy emphasis on sound and light levels in the gameplay, more so than other games in the genre. The Thief series is thought to have inspired such games as Hitman: Codename 47 (2000), Splinter Cell (2002) and Assassin's Creed (2007). The game has spawned an update with Thief Gold (1999) which included three more missions, five new enemies and several other additional features. Three sequels were released, Thief II: The Metal Age (2000), Thief: Deadly Shadows (2004) and Thief (2014). Thief: The Dark Project has often been cited as one of the best video games of all time.

Star Wars: Rogue Squadron

Date of release: December 1998

Region: USA

Developer: Factor 5 and LucasArts

Publisher: LucasArts

Platform: Nintendo 64 & Windows

Star Wars: Rogue Squadron is a single-player, third-person, action, flight combat game. Taking place between Star Wars: A New Hope and Star Wars: The Empire Strikes Back, the aim of the game is mission-dependent, but typically varies between four main categories, namely reconnaissance, rescue, protection, and search and destroy. You play as Luke Skywalker, flying the iconic X-Wing as part of the Rogue Squadron. There are also four other spacecraft that the player can fly depending on the mission at hand, namely the A-Wing, Y-Wing, V-Wing and Snowspeeder. The game also features the Millennium Falcon and TIE Interceptor as an unlockable craft. Each is handled differently, as well as having a different array of ordinance. Power-ups could be collected during each level to permanently upgrading various features of your fighter, from 'health' to firepower. Mission performance improves rank and awards medals, which unlock hidden content ranging from the aforementioned starfighters to bonus levels.

The game was one of the first to make use of the N64's Expansion Pak. The newly released Expansion Pak increased the console's RAM from 4MB to 8MB, allowing it to increase the game's original resolution of 320 x 240 (standard for consoles of the time) to a whopping 640 x 480, making it one of the best looking N64 titles at the time, if not the best.

The game was highly praised for its sound design, music and possible graphical enhancements (if purchased with the Expansion Pak), making for a fantastic gaming experience. However, it was criticised for its lack of multiplayer, which was expected for a game of this kind. Star Wars: Rogue Squadron sold over one million units and spawned two sequels with Star Wars Rogue Squadron II: Rogue Leader (2001) and Star Wars Rogue Squadron III: Rebel Strike (2003).

Baldur's Gate

Date of release: December 1998

Region: USA

Developer: BioWare

Publisher: Interplay Entertainment

Platform: Windows

Developed by Ray Muzyka and James Ohlen, Baldur's Gate is a single-player, isometric RPG, based on and licenced by popular tabletop RPG Advanced Dungeons and Dragons, and is the first in the Baldur's Gate series. As the game's title would imply, it is set in and around the city of Baldur's Gate in the Sword Coast region of western Faerûn, and part of the Forgotten Realms campaign setting. The initial aim of the game is to discover the cause behind the Iron Crisis, precipitated by the supernatural poisoning of the iron ore of the region, leading to increased diplomatic tensions and an explosion of banditry.

Baldur's Gate more or less follows the rules of tabletop AD&D, albeit with the standard paper doll interface with which to arm and equip characters. There are twenty-five characters the player can choose from to rotate in and out of the party throughout the game, the maximum party size is limited to six. The characters are some of the most stand-out features of the player's experience, featuring voice acting that was pretty good for the time and an engaging and witty script. Some characters get along and work well together, while others will not, and they make the player aware of this in no uncertain terms via amusing chatter and banter. Combat is in real-time; however, the player can easily pause the action and select their next commands, giving them the best of both worlds. The game also kept track of the player's morality. Performing actions perceived as good would cause NPCs to act more favourably towards the party, while actions perceived as evil would in turn see NPCs acting negatively as a consequence, ranging from a marked hike in shop prices and even being attacked. Multiplayer involved up to six players connecting online to form their party.

Baldur's Gate was Bioware's first successful game. It was highly praised for its rendered backgrounds, script, voice acting, story and gameplay and hailed as the best AD&D video game, if not the best fantasy RPG available on PC of its day.

The next year would see the release of an expansion pack with Baldur's Gate: Tales of the Sword (1999). The game's direct sequel, Baldur's Gate II: Shadows of Amn (2000), would prove to be even more popular and better respected than the original. Baldur's Gate: Dark Alliance (2004) proved to be a popular outing on the consoles of the time, and the original even received a remake with Baldur's Gate: Enhanced Edition (2012). Baldur's Gate III was released in Early Access in 2020 with a full release projected for 2023, at the time of writing.

Starsiege: Tribes

Date of release: December 1998

Region: USA

Developer: Dynamix

Publisher: Sierra On-Line

Platform: Windows

Developed by Tim Gift, Ken Embery, Scott Youngblood and Mark Frohnmayer, Starsiege: Tribes is a squad-based, multiplayer, first-person shooter and the first in the Tribes series of games. Set in the 40th century, the player's squad represents one of four of the largest factions, namely the Children of the Phoenix, Blood Eagle, Diamond Sword and Starwolf tribes. The player can choose a class as defined by their chosen Packs, which grant specific abilities, and their armour, being either Light, Medium or Heavy, and the type of match they want to play, namely Capture the Flag, Deathmatch, Capture and Hold, Defend and Destroy, or Find and Retrieve. At first glance, Tribes seems like just another online FPS. However, several features make it significantly different from its peers. For starters, players have a jetpack as part of their armour, by default you can make anywhere between a short jump to actual flight. Combat in Tribes was unlike anything at the time, taking place on huge maps that could cover several square kilometres. Maps would include each player's base as well as outlying sensor stations, generators and defence turrets to fight over. There are forty maps in Starsiege: Tribes, each featuring a variety of weather conditions, indoor zones and vast outdoor areas. A variety of weapons and items were available in the game which players could resupply at their base. More weapons and armour could be bought at inventory stations using points earned by achieving objectives and securing kills in the game. The Command Station at your base allowed you to view the map and, if the team's sensors were still intact, track the enemies' movement. This facilitated the possibility of using a good strategy to achieve the objective rather than just brute force. From the base, the player could also control powerful gun turrets. Players also had access to three different flying vehicles. Another impressive feature was the number of players the maps could support. The average map could accommodate thirty-two players while some maps were capable of supporting up to an astonishing 128 players.

Starsiege: Tribes was highly praised for its many features as well as its incredibly smooth gameplay and solid connectivity of the many servers. Although not always the front-runner when it came to online FPS games, it did have a strong following and for many years to come, it and its sequels, would be regarded as must play games for the PC platform. The other games in the Tribes series are Tribes 2 (2001), Tribes: Aerial Assault (2002), Tribes: Vengeance (2004) and Tribes: Ascend (2012).

1998 Notable Omissions

1080° Snowboarding. Academy of Interactive Arts & Sciences (AIAS) awards. Anno 1602. Atellier Marie Plus. Blasto. Blazing Lazers. Blazing Star. Blood 2: The Chosen. Body Harvest. Bomberman World. Burning Rangers. Caesar III. Crash Bandicoot: Warped. Cyber Troopers Virtual-On: Oratorio Tangram. Dark Vengeance. Daytona USA 2: Battle on the Edge. Deep Fear. Delta Force. Devil Dice. Dragon Quest Monsters. Dune 2000. Einhander. European Air War. FIFA World Cup 98. F-Zero X. Falcon 4.0. Fallout 2. Game Boy Camera. GameFront. Gex: Enter the Gecko. Grand Prix Legends. Heart of Darkness. International Superstar Soccer 98. Kartia: The World of Fate. Madden NFL 99. Mario Party. Marvel vs Capcom: Clash of Super-Heroes. MedEvil. Mega Man Legends. Microsoft Pinball Arcade. Myth II: Soulblighter. NCAA Football 99. N2O: Nitrous Oxide. Need for Speed III: Hot Pursuit. Neo Geo Pocket. NFL Blitz. Oddworld: Abe's Exodus. Pokémon Red and Blue. Pokémon Stadium. Railroad Tycoon II. R4: Ridge Racer Type 4. Rockstar Games is founded. Sanitarium. Shock Troopers: 2nd Squad. Shogo: Mobile Armour Division. SiN. Sonic Adventure. Space Station Silicon Valley. Star Wars: Rebellion. Street Fighter Alpha 3. Suikoden II. Tekken 3. The King of Fighters '98. The Settlers III. Thrill Kill. Tomb Raider III. Turok 2: Seeds of Evil. Warhammer: Dark Omen. Wario Land II. Wetrix. X-Men vs Street Fighter: EX Edition.

1999

Super Smash Bros.

Date of release: January 1999

Region: Japan

Developer: HAL Laboratory

Publisher: Nintendo

Platform: Nintendo 64

Conceived and developed by Masahiro Sakurai and Satoru Iwata, Super Smash Bros. is a single-player or multiplayer fighting game that takes characters and environments from popular Nintendo franchises. Both are modelled in 3D, but the fighting takes place on a 2D plane. The aim of the game is to defeat your opponents by way of knocking them off the stage, a goal made easier by the amount of damage inflicted. There are a few different modes in the game. The player can learn and practice a character's moves in Training Mode. By selecting 1P Mode, the player battles their way past various enemies and through bonus stages to reach the final boss. VS Mode is a free-for-all between two to four human players. There are also numerous rules and options for the players to choose from.

Super Smash Bros features eight selectable characters, with four more available to unlock. The initial roster is made up of Mario, Donkey Kong, Samus, Fox McCloud, Pikachu, Link, Kirby, and Yoshi. This character selection is further rounded out by the unlockable characters, namely Luigi, Ness, Jigglypuff and Captain Falcon. As well as being able to shield or grab an enemy, each character can perform a weak attack, strong attack, SMASH attack, and all have three unique special moves. There are nine stages in the game, these being Peach's Castle, Mushroom Kingdom, Congo Jungle, Planet Zebes, Sector Z, Saffron City, Hyrule Castle, Dream Land and Yoshi's Island. To make the battles more interesting, Super Smash Bros. includes several usable items that appear during gameplay. Throwing items include two different types of bombs and a Poké Ball that releases a random Pokémon that performs an attack associated with its type. Melee items for battering opponents include the Beam Sword, Fan, Hammer and Baseball Bat. Special Items include the Fire Flower used to blast opponents with a gout of fire, a Ray Gun, the Star which makes your character temporarily invincible, and the Green or Red Shell which slides around the stage damaging whoever they hit. There are also two items which you can use to recover your damage meter, namely the Maxim Tomato and Heart Container.

The game sold incredibly well and received high praise from both critics and consumers. There weren't many fighting games for the N64, which was a shame given that the console featured four controller ports making it perfect for the genre. So, when Smash Bros. was released, it filled a much-needed gap in the N64's library. Super Smash Bros. has spawned several popular sequels. Each major release has built on the base concept of the original, adding more game mechanics. The roster of characters and choice of stages has increased dramatically to 89 playable characters and 103 Stages in the most recent game! The published sequels at the time of writing are Super Smash Bros. Melee (2001), Super Smash Bros. Brawl (2008), Super Smash Bros. for 3DS and Wii U (2014) and Super Smash Bros. Ultimate (2018).

Sid Meier's Alpha Centauri

Date of release: February 1999

Region: USA

Developer: Firaxis Games

Publisher: Electronic Arts

Platform: Windows

Sid Meier's Alpha Centauri is a single-player or multiplayer, isometric, turn-based strategy game. In the year 2060, the colony ship Unity leaves the war-torn, famine-stricken, polluted and destitute Earth for the distant planet Chiron orbiting Alpha Centauri, our closest neighbouring star situated 4.37 light-years away. Only days away from planetfall, a reactor core malfunction forces the colonists to separate according to ideology and belief, landing on the new world in seven distinct groups. The player can choose from one of these seven different factions, namely the Spartan Federation, Gaia's Stepdaughters, the University of Planet, the Peacekeeping Forces, the Human Hive, the Lord's Believers and Morgan Industries, which each offer a variety of tech trees and playstyles. Alpha Centauri takes the popular civilisation game mechanics to the stars using the tried and tested 4X subgenre, standing for Explore, Expand, Exploit and Exterminate. The player must explore their environment, expand their empire, exploit the resources of the planet and exterminate any threats, although diplomacy can be used when encountering other factions. However, there is much more to the game than just that. As the player progresses through the campaign, several revelations about the planet and the native alien life that resides there are uncovered. Alpha Centauri offers a variety of gameplay options. As well as the campaign, players can choose specific scenarios to test their skills, play a random map and tweak the parameters to their heart's content or set up a multiplayer game.

This level of storytelling and the way it is presented was and still is rather rare in video games. Sid Meier's Alpha Centauri is a markedly unique game in that there has not been a game quite like it since its release back in 1999. The quality of its story and thought-provoking script, along with the different factions, their ideologies and how they developed into the future is fascinating, with each one very different from the next. The introduction of indigenous alien life was also quite a departure from most other 4X games of the time.

Unfortunately, there was never a sequel to this extraordinary game and no remake, only an expansion in the form of Sid Meier's Alien Crossfire (1999). Civilization: Beyond Earth (2014) was well-received and considered a spiritual successor to Sid Meier's Alpha Centauri, however, some might say it never achieved the heights of its forerunner. Sid Meier's Alpha Centauri has won numerous awards.

Crazy Taxi

Date of release: February 1999

Region: Japan

Developer: Hitmaker

Publisher: Sega

Platform: Arcade

Designed by Kenji Kanno, Crazy Taxi is a single-player driving game. The aim is to make as much money as possible as a taxi driver. To do this, the player must pick up any potential customers, who are indicated with a dollar sign above their head. Driving into the ringed area around the customer will prompt them to jump into the back of the player's bright yellow, open-top cab. A green arrow then indicates which direction to drive to reach their required destination. Players can earn more money through reckless driving and squeezing past other cars to get the customer there before the timer runs out. The fare given is dependent on the time remaining and added to the player's total. The game oozed cool with its colourful characters and a multiple hard rock and punk tracks featuring licensed music from groups such as Bad Religion.

The game was first released as a sit-down cabinet, with a stand-up version being released soon afterwards. Crazy Taxi was ported to the Sega Dreamcast in January 2000 and became one of its all-time best-selling games. It wasn't until two years later that it was ported to other platforms of the time. Crazy Taxi has spawned five sequels at the time of writing, with Crazy Taxi 2 (2001), being released exclusively for the Dreamcast, often considered to be the best.

Space Channel 5

Date of release: February 1999

Region: Japan

Developer: United Game Artists

Publisher: Sega

Platform: Dreamcast

Space Channel 5 is a single-player rhythm game. The aim of the game is to outdance the invading aliens called the Morolians. You play as Ulala, a reporter with an incredible talent for dancing. The gameplay is similar to other rhythm games of the time where the player must press the appropriate button in time with the music, resulting in Ulala performing the correct and corresponding dance move. Throughout the game, Ulala must build up her fan base who eventually become her backing dancers. Being able to have Ulala perform a flawless dance with her mass of followers to some great dance tracks made for a very satisfying gaming experience.

The initial concept for the game was to create an experience that would appeal chiefly to a female demographic. Ulala became an iconic video game character with her retro-future look, very long legs and smooth dance moves, which were created using both motion capture and the skills of a team of animators. Many different styles of music feature in Space Channel 5, ranging from jazz orchestras of the 1950s to more contemporary techno and trance, with some pieces being influenced by Peter Gabriel and Michael Jackson. The latter in particular would be included as an NPC character in the game with some of his signature moves.

The game didn't sell particularly well but has become a cult favourite due to its unique design. Space Channel 5 was later ported to the PlayStation 2 and Game Boy Advance and has spawned several sequels including Space Channel 5: Part 2 (2002).

Syphon Filter

Date of release: February 1999

Region: North America

Developer: Eidetic

Publisher: 989 Studios

Platform: PlayStation

Syphon Filter is a single-player, third-person, stealth action shooter. The aim of Syphon Filter is to stop the Black Baton terrorist group from using a newly developed bioweapon. The bioweapon is a virus, capable of being altered on a genetic level to target specific groups of people and is called Syphon Filter. You play as United States special agent Gabriel 'Gabe' Logan. The gameplay of Syphon Filter involves the player running about various locales, ranging from American cities to the plains of Kazakhstan and Ukrainian tundra, taking out enemies with numerous weapons. A green on-screen aim assist helps the player shoot the body or head of the target more reliably. There are also stages in the game which require the player to use stealth, silently dispatching enemies without raising the alarm. Doing so can result in failing the current mission and having to start again. This mix of action and stealth, as well as the flexible control over Gabe's movements like running, rolling and climbing, made for an engaging and fun, spy-orientated action game. The game also made for some memorable moments, ranging from shooting a terrorist with a silenced sniper rifle with an infra-red scope to using an overpowered Taser on an enemy and causing them to burst into flames.

The game was praised for its gameplay, story, enemy AI and the wide array of weapons and gadgets for the player to utilise. Syphon Filter has spawned five sequels, the most notable of these being Syphon Filter 2 (2000) and Syphon Filter 3 (2001). Syphon Filter: Logan's Shadow is the most recent game in the series and was released in 2007. Fans of the series are eagerly awaiting a new release of the franchise at some point in the future.

Silent Hill

Date of release: February/March 1999

Region: North America/Japan

Developer: Team Silent (Konami)

Publisher: Konami

Platform: PlayStation

Silent Hill is a single-player, third-person, survival horror game. Playing as Harry Mason, who awakes in the deserted town of Silent Hill, the aim of the game is to find his adopted daughter Cheryl, who has gone missing after Harry crashed his car late one night whilst attempting to avoid a mysterious woman standing in the middle of the road. Harry quickly discovers that Cheryl and another girl called Alessa are, in fact, two halves of the same person born to Dahlia, the leader of a zealous and demonic cult who intends to reunite the two girl's souls together to become their cult's deity. Unlike other survival horror games, Silent Hill didn't use fixed camera angles and pre-rendered backgrounds but full real-time 3D models for both characters and the environment. During the day, the titular town of Silent Hill is quiet, filled with dense fog and what appears to be unseasonal light snow, giving the game an unnatural and eerie feel. At night, things become even more unnerving as the player's torch can barely illuminate the gloomy darkness more than a few feet ahead of Harry. The lack of a HUD leads to even greater immersion in the game, with the sound design (masterfully done by sound director Akira Yamaoka) in certain areas making for an extremely disconcerting and tense gaming experience, as the environment becomes more disturbing throughout the game. As well as limited ammunition and use of a torch, the player also has a portable radio on their person which crackles with static when any of the various terrifying creatures of Silent Hill are nearby, warning or unnerving the player accordingly. Similar to the Resident Evil series, progress through the game is made by finding keys and solving puzzles to gain access to previously unexplored areas.

There are five possible endings in Silent Hill. In the Good ending, Harry defeats the deity and leaves Silent Hill with a reincarnated infant of Cheryl and Alessa. In the Good+ ending, Harry escapes with the infant and Cybil, the game's secondary main character. In the Joke ending, aliens are summoned to Silent Hill and abduct Harry. In the Bad ending, Harry defeats the deity but loses Cheryl, and after the credits is then seen dead in his wrecked car, suggesting perhaps it was all the hallucinations of a dying mind. In the Bad+ ending, Harry defeats the deity but loses Cheryl.

Silent Hill was often compared with Capcom's Resident Evil series, with which it shares several elements. However, it was noted for also being different in that it was a far more psychological and disturbing experience overall. That it was also a fully 3D survival-horror game rendered in real-time also helped serve to set it apart. The game is now seen as a significant milestone in the genre and is often cited as one of the best video games of all time. It has spawned several sequels, some of the most notable of which are Silent Hill 2 (2001) and Silent Hill 3 (2003). Silent Hill was also adapted into a film in 2006, broadly following the plot of the game.

EverQuest

Date of release: March 1999

Region: USA

Developer: Verant Interactive and 989 Studios

Publisher: Sony Online Entertainment

Platform: Windows

EverQuest is an MMORPG set in the fantasy world of Norrath. The player can choose from twelve different playable races, including humans, elves, dwarves, ogres and trolls, and must also choose their class, such as warrior, thief, rogue, assassin or wizard. Interestingly, players must also choose which deity they wish to pledge allegiance to, as Everquest features a wide arsenal of weapons and armour associated with a specific deity, and only those that worship that deity can use and equip their associated items. EverQuest allowed players to explore the vast world alongside others online and had them fight a vast array of enemies, collect treasure and items which could be used or sold, and subsequently gain experience, level up characters and acquire new abilities.

The phenomenon of spending real money to buy in-game items was prolific amongst players of NCSoft's own MMORPG Lineage (1989), yet Everquest would see this reach a new level with masses of players taking part in platinum farming, also known as plat farming, this involved acquiring in-game items to then be sold for real-world money. Companies employed teams of players to work as plat farmers. It is thought that there may have been as many as 400,000 plat farmers by 2008. The practice of platinum farming was frowned upon by the rest of the industry as not only were these businesses essentially sweatshops because of the apparent low wages and dismal working conditions, but the practice was also wreaking havoc on the in-game economy of EverQuest. In 2004, trading in Everquest would surpass the equivalent of $100 million.

EverQuest would become the most popular MMORPG in the United States, surpassing Ultima Online (1997) in terms of users. It was quite common to have hundreds of thousands of players spread out across the hundreds of servers which acted as simultaneous but separate instances of the EverQuest game world. However, as impressive as Everquest was in terms of player count, it could not overtake the South Korean game Lineage (1999).

The game has spawned twenty-seven expansions as well as other spin-off games and books and gave rise to a sequel with EverQuest II (2004). Some of the most notable of these expansions are Ruins of Kunark (2000), Planes of Power (2002) and Lost Dungeons of Norrath (2003). EverQuest is often cited as one of the most influential MMORPGs of all time and one of the best video games of all time.

As with Ultima Online (1997), EverQuest's dominance of MMORPGs in the West would be overtaken by the release of Blizzard's phenomenally successful World of Warcraft (2004). However, for a time it was EverQuest that was in the hearts and minds of players of this particular genre who sank huge amounts of time into it. It must be remembered, too, that World of Warcraft was very much built on the shoulders of these aforementioned giants.

RollerCoaster Tycoon

Date of release: March 1999

Region: North America

Developer: Chris Sawyer

Publisher: Hasbro Interactive

Platform: Windows

Developed almost entirely by Chris Sawyer of Transport Tycoon (1994), RollerCoaster Tycoon is a single-player, isometric, construction and management simulation game. The aim of the game is to play through one of the twenty-one pre-existing scenarios as, unfortunately, there is no free-build sandbox option included. The player can either use the prebuilt rollercoaster layouts that come with the game or design their own tracks. The game makes building a rollercoaster surprisingly easy and intuitive. The player can also test and edit various aspects of their rollercoaster, including its colour scheme and theme music, with RollerCoaster Tycoon even allowing the player to upload music of their own in the form of a .wav file to be used.

Once the theme park is open, hordes of little NPC guests will flock to the rides. The player can monitor whether their guests are impressed or disappointed, allowing the player to charge more money accordingly or expand and address the customers' issues and attempt to build the most awesome and successful rollercoaster theme park possible. Despite the name, RollerCoaster Tycoon isn't exclusively about managing rollercoasters, as it also includes a marked emphasis on the financial management of the park, and satisfying the many needs, expectations and requirements of guests. As such, the player can also construct transport rides to ferry guests between attractions, non-rollercoaster rides from categories such as Water Rides, Thrill Rides and Gentle

Rides, along with souvenir shops, food and drink stalls, vending machines, and bathrooms. Staff must also be managed, with four different kinds to hire from Handymen, Mechanics, Security Guards and Entertainers.

RollerCoaster Tycoon certainly built on the foundation of its predecessor, namely Coaster (1993) and Theme Park (1994). The only drawback was that the player was tragically unable to ride their rollercoaster in first-person view as was the case in the former game. However, when the raw scale of a RollerCoaster Tycoon park was taken into account, with all its multitude of rides and attractions, the hustle and bustle of the staff going about their allotted tasks and the screams of joy and fear alike from the guests on the rides, the game really did feel like a living, breathing amusement park. The game was very successful, selling over four million units.

The game spawned two expansion packs with RollerCoaster Tycoon: Added Attractions Pack (known as RollerCoaster Tycoon: Corkscrew Follies in the USA) (1999) and RollerCoaster Tycoon: Loopy Landscapes (2000) both of which added thirty more scenarios apiece to play through. The game also spawned several sequels, the best of which is often considered to be RollerCoaster Tycoon 3 (2004).

Team Fortress Classic

Date of release: April 1999

Region: USA

Developer: Valve

Publisher: Sierra Studios

Platform: Windows, OS X.

Team Fortress Classic is a multiplayer, first-person shooter. Players work together to achieve victory against the opposing team, the teams themselves being Red and Blue. The victory conditions of the match vary depending on the chosen game mode. These modes can range from the self-explanatory Capture the Flag to Control Point (which involves capturing one of several linked control point platforms and holding them against enemy attempts to recapture), and Assassination/Escort (which involves one team attempting to assassinate the designated VIP, while the other team act as bodyguards). Players can choose from one of the nine available classes. These are Scout, Sniper, Soldier, Demoman, Medic, Heavy Weapons Guy, Pyro, Spy or Engineer. There is also the Civilian class: however, this is only used in Assassination/Escort mode. Team Fortress could accommodate up to thirty-two players in teams of sixteen per side.

Team Fortress Classic received high praise for its fun and addictive gameplay. Players loved the fact that it was bundled in with Half-Life, and it soon gained a devoted user base. Surprisingly, there are still people who play it to this day.

The game was originally released as a Half-Life mod in April 1999 and was only published as a stand-alone game entitled Team Fortress Classic 1.5 and bundled with copies of Half-Life as of June 2000. Team Fortress spawned one sequel: the immensely popular Team Fortress 2 (2007) included as part of Valves Orange Box video game compilation bundle.

Street Fighter III: 3rd Strike

Date of release: May 1999

Region: Japan

Developer: Capcom

Publisher: Capcom

Platform: Arcade

Street Fighter III: 3rd Strike is a single-player or two-player, 2D fighting game, the nineteenth game to be bequeathed the Street Fighter name and the third of the Street Fighter III games. Street Fighter III: 3rd Strike brought back player favourite Chun-Li to the roster, as well as four new characters: Makoto, Remy, Twelve and Q.

At the time many viewed 3rd Strike as just another in a long line of Street Fighter games when most of the gaming world was focused on the next big 3D game. However, it is now often seen as one of the best Street Fighter games of all time with a fantastic roster of characters, great graphics and excellent gameplay.

Street Fighter III: 3rd Strike was ported a year later to the Dreamcast and, five years later, to both the PlayStation 2 and the Xbox.

Counter-Strike

Date of release: June 1999 (non-commercial release)

Region: USA

Developer: Minh Le and Jess Cliffe

Publisher: Minh Le and Jess Cliffe and later Valve

Platform: Windows

Counter-Strike is a multiplayer, first-person shooter, pitting terrorists against counter-terrorists. The aim of the game is to win via defusing or planting a bomb, or by rescuing or guarding hostages, or escorting or assassinating a target, though victory can also be achieved by killing everyone in the opposing team.

The first iteration of the game was created by Minh Le and Jess Cliffe as a mod for Half-Life (1998) using the GoldSrc engine. This first of many beta versions was available from June 1999 on a website created by Cliffe. In 2000, Valve hired both Le and Cliffe to continue work on Counter-Strike, which they released as a standalone game that same year. From its inception, Counter-Strike has inspired the community to put their own twist on the game, withs a plethora of mods available, tweaking or even overhauling everything from the graphics, sound design and even gameplay itself.

The game is renowned for being highly competitive. This trend first began in 2000, and continued with the first major tournament, the Cyberathlete Professional League (CPL), being held in Dallas, Texas in 2001, with a prize pool of $150,000. Counter-Strike was updated several times over the next few years with the final significant update released in 2003, Counter-Strike Version 1.6, also referred to as CS 1.6. Many Counter-Strike purists state that CS 1.6 had by far the highest skill ceiling of any other version of both Counter-Strike and any other FPS game around. It wasn't until the release of the highly lauded Counter-Strike: Global Offensive (2012) that the competitive community embraced the next generation of the game. There had been a few attempts at developing a successful sequel to Counter-Strike Version 1.6, however, none of these had been able to gain much traction with players.

Counter-Strike is often cited as one of the greatest first-person shooters and one of the best video games of all time.

System Shock 2

Date of release: August 1999

Region: USA

Developer: Irrational Games & LookingGlass Technologies

Publisher: Electronic Arts

Platform: Windows, OS X

System Shock 2 is a single-player or multiplayer, action, role-playing, first-person shooter and immersive sim, survival horror game. Set in the year 2114 (forty-two years after the events of the first game), the aim of System Shock 2 is to stop the rogue AI SHODAN once more, responsible for unleashing the 'Many', a biological hivemind created from a mutagenic virus jettisoned into space in the events of the original System Shock. The Many infect and mutate their human hosts, who have run amok throughout two spaceships, the UNN Von Braun and her escort, the UNN Rickenbacker.

You play as a soldier, awakened from their Cryo Tube and suffering from amnesia due to an unfortunate computer malfunction. The top section of the screen contains the player's inventory, including a drag and drop interface for weapons, armour and items. The lower left section displays status information, such as hit points, Psi Points, Nanites (System Shock 2's in-game currency) and upgrade points available. The bottom right section of the screen is reserved for general information, displaying the current weapon's ammo counter or options when interacting with a piece of the environment.

Gameplay essentially revolves around exploring the interior of each ship and gunning down various biological and mechanical monstrosities. However, there is far more to System Shock 2 than just running around and shooting things. Your character's statistics dictate how well they perform at any given action in much the same way as any RPG game. The player chooses a class at the beginning of the game and can customise their skillset from thereon out. The player can further supplement their character's specialisations through the use of cybernetic modules and upgrade units. The player can opt to focus on their raw combat skills (including weapon upgrades and modifications) to better mow down enemies, or instead choose to develop their psionic abilities that allow many avenues of offensive and defensive possibilities, very much akin to magic in a fantasy RPG. The player can also increase their technical skills, allowing players the option of hacking technological devices from High-Security Crates to Turrets.

The game qualifies as being of the survival-horror genre due to its psychological and unsettling themes, scarcity of resources such as ammunition, and directional sound. Played with the lights off and without the in-game sound (but the rest of the sound on), System Shock 2 made for quite the unnerving experience. The co-operative multiplayer mode of the game was added as a patch a month after the initial release of the game.

System Shock 2's flexible approach to gameplay, though not the first by any means, would help influence other developers to adopt such similar mechanics into their own games. Deus Ex (2000) and Fallout 3 (2008) are two games where the player has to specialise in their specific style of gameplay, whether this is melee combat, ranged combat or perhaps something even less orthodox, such as stealth or actively eschewing conflict. System Shock 2 afforded players the varied gameplay experience often only found in RPGs, even though it was primarily an FPS. System Shock 2 would define a new genre in gaming, that of the Immersive Sim – a game that is so flexible that the player can accomplish a goal in numerous and creative ways, some of which may have not even occurred to the developers. As well as its in-depth gameplay, System Shock 2 became renowned for being quite the challenge to complete. However, the game rewarded persistence with a hugely gratifying experience and has since become a cult game. System Shock 2 won multiple awards and is considered one of the greatest and most influential video games of all time. Bioshock (2007) is seen as the spiritual successor to System Shock 2.

Age of Empires II: The Age of Kings

Date of release: September 1998

Region: USA

Developer: Ensemble Studios

Publisher: Microsoft

Platform: Windows

Age of Empires II: The Age of Kings is a single-player or multiplayer, isometric RTS game and the sequel to the very successful Age of Empires (1997). The game is set during the Middle Ages but can cover a span of roughly a thousand years around this timeframe. As with the previous game, the core gameplay consists of gathering resources, building a civilization and raising an army to achieve victory through conquest.

There are five single-player campaigns to play through in Age of Empires II: William Wallace against the English, Joan of Arc against the English (again), Saladin against the English crusades (yet again), Genghis Khan against everyone he encountered, and Frederick Barbarossa's expansion across the Holy Roman Empire. Players can also choose to play single-player or multiplayer games in modes such as Deathmatch (victory through complete annihilation of the enemy) or Regicide (where the aim is to kill the enemy king), set on randomly generated maps or on specific map seeds.

New features for players of the Age of Kings included thirteen new civilizations with associated advantages and disadvantages and specific units, new units and buildings, unit formations which alter combat and movement behaviour, new ways to trade, eight new map types, more ways to control your military units, the ability to record and replay games and improved multiplayer features, making for the deepest RTS experience on the market at the time of its release.

Age of Empires II: The Age of Kings spawned one expansion pack in the form of The Age of Empires II: The Conquerors (2010) which includes five new civilizations. Two remakes have been released, namely Age of Empires II: HD Edition (2013) and Age of Empires II: Definitive Edition (2019). The game has received numerous accolades and is often cited as one of the best PC and video games of all time.

Outcast

Date of release: September 1999

Region: Belgium

Developer: Appeal

Publisher: Infogrames

Platform: Windows

Outcast is a single-player, third-person or first-person, action-adventure game. The aim is to repair the probe sent by the US Government to the alien world of Adelpha, situated in a parallel universe. You play as former US Navy SEAL Cutter Slade, who must escort three scientists to repair the probe on Adelpha before a black hole destroys the Earth. Gameplay primarily consists of exploration, which can be done on foot, by riding a twon-ha (a large, two-legged birdlike creature) or, later on in the game, through the use of a teleportation device, with objectives and points of interest given via conversing with NPCs. Available dialogue is highly dependent on the in-game morality meter. For example, if Cutter started shooting the alien Talan, they would be accordingly far less disposed to assist him.

Cutter has access to various weapons with which to deal with any enemies encountered, and even a few handy gadgets, one of which allows the player to become temporarily invisible. All these would be needed as Outcast boasts impressive enemy AI. Outcast also had several other remarkable features, such as a game world that was far larger than most of its contemporaries, a graphics engine capable of handling bloom lighting and depth of field, and real-time shadows rendered for all characters.

The game's graphics used a mix of traditional polygon and voxel-based technology, which served to give Outcast a rather unique look. Around the time of its release, some said that voxel graphics and not polygon-based 3D graphics were the future. However, the game's engine (which was made up of multiple engines, each dedicated to one specific aspect of rendering such as Polygons or Special Effects) relied solely on the CPU and RAM to render Outcast, as opposed to a dedicated graphics card, which had become more and more of a necessity by the late 1990s. The result was that the player needed an incredibly powerful CPU and a vast amount of RAM to run the game at any respectable framerate. Many initial critics and consumers reported very slow framerates, such was the game's demand on hardware. It seemed that this approach had turned out to be an evolutionary dead-end for video game graphics. Nevertheless, there were still those who championed it as a success, and since its release, more and more people have hailed it is a great and unique game. Outcast became far more playable as computers became more powerful, eventually reaching cult game status. It was also one of the first games ever to be advertised in the cinema.

Outcast has been re-released twice to work with more modern PCs: once in 2010 and then again in 2014. The game was also remade as Outcast: Second Contact (2017). A sequel was released in 2023, called Outcast 2 – A New Beginning.

Homeworld

Date of release: September 1999

Region: North America

Developer: Relic Entertainment

Publisher: Sierra Studios

Platform: Windows

Homeworld is a single-player or multiplayer, science-fiction RTS game. The aim is to reach the ancient ancestral homeworld of Hiigara with the few remaining survivors and colonists of the Kushan race after a brutal assault by the antagonist Taiidan Empire. The objective of each mission usually involves performing reconnaissance, gathering resources, building ships and destroying the enemy, as well as ensuring the defence of the mothership controlled by the scientist Karan S'jet who has had herself permanently integrated into the vessel thus bypassing the need for an unfeasibly large crew.

Homeworld shared many similarities to other RTS games of the time, yet it was its differences that set it apart, making for a markedly unique experience. For starters, the scope of the story was an amazing sci-fi narrative, with the desperation and hope of the Kushan colonists told through both gameplay and an evocative series of black and white hand-drawn cutscenes. Homeworld's writing truly was top-notch for a video game of its time. The gameplay, too, was entirely new to the genre. Every other RTS game took place on a relatively 2D plane, with flying units occupying their own plane a set distance above the ground. However, Homeworld presented combat in space where freedom of movement on all three axes needed to be taken into account and capitalised upon. In a similar vein, the game offered a degree of control over its units rarely seen in an RTS game. For instance, players could create squadrons and, via the use of hotkeys, command them quickly and efficiently in the heat of battle. The battles, too, were remarkably heated, immersive and very exciting as clusters of fighters and missiles all left trails behind them as powerful energy-based weapons lashed out from larger ships. Homeworld felt like an RTS version of one of the Freespace games, the second of which, FreeSpace 2, was also released in September 1999.

Homeworld was indeed ground-breaking, noted for its graphics, gameplay, difficulty, and the gamut of emotions it elicited from the presentation of its story and writing. Another contributing feature to the game's overall feel and identity was music by Paul Ruskay, whose addition of Samuel Barber's Adagio for Strings (1936) as the main theme was striking, and reminiscent of the effectiveness of the use of classical music in film, similar to 2001: A Space Odyssey (1968).

The game's source code was released in 2003, allowing players to create mods and facilitating ports to other platforms. Homeworld's popularity spawned several sequels, namely Homeworld: Cataclysm (2000), Homeworld 2 (2003) and Homeworld: Deserts of Kharak (2016). The original Homeworld and Homeworld 2 were re-released with greatly improved graphics in 2015. Homeworld 3 was released in 2023. As well as receiving multiple awards, Homeworld was rated as one of the best games of 1999 and is often cited as one of the best video games of all time.

Tony Hawk's Pro Skater/ Tony Hawk's Skateboarding

Date of release: September 1999

Region: USA

Developer: Neversoft

Publisher: Activision

Platform: Playstation & Dreamcast

Tony Hawk's Pro Skater is a single-player or multiplayer, third-person sports game. It offers a roster of ten professional skateboarders for the player to choose from. There are also nine game levels set all over the USA, in and around skate parks and other areas conducive to skateboarding. The controls are easy to learn yet difficult to master, and the courses, too, grew progressively more difficult. Each skateboarder can not only perform moves such as flips, grinds, ollies and boardslides but also has a unique special trick performed by inputting a specific button combo. In single-player mode, there is an option to either go Career Mode, Single Session or Free Skate. In Career Mode the player must achieve the goal shown on the loading screen. In Single Session, the player can attempt to set a new high score on that level, though only levels unlocked on Career mode can be accessed in Single Session mode. Finally, Free Skate is a mode with no restrictions and allows the player to practice their skills. Multiplayer also has three modes to choose from: Trick Attack, which allows players to compete for points; HORSE mode, where two players go head to head to perform tricks to earn the most points; and Graffiti mode, whereby players claim parts of the level's environment as their own by performing tricks upon them.

Tony Hawk's Pro Skater was highly praised for its gameplay, especially its control system, physics and punk rock and ska music soundtrack. The amalgamation of all these elements made for a skating game the likes of which had never been seen before, appealing to both skaters and non-skaters alike.

The game was soon ported to N64 and Game Boy Color in 2000 and the N-Gage in 2003. It was also remastered in 2020 along with its sequel, Tony Hawk's Pro Skater 1 + 2.

Medal of Honor

Date of release: October 1999

Region: North America

Developer: DreamWorks Interactive

Publisher: Electronic Arts

Platform: PlayStation

Medal of Honor is a single-player or multiplayer, first-person shooter. Set during World War 2, you play as Jimmy Patterson, recruited to the American Office of Strategic Service, or OSS. The aim of the game is to complete the missions given to Jimmy by the OSS, with most of them typically involving either stealing some important documents or blowing something up. There are also missions where Jimmy must go undercover as a German officer, donning disguises and acquiring the necessary papers of sufficient clearance to progress unhindered when challenged by guards. Patience and subterfuge are key during these missions as it is very easy to trigger the alarm and be accordingly gunned down. Most missions provide the player with a plethora of authentic World War 2 weapons and ammo from both the Allies and the Axis. These include the Colt M1911, the M1 Gerand, the BAR or Browning Automatic Rifle, the MP40 and the Thompson submachine gun. Scattered about the levels are also grenades and Panzerfausts or Bazookas. The game's multiplayer mode features a split-screen deathmatch, with each player able to choose a weapons loadout.

Medal of Honor's gameplay is uncannily similar to GoldenEye (1997), which is no bad thing. What set it apart, however, was its setting in World War 2. In between missions, authentic historical black and white footage drives the plot. Every effort was made to ensure that uniforms, weapons and environments were as authentic as possible. Extra effort was equally spent on small details in gameplay. The initial shot at an enemy soldier's head may knock their helmet off instead of killing them outright, should the calibre be insufficient or the angle too oblique. The player could throw grenades, but enemies could kick them away unless they were shot at or incapacitated. The Enemy AI was remarkably good for the time. Enemy soldiers could aggressively rush Jimmy, or run for cover, dive to the ground and roll away.

Medal of Honor's story was written by Steven Spielberg, who was inspired not only by the aforementioned GoldenEye (1997) but also by the film he had directed a year beforehand, namely Saving Private Ryan (1998). All these aforementioned qualities already made for a fine game, but Medal of Honor was enhanced yet further by its musical score. Composed by Michael Giacchino, who would go on to have a prolific career in scoring films, Medal of Honor's soundtrack was recorded using a full orchestra for a true cinematic flair and making for a unique and unmatched first-person shooter experience.

Medal of Honor would spawn many sequels and would become the point of reference in the more grounded historical subgenre of FPSs, until the release of Call of Duty (2003) and its subsequent cavalcade of sequels. Some of the most notable of the Medal of Honor games are Medal of Honor: Underground (2000), Medal of Honor: Allied Assault (2002) and Medal of Honor: Frontline (2002).

The Longest Journey

Date of release: November 1999

Region: Norway

Developer: Funcom

Publisher: IQ Media

Platform: Windows

The Longest Journey is a single-player, point-and-click adventure game. The player takes on the role of April Ryan, an 18-year-old student who is a Shifter, bequeathed with the unique ability to move between two parallel universes, Stark and Arcadia. Stark is April's world of origin, which is a fusion of Industrial and Art Deco styles, and Arcadia, a magical and fantasy-like world. The aim of the game is to restore the essential balance between the two worlds, lest they both perish. April must seek out the four different species of Arcadia and then fulfil their associated prophecies to gain four parts of a disc, replete with embedded jewels. The disc can then be used to restore balance and reunite the two worlds, which, it is revealed, used to be one, a long time ago. As with other games in this genre, the player must interact with objects and converse with NPCs, solving various puzzles to progress the plot.

Gameplay could be described as being either slow-paced or relaxing, depending on the player's temperament. The art style, however, is simply stunning. Great care and attention were taken to create the unique looking and intricately detailed environments, with some of these being arguably the most beautiful ever seen in a video game for the time. For fans of the point-and-click adventure genre, The Longest Journey became a firm favourite and an enduring classic. The game was also highly praised for its excellent voice acting, well-written story and memorable female protagonist.

The Longest Journey has spawned one sequel with Dreamfall: The Longest Journey (2006) and gave rise to a spin-off episodic crowd-funded game entitled Dreamfall Chapters (2014-2016).

Chrono Cross

Date of release: November 1999

Region: Japan

Developer: Square Product Development Division

Publisher: Square

Platform: PlayStation

Chrono Cross is a single-player, third-person JRPG, and is often cited as the spiritual sequel to the highly acclaimed Chrono Trigger (1995). The plot of Chrono Cross is complex and decidedly convoluted, even for a genre where this was typically commonplace. The player character is Serge, a young thief, who must uncover the mystery behind the divergence that has created two parallel worlds: one where he died as a child and the other where he survived. The player can shift between the two versions of the tropical archipelago of El Nido to find and recruit new members to their party, of which there are an incredible forty-five in total, along with finding plot-critical NPCs and items specific to each world and advancing the narrative. Gameplay is what one would expect from Square, characterised by turn-based combat, overworld exploration, interaction with NPCs and solving puzzles. The player can explore numerous locations and move around the overworld map both on foot and with a boat. Your party can fight with standard attacks, use Elements, Defend or attempt to flee. Chrono Cross features six Elements, namely fire/magma, water/ice, wind/flora, earth/lightning, light/cosmos and darkness/gravity. Each element tends to oppose another, dealing and receiving extra damage to and from sources of the opposing Element. Elements can also be used in combination for more powerful attacks or to revive a fallen party member. As with most JRPGs, should all party members go down, then it's game over and the player must reload from a previous save.

The game's combat is one of its most alluring features. Unlike many JRPGs, Chrono Cross features no experience point gain with which to level-up party members. Instead, the characters rely on their equipped weapons, armour and items to boost their stats. As well as unique gameplay, Chrono Cross also featured multiple endings (twelve in total), beautiful music by Yasunori Mitsuda and stunning CGI 3D cutscenes played during key moments of the game's story, akin to Final Fantasy VII (1997).

Whereas Chrono Trigger was released for several platforms, Chrono Cross was only available for the PlayStation. It was also only released in Japan and America, depriving the rest of the world of its unique experience until it was finally released for the PlayStation Network in 2011. Chrono Cross was met with exceptionally positive reviews by critics due to its many amazing features. The scope of its story, quality of graphics and music, the party composition with forty-five members to choose from, the parallel world mechanics and the fantastic combat system made for a game that felt comfortingly familiar yet strikingly different.

Pokémon Gold and Silver

Date of release: November 1999

Region: Japan

Developer: Game Freak

Publisher: Nintendo

Platform: Game Boy Color

Pokémon Gold and Silver is a single-player or multiplayer RPG. The goal is similar to that of its forebear: to earn the eight Gym Badges of the new Johto region, which in turn afford access to Indigo Plateau, allowing the player to challenge and defeat the Elite Four and dethrone the current Pokémon Master. As with previous Pokémon games, there was a plethora of Pokémon to fight, capture, train and evolve, with the game featuring 100 new Pokémon, bringing the overall total to 251, and it introduced two new types, namely Dark and Steel. The game also featured expansive post-game content, with the player able to visit the original Kanto region, challenge the eight original Gym Leaders and finally head to Mount Silver, populated by high-level wild Pokémon and challenge Red, the canon protagonist of Pokémon Red and Blue and the trainer with the highest-level Pokémon in the game. The gameplay is similar to the now tried-and-tested formula of the previous games. The player's character is viewed from a top-down perspective when exploring the overworld, with this changing to an over-the-shoulder view when battling against other trainers and wild Pokémon. However, one decidedly striking difference was that Pokémon Gold and Silver were the first Pokémon games to be in colour.

These two games were released a year later in Australia and North America, and a year after in Europe.

Pokémon Gold and Silver received similarly high acclaim as the original Pokémon Red and Green/Red and Blue. Nintendo released an enhanced version of the games entitled Pokémon Crystal (2000) and ten years later made remakes of the games for the Nintendo DS, entitled Pokémon HeartGold and SoulSilver (2009).

Unreal Tournament

Date of release: November

Region: North America

Developer: Epic Games

Publisher: GT Interactive Software

Platform: Windows, Mac OS

Unreal Tournament is a single-player or (primarily) multiplayer, first-person, arena shooter, albeit with a marked emphasis on the multiplayer aspect of the game. In the second Unreal game, but the first in the Unreal Tournament series, the aim of the game is to win matches, with the victory conditions dependent on the given game mode. Unreal Tournament can be played as a single-player game, but it is the multiplayer experience that it affords where it truly shines, allowing connection across a LAN or over the Internet. Game modes in Unreal Tournament are Deathmatch, Domination (where teams fight for possession of control points to amass the most points within a given time limit), Capture the Flag (won by scoring points by capturing the enemy's flag and successfully returning it to the player's base whilst successfully defending the team's flag), Assault (attempting to capture or destroy an objective) and Last Man Standing (a variation on Deathmatch where each player has a set number of respawns).

Games of Unreal Tournament afforded the players a broad degree of customisability, with options ranging from allowing Bots (computer-controlled players) and their associated difficulty (ranging from the hapless Novice to the terrifying Godlike) to game speed and weapon spawns, which opened up a huge amount of permutations for each possible game. Unreal Tournament has some great weapons, which range from the more conventional kinetic and explosive affairs like the Sniper Rifle, Minigun and Rocket Launcher to futuristic energy weapons, such as the Shock Rifle and Pulse Blaster. The game also featured some rather more unconventional weapons in the form of the Ripper which fires ricocheting discs, the Flak Cannon which fires a spray of red-hot shrapnel, the BioRifle which fires clumps of toxic sludge inflicting damage over time to the target, and the Redeemer, a one-use missile with a nuclear warhead and huge blast radius. Each weapon featured both primary and secondary fire modes.

As with other games of the emerging arena shooter genre, there were also numerous items scattered across the maps that a player could pick up to increase their chances of victory. These include Health Packs, Body Armor, Shield Belt, Damage Amplifier, Invisibility, Anti Grav Boots, and Scuba Gear. Unreal Tournament also featured a player-specific in-game announcer who called out specific actions, such as getting the first kill of the match (First Blood), killing two to six enemies within four seconds of each other (Double Kill, Multi Kill, Mega Kill, Ultra Kill and Monster Kill respectively) and earning killing sprees, which was killing increments of five enemies without dying (ranging from Killing Spree for five uninterrupted kills to WICKED SICK for thirty). These 'achievement announcements' acted as a very efficient audible reward and have been included in most FPS arena shooters since. The game featured a plethora of maps for players to fight across, which could be set anywhere from ancient castles to in and around a spacecraft. Unreal Tournament also came with a level editor so that players could create their own custom maps.

The game was a huge success, due in no small part to the vibrant community which took advantage of the free level editor. It was also somewhat inevitable that Unreal Tournament would be compared to id Software's Quake III Arena (1999), which was released about two weeks after Unreal. Of the two, it is difficult to say which is the better game, boiling down to personal preference above all else. However, Unreal Tournament no doubt offered more variety in terms of maps due to the variety of game types which arose from the tailoring of the rules that was possible, especially when coupled with the map editor.

A Playstation 2 version was released in late 2000, with a Dreamcast port arriving in early 2001. However, these weren't as well received, as the PC was seen as the game's home platform, and the keyboard and mouse were how it was supposed to be played. Unreal Tournament spawned several sequels including Unreal Tournament 2003 (2002), Unreal Tournament (2004) and Unreal Tournament 3 (2007). Unreal Tournament is often cited as one of the greatest video games of all time.

Ultima IX: Ascension

Date of release: November 1999

Region: North America

Developer: Origin Systems

Publisher: Electronic Arts

Platform: Windows.

Ultima IX: Ascension is a single-player, third-person RPG and the final game in the Ultima series which began with Ultima 1: The First Age of Darkness (1981), although some may argue that the first Ultima game is in fact Akalabeth: World of Doom (1979), sometimes referred to as Ultima 0. As is typical with the recent Ultima games, the player takes on the role of the Avatar. The aim of the game is to find and liberate the eight Runes of Virtue of the Shrines of Virtue, desecrating and twisting them into glyphs which are subsequently embedded into pillars in the hearts of various dungeons across Britannia by an evil being called the Guardian. The game contains similar elements to previous Ultima games and traditional RPGs alike, albeit with some notable differences. Perhaps the most striking of these is that the player doesn't gain experience points through combat, but rather can increase their ability scores and attributes by completing quests.

Unlike the recent isometric Ultima games, including its direct predecessor Ultima VIII (1994), the developers of Ultima IX were heavily influenced by the first three Tomb Raider games (1996-98) and The Legend of Zelda: Ocarina of Time (1998), and instead opted for a fully 3D third-person experience.

Ultima IX was unnecessarily buggy and poorly optimised due to Electronic Arts releasing it too early, it ran slowly even on the most cutting-edge PCs of the time. The game world may not have been as big as that of other games, but it made for a thrilling experience in that features visible far-off in the distance could not only be reached but also explored. While this degree of accessibility and exploration was something that would become rather common by the end of the next decade, in 1999 it was a rarity. Ultima IX was praised for its graphics, gameplay and sound design. The story, however, is a source of discontent amongst the fanbase. Some players were not satisfied by the final chapter of the Ultima series, while others thought it was excellent. The later versions of Ultima IX would have the bugs fixed, but the damage was already (and unfortunately) done and sales were low. Ultima IX would be the last in the Ultima series, yet there are those who thoroughly enjoyed what is an excellent RPG at its core.

Quake III: Arena

Date of release: December 1999

Region: USA

Developer: id Software

Publisher: Activision

Platform: Windows

Quake III: Arena is a multiplayer, first-person shooter, and more specifically an arena shooter, where the emphasis is on lightning-fast reactions, face-paced movement and tight gameplay. The premise is that the player is one of many great warriors fighting in the Arena Eternal for the amusement of the mysterious aliens known as the Vadrigar, where only survival matters. The game did include a single-player mode that gave the player the option to practice with thirty-two computer-controlled gladiators. However, Quake III is a multiplayer game at heart, to be played against other players across a LAN or over the internet. The weapons at the player's disposal in the arena are the Gauntlet, Machine Gun, Shotgun, Plasma Gun, Grenade Launcher, Rocket Launcher, Lightning Gun, Railgun and the BFG10K. Armour and health are also available in the arena as well as power-ups such as Flight, Haste, Invisibility, MegaHealth, Quad Damage and Regeneration. Players earn performance-based medals throughout the game, which appear on the player's HUD with a verbal praise award. Each arena contains several environmental features, such as acceleration pads and bounce pads, to afford players a greater degree of movement and options during engagements. The arenas also feature environmental hazards including the Fog of Death, Lava, Slime and bottomless pits. Games modes available in multiplayer are Free for All, Team Deathmatch, Tournament or Tourney (where players fought one-on-one deathmatches whilst others spectated, awaiting their turn to challenge the victor in the next round), and Capture the Flag.

Inspired by the huge mod scene from Quake II and its obvious popularity as a multiplayer game, id Software set out to create a multiplayer-only Quake experience. Quake III: Arena was a game that required a graphics card to play, but the result was that it ran incredibly well and at good framerates and made for a fast and exciting FPS gaming experience. Players could customise graphical settings to get the optimal balance between graphical quality and performance from their card. Such settings included field of view (FOV), model and texture detail and lighting settings. It wasn't long before certain maps would become firm favourites among the Quake community, with others proving to be far less popular.

The game was a solid favourite in the world of esports. Quake III: Team Arena was a team-based version of Quake III released in 2000. Interestingly enough, many FPS games of the early 2000s would use the Quake III engine such as Star Trek: Elite Force (2000), Return to Castle Wolfenstein (2001) and Call of Duty (2003). Quake III: Arena is often cited as one of the best video games of all time.

Planescape: Torment

Date of release: December 1999

Region: USA

Developer: Black Isle Studios

Publisher: Interplay Entertainment

Platform: Windows

Planescape: Torment is a single-player, isometric RPG. Set in the D&D campaign setting of Planescape, the setting is one of a confluence of overlapping planes of existence. The player wakes up in an otherworldly mortuary surrounded by corpses and suffering from amnesia. They are greeted in short order by a quirky flying skull that calls itself Morte, with the player only being referred to as the Nameless One. The overarching aim of the game is for the Nameless One to piece together the story of who they are and just what befell them previously, with exploring the environment and unravelling their past being what progress the plot and the game. The gameplay is typical of a PC isometric RPG game of the time. The player uses the mouse to direct the Nameless One and their maximum-sized party of five fascinating and compelling characters. Of particular note is the Tiefling rogue Annah-of-the-Shadows and her distinguishing Scottish accent, who was very well received and was considered one of the best female characters in PC gaming at the time. When levelling-up, characters could have certain attributes increased, resulting in them specking into a specific D&D class such as Fighter, Wizard or

Rogue. The game also features the typical Dungeons & Dragons character alignment system based on whether the Nameless One tended towards Good or Evil, and Lawful or Chaotic. Combat is based on the framework of preestablished D&D rules, the results thereof scroll across the screen as actions are undertaken, with an inbuilt degree of random-number generation mimicking the unpredictability of D&D's d20-based rules system. Unfortunately, the game's battle system didn't particularly excel, plagued as it was with below-average AI and often ineffective spells. Luckily, the narrative of Planescape: Torment is far more compelling.

Indeed, Planescape: Torment is often cited as one of the best stories ever told in a video game, an iteration of interactive literature at its finest. If the player is killed, then the Nameless One respawns but also forgets everything not otherwise recorded in their journal. Acting as an inherent dissuasion to an overly violent approach, Planescape: Torment placed a marked emphasis on the resolution of quests and encounters through dialogue or stealth. The game featured a plethora of NPC interactions and dialogue for the player to read through, making for an enriching gaming experience. This incredibly immersive game has also been praised for its cast of supporting characters, dark humour and unique atmosphere.

Planescape: Torment is regarded not only as one of the best PC games of all time but also as one of the best video games of all time. A remake of this acclaimed cult classic was released in 2017 with enhanced and updated graphics for a new generation of players. Torment: Tides of Numenera (2017) is considered Planescape: Torment's spiritual successor.

Shenmue

Date of release: December 1999

Region: Japan

Developer: Sega AM2

Publisher: Sega

Platform: Dreamcast

Spearheaded by legendary game designer Yu Suzuki (of Hang-On (1985), Space Harrier (1985), Out Run (1986) Virtua Racing (1992) and Virtua Fighter (1993)), Shenmue is a single-player or third-person, open-world, action-adventure game, although it transcends the boundaries of this genre as at times it also behaves like a life-simulation game, point and click adventure and RPG. Players will also find themselves being able to play arcade games and other minigames within Shenmue, the most iconic example of which perhaps is Sega's aforementioned classic Space Harrier (1985) at an arcade situated within the game world. The player character is teenage martial artist Ryo Hazuki, living in Yokosuka in 1986. The aim of Shenmue is to avenge Ryo's father's death at the hands of Lan Di. However, Lan Di is a master of martial arts and far stronger than Ryo, and so he must train by learning a myriad of different techniques taught by key characters throughout the game if he is to have any hope of victory and vengeance. Players are free to explore Yokosuka and interact not only with NPCs but also with a wide variety of objects making up the game world. Items such as a chest of drawers could be opened and examined, with their contents dutifully modelled and textured with a fantastic degree of fidelity and detail. The level of dedication and complexity of Shenmue went far beyond anything seen before. The game world featured a day-and-night system where four minutes in real time was equal to one hour within the game and also boasted a dynamic weather system, based on the annual weather of Yokosuka in 1986. The game was also populated with 250 distinctly different NPCs, each one programmed to have a 24-hour cycle behavioural pattern and follow their own routine from the moment they got up to the moment they went to bed. This was widely considered the next-level of detail in a video game.

Shenmue was also one of the first games to incorporate what would become known as Quick Time Events, more commonly abbreviated as QTEs. Distinct from player-controlled gameplay, QTEs take place in a scenario whereby the player must input the correct button or combination of buttons to have Ryo react accordingly and can range from combat to on-foot chases. A successful input progresses the scene, whereas an unsuccessful button press or failure to react in time can have a variety of negative outcomes. While QTEs had technically existed since the days of the LaserDisc arcade hit Dragon's Lair (1983), Shenmue codified and popularized their use as a game mechanic for many games to come.

Compared to other games at the time, Shenmue was graphically leaps and bounds ahead. It featured beautiful cinematics, an amazingly detailed open-world, high-resolution textures and models, impressive real-time lighting effects, intricate character movements and facial animation. It stretched credibility that Shenmue was a current-generation game at the time of release and served as a showcase for both Sega AM2 and the Dreamcast console. In some ways, Shenmue was Sega's last gambit to convince players that both Sega and their Dreamcast could provide a truly unique gaming experience, thus increasing sales and rising to challenge the dominance of Sony's PlayStation. Shenmue was a truly epic game in scope, costing a record $47 million to develop, which made it the most expensive game to develop for the time. Tragically, it only made $1.2 million in sales.

Being such a departure from many games of the time, Shenmue drew more than its fair share of both praise and criticism. For some players, it brought a level of immersion rarely experienced in a game, coupled with incredible graphics, sound design and overall scope. Yet for others, its life simulation erred rather too close to tedium, as Ryo works as a forklift operator and the player had to spend a significant amount of time stacking crates in a warehouse. The constant repetition of this and other everyday actions could lead to a rather mundane experience. Others complained about its controls, the lacklustre English voice acting, and the general lack of clarity when it came to finding out just where to go within the game world to advance the story. To this day, there are those who criticize the game and those who hold it in high regard. It is still often cited as one of the best video games of all time for everything it managed to achieve, and arguably paved the way for the games yet to come. The groundwork and inspiration laid down by Shenmue can be seen echoed years later in games such as Grand Theft Auto III (2001) and Yakuza (2005). Shenmue would spawn a more refined sequel with Shenmue II (2001) and decades later, Shenmue III (2019).

1999 Notable Omissions

Age of Wonders. Aliens Vs Predator. Ape Escape. Baldur's Gate: Tales of the Sword Coast. Bangai-O. Beetie: Adventure Racing. Bust a Move 2: Dance Tengoku Mix/Bust a Groove 2. ChuChu Rocket. Command & Conquer: Tiberian Sun. Crash Team Racing. Dead or Alive 2. Descent 3. Digimon World. Donkey Kong 64. Drakan: Order of the Flame. Driver. Dungeon Keeper 2. Earthworm Jim 3D. Earthworm Jim: Menace 2 the Galaxy. Faselei!. Fatal Fury: Mark of the Wolves. Final Fantasy VIII. Freespace 2. Front Mission 3. Gabriel Knight 3: Blood of the Sacred, Blood of the Damned. Garou: Mark of the Wolves. Gauntlet Legends. Grand Theft Auto 2. Growlanser. Guitar Freaks. Gran Turismo 2. Grandia. Half-Life: Opposing Forces. Harvest Moon 64. Heroes of Might and Might III. Hidden & Dangerous. ID TECH 3 Game Engine. ISS Pro Evolution. Jet Force Gemini. Koudelka. Legacy of Kain: Soul Reaver. Madden NFL 2000. Mario Golf 64. Mario Party 2. Might and Magic VII. Moorhuhn. NBA 2K. Mr. Driller. NCAA Football 2000. Neo Geo Pocket Color Handheld is released. Nocturne. Pac-Man World. Parasite Eve II. Pharaoh. Pokémon Snap. Pokémon Stadium. Prince of Persia 3D. Puyo Puyo~n. Quick & Crash. Rainbow Six: Rogue Spear. Rayman 2: The Great Escape. Resident Evil 3: Nemesis. Rocket: Robot on Wheels. Samba de Amigo. Seaman. Seven Kingdoms II: The Fryhtan Wars. Shadow Man. SimCity 3000. Sonic Adventure. Spyro 2: Ripto's Rage. Starship Titanic. Star Wars Episode 1: Racer. Star Wars: X-Wing Alliance. Tekken Tag Tournament. The Legend of Dragoon. Theme Park World/Sim Theme Park. Theme Park Inc/SimCoaster. The Nomad Soul. Threads of Fate. Tomb Raider: The Last Revelation. Vib-Ribbon. Virtua Tennis. Wipeout 3.

NOTES

Dear reader, as you may have guessed I love video games and lists alike. Here are some retrospective notes on the history of video games between 1990-99. It can be interesting and useful to collate information into categories such as game genres and console generations. I've only included the decade covered in this book. For notes pertaining the years before 1990 please refer to my previous book 'The Video Game Guide: Volume 1. 1947-1989'. Enjoy.

Significant Milestones in the Evolution of the First-Person Space Shooter

The first games in the multi-directional shooter genre were clones of the ground-breaking Spacewar (1962) such was the impact of Steve Russel's game. Berzerk (1980) is perhaps the first character-driven multi-directional shooter. By the nineties this genre wasn't as popular as it was in the previous two decades. Perhaps due to the ascent of 3D graphics. However, there are still some very popular, what are now termed twin-stick shooters to this day.

1990. Wing Commander. Origin Systems. Chris Roberts. MS-DOS.

1993. Star Wars: X-Wing. LucasArts. Lawrence Holland and Edward Kilham. Macintosh, MS-DOS & Windows.

1993. Frontier: Elite II. Gametek. David Braben. Amiga, Atari ST & MS-DOS.

1994. Star Wars: TIE Fighter. LucasArts. MS-DOS.

1995. Star Wars: Dark Forces. LucasArts. Daron Stinnet, Ray Gresko and Justin Chin. MS-DOS.

1995. Descent. Interplay Productions. Mike Kulas and Matt Toschlog of Parallax Software. MS-DOS.

1998. Descent: Freespace – The Great War. Volition, Hyperion Entertainment. Amiga & Windows.

1999. Freespace 2. Volition. Interplay Entertainment. Windows.

Significant Milestones in the Evolution of the (character driven) First-Person Shooter

Preceding Spasim (1974) by one year, Maze War (1973) is the first first-person game of any kind. Even though it could be argued that Corporation/Cyber-Cop (1991) was the first game to set off the modern-day FPS genre, it was really Tom Hall, John Carmack, John Romero and Adrian Carmack of the now legendary id software who popularised it with Wolfenstein 3D (1992), their Doom series (1993-1994) and Quake series (1999). The rest is history. See below.

1990. Corporation/Cyber-Cop. Virgin Games. Kevin Bulmer and Bill Allen of Synthetic Dimensions Core Design. Amiga.

1991. Hovertank 3D. Softdisk. Tom Hall, John Carmack, John Romero and Adrian Carmack. MS-DOS.

1991. Catacomb 3-D: The Descent. Softdisk. Tom Hall, John Carmack, John Romero and Jason Blochowiak of id Software. MS-DOS.

1992. Wolfenstein 3D. Apogee Software. Tom Hall, John Romero, John Carmack and Adrian Carmack of iD Software. MS-DOS.

1993. Doom. Id Software. John Romero, John Carmack, Tom Hall, Adrian Carmack, with music and sound by Bobby Prince. MS-DOS.

1994. System Shock. Origin Systems. Doug Church and Warren Spector of LookingGlass Technologies. MS-DOS.

1994. Doom II: Hell on Earth. GT Interactive Software. id Software. MS-DOS.

1994. Marathon. Bungie. Jason Jones and Alex Seropian. Macintosh.

1996. Duke Nukem 3D. FormGen. 3D Realms. MS-DOS.

1996. Quake. GT Interactive Software. id Software. MS-DOS and Microsoft Windows.

1997. Turok: Dinosaur Hunter. Iguana Entertainment. Acclaim Entertainment. David Dienstbier. Nintendo 64 & Microsoft Windows.

1997. GoldenEye 007. Rare. Nintendo. Martin Hollis. Nintendo 64.

1998. Unreal. Epic MegaGames. GT Interactive. Windows & Mac OS.

1998. Tom Clancy's Rainbow Six. Red Storm Entertainment. Red Storm Entertainment. Windows.

1998. Half-Life. Valve. Sierra Studios. Mike Harrington and Gabe Newell. Windows.

1998. Starsiege: Tribes. Dynamix. Sierra On-Line. Windows.

1999. Team Fortress Classic. Valve. Sierra Studios. Windows, OS X.

1999. Counter-Strike. Minh Le & Jess Cliffe, later Valve. Windows.

1999. Medal of Honor. DreamWorks Interactive. Electronic Arts. PlayStation.

1999. System Shock 2. Irrational Games & LookingGlass Technologies. Electronic Arts. Windows, OS X.

1999. Unreal Tournament. Epic Games. GT Interactive Software. Windows, Mac OS.

1999. Quake III: Arena. id Software. Activision. Windows.

Significant Milestones in the Shoot 'Em Up Genre

1990. Raiden. Tecmo. Seibu Kaihatsu. Arcade.

1991. SWIV. Random Access. Multi-Platform.

1992. Desert Strike: Return to the Gulf. Electronic Arts. Richard Robbins, Mike Posehn and John Manley. Various 16-bit platforms.

1993. Batsugun. Toaplan. Arcade and Sega Saturn.

1998. Radiant Silvergun. Treasure. Treasure. Arcade.

Significant Milestones in the Modern-Day Role-Playing Game Genre

1991. Eye of the Beholder. Strategic Simulations Inc. Westwood Associates. MS-DOS.

1991. Final Fantasy IV, known as Final Fantasy II in the west. Hironobu Sakaguchi and Takashi Tokita of Square. Super Famicom.

1991. Neverwinter Nights. Strategic Simulations. Stormfront Studios. MS-DOS.

1992. Ultima VII: The Black Gate. Origin Systems. Richard Garriot. MS-DOS.

1992. Lunar: The Silver Star. Game Arts. Toshiyuki Kubooka and Kei Shigema. Mega-CD/Sega CD (Genesis/Mega Drive add-on).

1992. Dragon Quest V: Hand of the Heavenly Bride. Enix. Chunsoft. Super Famicom.

1993. Gaia Gensoki/Illusion of Gaia. Enix. Masaya Hashimoto, Yasuyuki Sone and Tomoyoshi Miyazaki. Super Famicom/SNES.

1994. The Elder Scrolls: Arena. Bethesda Softworks. Vijay Lakshman, Christopher Weaver and Ted Peterson. MS-DOS.

1994. Final Fantasy VI, known as Final Fantasy III in the west. Square. Yoshinori Kitase and Hiroyuki Ito. Super Famicom/SNES.

1994. Mother 2: Giygas Strikes Back/Earthbound. Nintendo. Shigesato Itoi and Satoru Iwata. Super Famicom/SNES.

1995. Chrono Trigger. Square. Takashi Tokita, Yoshinori Kitase, Akihiko Matsui and Hironobu Sakaguchi. Super Famicom (SNES).

1995. Suikoden. Konami. PlayStation.

1995. Tales of Phantasia. Namco. Wolf Team. Super Famicom.

1996. Pokémon. Red and Green/Red and Blue. Game Freak. Nintendo.

1996. Super Mario RPG: Legend of the Seven Stars. Nintendo. Yoshihiko Maekawa, Chihiro Fujioka and produced by Shigeru Miyamoto. Square. Super Famicom/ Super Nintendo Entertainment System.

1996. Star Ocean. Enix. Tri-Ace. Directed by Joe Asanuma, Produced by Yoshinori Yamagishi and designed by Masaki Norimoto. Super Famicom.

1996. Tecmo's Deception: Invitation to Darkness. Tecmo. PlayStation.

1996. The Elder Scrolls II: Daggerfall. Bethesda Softworks. Developed by Julian Lefay and Christopher Weaver. MS-DOS.

1996. Revelations Persona. Atlus. Directed by Kouji Okada. PlayStation.

1997. Final Fantasy VII. Square. Sony Computer Entertainment. Yoshinori Kitase. Hironobu Sakaguchi. Kazushige Nojima. PlayStation.

1997. Fallout. Black Isle Studios. Interplay Productions. Tim Cain and Christopher Taylor. MS-DOS, Windows, Mac.

1998. Xenogears. Square. Squaresoft. PlayStation.

1998. Baldur's Gate. BioWare. Interplay Entertainment. Ray Muzyka and James Ohlen. Windows.

1999. Chrono Cross. Square Product Development Division. Square. PlayStation.

1996. Pokémon Red/ and Green/Red and Blue. Game Freak. Nintendo. Game Boy.

1999. Planescape: Torment. Black Isle Studios. Interplay Entertainment. Windows.

1999. Pokémon Gold and Silver. Game Freak. Nintendo. Game Boy Color.

1999. Ultima: Ascension. Origin Systems. Electronic Arts.

1999. Shenmue. Sega AM2. Sega. Dreamcast.

Evolution of the Sports Game Genre

1990. Speedball 2: Brutal Deluxe. Image Works. The Bitmap Brothers. Various 8-bit and 16-bit home computers and home consoles.

1991. 4D Boxing. Mindscape. Distinctive Software. Various 16-bit computers.

1993. NBA Jam. Midway. Mark Turmell. Arcade.

1993. Bill Walsh College Football. Visual Arts. Electronic Arts. Sega Genesis/Mega Drive, Sega CD and the Super NES.

1993. FIFA International Soccer. EA Sports. Extended Play Productions. Sega Genesis/Mega Drive.

1994. Sensible World of Soccer. Renegade GT Interactive. Jon Hare and Chris Chapman of Sensible Software. Amiga.

1999. Tony Hawk's Pro Skater. Neversoft. Activision. Playstation & Dreamcast.

Evolution of the Racing Game and Vehicular Combat Genre

1990. F-Zero. Nintendo. Super Famicom.

1990. Lotus Esprit Turbo Challenge. Gremlin Graphics. Magnetic Fields. Various 8-bit and 16-bit home computers.

1991. Micro Machines. Camerica. Codemasters. NES.

1991. Road Rash. Electronic Arts. Carl Mey, Keith McCurdy and Randy Breen. Sega Genesis/Mega Drive.

1992. Virtua Racing. Sega. Yu Suzuki. Arcade.

1992. Super Mario Kart. Nintendo. Tadashi Sugiyama, Hideki Konno and Shigeru Miyamoto. Super Famicom/SNES.

1993. Daytona USA. Sega. Toshihiro Nagoshi and Yu Suzuki. Arcade.

1993. Ridge Racer. Namco. Arcade.

1994. Need for Speed. Electronic Arts. EA Canada. 3DO.

1995. Wipeout. Psygnosis. John White, Dominic Mallinson, and Nick Burcome with music by Tim Wright. PlayStation.

1995. Twisted Metal. Sony Interactive Studios America. Mike Jackson and Scott Campbell of SingleTrac. PlayStation.

1996. Mario Kart 64. Nintendo. Directed by Hideki Konno and Produced by Shigeru Miyamoto. Nintendo 64.

1997. Carmageddon. Stainless Steel. Sales Curve Interactive. Mark Teal, Neil Barnden and Patrick Buckland. MS-DOS, Windows & Mac OS.

1997. Gran Turismo. Polys Entertainment. Sony Computer Entertainment. Kazunori Yamauchi, Takeshi Yokouchi and Hirotaka Komiyama. PlayStation.

1998. Colin McRae Rally. Codemasters. PlayStation & Windows.

1999. Crazy Taxi. Kenji Kanno. Hitmaker. Sega. Arcade & later multiple home platforms.

Evolution of the Fighting and Beat 'Em Up Genre

1990. Pit Fighter. Atari Games. Arcade.

1991. The Simpsons. Konami. Arcade & multi-platform.

1991. Battletoads. Tradewest. Rare. Chris Stamper, Gregg Mayles, Kev Bayliss, and music by David Wise. NES.

1991. Street Fighter II: The World Warrior. Konami. Hiroshi Matsumoto, Yoshiki Okamoto, with music by Yoko Shimomura. Arcade & multi-platform.

1991. Streets of Rage, known as 'Bare Knuckle: Furious Iron Fist' in Japan. Noriyoshi Ohba, Hiroaki Chino, Hiroshi Momota, with music by Yuzo Koshiro. Sega Genesis/Mega Drive.

1992. Mortal Kombat. Midway. Ed Boon, John Tobias, John Vogel with music by Dan Forden. Arcade.

1992. X-Men. Konami. Arcade.

1992. Street Fighter II Turbo: Hyper Fighter. Capcom. Yoshiki Okamoto, Akira Nishitani and Akira Yasuda of Capcom. Arcade.

1993. Mortal Kombat II. Midway. Arcade.

1993. Samurai Shodown. SNK. Eikichi Kawasaki, Tomoaki Fukui and Yasushi Adachi. Neo Geo Arcade and home platform.

1993. Virtua Fighter. Sega. Yu Suzuki. Arcade.

1994. King of Fighters '94. SNK. Neo Geo.

1994. Killer Instinct. Midway. Rare & Nintendo. Arcade.

1994. Tekken. Namco. Seiichi Ishii and Hajime Nakatani. Arcade.

1996. Dead or Alive. Tecmo. Team Ninja. Created by Tomonobu Itagaki. Arcade.

1997. Sangokumusou/Dynasty Warriors. Omega Force. Koei. PlayStation.

1997. Bushido Blade. Light Weight. Square. PlayStation.

1997. Tekken 3. Namco. Arcade.

1998. Project Soul. Namco. Arcade.

1998. Soulcalibur. Project Soul. Namco.

1999. Super Smash Bros. HAL Laboratory. Nintendo. Nintendo 64.

1999. Street Fighter III: 3rd Strike. Capcom. Capcom. Arcade.

Significant Milestones in the Platform Game Genre

1990. Castle of Illusion Starring Mickey Mouse. Sega. Emiko Yamamoto, Yoshio Yoshida and Stephen L. Butler. Sega Genesis/Mega Drive.

1990. Super Mario World/Super Mario World: Super Mario Bros. 4. Nintendo. Takashi Tezuka and Shigeru Miyamoto with music by Koji Kondo. Super Famicom.

1990. Commander Keen in Invasion of the Vorticons. Apogee Software. Id Software. Tom Hall, John Carmack, John Romero, Adrian Carmack, with music by Robert Prince. MS-DOS.

1991. Sonic the Hedgehog. Sega. Yuji Naka, Shinobu Toyoda and Hirokazu Yasuhara. Sega Genesis/Mega Drive.

1991. Battletoads. Tradewest. Time and Chris Stamper, Gregg Mayles, Kev Bayliss, and music by David Wise, of RARE. NES.

1991. Duke Nukem. Apogee Software. MS-DOS.

1991. Super Castlevania. Konami. Masanori Adachi and Taro Kudo. Super Famicom.

1991. Another World, known as Out of this World in North America. Delphine Software. Eric Chahi with music by Jean-Francois Freitas. Amiga and Atari ST.

1992. The Lost Vikings. Interplay Productions. Silicon & Synapse. SNES.

1992. Kirby's Dream Land. Nintendo. Masahiro Sakurai and Makoto Kanai of HAL Laboratory. Game Boy.

1992. Flashback/Flashback: The Quest for Identity. U.S. Gold. Paul Cuisset of Delphine Software. Amiga.

1992. Sonic the Hedgehog 2. Sega. Masaharu Yoshi, Shinobu Toyoda, Hirokazu Yasuhara, Yuji Naka and music by Masato Nakamura. Sega Genesis/Mega Drive.

1993. Sonic CD. Sega. Sega Genesis/Mega Drive' Sega CD.

1993. Akumajō Dracula X: Chi no Rondo/Castlevania: Rondo of Blood. Konami. PC Engine CD.

1993. Disney's Aladdin. Capcom. Super Famicom/SNES.

1993. Disney's Aladdin. Sega. Virgin Games. Genesis/Mega Drive.

1994. Sonic the Hedgehog 3. Sega. Sega Technical Institute. Genesis/Mega Drive.

1994. Super Metroid. Nintendo. Yoshio Sakamoto, Gunpei Yokoi and Makoto Kano. Super Famicom/SNES.

1994. Sonic & Knuckles. Sega. Sega Technical Institute. Genesis/Mega Drive.

1994. Earthworm Jim. Playmates Interactive and Virgin Interactive Entertainment. Shiny Entertainment. Sega Genesis/Mega Drive and Super Famicom/SNES.

1994. Donkey Kong Country. Nintendo. Rare. Famicom/SNES.

1995. Magical Pop'n. Pack-In-Video. Polestar. Super Famicom.

1995. Super Mario World 2: Yoshi's Island. Nintendo. by Takashi Tezuka and Shigeru Miyamoto with music by Koji Kondo. Super Famicom.

1995. Rayman. Ubi Studios. Gerard Guillemot and Michel Ancel. Atari Jaguar and PlayStation.

1995. Donkey Kong Country 2: Diddy's Kong Quest. Nintendo. Rare. SNES.

1996. Super Mario 64. Nintendo. Nintendo EAD. Directed and produced by Shigeru Miyamoto with music by Koji Kondo. Nintendo 64.

1996. Crash Bandicoot. Sony Computer Entertainment. Naughty Dog. Developed by Jason Rubin, David Siller and Andy Gavin. PlayStation.

1997. Castlevania: Symphony of the Night. Konami Computer Entertainment Tokyo. Konami. PlayStation.

1997. Oddworld: Abe's Oddysee. Oddworld Inhabitants. GT Interactive Software. Lorne Lanning. PlayStation.

1998. Banjo-Kazooie. Rare. Nintendo. Nintendo 64.

1998. Spyro the Dragon. Insomniac Games. Sony Computer Entertainment. PlayStation.

Significant Milestones in the Run and Gun Genre

1990. Out Zone. Tecmo, Romstar and Toaplan. Arcade.

1991. Alien Breed. Team17. Martyn Brown, Rico Holmes, Andreas Tadic, and Peter Tuleby with sound and music by Alister Brimble. Amiga.

1992. Contra III: The Alien Wars/Super Probector: Alien Rebels. Konami. Nobuya Nakazato and Kazumi Kitaue. Super Famicom/SNES.

1992. Super Star Wars. LucasArts. Sculptured Software. Super Famicom/SNES.

1993. Gunstar Heroes. Sega. Sega Genesis/Mega Drive.

1993. Cannon Fodder. Virgin Interactive Entertainment. Sensible Software. Amiga.

1996. Metal Slug. SNK. Nazca Corporation. Produced by Takashi Nishiyama and designed by Kazuma Kujo Meeher. Arcade (Neo-Geo).

Significant Milestones in the Point and Click Graphic Adventure Genre

1990. The Secret of Monkey Island. Lucasfilm Games. Ron Gilbert, Greg Hammond, Dave Grossman and Tim Shafer. 16-bit home computers.

1990. King's Quest V: Absence Makes the Heart Go Yonder. Sierra On-Line. Various home computers.

1991. Monkey Island 2: LeChucks's Revenge. LucasArts. Ron Gilbert, Shelley Day, Dave Grossman and Tim Schafer. Amiga, Mac OS and MS-DOS.

1992. Dune. Virgin Games. Remi Herbulot, Stephen Clarke-Wilson of French studio, Cryo Interactive. Amiga and MS-DOS.

1992. Lure of the Temptress. Revolution Software. Amiga, Atari ST and MS-DOS.

1992. Indiana Jones and the Fate of Atlantis. LucasArts. Hal Barwood, Noah Falstein and Shelly Day. 16-bit home computers.

1993. The 7th Guest. Virgin Interactive Entertainment. Trilobyte. MS-DOS.

1993. Maniac Mansion II: Day of the Tentacle. LucasArts. by Dave Grossman, Tim Schafer, Ron Gilbert and art by Peter Chan. MS-DOS.

1993. Myst. Broderbund. Rand and Robyn Miller of Cyan. Macintosh.

1993. Sam & Max Hit the Road. LucasArts. Sean Clark and Mike Stemmie. MS-DOS.

1993. Gabriel Knight: Sins of the Father. Sierra On-Line. Jane Jensen, Bill Crow, Robert Holmes and John E. Grayson. MS-DOS and Macintosh.

1994. Beneath a Steel Sky. Virgin Interactive Entertainment. Revolution Software. Amiga and MS-DOS.

1996. The Neverhood. DreamWorks Interactive. The Neverhood, Inc. Designed by Doug TenNapel and Mark Lorenzen. Windows.

1996. Broken Sword: The Shadow of the Templars. Revolution Software. Windows and Mac OS.

1997. Blade Runner. Westwood Studios. Virgin Interactive. Windows.

1997. The Curse of Monkey Island. LucasArts. Windows.

1997. Broken Sword II: The Smoking Mirror. Revolution Software. PlayStation, Windows and Mac OS.

1998. Grim Fandango. LucasArts. Tim Schafer. Windows.

1999. The Longest Journey. Funcom. IQ Media. Windows.

Significant Milestones in the Turn-Based Strategy Game Genre

With their principles based in table-top war-games, which had been played for the last two centuries and even on older traditional games such as Chess (whose origins go back much further), Turn-based strategy/tactics games with their underlying principles in maths lent themselves very well to the workings of the computer and there would always be a willing participant to play with, even if it had to be a silicon-based one.

1990. Powermonger. Electronic Arts. Bullfrog Productions. Amiga & Atari ST.

1990. Fire Emblem: Ankoku Ryu to Hikari No Tsurugi/Fire Emblem: Shadow Dragon and the Blade of Light. Intelligent Systems and Nintendo. Famicom/NES.

1991. Sid Meier's Civilization. Microprose. Sid Meier and Bruce Shelly. MS-DOS.

1991. Mega Lo Mania, also known as 'Tyrants: Fight through Time'. Sensible Software. Amiga.

1992. Shining Force. Sega. Climax Entertainment and Sonic! Software Planning. Sega Genesis/Mega Drive.

1993. Master of Orion. MicroProse. Stephen Barcia Jeff Johannigman of Simtex. MS-DOS and the Macintosh.

1994. UFO: Enemy Unknown. Microprose. Tim Roberts, Julian Gollop and Nick Gollop of Mythos games. Amiga and MS-DOS.

1995. Tactics Ogre Let Us Cling Together. Yasumi Matsuno. Quest Corporation. Super Famicom. Super Famicom.

1997. Final Fantasy Tactics. Squaresoft. Square. PlayStation.

1999. Sid Meier's Alpha Centauri. Firaxis Games. Electronic Arts. Windows.

Significant Milestones in the Stealth Game Genre

The Stealth genre did not really see a rise in popularity until 1998, when there was a sudden explosion of titles with an emphasis of sneaking up and silently taking out your enemies. Each of these games brought some unique mechanic to the table. The late nineties and early two thousands was without doubt the golden age of the stealth game.

1998. Tenchu: Stealth Assassins. Acquire. Sony Music Entertainment Japan/Activision. PlayStation.

1998. Metal Gear Solid. Konami Computer Entertainment Japan. Konami. PlayStation.

1998. Thief: The Dark Project. Looking Glass Studios. Eidos Interactive. Windows.

1999. Syphon Filter. Eidetic. 989 Studios. PlayStation.

Evolution of the Action-Adventure Game Genre

RPG elements can be found in the action-adventure genre, (such as The Legend of Zelda: A Link to the Past (1991)) while some are more purely action-adventure games (Tomb Raider (1996)). Action-adventure could also include almost any element from other genres that including strategy, puzzles, stealth and often a strong narrative.

1990. StarTropics. Nintendo. NES.

1991. Hunter. Activision. Paul Holmes. Amiga and Atari ST.

1991. The Legend of Zelda: A Link to the Past, (known as 'The Legend of Zelda: Triforce of the Gods' in Japan). Nintendo. Takashi Tezuka, Shigeru Miyamoto with music by Koji Kondo. Super Famicom/SNES.

1992. Eco the Dolphin. Sega. László Szenttornyai and Edward Ettore Annunziata of Novotrade International. Sega Genesis/Mega Drive.

1993. The Legend of Zelda: Link's awakening. Nintendo. Takashi Tezuka and Shigeru Miyamoto. Game Boy.

1993. Seiken Densetsu 2/Secret of Mana. Square. Koichi Ishi and Hiromichi Tanaka. Super Famicom/SNES.

1994. System Shock. Origin Systems. Doug Church and Warren Spector of LookingGlass Technologies. MS-DOS.

1994. Little Big Adventure/Relentless: Twinsen's Adventure. Electronic Arts. Adeline Software International. MS-DOS.

1996. Tecmo's Deception: Invitation to Darkness. Tecmo. PlayStation.

1996. Tomb Raider. Eidos Interactive. Core Design. Programmed by Paul Douglas, written by Vicky Arnold, Art by Toby Gard (the creator of Lara) and music by Nathan McCree. Sega Saturn and PlayStation.

1997. Grand Theft Auto. DMA Design Limited. Microsoft. MS-DOS, Windows, PlayStation, Game Boy Color.

1998. Panzer Dragoon Saga. Team Andromeda. Sega. Sega Saturn.

1998. The Legend of Zelda: Ocarina of Time. Nintendo EAD. Nintendo 64.

1999. Outcast. Appeal. Infogrames. Windows.

1999. Shenmue. Sega AM2. Sega. Dreamcast.

Evolution of the Real-Time Strategy/Tactics Game Genre

The game to hold the accolade of the first RTS game is a matter of much contention, which will never be agreed upon. The turn-based strategy game Utopia (1981) indeed has a real-time feature. Also Cytron Masters (1982) is a strong contender. However, many see The Ancient Art of War (1984) as the first true RTS. You may disagree. Throughout the eighties there was always a steady trickle of RTS games. Yet it wasn't until the release of Dune II: The Building of a Dynasty/Dune II: The Battle of Arrakis (1992) that almost single-handedly inspired a whole generation of game developers to create their own RTS games. The late nineties and early two-thousands became a golden age for the genre.

1990. Powermonger. Electronic Arts. Bullfrog Productions. Amiga & Atari ST.

1992. Dune. Virgin Games. Remi Herbulot, Stephen Clarke-Wilson of French studio, Cryo Interactive. Amiga and MS-DOS.

1992. Dune II: The Building of a Dynasty/Dune II: The Battle of Arrakis. Virgin Games. Westwood Studios. MS-DOS.

1994. Warcraft: Orcs & Humans. Blizzard Entertainment. Bill Roper and Patrick Wyatt. MS-DOS.

1995. Command and Conquer. Virgin Interactive Entertainment. Westwood Studios. MS-DOS and Mac OS.

1995. Warcraft II: Tides of Darkness. Blizzard Entertainment. Sam Didier, Michael Morhaime, Patrick Wyatt and Ron Miller. Mac OS and Windows.

1996. Dragon Force. Sega. J-Force. Sega Saturn.

1997. Total Annihilation. Cavedog Entertainment. Ron Gilbert, Chris Taylor and Clayton Kauzlaric. Windows.

1997. Age of Empires. Ensemble Studios. Microsoft. Brice Shelly, Brian Sullivan, Rick Goodman and Stephen Rippy. Windows.

1997. Myth. The Fallen Lords. Bungie. Mac and Windows.

1997. Sid Meier's Gettysburg! Firaxis Games. Windows.

1998. StarCraft. Blizzard Entertainment. Windows.

1998. Commandos: Behind Enemy Lines. Pyro Studios. Gonzalo Suárez and Ignacio Pérez

Dolset. Windows.

1999. Age of Empires II: The Age of Kings. Ensemble Studios. Microsoft. Windows.

1999. Homeworld. Relic Entertainment. Sierra Studios. Windows.

Evolution of the Modern-Day Survival Horror Game Genre

The definition of the Survival Horror Genre contains several elements including, of course, a spooky/horror theme. The typical elements found in these games are an emphasis on a limited inventory, lack of resources such as weapon ammunition, health items and save points. Players must sometimes evade monsters to survive. Resident Evil/Bio Hazard (1996) though not the first such game, is often seen as a watershed moment in the genre, establishing many of the elements seen from that moment on.

1992. Alone in the Dark. Infogrames. Frédérick Raynal and Bruno Bonnell. MS-DOS.

1994. Doctor Hauzer. Riverhillsoft. 3DO

1995. D/ D's Dining Table. Panasonic Acclaim. 3DO.

1996. Resident Evil/Bio Hazard. Capcom. Shinji Mikami and Tokuro Fujiwara. PlayStation.

1998. Resident Evil 2. Capcom. Hideki Kamiya and Shinji Mikami. PlayStation.

1998. Parasite Eve. Square. Square. PlayStation.

1999. Silent Hill. Team Silent (Konami). Konami. PlayStation.

1999. System Shock 2. Irrational Games & LookingGlass Technologies. Electronic Arts. Windows, OS X.

Significant Milestones in the Puzzle Game Genre

Precursors to the puzzle genre include many primitive strategy games throughout the fifties, sixties and seventies, games such as Nim, Chequers or Chess. By the eighties programmers/designers were either mimicking real-life puzzles such as Blockbuster (1981) which is a digital version of a Rubik's Cube, or were highly original concepts like Qix (1981) and Tetris (1984). Tetris being the most successful puzzle game of all time.

1990. Klax. Atari Games. Dave Akers and Mark Stephen Pierce. Arcade.

1991. Lemmings. Psygnosis. David Jones, Russel Kay and Mike Daily of DMA Design. Multi-platform.

1991. Puyo Puyo. Compile. Masamitsu Niitani. MSX2.

1994. Puzzle Bobble/Bust-a-Move. Taito. Arcade.

Significant Milestones in the Simulation Game Genre

This category is assigned to games which simulate real-life people doing (more or less) real-life things. These are the games which bucked the trend. Some of these games weren't even considered proper video games and were frowned upon at the time of their conceptualisation and development. Titles like SimCity (1989) and The Sims (2000) went on to become some of the best-selling games of their time.

1990. Railroad Tycoon. Microprose. Sid Meier. 16-bit home computers.

1991. Championship Manager. Paul and Oliver Collyer. Amiga, Atari ST and MS-DOS.

1993. SimCity 2000. Maxis. Fred Haslam and Will Wright. Apple Macintosh.

1994. Theme Park. Bullfrog Productions. Peter Molyneux and Demis Hassabis. 3DO, Amiga and MS-DOS.

1996. Harvest Moon. Pack-In-Video. Amccus. SNES.

1999. RollerCoaster Tycoon. Chris Sawyer. Hasbro Interactive. Windows.

1999. Shenmue. Sega AM2. Sega. Dreamcast.

Significant Milestones in the Rail Shooter Game Genre

Rail Shooters have never been as prolific as the standard FPS, where the player is allowed to roam freely. The Rail Shooter restricts that freedom a little or completely, so that the developers can control the pacing of the game. This can lead to a very exciting and immersive experience as anyone who played the cinematic Star Wars (1983) or Starblade (1991) Arcade cabinets would contest. In the nineties two player co-op cabinets such as Virtua Cop (1994), Time Crisis (1995) and The House of the Dead (1996) (and their respective sequels) were immensely popular despite the decline of the

Arcade industry.

1991. Starblade. Namco. Hajime Nakatani. Arcade.

1993. Star Fox. Nintendo. Katsuya Eguchi and Shigeru Miyamoto. Super Famicom/SNES.

1993. Star Wars: Rebel Assault. LucasArts. Vince Lee. Multi-Platform.

1994. Virtua Cop. Sega. Jun'etsu Kakuta, Toshinori Asai and Yu Suzuki. Arcade.

1995. Panzer Dragoon. Sega. Yukio Futatsugi of Sega's, Team Andromeda. Sega Saturn.

1995. Time Crisis. Namco. Arcade.

1996. The House of the Dead. Sega. Sega AM Research & Development No.1. Arcade.

1997. Star Fox 64/Lylat Wars. Nintendo EAD. Nintendo. Takao Shimizu and Shigeru Miyamoto. Nintendo 64.

Evolution of the Massive Multiplayer Online Role-Playing Games (MMORPG) Genre

The MMORPG differentiates itself from any other online game with the large number of players that can play within the game world and its persistent world, meaning that even when you and your friends leave, time and the game continue to change and evolve. Surprisingly the first ever online multiplayer game over a somewhat primitive 'inter' network was the RPG Essex MUD (1980). Over the next ten years there would be numerous Multi-User Dungeon (MUD) games using what would eventually become the internet. Eleven years after Essex MUD saw the release of Neverwinter Nights (1991), the first fully graphical MMORPG. Every game on this list was revolutionary in its day, giants of their time, drawing huge numbers of players who sunk hundreds or even thousands of hours immersing themselves into these worlds.

1991. Neverwinter Nights. Strategic Simulations. Stormfront Studios. MS-DOS.

1991. The Shadow of Yserbius. Sierra On-Line. Ybarra Productions. MS-DOS.

1996. Meridian 59. The 3DO Company. Archetype Interactive. Designed by brothers Andrew and Chris Kirmse and produced by John Hanke. Windows.

1997. Ultima Online. Origin Systems. Electronic Arts. Starr Long, Richard Garriot and Raphael Koster. Windows.

1998. Lineage. NCSoft. Jake Song. Windows.

1999. Everquest. Verant Interactive and 989 Studios. Sony Online Entertainment. Windows.

Significant Milestones in the Open World/Sandbox Game Genre

The futuristic Space Simulator Elite (1984) is possibly the first game where the player could choose such a diverse range of playstyles that would change the game world and how it reacted to them. No mean feat. Today Open World or Sandbox Games are common. Back then, the concept was difficult for some players and developers to get their head around. Perhaps that is why it took a while for them to catch on, although it could be argued that this kind of gameplay was alive and well in the Massive Multiplayer Online Role-Playing Game (MMORPG) community which began in the early Nineties.

1991. Hunter. Activision. Paul Holmes. Amiga and Amiga ST.

1993. Frontier: Elite II. David Braben. GameTek. Amiga. Amiga CD32, Atari ST, DOS.

1994. Theme Park. Bullfrog Productions. Electronic Arts. 3DO, the Amiga and MS-DOS.

1999. Shenmue. Sega AM2. Sega. Dreamcast.

Significant Milestones in the Rhythm Game Genre

The Rhythm game is a relatively new genre (compared to many others), brought to the public's attention by the ground-breaking Parappa the Rapper (1996). From this point it became a matter of bringing in new innovations. There were plenty of titles on the home consoles, though it was the Arcade cabinets which would first feature prominently in the public's consciousness with highly skilled players amazing people with their moves.

1996. Parappa the Rapper. Sony Computer Entertainment. NanaOn-Sha. Produced and directed by Masaya Matsuura. PlayStation.

1998. Bust a Move: Dance & Rhythm Action/Bust a Groove. Metro Graphics. Enix. PlayStation.

1998. Dance Dance Revolution. Konami. Arcade.

Most Successful Fourth-Generation Gaming Platforms

49 million units. Nintendo Super Famicom/SNES. 1990.

31 million+ units. Sega Mega Drive/Genesis. 1988.

18 million units. NEC PC-98. 1982.

11 million units. PC Engine/TurboGrafx-16. 1987

4.9 million. Commodore Amiga. 1985.

1 million. SNK Neo Geo/Neo Geo AES. 1990.

Most Successful Fifth-Generation Gaming Platforms

118 million units. Nintendo Game Boy and Game Boy Color. 1990.

102 million units. Sony PlayStation. 1994.

33 million units. Nintendo 64. 1996.

9.3 million. Sega Saturn. 1994.

2 million. 3DO. 1993.

Most notable Amiga Games

1986. Defender of the Crown.

1987. International Karate +.

1988. F18 Interceptor.

1989. Batman.

1989. Shadow of the Beast.

1991. Alien Breed.

1991. Lemmings.

1991. Turrican II: The Final Fight.

1993. Cannon Fodder.

1993. Dune II: The Fight for Arrakis.

1993. Speedball 2: Brutal Deluxe.

Most notable PC Engine/TurboGrafx-16 games

1988. Military Madness.

1989. Blazing Lazers.

1989. Bonk's Revenge.

1991. Neutopia II.

1990. Splatterhouse.

Most notable Turbo Express/PC Engine GT games

1989. Military Madness.

1989. Blazing Lazers.

1989. Bonk's Revenge.

1990. Splatterhouse.

1991.Neutopia II.

1992. Bomberman '93.

1993. Street Fighter II: Championship Edition.

Most notable Sega Mega Drive/Genesis games

1991. Sonic the Hedgehog.

1992. Sonic the Hedgehog 2.

1993. Gunstar Heroes.

1993. Shining Force.

1993. Streets of Rage 2.

1994. Castlevania: Bloodlines.

1994. Earthworm Jim.

1994. Ecco: The Tides of Time.

1994. Super Street Fighter II.

1995. Comix Zone.

1995. Phantasy Star IV.

Most notable Nintendo Game Boy games

1989. Tetris.

1992. Kirby's Dream Land.

1993. Super Mario Land 2: 6 Golden Coins.

1993. The Legend of Zelda: Link's Awakening.

1994. Donkey Kong.

1994. Wario Land: Super Mario Land 3.

1998. Pokémon Red & Blue.

1998. Wario Land II.

Most notable Neo Geo games

1994. Samurai Showdown II.

1996. Metal Slug (1996)

1997. The Last Blade.

1998. Blazing Star.

1998. King of Fighters 98: The Slugfest.

1998. Shock Troopers: 2nd Squad.

1999. Garou: Mark of the Wolves.

Most notable Game Gear games

1992. Prince of Persia.

1992. Shinobi II: The Silent Fury.

1992. Sonic the Hedgehog 2.

1993. Land of Illusion starring Micky Mouse.

1993. Streets of Rage 2.

1994. Shining Force II: The Swords of Hajya.

1995. Gunstar Heroes.

Most notable Super Famicom/Super Nintendo Entertainment System games

1991. Super Castlevania IV.

1991. The Legend of Zelda: A Link to the Past.

1992. Super Mario World.

1992. Super Mario Kart.

1993. Star Fox.

1993. Street Fighter II Turbo: Hyper Fighting .

1994. Donkey Kong Country.

1994. Final Fantasy III.

1994. Super Metroid.

1995. Chrono Trigger.

1995. Earthbound.

1996. Super Mario RPG: Legend of the Seven Stars.

Most notable Sega Saturn games

1995. Sega Rally Championship.

1995. Virtua Cop.

1996. Virtual Fighter 2.

1996. Dragon Force.

1996. Night into Dreams.

1996. Guardian Heroes.

1997. Saturn Bomberman.

1997. Die Hard Trilogy/Arcade.

1997. Shining Force III.

1997. X-Men Vs Street Fighter.

1998. Panzer Dragoon Saga.

1998. Radiant Silvergun.

1999. Street Fighter Zero 3.

Most notable PlayStation games

1996. Wipeout XL.

1996. PaRappa the Rapper.

1997. Castlevania: Symphony of the Night.

1997. Tomb Raider.

1997. Final Fantasy VII.

1998. Metal Gear Solid.

1998. Resident Evil 2.

1998. Tekken 3.

1998. Crash Bandicoot: Warped.

1999. Street Fighter Alpha 3.

1999. Medal of Honor.

2001. Tony Hawk's Pro Skater 2 (2001).

Most notable Nintendo 64 games

1996. Super Mario 64.

1996. Mario Kart 64.

1997. Star Fox 64.

1997. GoldenEye 007.

1998. The Legend of Zelda: Ocarina of Time.

1998. Banjo-Kazooie.

1999. Super Smash Bros.

2000. Perfect Dark.

2000. Paper Mario.

2000. The Legend of Zelda: Majora's Mask.

Glossary

1-up. An extra life.

8-Bit. Referring to computer hardware that processes 8 bits (see Bit) of information at a time.

16-Bit. Referring to computer hardware that processes 16 bits (see Bit) of information at a time.

3D Wireframe. A graphical representation of a 3D object which only displays the edges of said object. For example, a cube is displayed with 12 lines. This technique requires the least amount of computational resources to display a 3D object.

3D Wireframe with Hidden Line Removal. A 3D wireframe of a 3D object, except the internal lines, are removed giving the impression that the object is more solid. To remove the internal lines of an object requires more computational resources.

Action-Adventure Game. A video game in which the emphasis is on high action, exploration and puzzle-solving with an intriguing narrative.

Anti-Aliasing. The smoothing of the edges of a digital image by averaging the colours of the pixels at the boundary

ASCII. Abbreviation for American Standard Code for Information: a way of storing numbers, letters, or symbols for exchanging information between computer systems. In games has been a way to represent dungeons on-screen using little memory. For example, dots and lines make up the structure of the rooms, the player's character is displayed as an @ symbol, a snake is represented by an S, and so on and so forth.

Axonometric Projection. An efficient way for the hardware of the time to display 3D isometric-looking graphics.ing

BASIC. A Common computer programming language that uses instructions that are similar to English. Basic is an acronym for Beginner's All-purpose Symbolic Instruction Code.

Beat 'em up. Refers to a genre of game where the player/s must frequently use hand to hand combat to defeat numerous waves of enemies.

Bedroom Coder/s. A term used to describe either a very small team, often just one person, writing code for a game in their bedroom.

Bit. A unit of information in a computer that must be either 1 or 0.

Bitmap. A computer image formed from pixels.

Boss. An enemy often found at the end of a level or game that is significantly stronger and more difficult to beat than other enemies.

Buff. A temporary beneficial status effect.

Bullet Hell. A sub-genre of the shoot 'em up where the screen is almost filled with enemy bullets.

Byte. A unit of information consisting of eight bits e.g. 10101110. A byte of information can represent one character e.g. the letter 'a'.

CAD. Abbreviation for Computer-Aided Design. The use of computers to design objects.

CD-ROM. Abbreviation for Compact Disc Read-Only Memory. This is a compact disc that holds large amounts of information that can be read by a computer but cannot be changed.

City Building Game. A game where the player acts as the city planner managing resources, keeping citizens happy and expanding/evolving the city.

Clone. An unlicensed copy of a video game.

Colour Overlay. A primitive way of creating colour graphics by placing a coloured acetate overlay onto a monochromatic screen.

Copy Protection. A technique used to prevent the use of copied games. In the early days of video games, this might mean having the player refer to a code or specific location in a guide book included with a genuine copy of the game.

CRT. A monitor, television or projector that displays an image using a Cathode-Ray-Tube.

Cut-Scene. An in-game movie where the player has little to no control over the characters. The cut-scene is often a way to inform the player and progress story.

Debuff. Effects that negatively impact the player character or non-player character, which can result in anything from slower attack speed to reducing stats or lowering defences and resistances.

Demo Scene. Referring to audio-visual demonstrations emphasising and pushing the boundaries of what specific computer hardware can do.

Dogfighting. Close-range aerial or space battle.

D-Pad. Short for directional pad, the D-pad is a four-way (although there are models which operate in more than four directions) directional button, usually operated by the player's left thumb.

Dungeon Crawl. A genre of game that involves the player navigating through a labyrinthian game world.

Eighth Generation. Refers to the eighth generation of home video game consoles (Sony Playstation 4, Nintendo Wii U & Switch and Microsoft Xbox One) and their games, between 1998-2015.

Eroge. A Japanese genre of erotic games.

Esports. An organised video game competition where players or teams of players compete against one another.

Experience Points. Also known as XP. A number that conveys a character's experience. A player's character gains experience points through battle and other encounters, or by fulfilling a quest. More XP results in higher stats such as attack strength, speed, defence etc.

Fantasy Text-Based RPG. An RPG that exclusively or mainly uses text for input and output, set against a fantasy-themed backdrop.

Feelies. Objects such as a map, coins, models, badges etc included with a video game.

Fifth Generation. Also known as the 32-bit era, refers to the fifth generation of home video game consoles - Sony Playstation, Sega Saturn & Nintendo 64 and their games, between 1993-2006.

Final Boss. An enemy, often at the end of the game and the game's main antagonist, which is stronger and more difficult to beat than any other enemy in a game.

First Generation. Refers to the first generation of home video game consoles (Magnavox Odyssey, Atari Home Pong & Nintendo Color TV-Game series) and their games, between 1972-1983.

First-Person. Refers to a video game where you play/see as though you are the character in the game.

Fixed Shooter. A sub-genre of the shooter, where the player's movement is restricted to only two directions of movement, often left and right.

Flat-Shaded. A graphical representation of a 3D object which displays each side, known as a polygon, as a uniform colour. For example, a cube is displayed with 6 polygons, though often only between one- three sides are displayed at one time. This requires more computational resources to display than a wireframe 3D object.

Flight Simulator. A game or simulation, the purpose of which is to emulate as many characteristics between the pilot, plane and the environment.

Flip-Screen. A game world larger than the screen, so that the next part of the environment 'flips' to reveal the next screen, when the player reaches the edge of the screen.

FOCAL. A computer programming language that uses instruction that is similar to English. FOCAL is an acronym for Formulating On-Line Calculation in Algebraic Language.

Fourth Generation. Also known as the 16-bit era, refers to the fourth generation of home video game consoles (Super Famicom/SNES, Sega Mega Drive/Genesis, PC Engine/TurboGrafx- 16 & SNK Neo Geo) and their games, between 1987-2004.

FPS. Abbreviation for Frames Per Second: the rate at how many frames are displayed per second. It is also an abbreviation for First Person Shooter, popularised in the Nineties.

Free-Roaming. Allowing the player to move freely through the game world and/or choose the game narrative and objectives at will.

Game Engine. Software specifically built for game development, often includes its own scripting, 3D editor, physics engine, lighting editor, sound editor, cutscene editor and a level editor.

Game Mechanic. The underlying rules of a game.

Gameplay. How the game feels through its interface and the character/s they play, to interact with the game.

GG. Abbreviation for Good Game/Great Game. Often used (in the in-game chat facility) by players at the end of a multiplayer game.

God Game. A game where the player takes the role of a powerful deity who manipulates NPCs and the environment to achieve their aims.

Graphical Adventure Game. An adventure game that relies heavily or exclusively on graphics with a graphical user interface (GUI) for issuing commands.

Grind/Grinding. A term used when a player resorts to a repetitive task for long periods of time, whether that be combat or acquiring loot, to gain abilities, XP or level-up.

GUI. Abbreviation for Graphical User Interface. It is an interface that allows users to interact with electronic devices through graphical icons and audio indicators instead of text-based user interfaces, typed command labels or text navigation.

Hack and Slash. Refers to a genre of game where the emphasis is put on the player violently dispatching a massive number of enemies. It distinguishes itself from the 'beat 'em up' as being more violent and often involves more elaborate weapons and magic.

Homebrew. Referring to a game written by a hobbyist.

Hot Seat. Refers to a mode of multiplayer gaming, often found in turn-based games, where players use the same machine to play the game and so must take turns, sitting down and then getting up.

IP. Abbreviation for Intellectual Property. An idea, invention or creation protected by law.

Isometric. A method of drawing three-dimensional shapes using two dimensions.

Isometric Shooter. A shooter game taking place on an isometric grid.

JRPG. Acronym for a Japanese Role-Playing Game.

Killer App. In this case, a video game that will cause a consumer to buy a console or computer to play that game, often exclusive to that or only a select few platforms.

Kilobyte (K or KB). A unit of computer information consisting of 1,024 Bytes or 8,192 Bits of data.

LaserDisc. An optical disc storage for video and audio, that can be read using a laser, first released in 1978.

LCD. Abbreviation for Liquid Crystal Display. Refers to an electronic display.

Level Editor. A development tool to more easily facilitate the building of levels, maps or environments for a specific game.

Levelling Up. An in-game event which means that the player's character has reached a new level e.g. risen from level 8 to level 9. It results in higher stats or access to new, usable items and quests only available for characters above a certain level.

Light Gun. A device resembling a gun that allows players to shoot at and thus interact with pixels on a screen.

Local Area Network (LAN). A term to describe several computers which are linked together in relatively close proximity.

Mainframe. A very large, powerful computer with a lot of memory that many people can use at the same time.

Maze Game. A genre of game where the player is placed within a maze.

Memory. The part of a computer in which information or programs are stored either permanently or temporarily, or the amount of space available on it for storing information.

Menu-Driven Adventure. An adventure game which has the player utilise a set menu of commands (as opposed to inputting text) to control characters, solve puzzles and progress the narrative.

Microcomputer. A small computer containing a microprocessor, often used in homes.

Microprocessor. A part of a computer that controls its main operations.

Minicomputer. A computer that is smaller than a mainframe computer, yet larger than a microcomputer.

MMORPG. (Massively Multiplayer Online Role-

Playing Game.) A role-playing game that involves hundreds or thousands of players, playing at the same time in the same world.

MOBA. (Multiplayer Online Battle Arena.) A genre of video game in which you play as a specific class of character working with a small team to destroy the enemy base, against another group of human players with the same aim.

Modular PC. Where each major component of the PC can easily be removed and replaced or upgraded, thus removing the need to replace the entire unit.

MUD. Abbreviation for Multi-User Dungeon.

Multiplayer (Game). A game in which more than one person can play within the same gaming environment, whether working in teams or on your own against the other players.

Multi-Scrolling. A game that scrolls in any four directions, rather than being restricted to only two.

NPC (Non-Player Character). Any character in a video game not controlled by a player.

Open Architecture. Hardware or software architecture that easily facilitates changes by other users.

Oscilloscope. A device that represents oscillations by displaying them on a Cathode Ray Tube.

Parallax Scrolling. An animation technique often used in 2D side-scrolling games where different layers, e.g. foreground, midground and background, move at different speeds to give the illusion of depth.

Parser. A program or part of a program that interprets input to a computer by recognising keywords or analysing sentence structure.

Party-Based System. A system in a game where the player controls one character (in which case the AI controls the other players), or more than one character, in a group, working together for a common goal.

PC. Personal Computer.

Pixel. The smallest area of illumination on a display from which graphics are composed.

Platform. The type of system you are using. Examples are PC, Playstation, IOS and Arcade.

Platformer. A platformer or platform game is a game with an emphasis on jumping, climbing and sometimes combat, in an environment of platforms of varying height.

Polygon. A polygon is a 2D geometric shape. These can be used to make a 3D object. For example, six quadrilaterals can form a cube. Though most shapes are broken down into triangles. Very complex 3D objects made of thousands or millions of polygons, called meshes, can be used in the development of video games.

Port. Adapting a game to run on a different platform.

Power-Up. An item that adds benefits for the player. Examples are extra firepower or temporary invulnerability.

Pre-Rendered Graphics. Computer graphics that are not rendered in real-time. Video footage, where each frame is rendered beforehand and played back later.

Procedurally Generated. Graphics or assets which are generated using algorithms rather than created by human input.

PvE. Short for player versus environment, the environment is controlled by the computer hardware.

PvP. Short for player versus player. Can refer to just two players competing head to head or multiple players.

RAM. Abbreviation for Random Access Memory. A type of computer memory that can be searched in any order and changed, as necessary. Also, known as active memory.

Raster. A type of computer image made of pixels.

Real-Time Strategy (RTS). RTS games usually involve gathering resources, building armies and then defeating your opponent's army in real-time, as opposed to turn-based strategy games where the player can take their time to make a move.

Roguelike. A genre of game characterized by level randomisation, turn-based movement and permanent death.

ROM. Abbreviation for Read-Only Memory. A type of memory that holds information that can be accessed but not changed or added to.

Rotoscoping. The tracing of a series of still images from footage of people or animals in motion (for example) to present more natural-looking animation.

RPG. Acronym for a Role-Playing Game.

Run & Gun. A sub-genre of the shoot 'em up or shooters, where the player is on foot running and shooting a multitude of various enemies.

Sandbox Game. A game with an emphasis on freedom and creativity and allowing the player to go anywhere and do anything, as opposed to a game that is linear or requires something from the player to progress to another level or area.

Scaling Sprites. The technique of scaling graphics in quick succession over a series of frames to give the illusion of three-dimensional movement.

Screen Resolution. The ability of a display to show things clearly and with a lot of detail. The higher the resolution, the clearer the image.

Scrolling. The continuous movement of text or images on a display screen in either a horizontal or vertical direction.

Second Generation. Refers to the second generation of home video game consoles (Fairchild Channel F, Atari 2600 & Intellivision) and their games, between 1976-1992.

Seventh Generation. Refers to the seventh generation of home video game consoles (Sony Playstation 3, Nintendo Wii & Microsoft Xbox 360) and their games, between 2005-2021.

Shooter. A genre of video game where the main conceit is that of shooting the enemy.

Side-Scrolling. In reference to a game that is viewed from the side and the camera scrolls left or right with the player's character.

Single-Player. A game that involves only one player's input.

Sixth Generation. Refers to the sixth generation of home video game consoles (Sega Dreamcast, Sony Playstation 2, Nintendo Gamecube & Microsoft Xbox) and their games, between 1998-2015.

Speech Synthesis. The artificial electronic reproduction of human speech.

Sprite. A two-dimensional image or animation that is integrated into a larger scene.

Stealth Game. A game with an emphasis on stealth to avoid or overcome opponents to achieve the aims of the game.

Strategy Video Game. A game with an emphasis on planning and strategy to win the game.

Survival Horror. A game that contains strong horror elements with action adventure. The emphasis is often on lack of resources thus heightening the survival aspect of the game.

Tape/Cassette. Thin plastic in a long, narrow strip with a magnetic covering that allows sounds and data to be recorded/stored and played/loaded.

Tape Recorder. A machine that is used for playing/loading and recording/storing sound/information onto a tape.

Texture-Mapped. Mapping a textured image onto a 3D polygon model.

Third Generation. Also known as the 8-bit era, refers to the third generation of home video game consoles (Famicom/NES, SG-1000, Sega Master System & Atari 7800) and their games, between 1983-2003.

Third Person. Refers to a video game where you view the character or object that you control in the game.

Tile-Based. Often referring to games where movement and attack range is restricted to tile-based blocks.

Tube Shooter. Refers to a sub-genre of the shoot 'em up games where the player can move around the entirety of the screen shooting towards the middle at enemies as if they were flying down a giant tube.

Turn-Based Strategy. A game where players take turns playing.

Twin-Stick Shooter. Also referred to as multi-directional shooters, the twin-stick shooter features two joysticks, one for movement and one for firing, allowing the player to fire in any direction independent of their movement.

Vector Graphics. The use of mathematical equations to draw computer graphics.

Virtual Reality. (VR). Virtual Reality involves using hardware and software to immerse a player in a simulated world.

Vision Cone. A visual representation of a character's vision range.

Wireframe. A method of displaying a 3D digital model of something in which only lines are displayed.

Sources Used

Books

Martin Amis. Invasion of the Space Invaders. (1982). Published by Johnathan Cape Vintage Publishing.

Steven L. Kent. The Ultimate History of Video Games. (2001). Three Rivers Press.

Dave Morris & Leo Haratas. The Art of Game Worlds. (2004). ILEX Press Limited.

Triston Donovan. Replay: The History of Video Games. (2010). UK. Yellow Ant.

Frans Mayra. An Introduction to Game Studies, Games in Culture. (2010). SAGE Publications Ltd.

Larissa Hjorth. (2011). Games and Gaming, An Introduction to new media. Berg.

Jane McGonical. Reality is Broken: Why Games Make Us Better and How They Can Change the World. (2011). Vintage Digital.

Harold Goldberg. All Your Base Are Belong To Us: How Fifty Years of Videogames Conquered Pop Culture. (2011). USA. Three Rivers Press.

Tony Mott. 1001 Video Games You Must Play Before You Die. (2013).UK. Cassell.

Steven Howlett. Diary of An 80s Computer Geek: A Decade of Micro Computers, Video Games and Cassette Tape. (2014). CreateSpace.

Scott Rogers. Level Up! The Guide to Great Video Game Design. (2014). Wiley.

Kurt Kalata. Hardcore Gaming 101 Presents: The 200 Best Games of All Time. (2015). CreateSpace.

Chris Kohler. power-up how Japanese video games gave the world an extra life. (2016). Dover Publications Inc.

Katherine Isbister. How Games Move Us: Emotion by Design (Playful Thinking). (2016). The MIT Press.

Kurt Kalata. Hardcore Gaming 101 Presents: The Guide to Retro Indie Games Vol 1.

(2017). CreateSpace.

Simon Parkin. An illustrated History of 151 Video Games. (2017). USA. Annes Publishing Ltd.

Nicholas Sinard. A short History of Video Games. (2017). Independently Published.

Kurt Kalata. Hardcore Gaming 101 Digest Vol. 3: The Guide to Retro Horror. (2018). CreateSpace.

Iain Simons & James Newman. A History of Videogames. (2018). Carlton Books Ltd.

Marty Allen. Retro Games. (2018). Dog 'n' Bone.

Dustin Hansen. Game On!: Video Game History from Pong and Pac-Man to Mario, Minecraft, and More. (2019). Square Fish.

Richard Stanton. (2019). A Brief History of Video Games: From Atari to Virtual Reality. (2019). UK. Robinson.

Mike Diver. Retro Gaming: A Byte-sized History of Video Games. (2019). Michael O'Mara Books Limited.

Magazines

Edge Magazine. (1993-present.) Future Publishing.

Games TM. (2002-2018). Highbury Entertainment and then Future Publishing.

PC Gamer Magazine. (2016-present). Future Publishing.

Retro Gamer Magazine. (2004-present). Live Publishing (2004-2005). Future Publishing (2005-2016). Future Publishing (2016-present).

Online

To cite every website that has had bearing on this book would be an exercise in futility, however, here are some example of some of the most valuable resources.

https://www.computerhistory.org/timeline/

https://listverse.com/2010/05/11/15-firsts-in-video-game-history/

https://en.wikipedia.org/wiki/History_of_video_games

https://bigboxcollection.com/#CollectionOverview

https://vgsales.fandom.com/wiki/Video_Game_Sales_Wiki

https://www.giantbomb.com/

https://virtualspeech.com/blog/history-of-vr

https://www.arcade-museum.com/

https://videogamehistorian.wordpress.com/2014/01/22/the-priesthood-at-play-computer-games-in-the-1950s/

http://self.gutenberg.org/articles/video_game_crash_of_1977#Early_arcade_video_games_.281971.E2.80.931977.29

https://retroconsole.xyz/history-of-video-games/video-games-1988/

https://docs.google.com/file/d/0BxIuaTgKKEs4MGFsZ2NpSHctVVE/edit

mobygames.com

The Angry Video Game Nerd

Kim Justice

Metal Jesus Rocks

John's Arcade Game Reviews & Tech

Ashens

LGR

TNT Amusements Inc

Retro Game On

Retroware

Index

2

21st Century Entertainment · 64

3

32X · 136
3D Realms · 45, 168, 290
3D wireframe · 313
3DO · 49, 106, 123, 128, 150, 187, 294, 303, 304, 305, 306, 307
3DO Interactive Multiplayer · 106

4

4D Sports Boxing · 41

9

989 Studios · 265, 267, 300, 305

A

Acclaim Entertainment · 91, 201, 290
Activision · 46, 222, 231, 253, 254, 276, 284, 291, 293, 300, 306
AD&D · 42, 257, 258
Adam Pletcher · 238
Adeline Software International · 131, 301
Adrian Carmack · 27, 32, 37, 67, 113, 222, 290, 296
Advanced Dungeons & Dragons · 36, 42
Age of Empires · 217
Age of Empires II: The Age of Kings · 273
Aki Maita · 190
Akihiko Matsui · 149, 292
Akihiro Yokoi · 190
Akira Nishitani · 33, 83, 295
Akira Toriyama · 149
Akira Yasuda · 33, 83, 295
Akumajō Dracula X: Chi no Rondo · 105
Alex Seropian · 38, 142, 290
Alien Breed · 53
Alister Brimble · 53, 297
Allen Adham · 32
Alone in the Dark · 77
Alpha Waves · 13
Amccus · 181, 304
American McGee · 222
Amiga · 14, 17, 19, 31, 36, 38, 41, 46, 50, 52, 53, 55, 56, 57, 61, 64, 72, 73, 76, 82, 89, 93, 103, 104, 112, 115, 120, 121, 123, 137, 150, 157, 158, 254, 289, 290, 293, 296, 297, 298, 299, 300, 302, 304, 306, 307
Amis, Martin · 325
Andreas Tadic · 53, 297
Andy Gavin · 183, 297
Another World · 55
Anthony Crowther · 17
anti-aliasing · 118
Apogee Software · 27, 44, 67, 290, 296
Apple Macintosh · 87, 304
Arcade · 8, 10, 12, 13, 15, 18, 25, 32, 33, 34, 38, 41, 47, 48, 51, 70, 71, 75, 80, 90, 91, 97, 102, 103, 118, 124, 126, 128, 132, 139, 141, 163, 173, 185, 191, 192, 223, 235, 242, 243, 248, 259, 263, 270, 291, 293, 294, 295, 297, 298, 303, 304, 305, 306,

311
Archetype Interactive · 187, 305
Argonaut Software · 86, 87
ASCII · 313
Atari · 316, 322, 324, 326
Atari 2600 · 322
Atari 7800 · 324
Atari games · 48
Atari Games · 7, 14, 15, 18, 294, 303
Atari Jaguar · 108, 155, 297
Atari ST · 13, 14, 17, 19, 48, 55, 72, 104, 254, 289, 296, 298, 299, 300, 302, 304, 306
Atelier Marie: The Alchemist of Salburg · 205
Atlus · 186, 292
Axonometric Projection · 313
Ayami Kojima · 203, 204

B

Baldur's Gate · 257
Bandai. · 190
Banjo-Kazooie · 239
Bare Knuckle: Furious Iron Fist · 45
BASIC · 314
Battletoads · 40
Beam Software · 92
beat 'em up · 318
Beneath a Steel Sky · 121
Bethesda Softworks · 119, 184, 292
Bill Allen · 14
Bill Crow · 111, 298
Bill Roper · 135, 197, 302
Bill Walsh College Football · 95
Bio Hazard · 170
Bioware · 42, 145, 258
BioWare · 257, 293
Black Isle Studios · 218, 285, 292, 293
Blizzard Entertainment · 32, 89, 135, 161, 197, 232, 302
Blizzard North · 197
Bobby Prince · 113, 290
Bomberman '93 · 83
Bomberman 64 · 212
Brian Sullivan · 217, 302
Broderbund · 99, 298
Bruce Shelly · 9, 49, 151, 217, 299
Bruno Bonnell · 77, 303
Bullfrog Productions · 18, 93, 123, 206, 299, 302, 304, 306
Bungie · 38, 142, 290, 302
Bushido Blade · 201
Bust a Groove · 228
Bust a Move: Dance & Rhythm Action · 228

C

Camerica · 8, 37, 294
Cannon Fodder · 112
Capcom · 33, 83, 109, 170, 171, 181, 227, 251, 259, 266, 270, 295, 296, 303
Captive · 17
Carl Mey · 48, 294
Carmageddon · 209
Castle of Illusion Starring Mickey Mouse · 22
Castlevania: Rondo of Blood · 105
Castlevania: Symphony of the Night · 203
Catacomb 3-D · 54
Cavedog Entertainment · 216, 302
Championship Manager · 72
Charles Cecil · 121
Chihiro Fujioka · 172, 292
Chris Anderson · 183
Chris Chapman · 137, 293
Chris Crowther · 17
Chris Metzen · 232
Chris Roberts · 16, 289

Chris Sawyer · 268, 304
Chris Stamper, · 40, 295, 296
Chris Taylor · 216, 302
Christophe de Dinechin · 13
Christopher Taylor · 218, 292
Christopher Weaver · 119, 184, 292
Chrono Cross · 279
Chrono Trigger · 149
Chunsoft · 74, 292
Civilization · 49
CivNet · 151
Clayton Kauzlaric · 216, 302
Climax Entertainment · 34, 63, 299
Codemasters · 8, 37, 241, 294
Colin McRae Rally · 241
Command and Conquer · 156
Commander Keen in Invasion of the Vorticons trilogy · 27
Commandos: Behind Enemy Lines · 238
Continuum · 13
Contra III: The Alien Wars · 63
Core Design · 189, 220, 290, 301
Cosplay · 181
Counter-Strike · 270
Crash Bandicoot · 182
Crazy Taxi · 263
Cryo · 61, 272, 298, 302
Cyan · 99, 298

D

D's Diner · 150
Dan Forden · 75, 295
Dance Dance Revolution · 248
Daron Stinnet · 145, 289
Data East · 92
Dave Akers · 8
Dave Grossman · 19, 57, 94, 298
David Braben · 103, 289, 306
David Brevik · 197
David Dienstbier · 201, 290
David Jones · 31, 303
David Siller · 183, 297
David Wise · 40, 295, 296
Davidson & Associates · 161
Day of the Tentacle · 95
Daytona USA · 118
Dead or Alive · 191
Delphine Software · 55, 73, 296
Demis Hassabis · 123, 304
Descent · 147
Descent: FreeSpace – The Great War · 237
Desert Strike · 62
Diablo · 197
Digimon · 207
Digital Illusion · 64
Digital Pictures · 78
Disney's Aladdin · 109
Distinctive Software · 41, 293
DMA Design · 31, 221, 301, 303
Domark · 72
Dominic Mallinson · 154, 294
Donkey Kong Country · 136
Donkey Kong Country 2: Diddy's Kong Quest · 160
Doom · 112
Doom II: Hell on Earth · 134
Doug Church · 129, 290, 301
Doug TenNapel · 188, 299
D-pad · 315
Dragon Force · 172
Dragon Quest V · 74
Dreamcast · 206, 223, 228, 243, 244, 250, 251, 263, 264, 270, 276, 282, 286, 287, 293, 301, 304, 306
DreamHack · 117
DreamWorks Interactive · 188, 277, 291, 299
Duke Nukem · 45
Duke Nukem 3D · 168
Duncan Botwood · 210
Dune · 61

Dune II: The Battle of Arrakis · 82
Dune II: The Building of a Dynasty · 82
Dungeon Keeper · 206
Dynamix · 258, 291
Dynasty Warriors · 200

E

E3 · 150
Earthbound · 127
Earthworm Jim · 133
Ecco the Dolphin · 81
Ed Boon · 75, 295
Edge Magazine · 104
Edward Kilham · 85, 289
Eidetic · 265, 300
Eidos Interactive · 29, 189, 220, 239, 255, 300, 301
Eiji Aonuma · 253
Eikichi Kawasaki, · 97, 295
Electronic Arts · 19, 48, 62, 93, 95, 106, 110, 123, 128, 131, 145, 206, 213, 262, 271, 277, 283, 291, 293, 294, 299, 300, 301, 302, 303, 305, 306
Elite II · 103
Emiko Yamamoto · 22, 296
Enix · 74, 98, 107, 179, 228, 292, 306
Ensemble Studios · 217, 273, 302
Entertainment Software Rating Board · 130
Epic MegaGames · 236, 290
Éric Chahi · 55
Erin Schroeder · 9
Eroge · 315
ESRB · 130
Eugene Jarvis · 12
EverQuest · 266
Extended Play Productions · 110, 293
Eye of the Beholder · 36

F

Fairchild Channel F · 322
Fallout · 218
Famicom · 11, 21, 23, 24, 43, 53, 54, 57, 63, 71, 74, 79, 86, 98, 109, 147, 149, 165, 172, 176, 179, 180, 291, 292, 293, 294, 296, 297, 298, 299, 300, 301, 304, 306, 310, 317, 323
FIFA International Soccer · 110
Final Fantasy Adventure · 43
Final Fantasy II · 43
Final Fantasy III · 122
Final Fantasy IV · 43
Final Fantasy Tactics · 207
Final Fantasy VI · 122
Final Fantasy VII · 198
Firaxis Games · 194, 262, 300, 302
Fire Emblem: Ankoku Ryu to Hikari no Tsurugi · 11
Fire Emblem: Shadow Dragon and the Blade of Light · 11
Flashback · 73
flat-shaded · 47, 48, 52, 86, 104, 141, 193
Flight Simulator · 316
FOCAL · 317
FormGen · 168, 290
Frank Pearce · 32
Fred Haslam · 87, 304
Frédérick Raynal · 77, 303
FreeCell · 7
FreeSpace · 237
Full Motion Video · 49, 90, 128
Funcom · 278, 299
F-Zero · 24

G

Gabe Newell · 182, 251, 291
Gabriel Knight: Sins of the Father · 111

Gaia Gensoki · 107
Game Arts · 68, 292
Game Boy · 8, 20, 21, 25, 43, 64, 66, 89, 94, 97, 123, 137, 143, 153, 160, 165, 169, 221, 224, 244, 259, 264, 277, 280, 293, 296, 301, 307, 309
Game Boy Color · 249
Game Freak · 169, 280, 292, 293
Game Gear · 8, 20, 21, 22, 41, 81, 97, 101, 310
Game Genie · 8
Game Zero · 135
Game.com · 211
GameFAQs · 159
Gamespot · 174
GameTek · 103, 306
Gary Stark · 15
Genesis · 8, 14, 21, 22, 34, 39, 45, 46, 48, 56, 58, 63, 69, 71, 73, 76, 79, 81, 82, 89, 93, 95, 97, 98, 101, 102, 108, 109, 110, 117, 118, 132, 133, 136, 138, 139, 251, 292, 293, 294, 295, 296, 297, 298, 299, 301, 306, 308, 317
Genesis32X · 136
Gerard Guillemot · 155, 297
Get Bass · 223
G-Loc · 25
Gold Box · 42
Golden Joystick Awards · 11, 35, 65, 123, 220
GoldenEye 007 · 210
Gonzalo Suárez · 239, 302
Gran Turismo · 223
Grand Theft Auto · 221
Greame Whittle · 17
Greg Hammond · 19, 298
Greg Zeschuk · 145
Gregg Mayles · 40, 295, 296
Grim Fandango · 249
GT Interactive · 134, 175, 214, 236, 281, 290, 291, 293, 297
GT Interactive Software · 134, 214, 281, 290, 291, 297
Guardian Heroes · 167
GUI · 317, 318
Gunpei Yokoi · 11, 122, 297
Gunstar Heroes · 101
Gust Co. Ltd · 205

H

Hajime Nakatani · 47, 141, 295, 304
Hal Barwood · 69, 298
HAL Laboratory · 66, 261, 295, 296
Half-Life · 251
Harvest Moon · 181
Hasbro Interactive · 268, 304
Hideki Kamiya · 227, 303
Hideki Konno · 71, 193, 294
Hideo Kojima · 245
Hiroaki Chino · 45, 295
Hirokazu Yasuhara · 39, 79, 132, 296
Hironobu Sakaguchi · 43, 149, 198, 234, 291, 292
Hiroshi Momota · 45, 295
Hirotaka Komiyama · 223, 294
Hiroyuki Ito · 122, 292
Hi-Ten Bomberman · 96
Homebrew · 318
Homeworld · 275
Hovertank 3D · 37
Hudson Soft · 83, 96, 212
Hunter · 46

I

id Software · 27, 32, 36, 37, 54, 55, 67, 68, 113, 114, 134, 175, 176, 222, 252, 282, 284, 290, 291
Id Software · 113, 290, 296
IGN · 183

Ignacio Pérez Dolset · 239, 302
Iguana Entertainment · 201, 290
Illusion of Gaia · 107
Illusion of Time · 107
Image Works · 28, 50, 293
Imagine Games Network · 183
Indiana Jones and the Fate of Atlantis · 69
Infogrames · 13, 42, 77, 274, 301, 303
Insomniac Games · 246, 297
Intelek · 72
Intelligent Systems · 10, 299
Intellivision · 322
Interplay Entertainment · 257, 285, 289, 293
Interplay Productions · 88, 147, 218, 219, 237, 289, 292, 296
IQ Media · 278, 299
Irrational Games · 271, 291, 303

J

Jake Song · 247, 305
James Ohlen · 257, 293
James Phinney · 232
Jane Jensen · 111, 298
Jason Blochowiak · 54, 290
Jason Jones · 142, 290
Jason Rubin · 183, 297
Jean-Francois Freitas · 55, 296
Jeff Dee · 65
Jeff Johannigman · 100, 299
Jess Cliffe · 270, 271, 291
Joe Asanuma · 179, 292
John Carmack · 27, 32, 37, 54, 67, 68, 113, 175, 222, 290, 296
John E. Grayson · 111, 298
John Manley · 62, 291
John Romero · 27, 32, 37, 54, 67, 68, 113, 175, 290, 296
John Salwitz · 18
John Tobias · 75, 295
John Vogel · 75, 295
John White · 154, 294
Johnathan Waldern · 51
Jon Hare · 137, 293
Jonathan Simpson · 183
JRPG · 318
Julian Gollop · 120, 300
Julian Lefay · 184, 292
Jun'etsu Kakuta · 128, 304
Justin Chin · 145, 289

K

Katsuya Eguchi · 86, 304
Kazuma Kujo Meeher · 174, 298
Kazumi Kitaue · 53, 63, 298
Kazunori Yamauchi · 223, 294
Kazushige Nojima · 198, 292
Kei Shigema · 69, 292
Keisuke Terasaki · 11
Ken Demarest · 65
Ken Embery · 258
Kenji Eno · 150
Kenji Kanno · 263, 294
Kev Bayliss · 40, 295, 296
Kevin Bulmer · 14
Kevin Cloud · 222
Killer Instinct · 132
King's Quest V · 22
Kirby's Dream Land · 66
Klax · 7, 8, 303
Klaymen: The Mystery of Neverhood · 188
Koei · 200, 295
Koichi Ishii, · 43
Koji Kondo · 23, 57, 153, 177, 205, 253, 296, 297, 301
Kokumeikan · 180
Konami · 32, 33, 53, 63, 80, 105, 160, 203, 245, 248, 265, 292, 294, 295,

296, 297, 298, 300, 303, 306
Kouji Okada · 186, 292

L

LaserDisc · 38, 39, 287
Lawrence Holland · 85, 289
LCD · 319
Lego Fun to Build · 164
Lemmings · 31
Light Weight · 202, 295
Lineage · 247
Little Big Adventure · 131
Looking Glass Studios · 255, 300
LookingGlass Technologies · 129, 271, 290, 291, 301, 303
LucasArts · 16, 57, 69, 85, 94, 95, 107, 125, 145, 249, 250, 256, 289, 298, 299, 304
Lucasfilm Games · 19, 20, 298
Lunar: The Silver Star · 69
Lylat Wars · 204

M

Macintosh · 85, 99, 100, 111, 126, 142, 147, 289, 290, 298, 300
Magical Pop'n · 146
Magnavox · 316
Magnavox Odyssey · 316
Manabu Kusunoki · 229
Marathon · 142
Marc Laidlaw · 251
Mario · 326
Mario Kart 64 · 193
Mark Frohnmayer · 258
Mark Healy · 206
Mark Lorenzen · 188, 299
Mark Pierce · 15
Mark Teal · 209, 294
Mark Turmell · 91, 293
Marooned on Mars · 27
Martin Hollis · 210, 290
Martyn Brown · 53, 297
Masahiro Sakurai · 66, 261, 296
Masahiro Ueno · 53
Masaki Norimoto · 179, 292
Masaki Ukyo · 167
Masamitsu Niitani · 51, 303
Masanori Adachi · 53, 296
Masato Nakamura · 79, 296
Masaya Hashimoto · 107, 292
Masaya Matsuura · 192, 306
Masayuki Uemura · 21
Master of Orion · 100
Matt Toschlog · 147, 289
Maxis · 87, 304
Medal of Honor · 277
Mega Drive · 8, 14, 22, 34, 39, 46, 58, 69, 71, 73, 76, 79, 81, 82, 89, 93, 97, 101, 102, 108, 109, 110, 117, 118, 132, 133, 136, 138, 251, 292, 293, 294, 295, 296, 297, 298, 299, 301, 306, 308, 317
Mega Lo Mania · 50
Mega-CD · 58
Megami Ibunroku Persona · 186
Meridian 59 · 187
Metal Gear Solid · 244
Metal Slug · 173
Metro Graphics · 228, 306
Michael Morhaime · 32, 161, 302
Michel Ancel · 155, 297
Michiru Yamane · 203
Micro Machines · 37
microprocessor · 319
MicroProse · 9, 49, 100, 120, 151, 299
Microsoft · 7, 82, 108, 152, 161, 175, 206, 213, 215, 217, 221, 251, 259, 273, 290, 301, 302, 315, 323
Microsoft Entertainment Pack · 7
Midway · 75, 90, 91, 92, 132, 293, 295

Mike Daily · 31, 303
Mike Harrington · 182, 251, 291
Mike Jackson · 159, 294
Mike Kulas · 147, 289
Mike Posehn · 62, 291
Mike Stemmle · 107
Mindscape · 16, 17, 41, 293
Minesweeper · 7
Minh Le · 270, 271, 291
Mode 7 · 23, 24, 72, 79
Monkey Island 2: LeChucks's Revenge · 57
Mortal Kombat · 75
Mortal Kombat II · 91
Mother 2 · 127
MPS Labs · 9
MS-DOS · 14, 16, 17, 27, 33, 36, 37, 45, 49, 53, 54, 59, 61, 65, 67, 72, 73, 76, 77, 82, 83, 85, 90, 94, 100, 107, 111, 113, 119, 120, 121, 123, 125, 129, 131, 134, 135, 145, 147, 150, 151, 152, 156, 168, 175, 184, 189, 190, 206, 209, 218, 221, 289, 290, 291, 292, 294, 296, 298, 299, 300, 301, 302, 303, 304, 305, 306
MSX2 · 51, 303
MUD · 320
Myst · 99
Mystic Quest · 43
Mythos Games · 120

N

Namco · 47, 102, 103, 118, 141, 163, 164, 192, 242, 292, 294, 295, 304, 305
NanaOn-Sha · 192, 306
Naoto Ohshima · 178
Nathan McCree · 189, 301
Naughty Dog · 182, 297
Nazca Corporation · 173, 298
NBA Jam · 91
NCSoft · 247, 267, 305
Neil Barnden · 209, 294
Neo Geo · 10, 97, 126, 143, 173, 224, 259, 288, 295, 307, 309
Neo Geo Advanced Entertainment System home console · 10
Neo Geo Multi Video System Arcade Cabinet · 10
NES · 8, 9, 21, 22, 24, 26, 33, 37, 40, 47, 74, 97, 115, 178, 293, 294, 295, 296, 299, 300, 323
Neversoft · 276, 293
Neverwinter Nights · 42
Nick Burcome · 154, 294
Nick Gollop · 120, 300
Night Trap · 78
Nights into Dreams · 178
Nintendo · 8, 9, 10, 20, 21, 23, 24, 25, 26, 29, 40, 47, 54, 56, 57, 63, 66, 71, 74, 78, 79, 86, 94, 108, 121, 122, 127, 132, 136, 138, 140, 143, 149, 152, 160, 162, 163, 169, 171, 172, 176, 177, 178, 193, 194, 199, 201, 204, 205, 210, 211, 212, 240, 246, 249, 251, 253, 254, 256, 261, 280, 281, 290, 292, 293, 294, 295, 296, 297, 299, 300, 301, 304, 305, 306, 307, 309, 310, 312, 315, 316, 323
Nintendo 64 · 108, 138, 140, 176, 177, 178, 193, 194, 201, 204, 210, 212, 240, 253, 256, 261, 290, 294, 295, 297, 301, 305, 307, 312
Noah Falstein · 69, 298
Nobuo Uematsu · 123, 149, 199
Nobuya Nakazato · 63, 298
Nokia · 241
Noritaka Funamizu · 33
Noriyoshi Ohba · 45, 295
Noriyuki Asakura · 231
Novotrade International · 81, 301
NPC · 320

Nvidia · 89

O

Ocean Software · 157
Oddworld Inhabitants · 214, 297
Oddworld: Abe's Oddysee · 214
Omega Force · 200, 295
Origin Systems · 16, 65, 129, 213, 283, 289, 290, 291, 293, 301, 305
Out of this World · 55
Out Zone · 15
Outcast · 274

P

Pack-In-Video · 181, 297, 304
Pac-Man · 326
Panzer Dragoon · 148
Panzer Dragoon Saga · 229
Parallax Software · 147, 289
Parappa the Rapper · 192
Parasite Eve · 234
Patrick Buckland · 209, 294
Patrick Wyatt · 135, 161, 302
Paul Cuisset · 73, 296
Paul Douglas · 189, 301
Paul Holmes · 46, 300, 306
Paul Kwinn · 15
PC Engine · 21, 25, 26, 29, 83, 105, 106, 296, 306, 308, 317
PC Gamer · 88
Peter Chan · 94, 298
Peter Maris · 152
Peter Molyneux · 123, 206, 304
Peter Tuleby · 53, 297
Phantasmagoria · 152
Phillips CD-i system · 56
Pinball Dreams · 64
Pipe Dream · 7
Pit Fighter · 15
Planescape: Torment · 285
platform game · 321
platformer · 321
platinum farming · 267
Playmates Interactive · 133, 297
PlayStation · 49, 69, 74, 81, 95, 101, 108, 118, 120, 123, 126, 129, 131, 138, 139, 140, 141, 146, 147, 148, 149, 150, 154, 155, 157, 159, 160, 163, 165, 170, 171, 172, 173, 176, 179, 180, 183, 186, 187, 188, 189, 190, 191, 192, 193, 198, 199, 200, 202, 203, 205, 206, 208, 211, 214, 220, 221, 222, 223, 224, 227, 228, 229, 230, 231, 234, 241, 242, 243, 244, 245, 246, 248, 250, 264, 265, 270, 277, 279, 280, 287, 291, 292, 293, 294, 295, 297, 299, 300, 301, 303, 306, 307, 311
Pocket Monsters · 169
Pokémon Gold and Silver · 280
Pokémon Red and Blue · 170
Pokémon Red and Green · 169
Pong · 316, 326
Postal · 215
Powermonger · 19
Project Reality · 176
Psygnosis · 31, 154, 294, 303
Puyo Pop · 51
Puyo Puyo · 51
Puzzle Bobble · 124
PvP · 321
Pyro Studios · 239, 302

Q

Quake · 175
Quake II · 222
Quake III: Arena · 284
Quest Corporation · 157, 300

R

Radiant Silvergun · 235
Raiden · 13
Railroad Tycoon · 8
Rampart · 18
Rand and Robyn Miller · 99
Randy Breen · 48, 294
Rare · 40, 132, 133, 136, 137, 160, 210, 211, 240, 290, 295, 297
Ray Gresko · 145, 289
Ray Muzyka · 145, 257, 293
Rayman · 155
Raymond Benson · 65
Real-Time Strategy · 322
Red Storm Entertainment · 244, 290
Relentless: Twinsen's Adventure · 131
Relic Entertainment · 275, 302
Remi Herbulot · 61, 298, 302
Renegade GT Interactive · 137
Resident Evil · 170
Resident Evil 2 · 227
Revelations Persona · 186
Revolution Software · 29, 121, 298, 299
Richard Garriot · 65, 213, 291, 305
Richard Robbins · 62, 291
Rick Dyer · 38
Rick Goodman · 217, 302
Rico Holmes · 53, 297
Ridge Racer · 103
Road Rash · 48
Rob Rowe · 15
Robert Holmes · 111, 298
Robert Prince · 27, 296
Robert Whitemanin · 9
Roberta Williams · 152
Roger Keating · 17
RollerCoaster Tycoon · 268
Ron Gilbert · 19, 57, 94, 216, 298, 302
Ron Miller · 161, 302
RPG · 316, 322
RTS · 322
Rumble Pak · 205
Russel Kay · 31, 303

S

Sales Curve Interactive · 209, 294
Sam & Max Hit the Road · 107
Sam Didier · 161, 302
Samurai Shodown · 97
Sangokumusou · 200
Satoru Iwata · 127, 261, 292
Satoshi Tajiri · 169
Saturn 3D Control Pad · 179
Scott Campbell · 159, 294
Scott Youngblood · 258
Sculptured Software · 78, 298
SCUMM engine · 58, 69, 95, 107
S-DD1 compression chip · 179
Sean Clark · 107, 298
Secret of Mana · 98
Sega · 8, 14, 20, 21, 22, 25, 29, 34, 36, 38, 39, 40, 41, 45, 48, 49, 58, 61, 63, 69, 70, 71, 76, 78, 79, 81, 82, 89, 93, 95, 97, 98, 99, 101, 102, 103, 108, 109, 110, 115, 117, 118, 128, 129, 132, 133, 136, 138, 139, 140, 148, 150, 154, 157, 161, 163, 164, 167, 171, 173, 176, 178, 179, 185, 189, 190, 191, 204, 206, 223, 229, 236, 250, 251, 263, 264, 286, 287, 291, 292, 293, 294, 295, 296, 297, 298, 299, 301, 302, 304, 305, 306, 307, 308, 311, 316, 317, 323
Sega AM2 · 25, 102, 118, 128, 286, 287, 293, 301, 304, 306
Sega Bass Fishing · 223
Sega CD · 58
Sega Channel · 139
Sega Master System · 324
Sega Model 1 · 70, 71, 102
Sega Saturn · 22, 49, 69, 97, 102, 108,

118, 129, 136, 138, 139, 140, 148, 150, 154, 157, 161, 167, 171, 173, 176, 178, 179, 185, 189, 190, 191, 204, 206, 229, 236, 250, 291, 301, 302, 304, 307, 311
Sega Technical Institute · 79, 117, 132, 297
Seiichi Ishii · 141, 295
Seiken Densetsu 2 · 98
Seiken Densetsu: Final Fantasy Gaiden · 43
Sensible Software · 50, 111, 112, 137, 138, 293, 298, 299
Sensible World of Soccer · 137
SG-1000 · 323
Shadowrun · 92
shareware · 27, 68, 114, 147, 167
Shelly Day · 69, 298
Shenmue · 286
Shigeki Fujiwara · 83
Shigeru Miyamoto · 23, 57, 71, 86, 94, 153, 169, 172, 177, 193, 204, 253, 292, 294, 296, 297, 300, 301, 304, 305
Shigesato Itoi · 127, 292
Shin Megami Tensei: Persona · 186
Shin Sangokumusou · 200
Shining and the Darkness · 34
Shining Force · 63
Shining in the Darkness · 34
Shinji Mikami · 170, 227, 303
Shinobu Toyoda · 39, 79, 296
Shiny Entertainment · 133, 297
shoot 'em up · 314, 322, 324
Shouzou Kaga · 11
Sid Meier · 9, 49, 50, 101, 151, 165, 224, 239, 262, 263, 299, 300, 302, 304
Sid Meier's Alpha Centauri · 262
Sierra On-Line · 22, 59, 111, 152, 258, 291, 298, 305
Sierra Studios · 251, 269, 275, 291, 302
Silent Hill · 265
Silicon & Synapse · 88, 89, 296
Silicon Graphics · 133, 137, 171, 172, 176, 183
Silicon Synapse · 32
SimCity 2000 · 87
Simon Carter · 206
Simtex · 100, 299
Smash TV · 12
Snake · 240
SNES · 21, 23, 24, 36, 47, 56, 57, 63, 65, 72, 73, 76, 86, 87, 88, 89, 92, 95, 98, 106, 107, 108, 109, 110, 123, 127, 133, 136, 140, 149, 160, 164, 172, 178, 181, 194, 292, 294, 296, 297, 298, 301, 304, 306
SNK · 10, 97, 126, 173, 295, 298, 307, 317
Softdisk · 36, 54, 55, 290
Sonic & Knuckles · 132
Sonic CD · 98
Sonic Mayhem · 222
Sonic Team · 39, 178
Sonic the Hedgehog · 39
Sonic the Hedgehog 2 · 79
Sonic the Hedgehog 3 · 117
Sony Computer Entertainment · 183, 192, 198, 223, 246, 292, 294, 297, 306
Sony Interactive Entertainment · 158
Sony Online Entertainment · 267, 305
Soul Edge · 242
Soulcalibur · 242
Space Channel 5 · 264
Space Invaders · 325
Spec Ops: Ranger Assault · 235
Spec Ops: Rangers Lead the Way · 235
Speedball 2: Brutal Deluxe · 28
Spyro the Dragon · 246
Square · 43, 76, 97, 98, 122, 149, 157, 172, 198, 199, 202, 208, 230, 234, 279, 291, 292, 293, 295, 300, 301,

303, 326
Squaresoft · 230, 293, 300
Stainless Games · 209, 210
Star Fox · 86
Star Fox 64 · 204
Star Ocean · 179
Star Wars: Dark Forces · 145
Star Wars: Rogue Squadron · 256
Star Wars: TIE Fighter · 125
Star Wars: X-Wing · 85
Starblade · 47
StarCraft · 232
Starr Long · 213, 305
Starsiege: Tribes · 258
StarTropics · 26
Starwing · 86
Steel Talons · 48
Stephen Barcia · 100, 299
Stephen Clarke-Wilson · 61, 298, 302
Stephen Hart · 17
Stephen L. Butler · 22, 296
Stephen Pierce · 8
Stephen Rippy · 217, 302
Steve Fawkner · 17
Strategic Simulations · 36, 291, 305
Strategic Studies Group · 17
Street Fighter II Turbo: Hyper Fighting · 83
Street Fighter II: The World Warrior · 33
Street Fighter III: 3rd Strike · 270
Streets of Rage · 45
Suikoden · 161
Super 32X · 136
Super Castlevania IV · 53
Super Famicom · 21, 24, 74, 122, 127, 136, 146, 149, 153, 157, 160, 164, 300
Super Mario 64 · 177
Super Mario Kart · 71
Super Mario RPG: Legend of the Seven Stars · 171
Super Mario USA · 74
Super Mario World · 23, 46
Super Mario World 2: Yoshi's Island · 153
Super Mario World: Super Mario Bros. 4 · 23
Super Metroid · 122
Super Nintendo Entertainment System · 8, 10, 21, 71, 74, 79, 172, 292, 310
Super Nintendo System · 21
Super Probector: Alien Rebels · 63
Super Smash Bros. · 261
Super Star Wars · 79
Syndicate · 93
Synthetic Dimensions · 14, 290
Syphon Filter · 264
System Shock · 129
System Shock 2 · 271

T

Tactics Ogre: Let Us Cling Together · 157
Tadashi Sugiyama · 71, 294
Taito · 124, 303
Takao Shimizu · 204, 305
Takashi Iizuka · 178
Takashi Nishiyama · 174, 298
Takashi Tezuka · 23, 57, 94, 153, 296, 297, 300, 301
Takashi Tokita · 43, 149, 234, 291, 292
Takeshi Yokouchi · 223, 294
Takuma Endo · 231
Tales of Phantasia · 164
Tamagotchi · 190
Taneli Armanto · 241
Taro Kudo · 53, 296
Team 17 · 29, 157, 158
Team Fortress Classic · 269
Team Ninja · 191, 295
Team17 · 52, 297

Tecmo · 12, 15, 59, 180, 191, 207, 291, 292, 295, 297, 301
Tecmo's Deception: Invitation to Darkness · 180
Ted Peterson · 119, 292
Tekken · 141
Tekken 3 · 191
Tencent · 253
Tenchu: Stealth Assassins · 231
Tetris · 7, 9, 51, 249, 303, 309
Tetsuhiko Kikuchi · 167
texture-mapped · 104, 141, 175
The 7th Guest · 90
The Bitmap Brothers · 28, 293
The Elder Scrolls II: Daggerfall · 184
The Elder Scrolls: Arena · 119
The House of the Dead · 185
The King of Fighters '94 · 126
The Legend of Zelda: A Link to the Past · 57
The Legend of Zelda: Link's Awakening · 94
The Legend of Zelda: Ocarina of Time · 253
The Legend of Zelda: Triforce of the Gods · 57
The Longest Journey · 278
The Lost Vikings · 88
The Need for Speed · 128
The Neverhood · 188
The Neverhood Chronicles · 188
The Neverhood, Inc. · 188, 299
The Nintendo World Championship · 9
The Secret of Monkey Island · 19
The Shadow of Yserbius · 59
The Simpsons · 32
The Virtual Boy · 162
Theme Park · 123
Thief: The Dark Project · 255
Thor Aackerlund · 9
Tim Cain · 218, 292
Tim Gift · 258
Tim Roberts · 120, 300
Tim Schafer · 57, 94, 249, 298, 299
Tim Shafer · 19, 298
Tim Stamper · 40
Tim Sweeny · 237
Tim Wright · 154, 294
Time Crisis · 163
Time Traveller · 38
Toaplan · 15, 291, 297
Toby Gard · 189, 301
Tokuro Fujiwara · 170, 303
Tokyo Game Show · 181
Tom Clancy's Rainbow Six · 243
Tom Hall · 27, 32, 37, 54, 67, 113, 290, 296
Tomb Raider · 189
Tomb Raider II · 220
Tomoaki Fukui · 97, 295
Tomonobu Itagaki · 191, 295
Tomoyoshi Miyazaki · 107, 292
Tony Hawk's Pro Skater · 276
Tony Hawk's Skateboarding · 276
Toru Hagihara · 203
Toru Osawa · 253
Toshihiro Nagoshi · 118, 294
Toshinori Asai · 128, 304
Toshio Iwawaki · 253
Toshiyuki Kubooka · 69, 292
Total Annihilation · 216
Totally Games · 125
Tradewest · 40, 295, 296
tri-Ace · 179
Trilobyte · 89, 298
Trip Hawkins · 106
Tsukasa Kuwahara · 83
Tube Shooter · 324
Turbo Express · 20, 21, 25, 308
TurboGrafx- 16 · 83
TurboGrafx-16 · 21, 306, 308
turn-based strategy · 322
Turok: Dinosaur Hunter · 201
Twisted Metal · 159

U

U.S. Gold · 73, 296
Ubi Soft Entertainment · 155
Ubi Studios · 155, 297
UFO: Enemy Unknown · 120
Ultima IX: Ascension · 283
Ultima Online · 213
Ultima VII: The Black Gate · 65
Ultra Famicom · 176
United Game Artists · 264
Unreal · 236
Unreal Engine · 237
Unreal Tournament · 281

V

Valve · 176, 182, 251, 252, 269, 270, 271, 291
Valve Corporation · 182
Vicky Arnold · 189, 301
Victor Kislyi · 243
Vijay Lakshman · 119, 292
Virgin Games · 14, 61, 82, 109, 290, 296, 298, 302
Virgin Interactive Entertainment · 90, 112, 121, 133, 156, 297, 298, 299, 302
Virtua Cop · 128
Virtua Fighter · 102
Virtua Racing · 70
Virtual Image Productions · 38
virtual reality · 51, 52, 108, 163, 182
Virtual Reality · 51
Virtuality 1000 · 51
Visual Concepts · 95
Volition · 237, 289
voxel · 274
VR · 108, 115

W

Warcraft II: Tides of Darkness · 161
Warcraft: Orcs & Humans · 135
Wargaming · 243
Warlords · 17
Warren Spector · 129, 290, 301
Westwood Associates · 36, 291
Westwood Studios · 82, 156, 299, 302
Will Wright · 87, 304
Wing Commander · 16
Wipeout · 154
wireframe · 316
Wolf Team · 164, 292
Wolfenstein 3D · 67
Worms · 158

X

X-COM: UFO Defense · 120
Xenogears · 229
X-Men · 80

Y

Yasumi Matsuno · 157, 209, 300
Yasunori Mitsuda · 149, 280
Yasushi Adachi · 97, 295
Yasuyuki Sone · 107, 292
Ybarra Productions · 58, 305
Yoichi Yamada · 253
Yoko Shimomura · 33, 172, 234, 295
Yoshiaki Koizumi · 253
Yoshihiko Maekawa · 172, 292
Yoshiki Okamoto · 33, 83, 295
Yoshinori Kitase · 122, 149, 198, 292
Yoshinori Yamagishi · 179, 292
Yoshio Sakamoto · 122, 297
Yoshio Yoshida · 22, 296
Yu Suzuki · 25, 70, 102, 118, 128, 286,

294, 295, 304
Yuji Horii · 149
Yuji Naka · 39, 40, 79, 132, 178, 296
Yuka Tsujiyoko · 11
Yukio Futatsugi · 148, 229, 304
Yuzo Koshiro · 45, 295

Z

Zenithian trilogy · 74

www.ingramcontent.com/pod-product-compliance
Lightning Source LLC
LaVergne TN
LVHW100135061126
851857LV00010B/95
9781739238407